CHERRY TOMATO

Thank you for purchasing [this]... The illustration is a horse... Notes... from the 50th anniversary issue of *Weekly Shonen Jump*. The horse's name is Cascade, and he's from the old series *Midori no Makibao*. I was told I could draw any character from any legendary *Weekly Shonen Jump* series I wanted. Cascade sprung to mind. Immediately! So I drew him.

**HARUICHI FURUDATE** began his manga career when he was 25 years old with the one-shot *Ousama Kid* (King Kid), which won an honorable mention for the 14th Jump Treasure Newcomer Manga Prize. His first series, *Kiben Gakuha, Yotsuya Sensei no Kaidan* (Philosophy School, Yotsuya Sensei's Ghost Stories), was serialized in *Weekly Shonen Jump* in 2010. In 2012, he began serializing *Haikyu!!* in *Weekly Shonen Jump*, where it became his most popular work to date.

# HAIKYU!!

VOLUME 40

SHONEN JUMP Manga Edition

Story and Art by

**HARUICHI FURUDATE**

Translation ■ **ADRIENNE BECK**
Touch-Up Art & Lettering ■ **ERIKA TERRIQUEZ**
Design ■ **JULIAN [JR] ROBINSON**
Editor ■ **MARLENE FIRST**


First published in Japan in 2012 by SHUEISHA Inc., Tokyo.
English translation rights arranged by SHUEISHA Inc.



Printed in Canada

Published by VIZ Media, LLC
P.O. Box 77010
San Francisco, CA 94107

10 9 8 7 6 5 4 3 2 1
First printing, September 2020

VIZ MEDIA
viz.com

ratings.viz.com RATED T TEEN

**PARENTAL ADVISORY**
HAIKYU!! is rated T for Teen and is recommended for ages 13 and up for mild language.

SHONEN JUMP
shonenjump.com

# HAIKYU!!

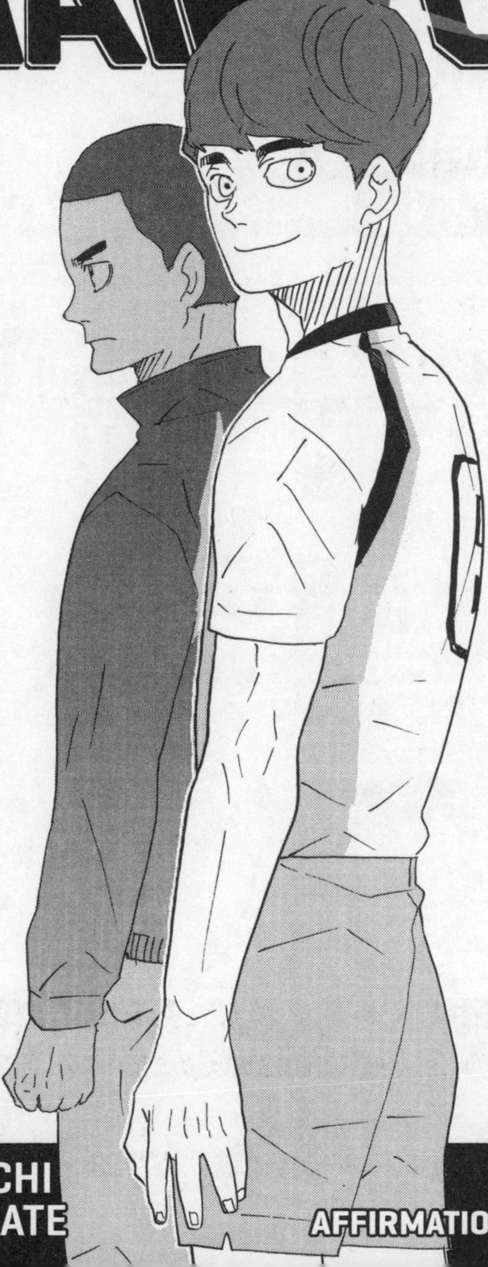

HARUICHI
FURUDATE

AFFIRMATION

40

# Karasuno High School Volleyball Club

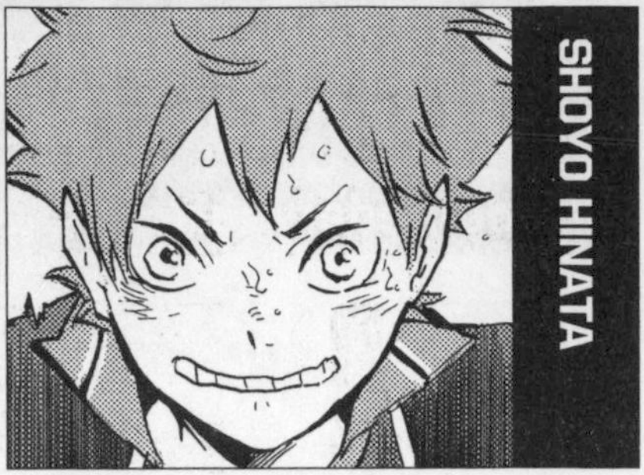
SHOYO HINATA

**1ST YEAR / MIDDLE BLOCKER**
Even though he doesn't have the best body type for volleyball, he is super athletic. Gets nervous easily.

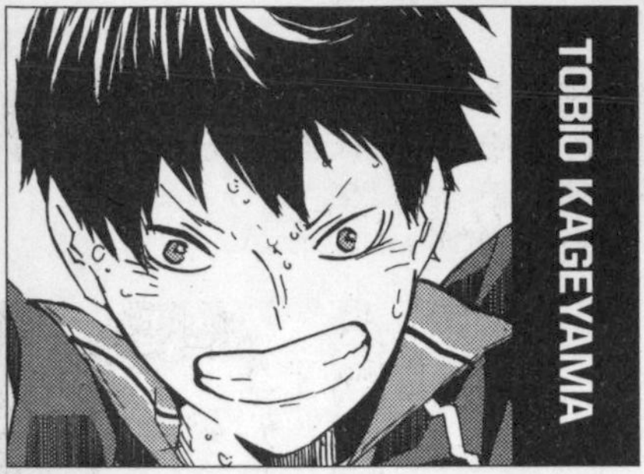
TOBIO KAGEYAMA

**1ST YEAR / SETTER**
His instincts and athletic talent are so good that he's like a "king" who rules the court. Demanding and egocentric.

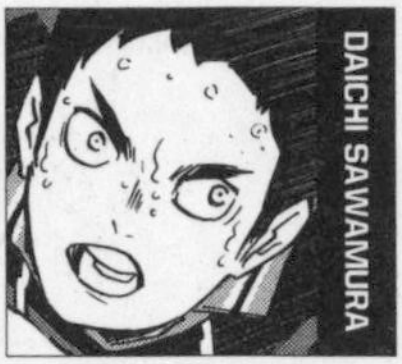
DAICHI SAWAMURA

**3RD YEAR (CAPTAIN)**
**WING SPIKER**

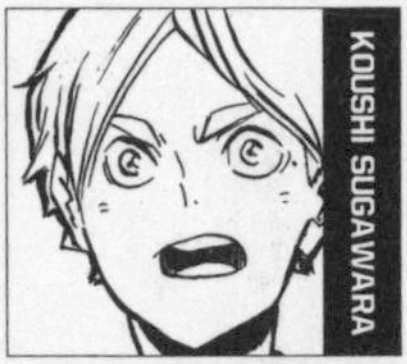
KOUSHI SUGAWARA

**3RD YEAR (VICE CAPTAIN)**
**SETTER**

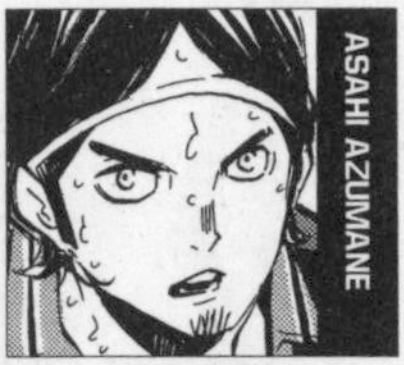
ASAHI AZUMANE

**3RD YEAR**
**WING SPIKER**

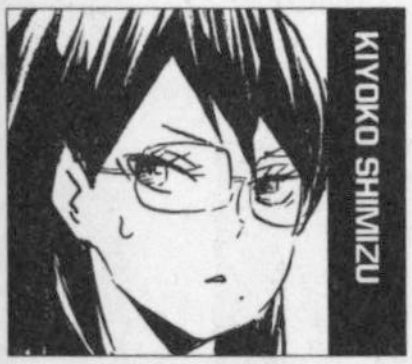
KIYOKO SHIMIZU

**3RD YEAR**
**MANAGER**

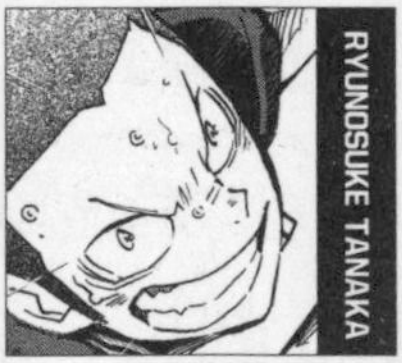
RYUNOSUKE TANAKA

**2ND YEAR**
**WING SPIKER**

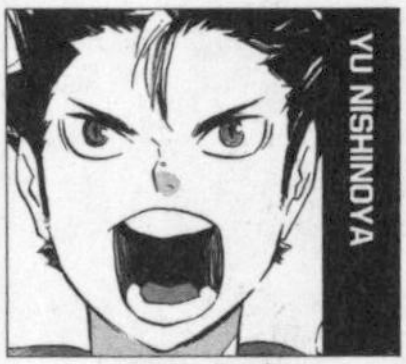
YU NISHINOYA

**2ND YEAR**
**LIBERO**

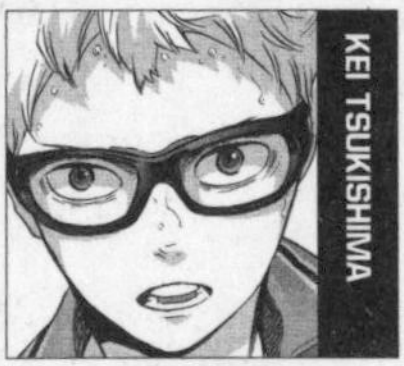
KEI TSUKISHIMA

**1ST YEAR**
**MIDDLE BLOCKER**

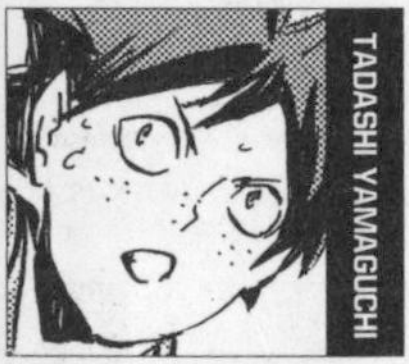
TADASHI YAMAGUCHI

**1ST YEAR**
**MIDDLE BLOCKER**

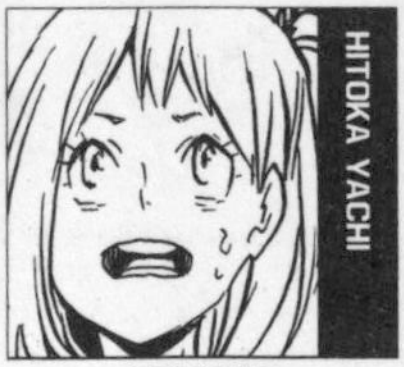
HITOKA YACHI

**1ST YEAR**
**MANAGER**

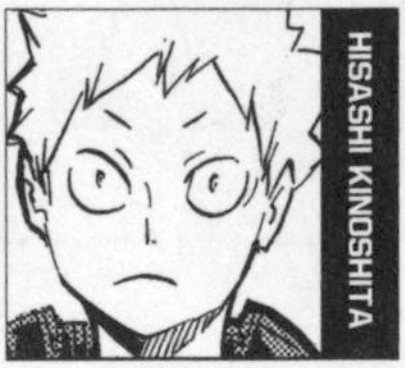
HISASHI KINOSHITA

**2ND YEAR**
**WING SPIKER**

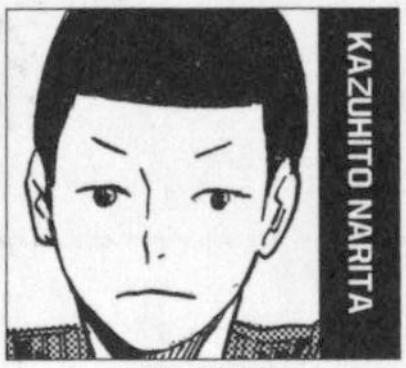
KAZUHITO NARITA

**2ND YEAR**
**MIDDLE BLOCKER**

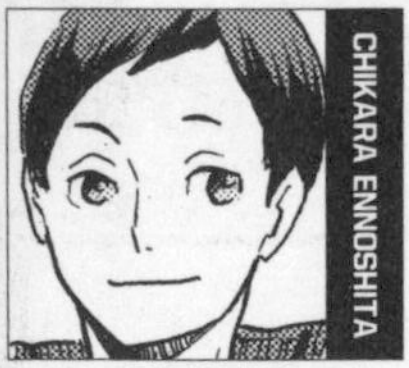
CHIKARA ENNOSHITA

**2ND YEAR**
**WING SPIKER**

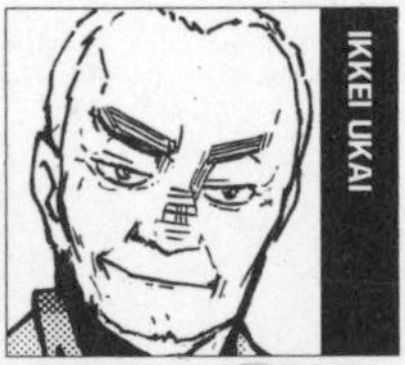
IKKEI UKAI

**FORMER HEAD COACH**

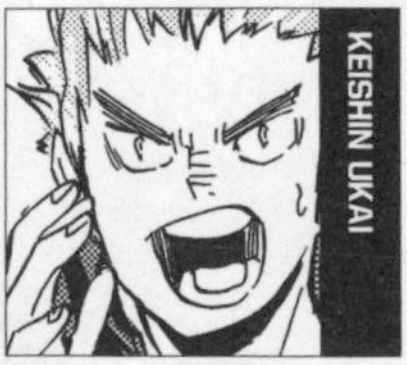
KEISHIN UKAI

**COACH**

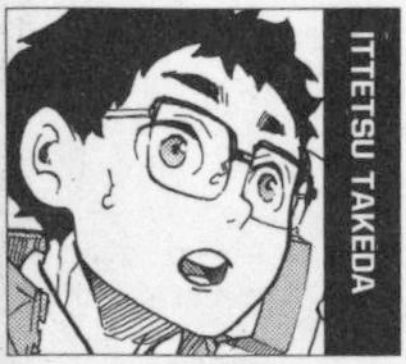
ITTETSU TAKEDA

**ADVISER**

# CHARACTERS

## NATIONAL SPRING TOURNAMENT ARC

### Kamomedai High School Volleyball Club

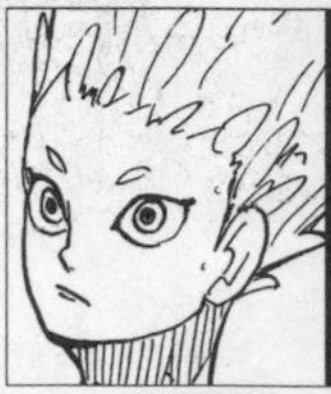
KORAI HOSHIUMI
2ND YEAR
WING SPIKER

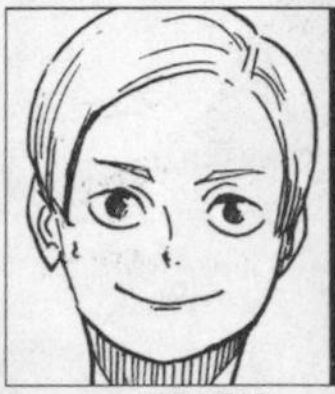
KEIICHIRO KANBAYASHI
3RD YEAR
LIBERO

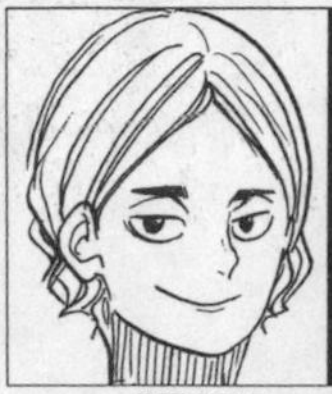
IZURU NOZAWA
3RD YEAR
WING SPIKER

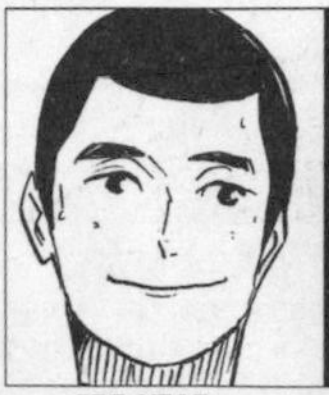
AIKICHI SUWA
3RD YEAR (CAPTAIN)
SETTER

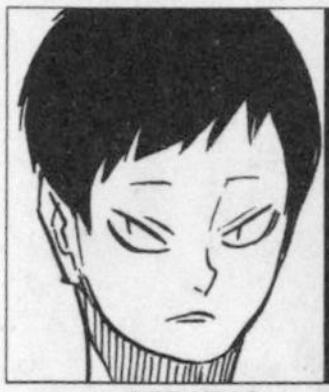
KAZUYOSHI BESSHO
1ST YEAR
MIDDLE BLOCKER

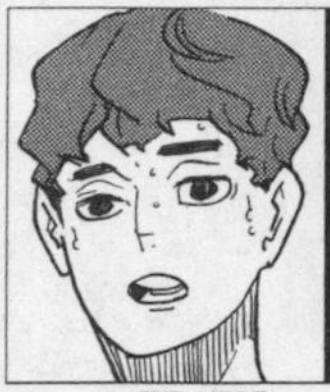
SACHIRO HIRUGAMI
2ND YEAR
MIDDLE BLOCKER

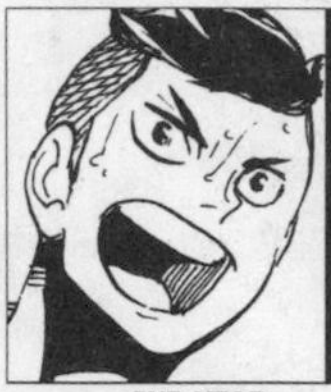
GAO HAKUBA
2ND YEAR
WING SPIKER

### Nekoma Volleyball Club

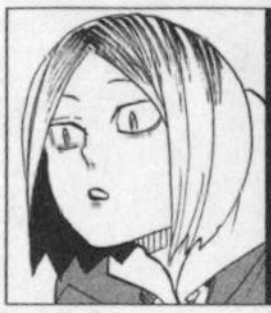
KENMA KOZUME

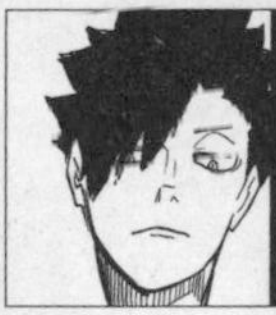
TETSURO KUROO

### Karasuno Cheering Section

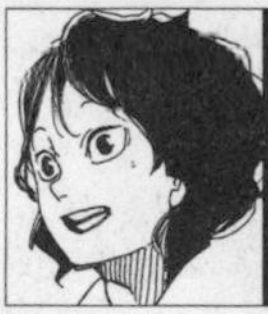
TENMA UDAI

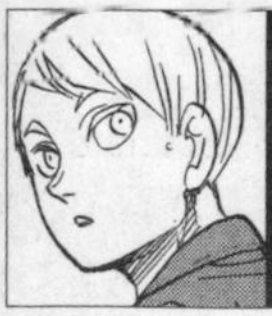
AKITERU TSUKISHIMA

Ever since he saw the legendary player known as "the Little Giant" compete at the national volleyball finals, Shoyo Hinata has been aiming to be the best volleyball player ever! He decides to join the volleyball club at his middle school and gets to play in an official tournament during his third year. His team is crushed by a team led by volleyball prodigy Tobio Kageyama, also known as "the King of the Court." Swearing revenge on Kageyama, Hinata graduates middle school and enters Karasuno High School, the school where the Little Giant played. However, upon joining the club, he finds out that Kageyama is there too! The two of them bicker constantly, but they bring out the best in each other's talents and become a powerful combo. It's the Spring Tournament quarterfinals. Karasuno's attacks are being relentlessly shut down by Kamomedai's highly disciplined read-blocking strategy. Tsukishima manages to stop Hoshiumi a few times with some good decision-making, but Kamomedai's overall skill level causes the whole Karasuno team to realize just how behind they are. In the end, Hoshiumi's polished performance across the board gives Kamomedai the win in set 1. At the start of set 2, both teams switch up their rotations. Karasuno positions Hinata in just the spot to face Kamomedai's strongest rotation head-on, but Kamomedai ignores him and keeps focusing on Azumane...

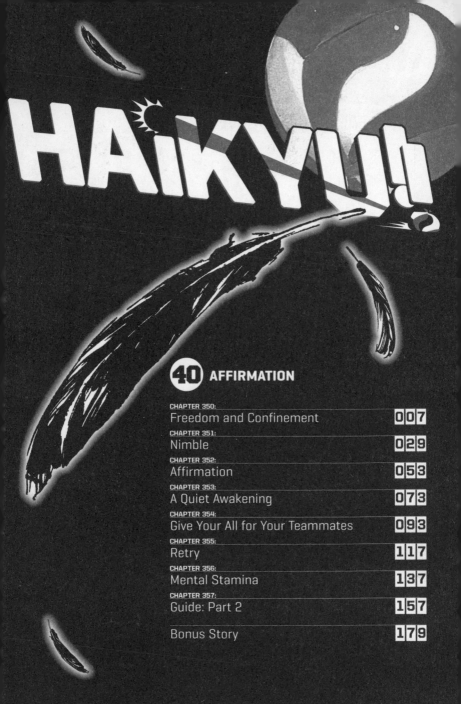

# HAIKYU!!

## 40 AFFIRMATION

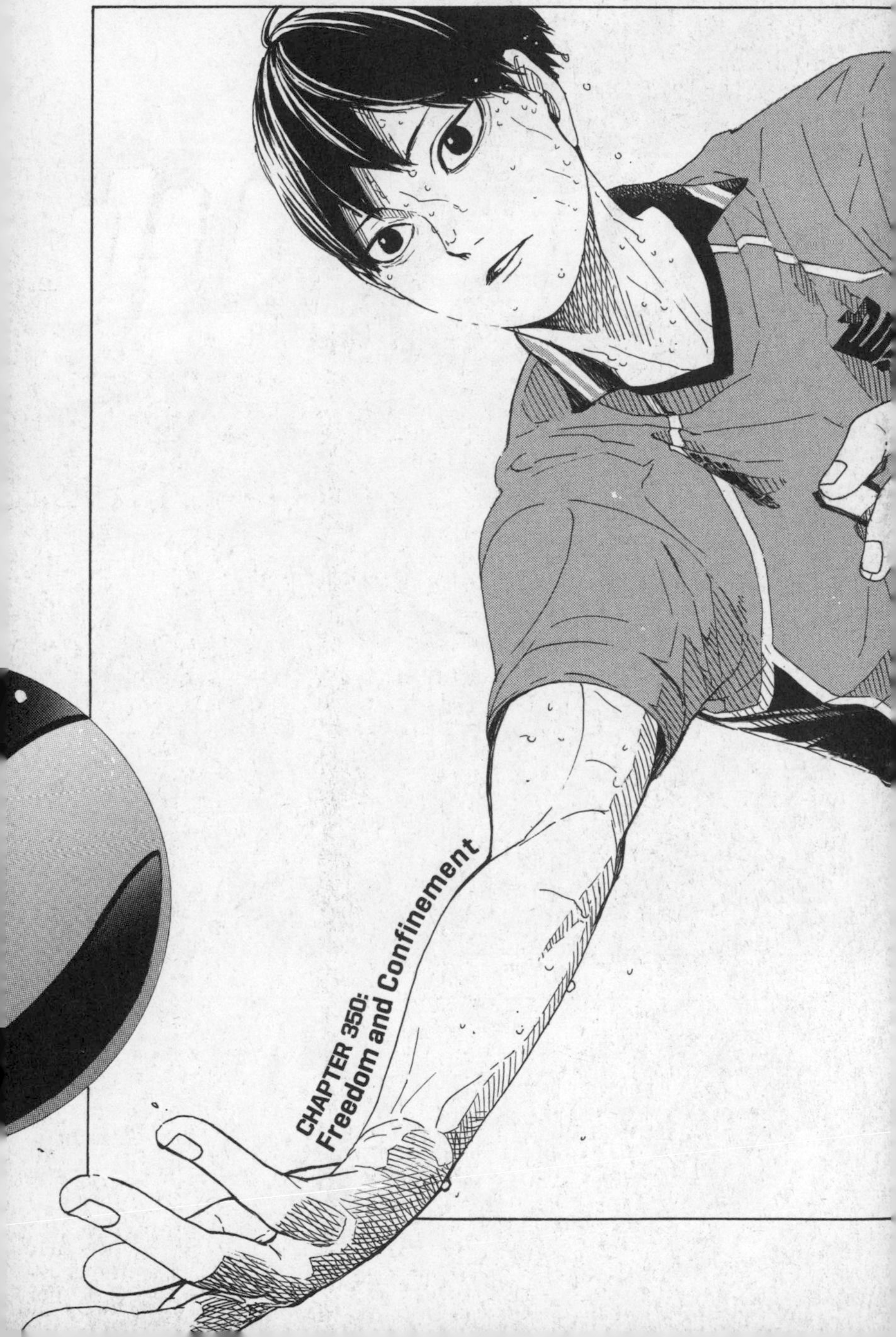
CHAPTER 350:
Freedom and Confinement

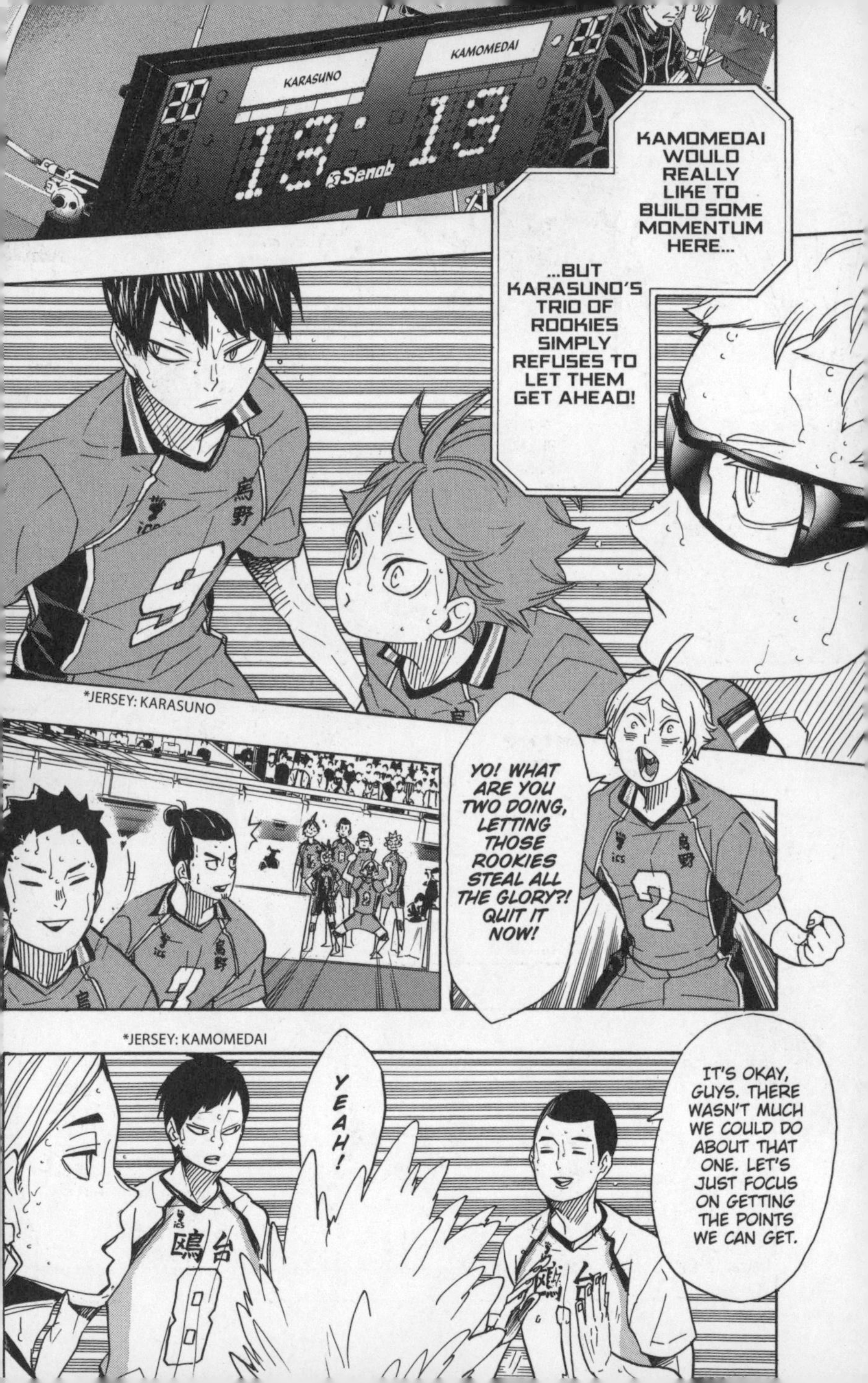
KAMOMEDAI
KARASUNO
KAMOMEDAI WOULD REALLY LIKE TO BUILD SOME MOMENTUM HERE...
...BUT KARASUNO'S TRIO OF ROOKIES SIMPLY REFUSES TO LET THEM GET AHEAD!
*JERSEY: KARASUNO
YO! WHAT ARE YOU TWO DOING, LETTING THOSE ROOKIES STEAL ALL THE GLORY?! QUIT IT NOW!
*JERSEY: KAMOMEDAI
IT'S OKAY, GUYS. THERE WASN'T MUCH WE COULD DO ABOUT THAT ONE. LET'S JUST FOCUS ON GETTING THE POINTS WE CAN GET.
YEAH!

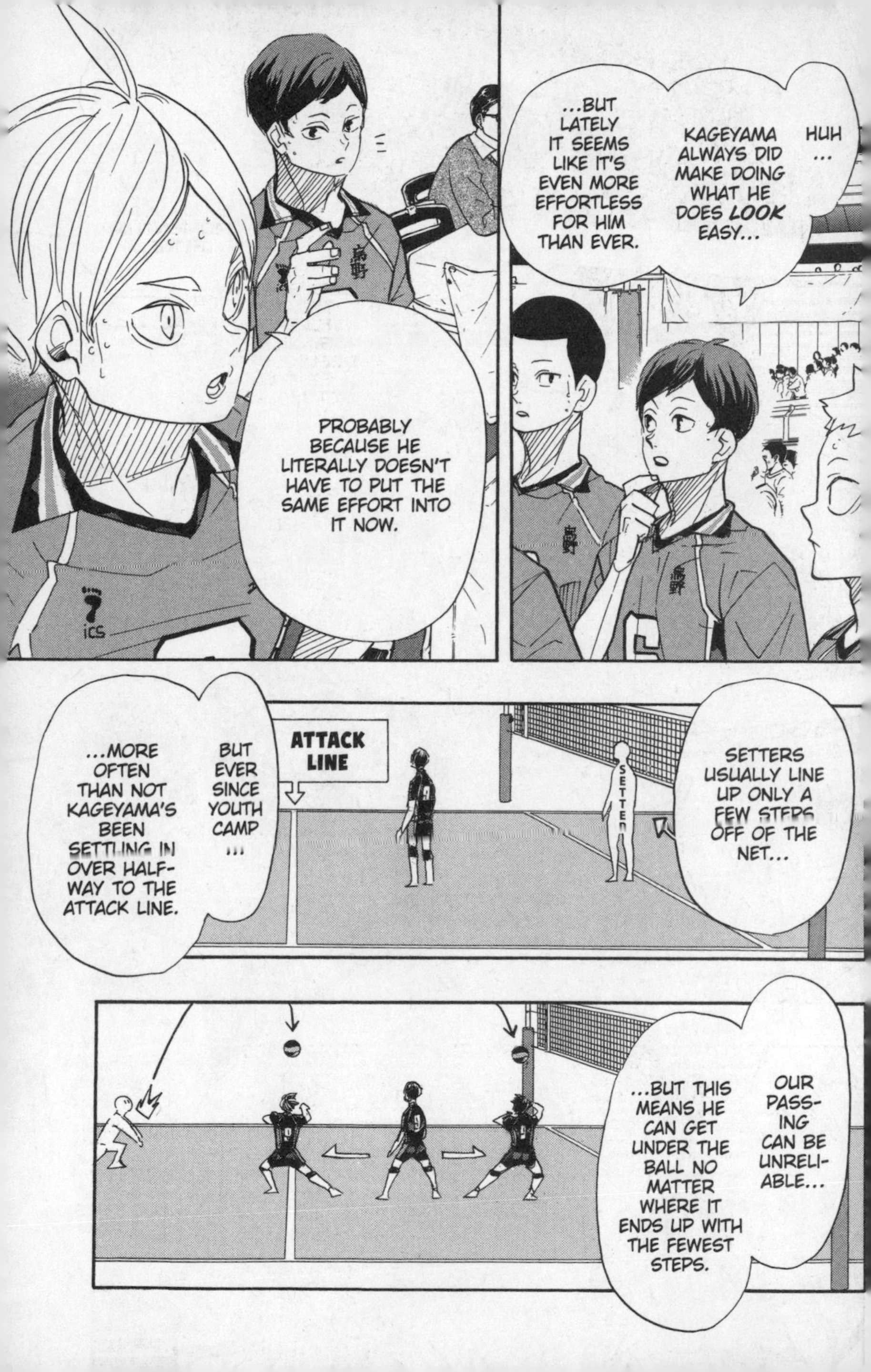
HUH ...
KAGEYAMA ALWAYS DID MAKE DOING WHAT HE DOES *LOOK* EASY...
...BUT LATELY IT SEEMS LIKE IT'S EVEN MORE EFFORTLESS FOR HIM THAN EVER.
PROBABLY BECAUSE HE LITERALLY DOESN'T HAVE TO PUT THE SAME EFFORT INTO IT NOW.
SETTERS USUALLY LINE UP ONLY A FEW STEPS OFF OF THE NET...
SETTER
ATTACK LINE
BUT EVER SINCE YOUTH CAMP ...
...MORE OFTEN THAN NOT KAGEYAMA'S BEEN SETTLING IN OVER HALF-WAY TO THE ATTACK LINE.
OUR PASSING CAN BE UNRELIABLE...
...BUT THIS MEANS HE CAN GET UNDER THE BALL NO MATTER WHERE IT ENDS UP WITH THE FEWEST STEPS.

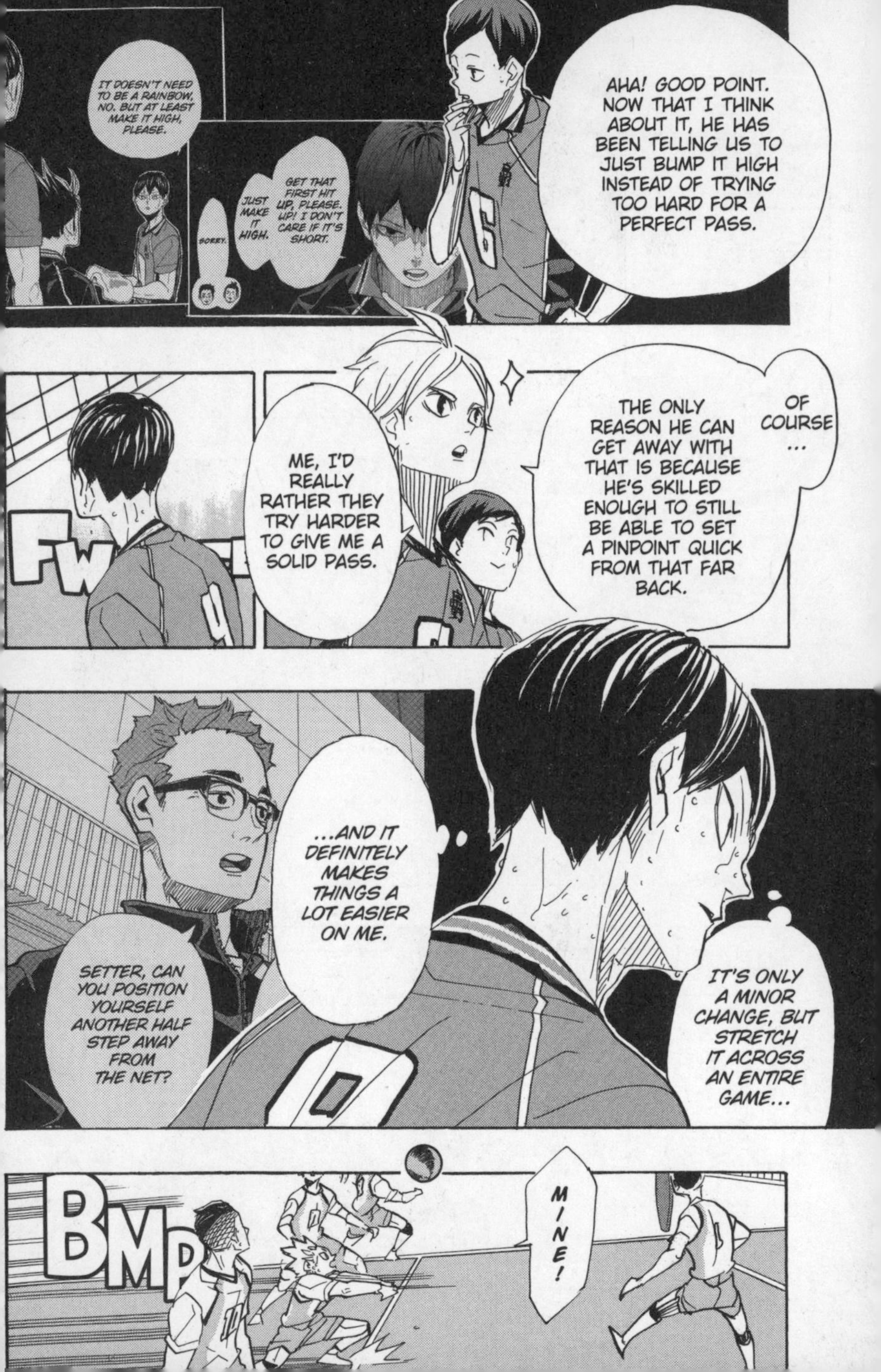
AHA! GOOD POINT. NOW THAT I THINK ABOUT IT, HE HAS BEEN TELLING US TO JUST BUMP IT HIGH INSTEAD OF TRYING TOO HARD FOR A PERFECT PASS.
GET THAT FIRST HIT UP, PLEASE. UP! I DON'T CARE IF IT'S SHORT.
JUST MAKE IT HIGH.
SORRY.
IT DOESN'T NEED TO BE A RAINBOW, NO. BUT AT LEAST MAKE IT HIGH, PLEASE.
OF COURSE...
THE ONLY REASON HE CAN GET AWAY WITH THAT IS BECAUSE HE'S SKILLED ENOUGH TO STILL BE ABLE TO SET A PINPOINT QUICK FROM THAT FAR BACK.
ME, I'D REALLY RATHER THEY TRY HARDER TO GIVE ME A SOLID PASS.
FW
...AND IT DEFINITELY MAKES THINGS A LOT EASIER ON ME.
SETTER, CAN YOU POSITION YOURSELF ANOTHER HALF STEP AWAY FROM THE NET?
IT'S ONLY A MINOR CHANGE, BUT STRETCH IT ACROSS AN ENTIRE GAME...
MINE!
BMP

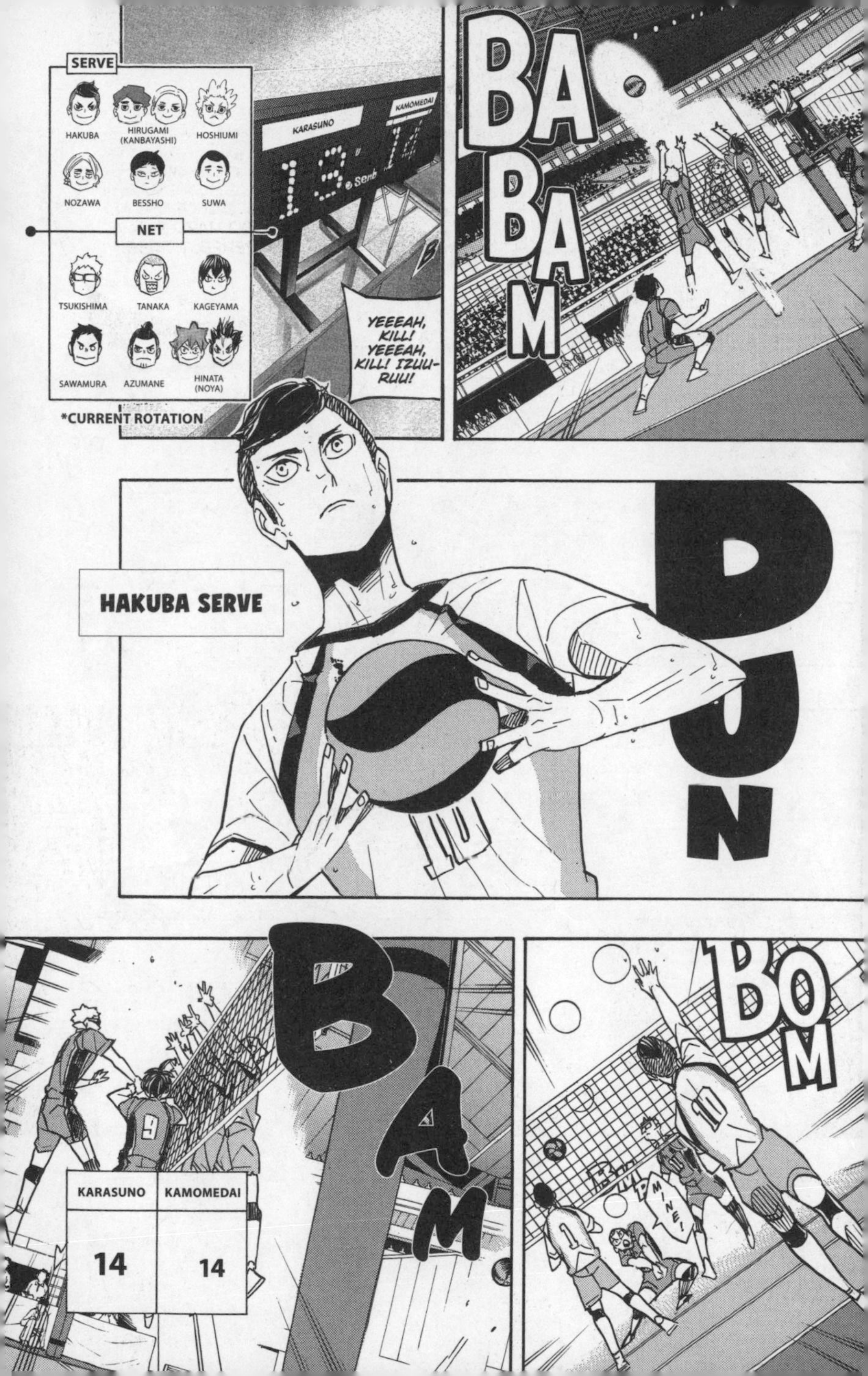
BABABAM
SERVE
HAKUBA
HIRUGAMI (KANBAYASHI)
HOSHIUMI
NOZAWA
BESSHO
SUWA
NET
TSUKISHIMA
TANAKA
KAGEYAMA
SAWAMURA
AZUMANE
HINATA (NOYA)
*CURRENT ROTATION
YEEEAH, KILL! YEEEAH, KILL! IZUU-RUU!
DUN
HAKUBA SERVE
BOM
MINE!
BAM
KARASUNO 14
KAMOMEDAI 14

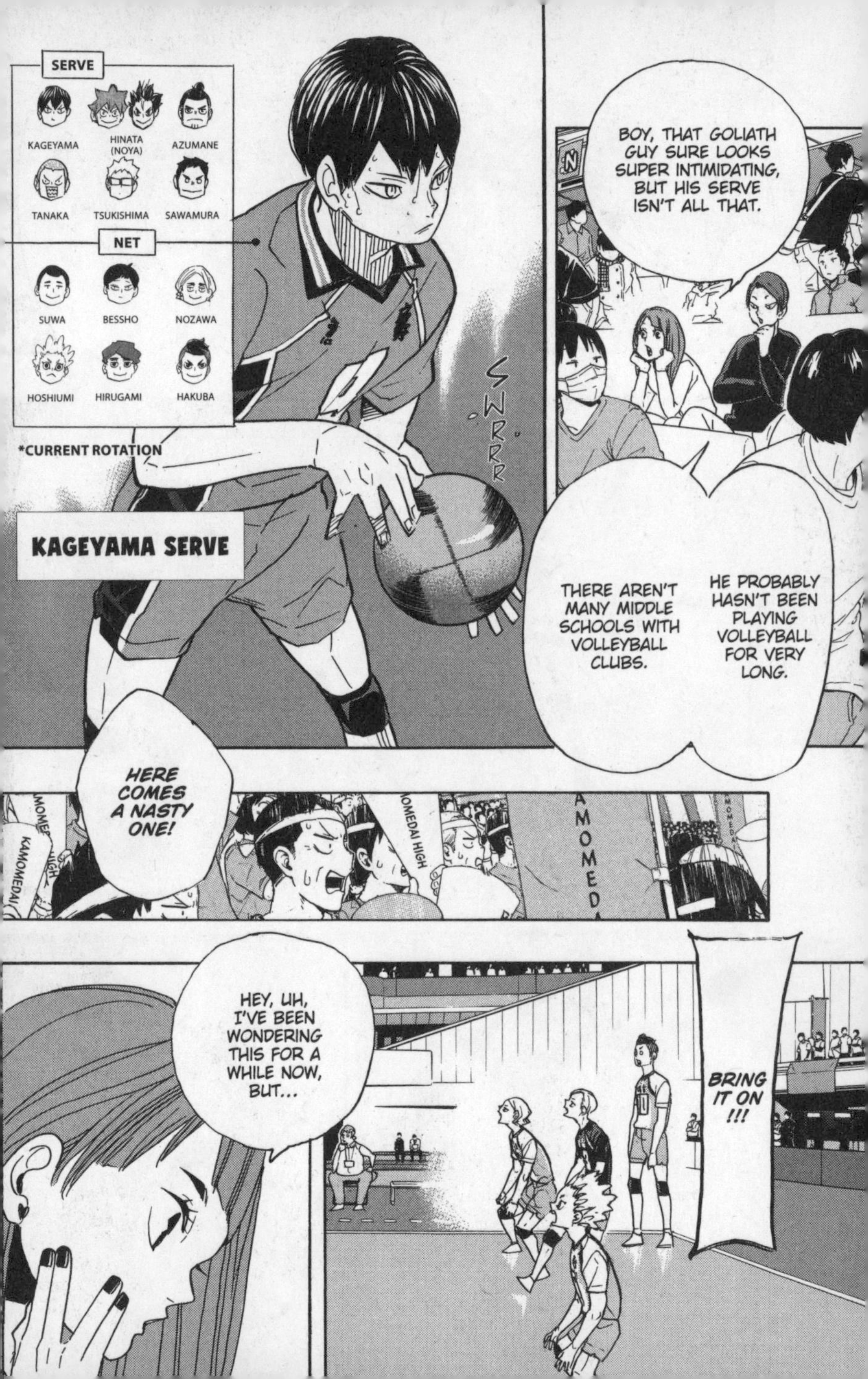
BOY, THAT GOLIATH GUY SURE LOOKS SUPER INTIMIDATING, BUT HIS SERVE ISN'T ALL THAT.
HE PROBABLY HASN'T BEEN PLAYING VOLLEYBALL FOR VERY LONG.
THERE AREN'T MANY MIDDLE SCHOOLS WITH VOLLEYBALL CLUBS.
SERVE
KAGEYAMA
HINATA (NOYA)
AZUMANE
TANAKA
TSUKISHIMA
SAWAMURA
NET
SUWA
BESSHO
NOZAWA
HOSHIUMI
HIRUGAMI
HAKUBA
*CURRENT ROTATION
KAGEYAMA SERVE
SWRRR
HERE COMES A NASTY ONE!
BRING IT ON!!!
HEY, UH, I'VE BEEN WONDERING THIS FOR A WHILE NOW, BUT...

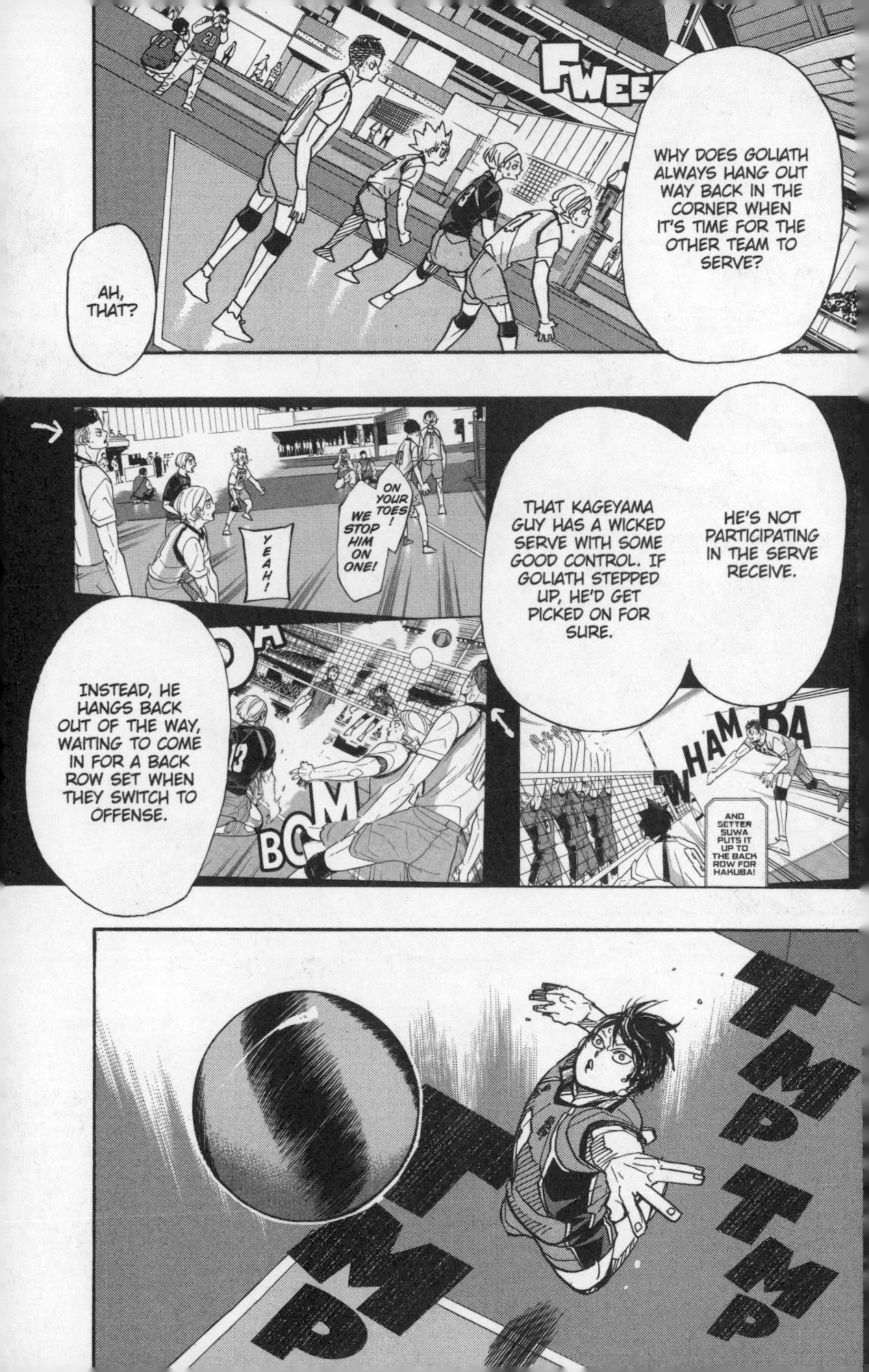
FWEE
WHY DOES GOLIATH ALWAYS HANG OUT WAY BACK IN THE CORNER WHEN IT'S TIME FOR THE OTHER TEAM TO SERVE?
AH, THAT?
HE'S NOT PARTICIPATING IN THE SERVE RECEIVE.
THAT KAGEYAMA GUY HAS A WICKED SERVE WITH SOME GOOD CONTROL. IF GOLIATH STEPPED UP, HE'D GET PICKED ON FOR SURE.
ON YOUR TOES! WE STOP HIM ON ONE!
YEAH!
BA
WHAM
AND SETTER SUWA PUTS IT UP TO THE BACK ROW FOR HAKUBA!
INSTEAD, HE HANGS BACK OUT OF THE WAY, WAITING TO COME IN FOR A BACK ROW SET WHEN THEY SWITCH TO OFFENSE.
BOM
TMP TMP TMP
TMP TMP

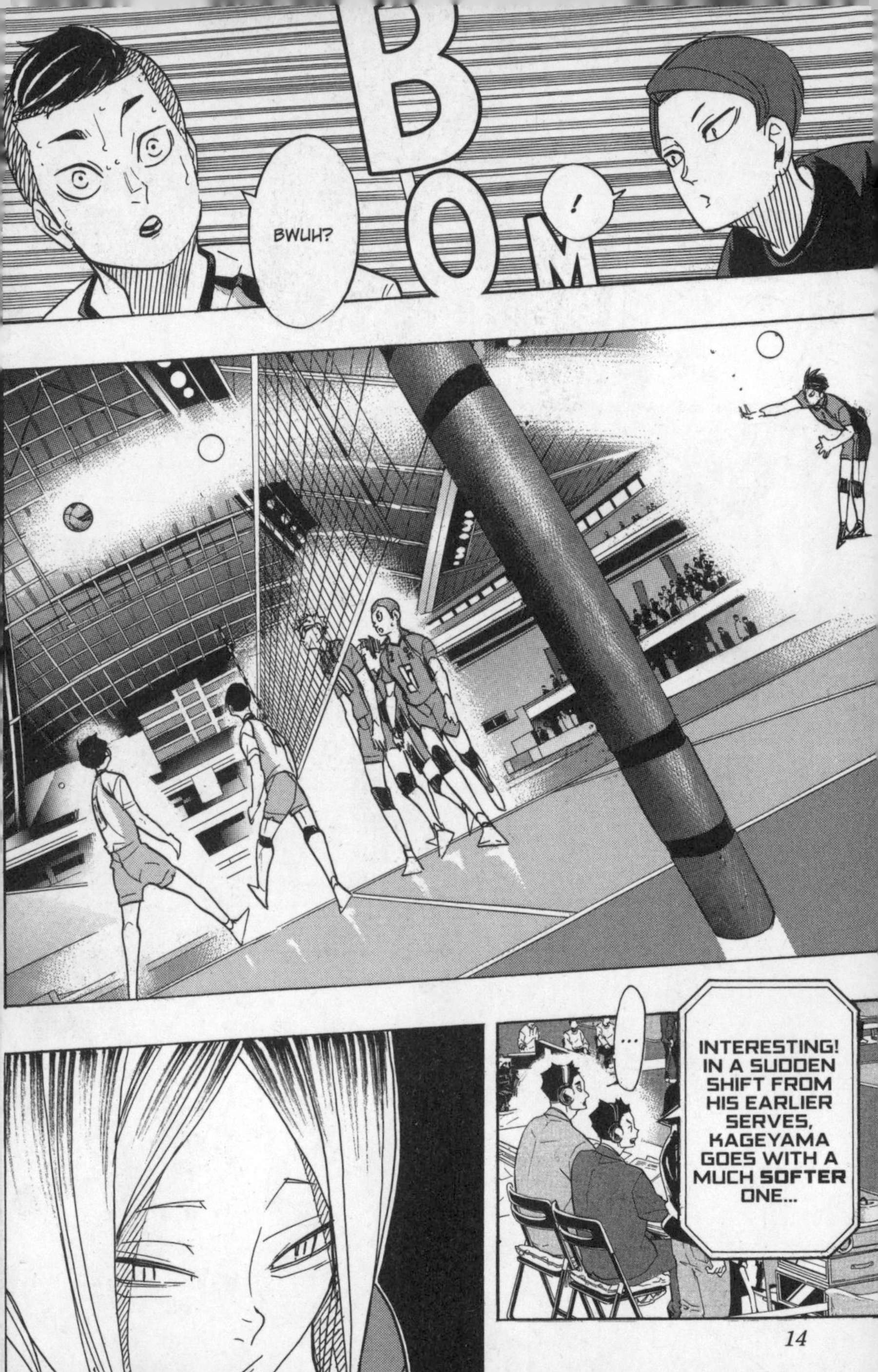
!
BOOM
BWUH?
INTERESTING! IN A SUDDEN SHIFT FROM HIS EARLIER SERVES, KAGEYAMA GOES WITH A MUCH SOFTER ONE...
...

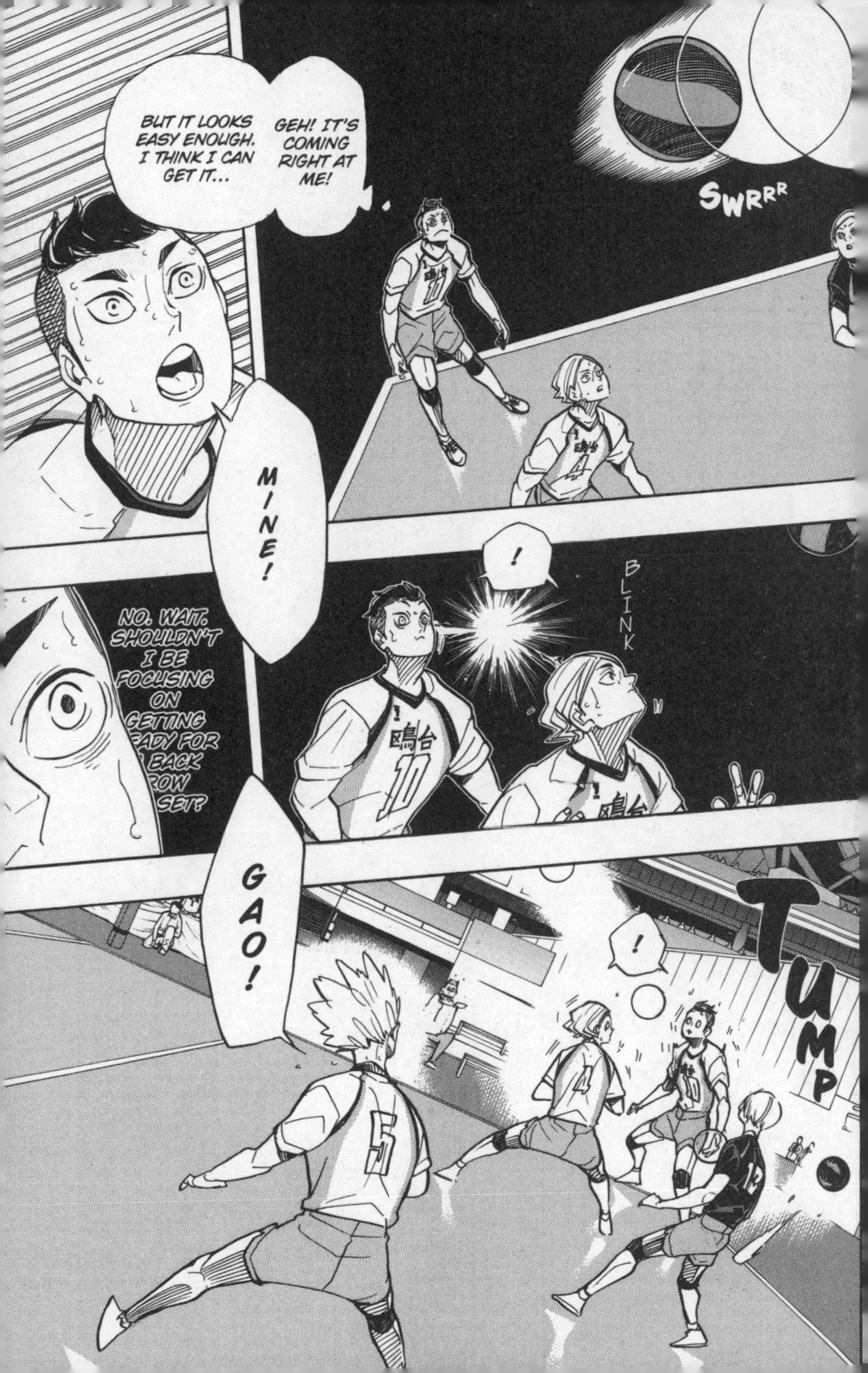
SWRRR
GEH! IT'S COMING RIGHT AT ME!
BUT IT LOOKS EASY ENOUGH. I THINK I CAN GET IT...
MINE!
!
BLINK
NO. WAIT. SHOULDN'T I BE FOCUSING ON GETTING EADY FOR BACK ROW SET?
TUMP
!
GAO!

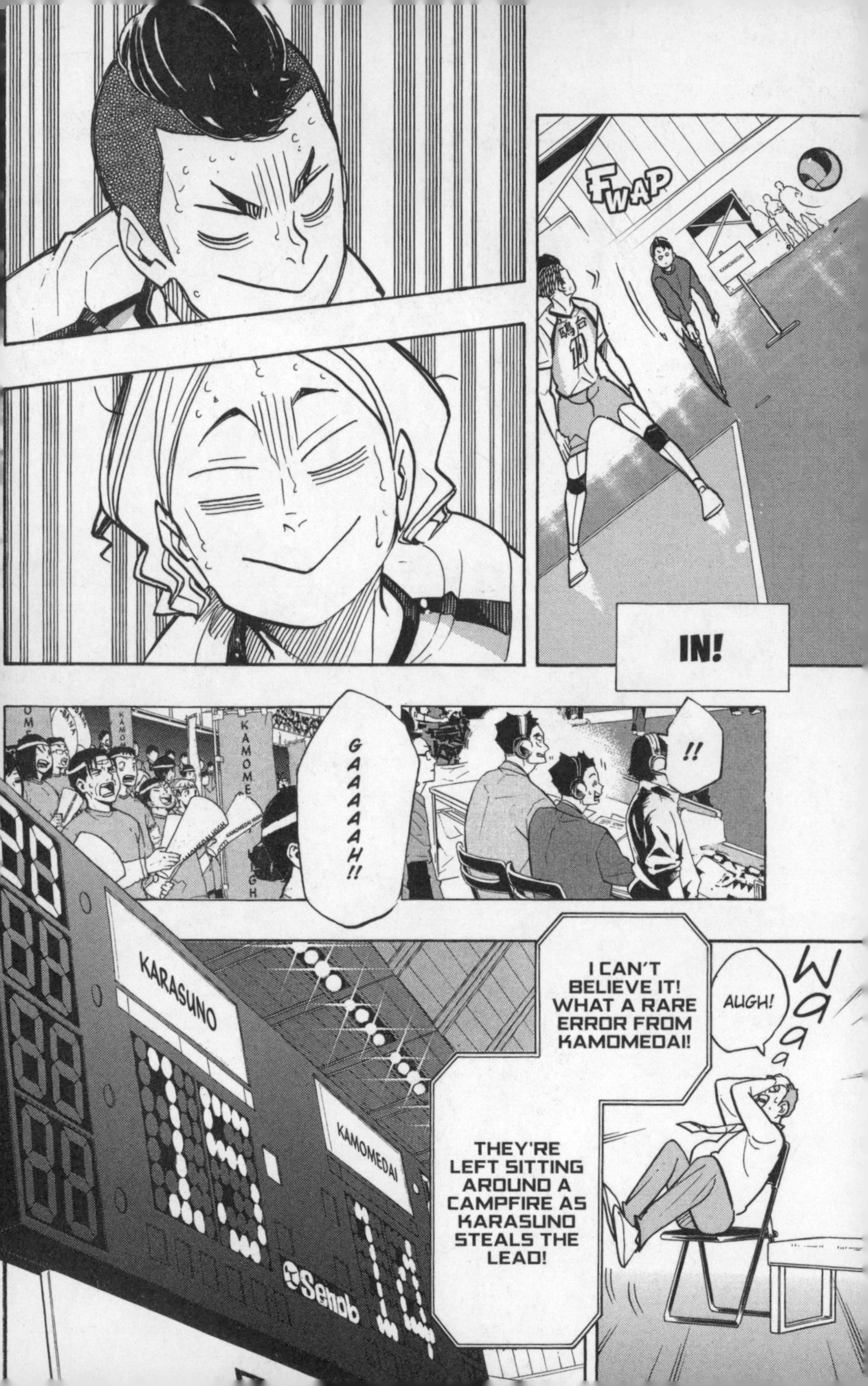
FWAP
IN!
!!
GAAAAAAH!!
Waaa
AUGH!
I CAN'T BELIEVE IT! WHAT A RARE ERROR FROM KAMOMEDAI!
THEY'RE LEFT SITTING AROUND A CAMPFIRE AS KARASUNO STEALS THE LEAD!
KARASUNO
KAMOMEDAI

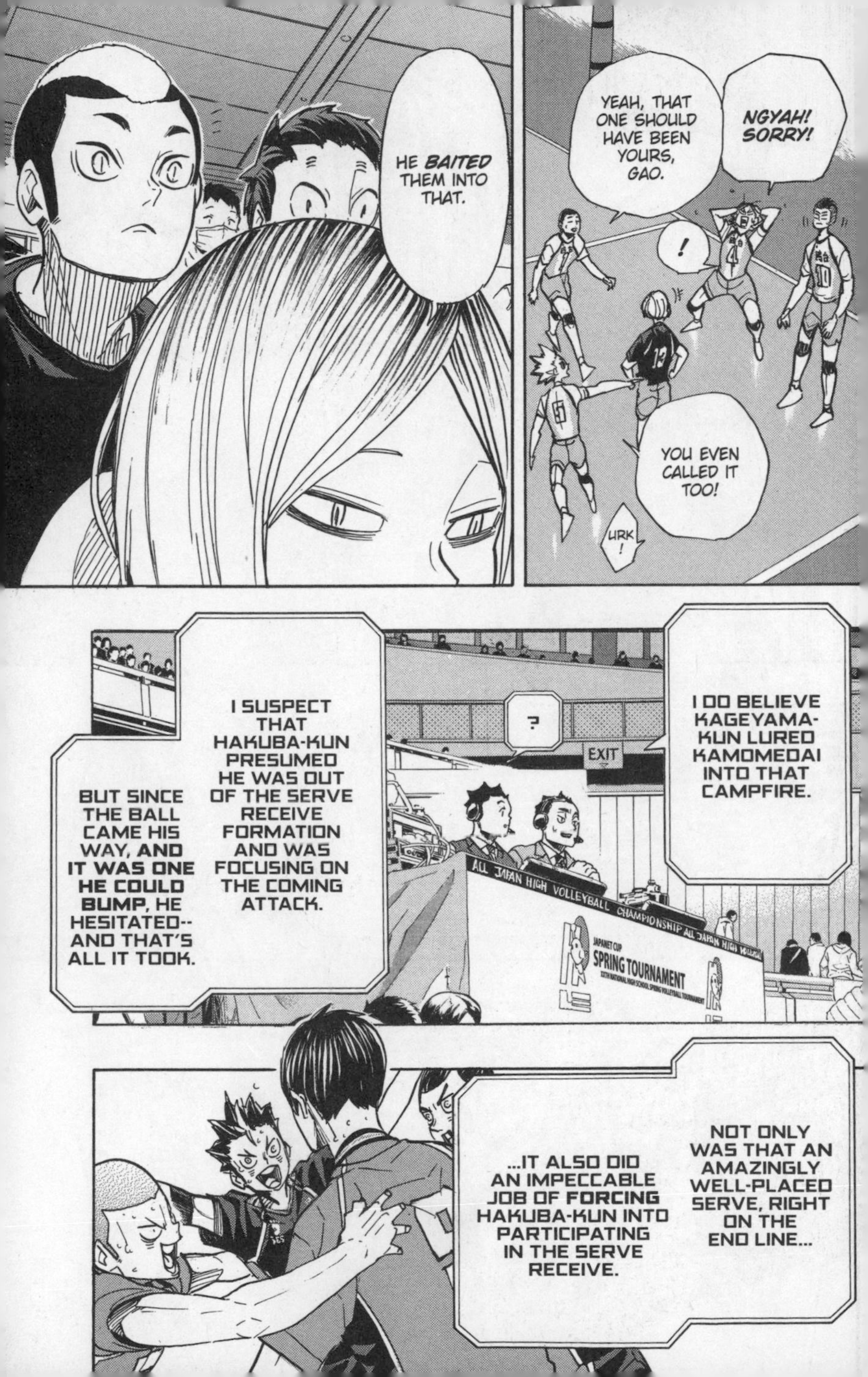
NGYAH! SORRY!
YEAH, THAT ONE SHOULD HAVE BEEN YOURS, GAO.
!
YOU EVEN CALLED IT TOO!
URK!
HE BAITED THEM INTO THAT.
I DO BELIEVE KAGEYAMA-KUN LURED KAMOMEDAI INTO THAT CAMPFIRE.
?
EXIT
I SUSPECT THAT HAKUBA-KUN PRESUMED HE WAS OUT OF THE SERVE RECEIVE FORMATION AND WAS FOCUSING ON THE COMING ATTACK.
BUT SINCE THE BALL CAME HIS WAY, AND IT WAS ONE HE COULD BUMP, HE HESITATED-- AND THAT'S ALL IT TOOK.
ALL JAPAN HIGH VOLLEYBALL CHAMPIONSHIP
JAPANET CUP
SPRING TOURNAMENT
NOT ONLY WAS THAT AN AMAZINGLY WELL-PLACED SERVE, RIGHT ON THE END LINE...
...IT ALSO DID AN IMPECCABLE JOB OF FORCING HAKUBA-KUN INTO PARTICIPATING IN THE SERVE RECEIVE.

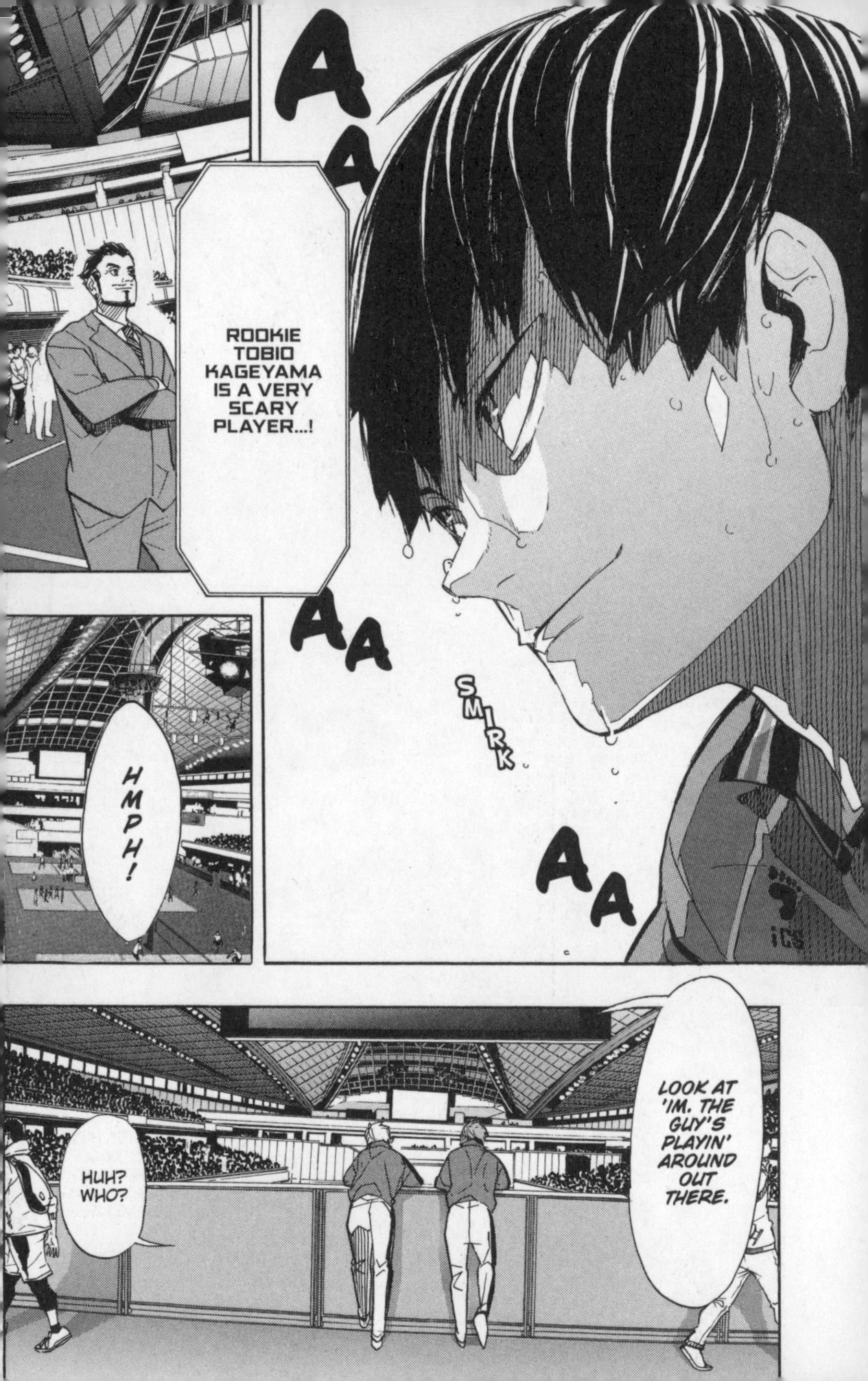
AA
AA
SMIRK
AA
ROOKIE TOBIO KAGEYAMA IS A VERY SCARY PLAYER...!
HMPH!
LOOK AT 'IM. THE GUY'S PLAYIN' AROUND OUT THERE.
HUH? WHO?

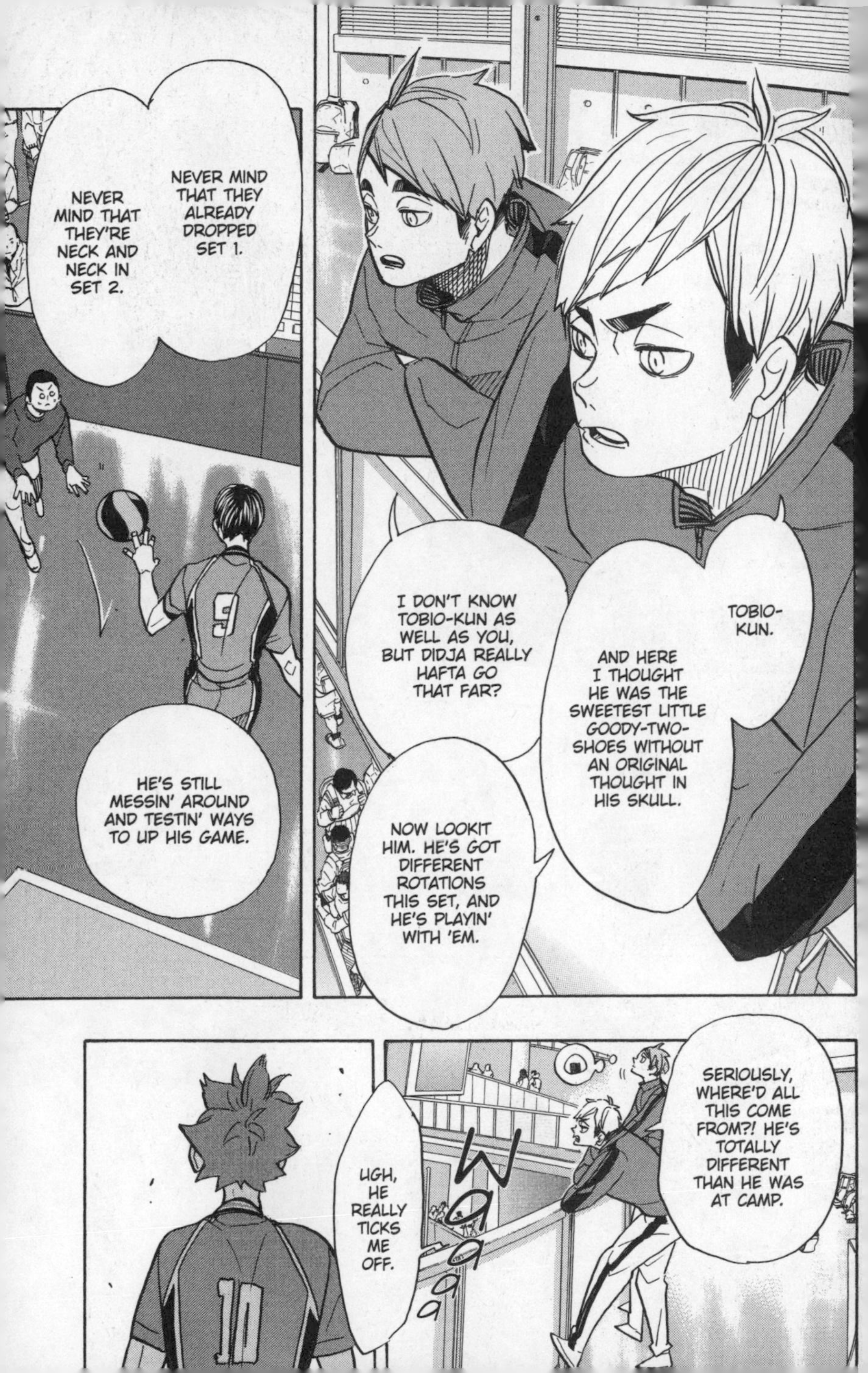
TOBIO-KUN.
AND HERE I THOUGHT HE WAS THE SWEETEST LITTLE GOODY-TWO-SHOES WITHOUT AN ORIGINAL THOUGHT IN HIS SKULL.
I DON'T KNOW TOBIO-KUN AS WELL AS YOU, BUT DIDJA REALLY HAFTA GO THAT FAR?
NOW LOOKIT HIM. HE'S GOT DIFFERENT ROTATIONS THIS SET, AND HE'S PLAYIN' WITH 'EM.
NEVER MIND THAT THEY ALREADY DROPPED SET 1.
NEVER MIND THAT THEY'RE NECK AND NECK IN SET 2.
HE'S STILL MESSIN' AROUND AND TESTIN' WAYS TO UP HIS GAME.
SERIOUSLY, WHERE'D ALL THIS COME FROM?! HE'S TOTALLY DIFFERENT THAN HE WAS AT CAMP.
UGH, HE REALLY TICKS ME OFF.

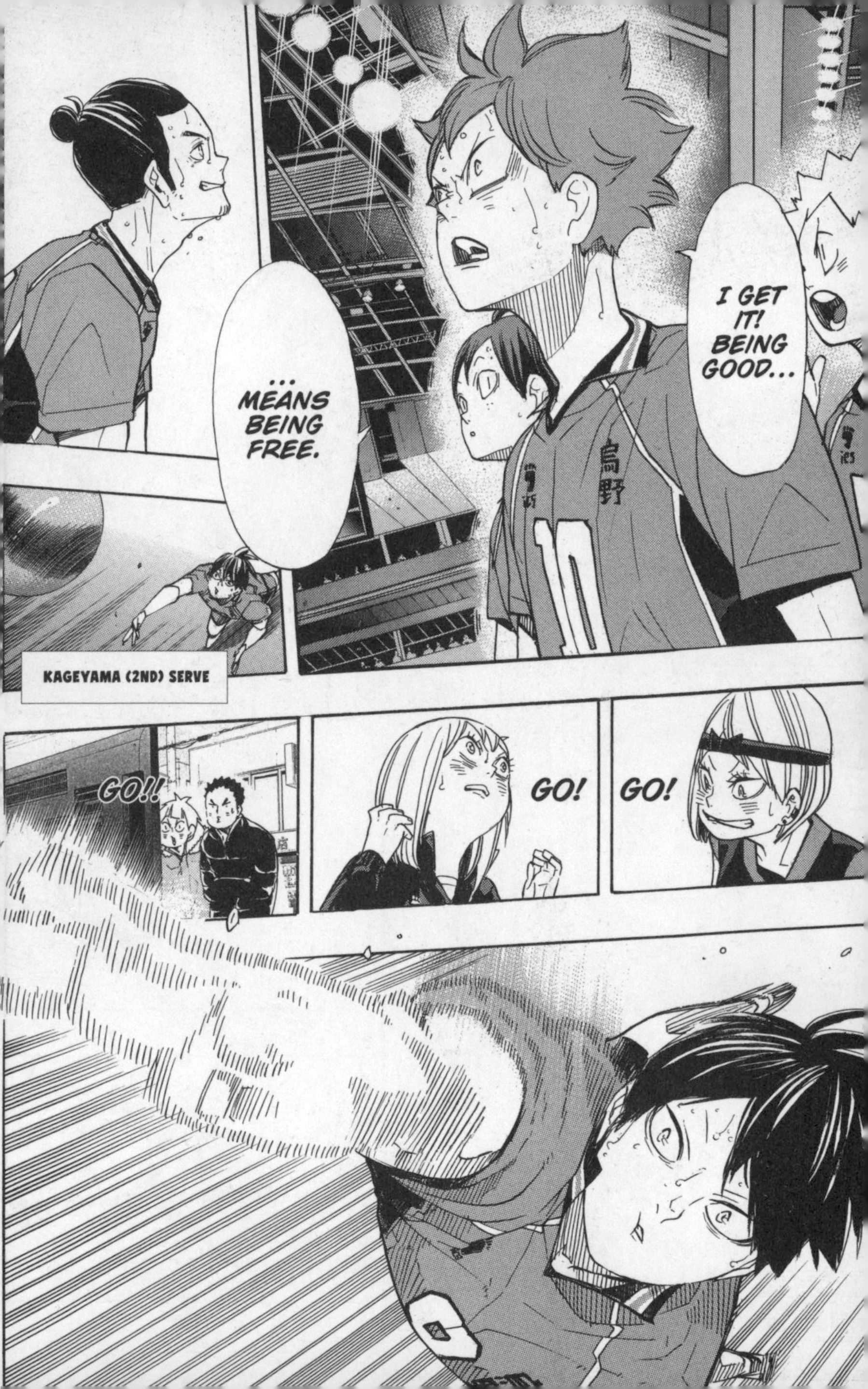
I GET IT! BEING GOOD...
...MEANS BEING FREE.
KAGEYAMA (2ND) SERVE
GO!
GO!
GO!!

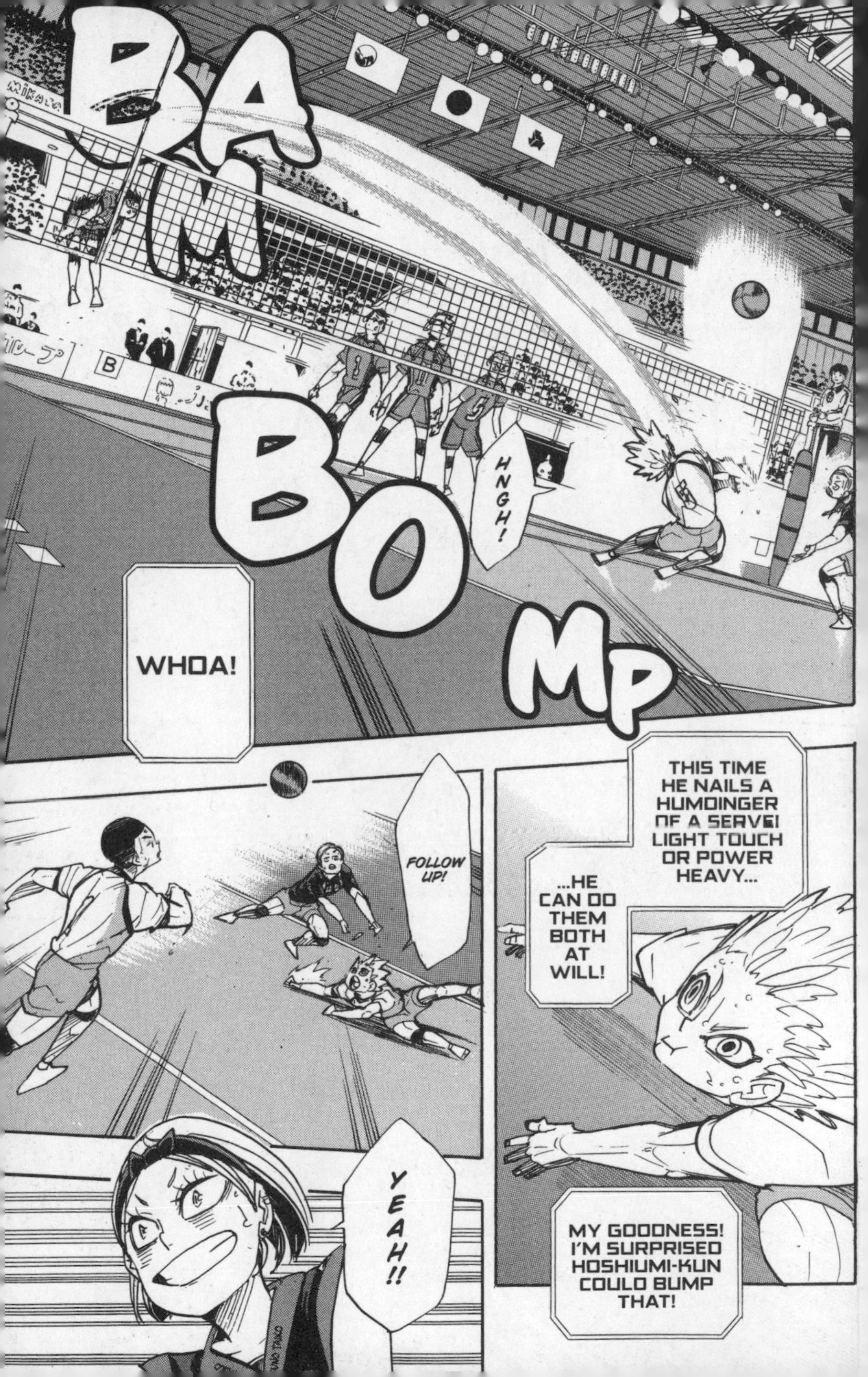
BAM
BOMP
HNGH!
WHOA!
THIS TIME HE NAILS A HUMDINGER OF A SERVE! LIGHT TOUCH OR POWER HEAVY...
...HE CAN DO THEM BOTH AT WILL!
MY GOODNESS! I'M SURPRISED HOSHIUMI-KUN COULD BUMP THAT!
FOLLOW UP!
YEAH!!

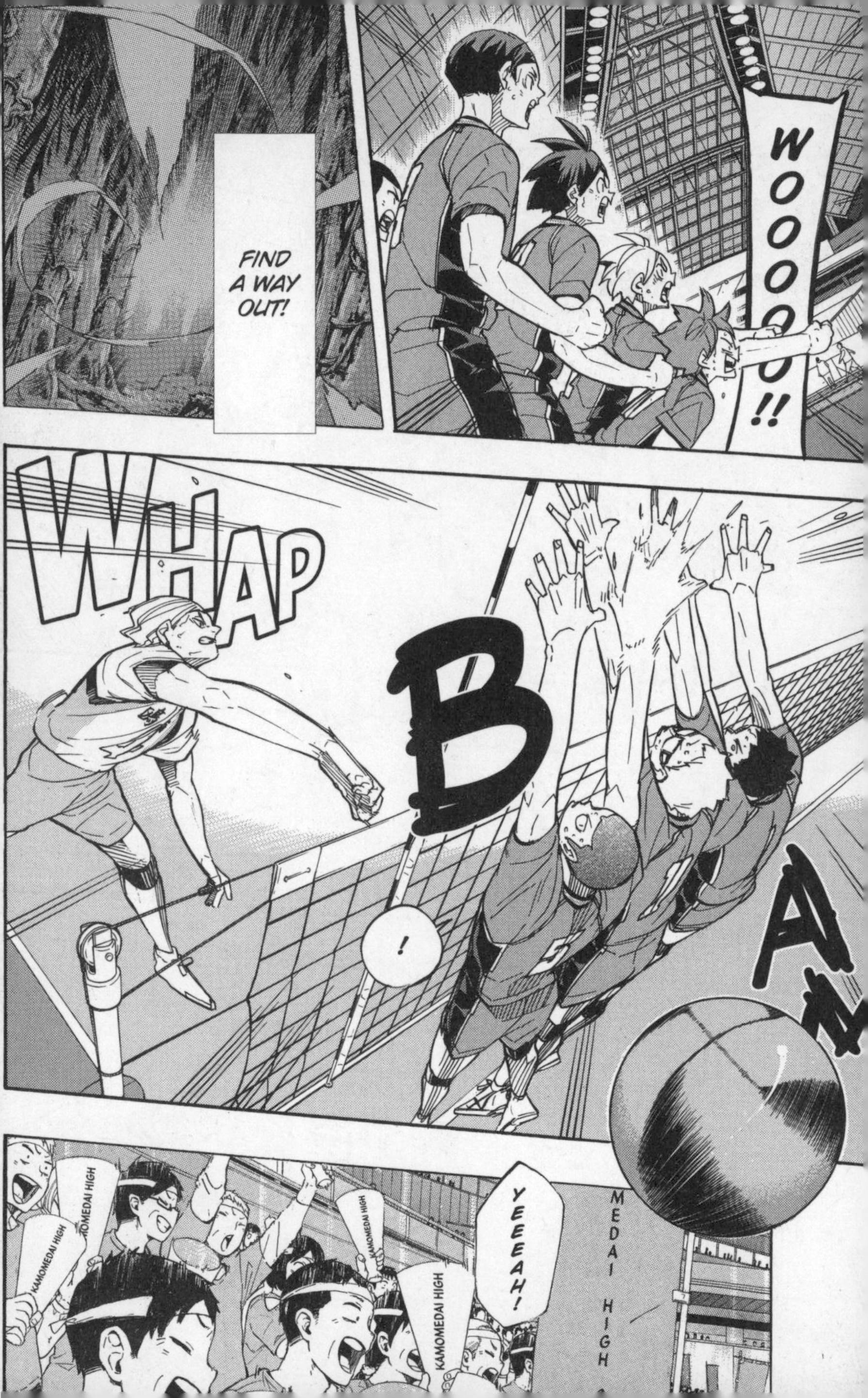
WOOOOOO!!
FIND A WAY OUT!
WHAP
B
A
!
YEEEAH!
MEDAI HIGH
KAMOMEDAI HIGH
KAMOMEDAI HIGH
KAMOMEDAI HIGH
KAMOMEDAI HIGH

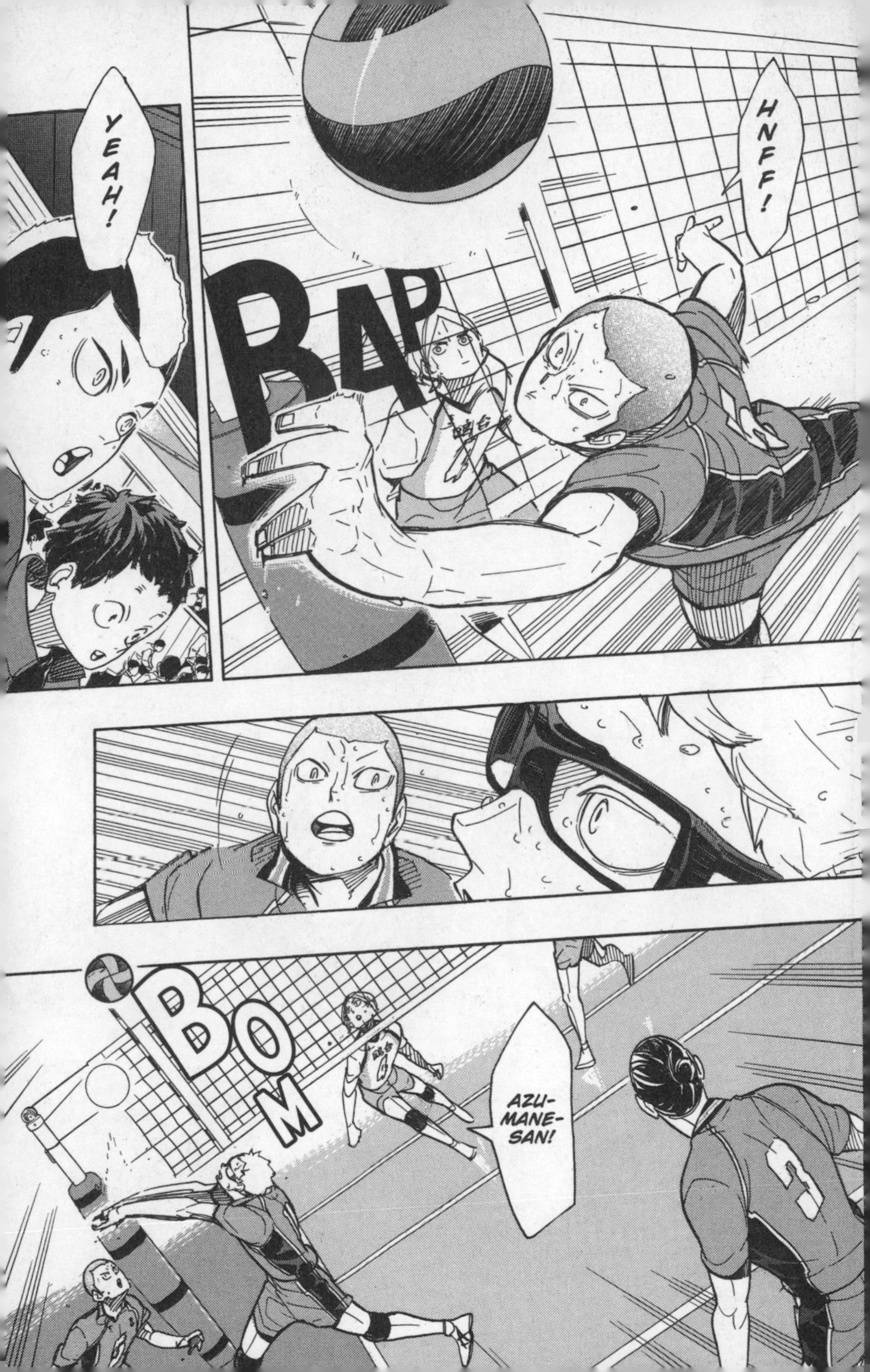
HNFF!
BAP
YEAH!
BOOM
AZUMANE-SAN!

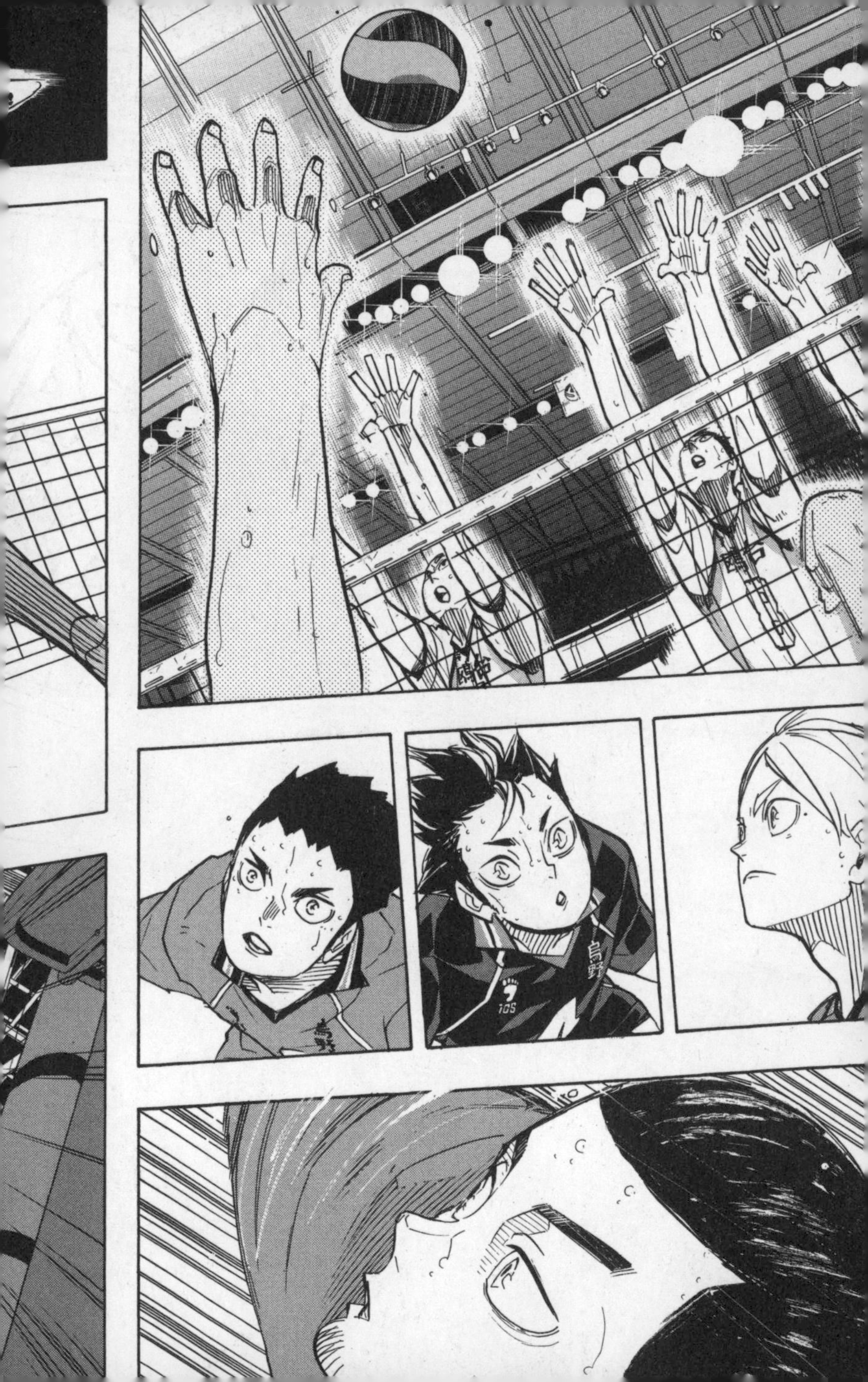
烏野

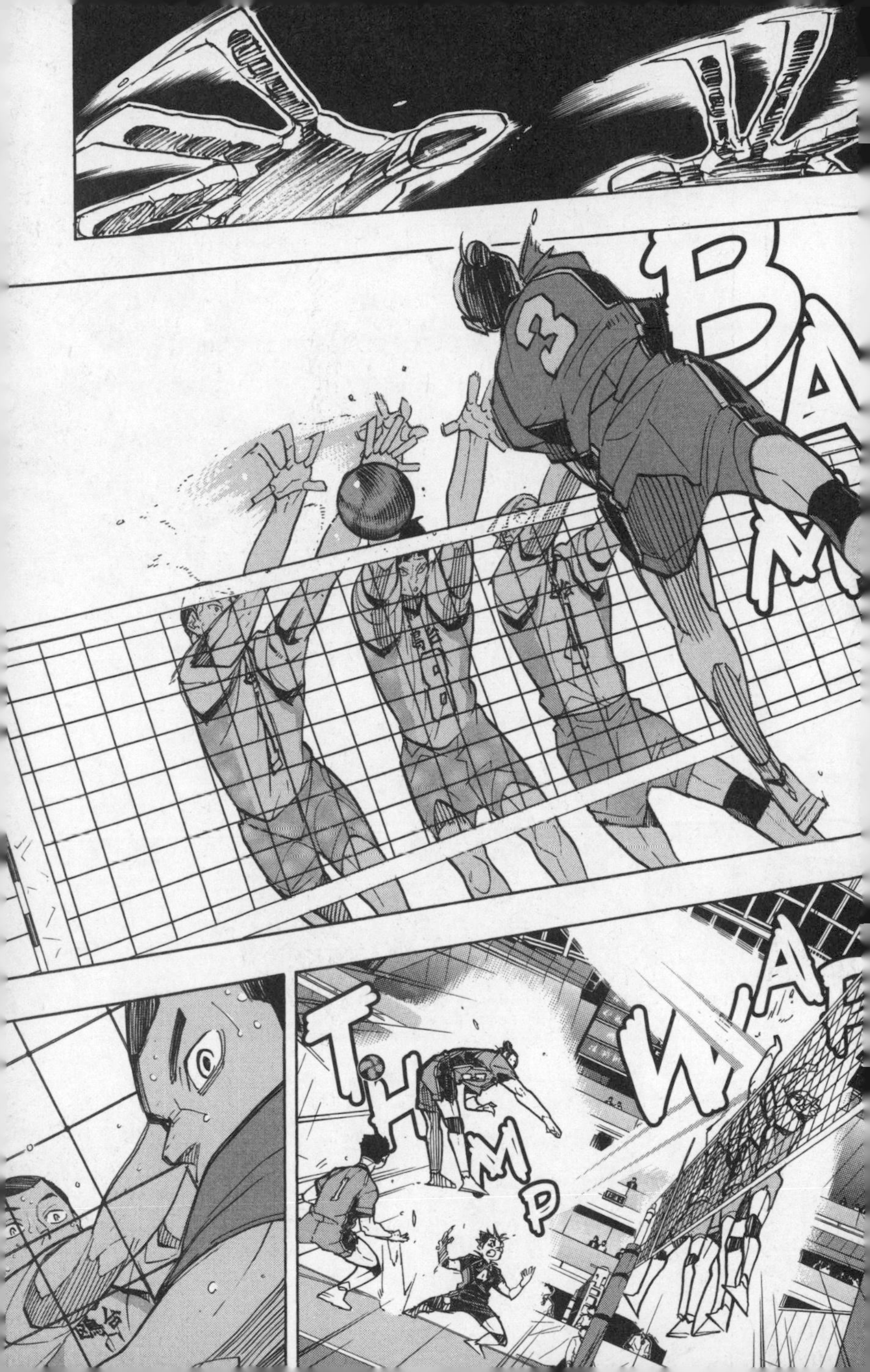
BAM
WA
THUMP

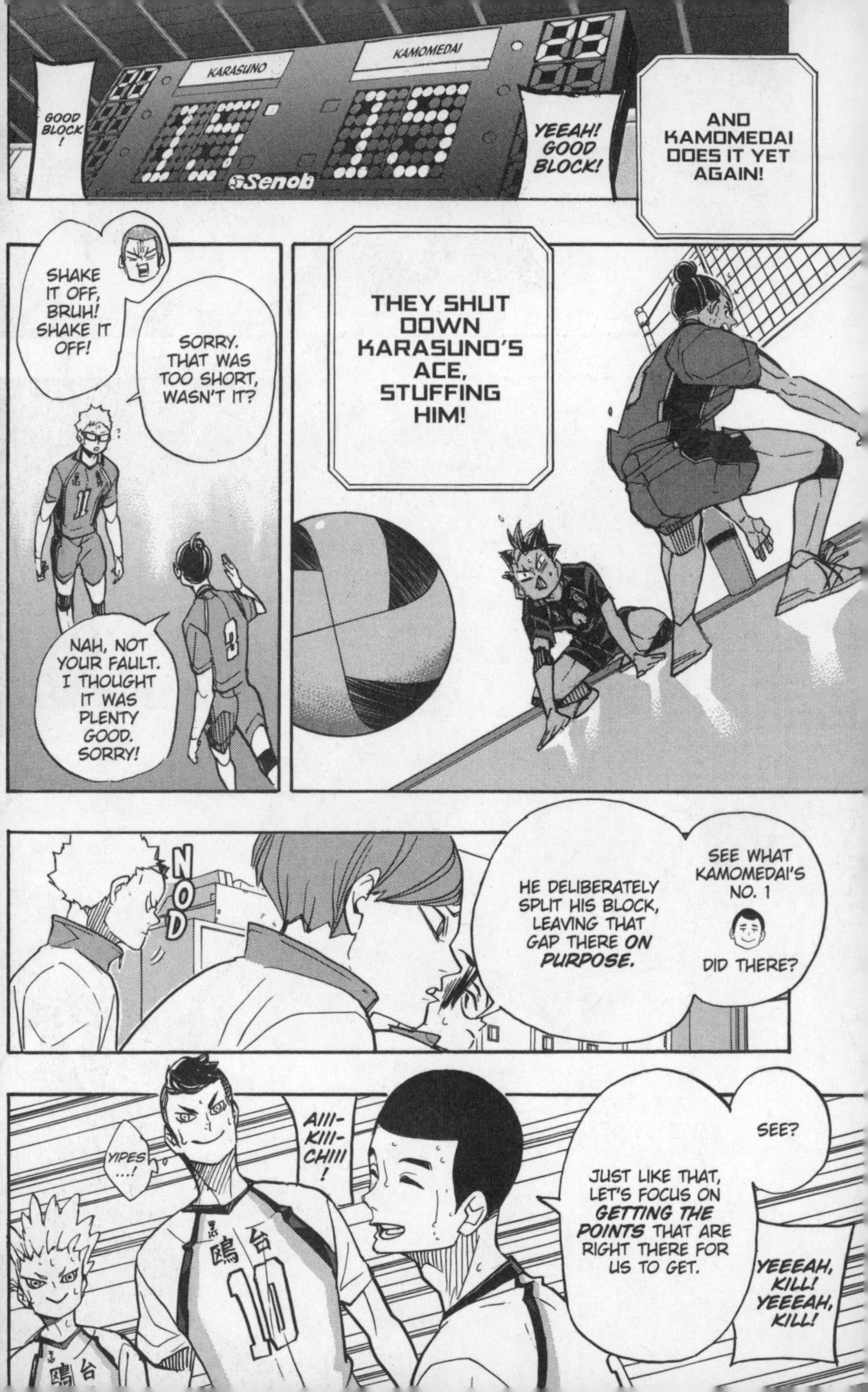
AND KAMOMEDAI DOES IT YET AGAIN!
YEEAH! GOOD BLOCK!
KAMOMEDAI
KARASUNO
Senob
GOOD BLOCK!
THEY SHUT DOWN KARASUNO'S ACE, STUFFING HIM!
SHAKE IT OFF, BRUH! SHAKE IT OFF!
SORRY. THAT WAS TOO SHORT, WASN'T IT?
NAH, NOT YOUR FAULT. I THOUGHT IT WAS PLENTY GOOD. SORRY!
SEE WHAT KAMOMEDAI'S NO. 1 DID THERE?
HE DELIBERATELY SPLIT HIS BLOCK, LEAVING THAT GAP THERE ON PURPOSE.
NOD
SEE?
JUST LIKE THAT, LET'S FOCUS ON GETTING THE POINTS THAT ARE RIGHT THERE FOR US TO GET.
YEEEAH, KILL! YEEEAH, KILL!
AIII-KIII-CHIII!
YIPES...!

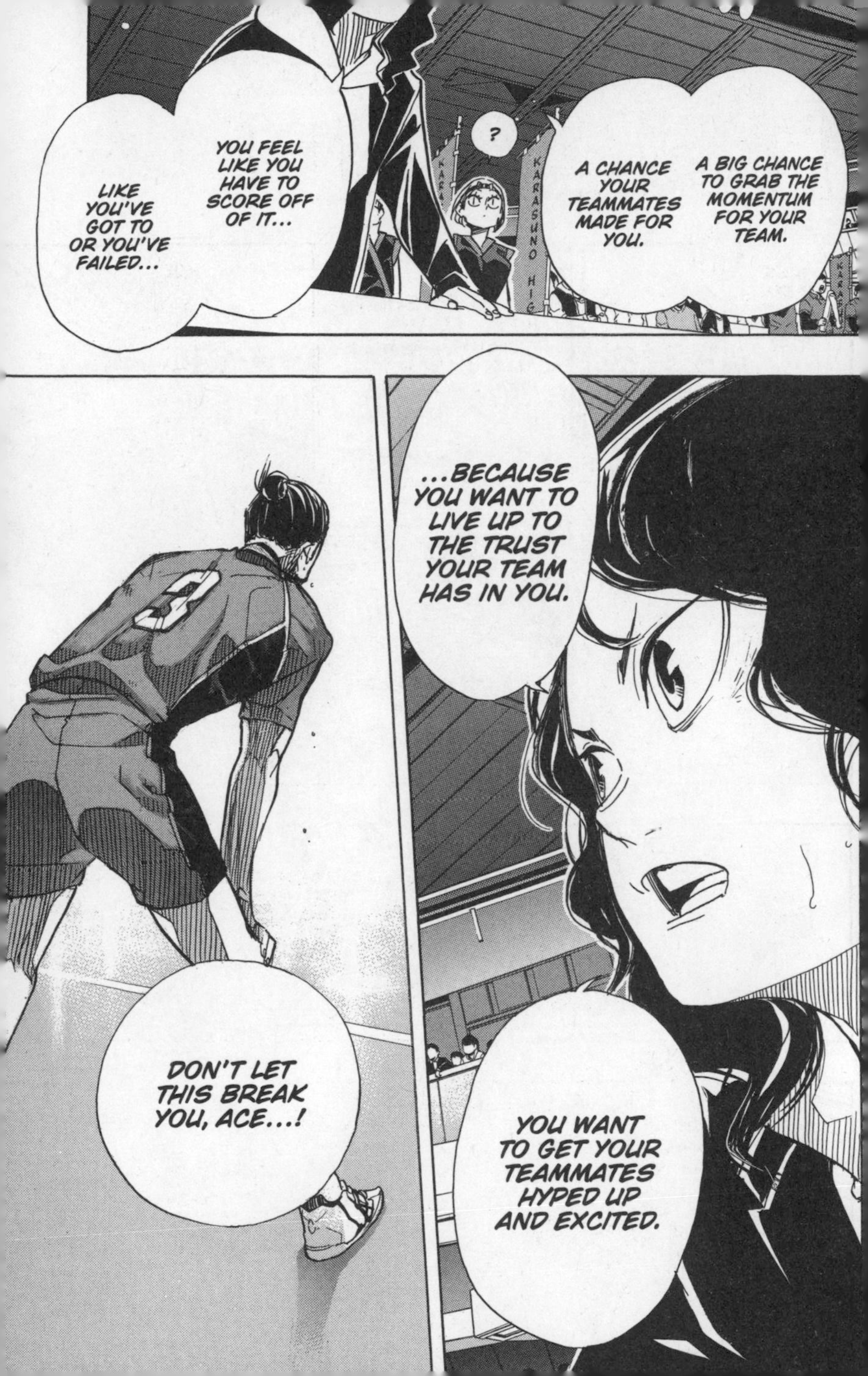
A BIG CHANCE TO GRAB THE MOMENTUM FOR YOUR TEAM.
A CHANCE YOUR TEAMMATES MADE FOR YOU.
?
YOU FEEL LIKE YOU HAVE TO SCORE OFF OF IT...
LIKE YOU'VE GOT TO OR YOU'VE FAILED...
...BECAUSE YOU WANT TO LIVE UP TO THE TRUST YOUR TEAM HAS IN YOU.
YOU WANT TO GET YOUR TEAMMATES HYPED UP AND EXCITED.
DON'T LET THIS BREAK YOU, ACE...!

HELLO FROM BEYOND THE (PAGE) EDGE!! GUESS WHICH PANEL THIS IS!!

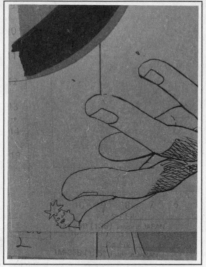

**FROM CHAPTER 350**

**LIFTOFF!**

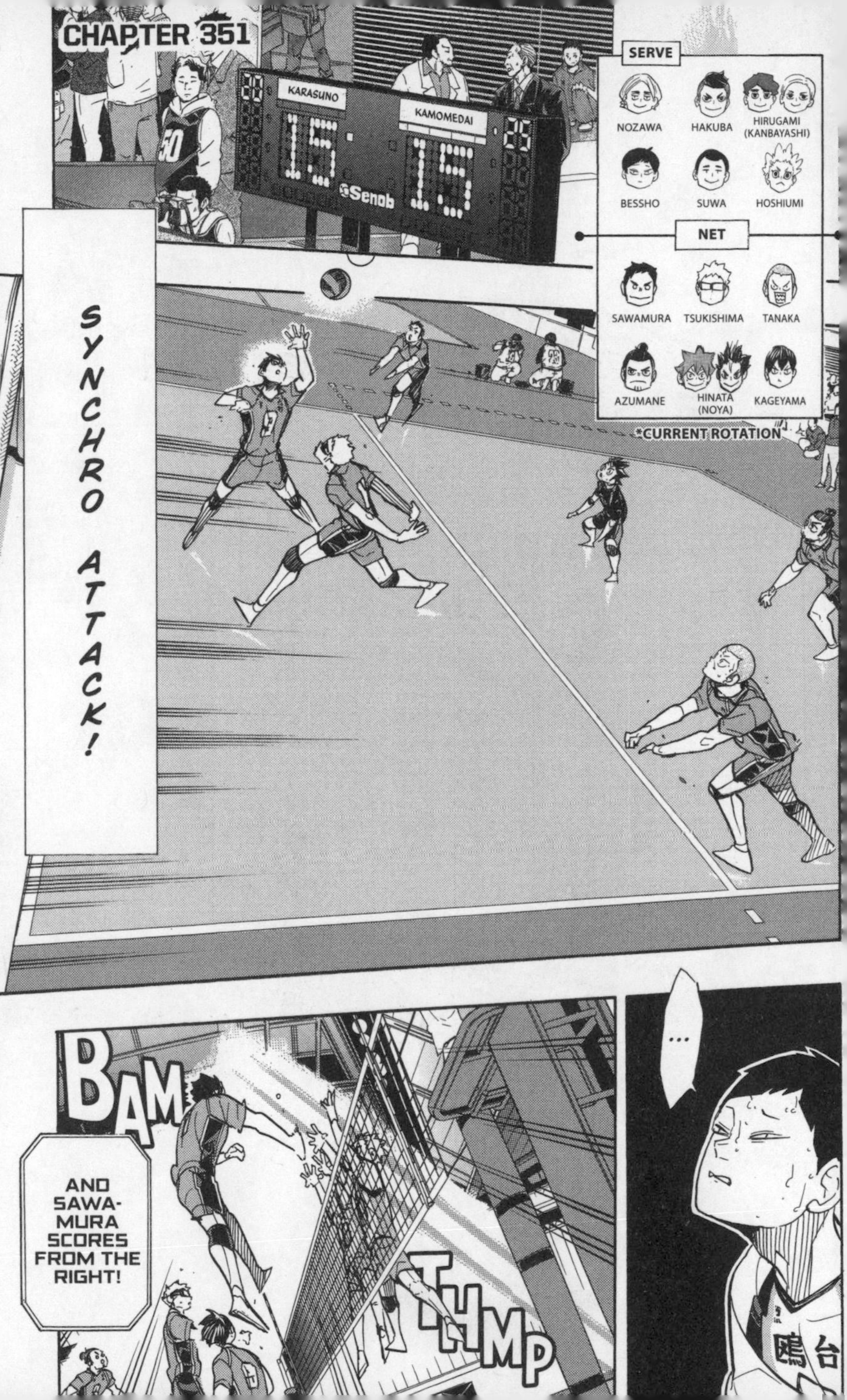
CHAPTER 351
KARASUNO
15
KAMOMEDAI
15
Senob
SERVE
NOZAWA
HAKUBA
HIRUGAMI (KANBAYASHI)
BESSHO
SUWA
HOSHIUMI
NET
SAWAMURA
TSUKISHIMA
TANAKA
AZUMANE
HINATA (NOYA)
KAGEYAMA
*CURRENT ROTATION
SYNCHRO ATTACK!
...
鴎台
BAM
AND SAWAMURA SCORES FROM THE RIGHT!
THMP

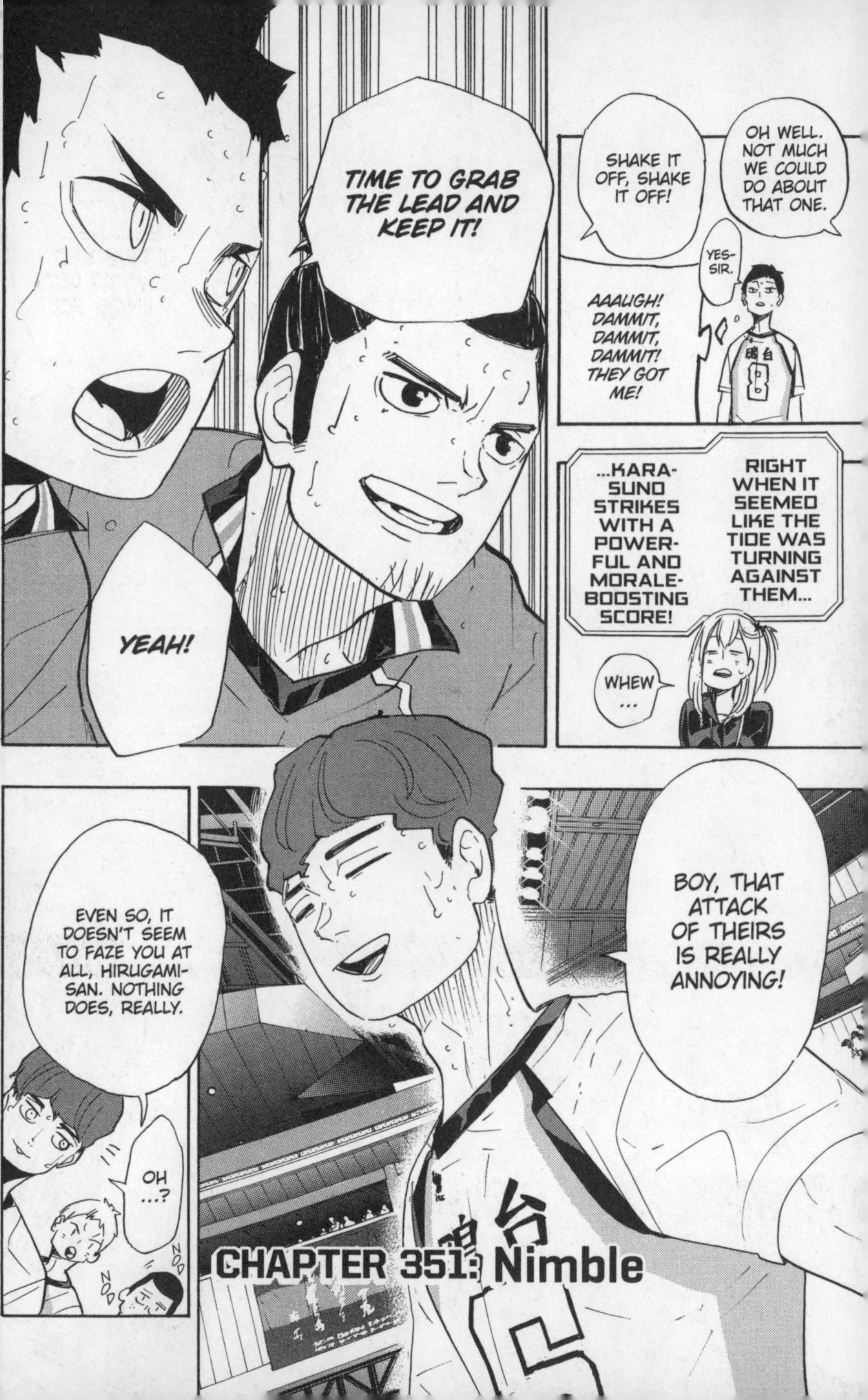
OH WELL. NOT MUCH WE COULD DO ABOUT THAT ONE.
SHAKE IT OFF, SHAKE IT OFF!
YES-SIR.
AAAUGH! DAMMIT, DAMMIT, DAMMIT! THEY GOT ME!
RIGHT WHEN IT SEEMED LIKE THE TIDE WAS TURNING AGAINST THEM...
...KARASUNO STRIKES WITH A POWERFUL AND MORALE-BOOSTING SCORE!
WHEW...
TIME TO GRAB THE LEAD AND KEEP IT!
YEAH!
BOY, THAT ATTACK OF THEIRS IS REALLY ANNOYING!
EVEN SO, IT DOESN'T SEEM TO FAZE YOU AT ALL, HIRUGAMI-SAN. NOTHING DOES, REALLY.
OH ...?
NOD
NOD
CHAPTER 351: Nimble

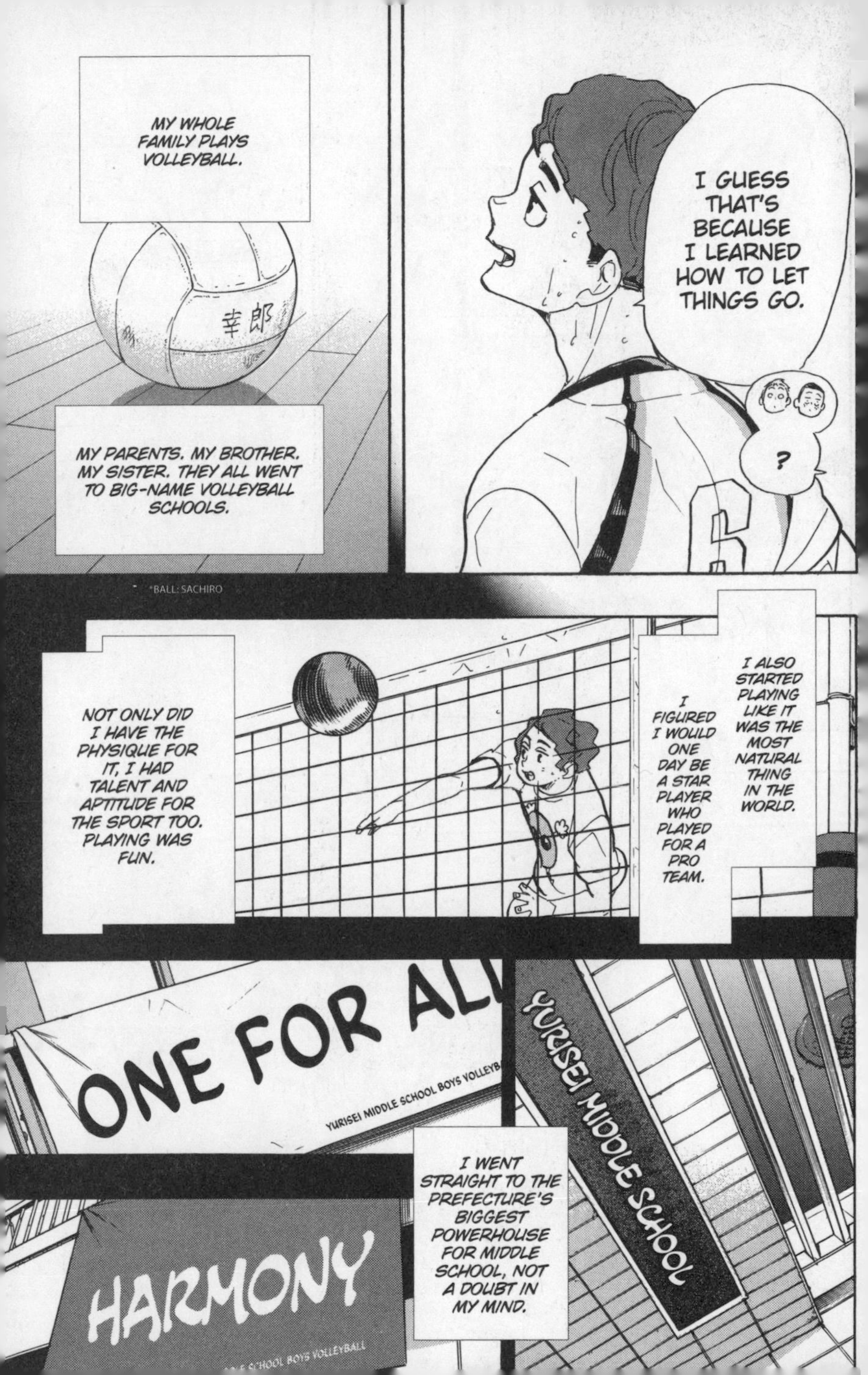

I GUESS THAT'S BECAUSE I LEARNED HOW TO LET THINGS GO.
?
MY WHOLE FAMILY PLAYS VOLLEYBALL.
幸郎
MY PARENTS. MY BROTHER. MY SISTER. THEY ALL WENT TO BIG-NAME VOLLEYBALL SCHOOLS.
*BALL: SACHIRO
I ALSO STARTED PLAYING LIKE IT WAS THE MOST NATURAL THING IN THE WORLD.
I FIGURED I WOULD ONE DAY BE A STAR PLAYER WHO PLAYED FOR A PRO TEAM.
NOT ONLY DID I HAVE THE PHYSIQUE FOR IT, I HAD TALENT AND APTITUDE FOR THE SPORT TOO. PLAYING WAS FUN.
YURISEI MIDDLE SCHOOL
I WENT STRAIGHT TO THE PREFECTURE'S BIGGEST POWERHOUSE FOR MIDDLE SCHOOL, NOT A DOUBT IN MY MIND.
ONE FOR AL
YURISEI MIDDLE SCHOOL BOYS VOLLEYBA
HARMONY

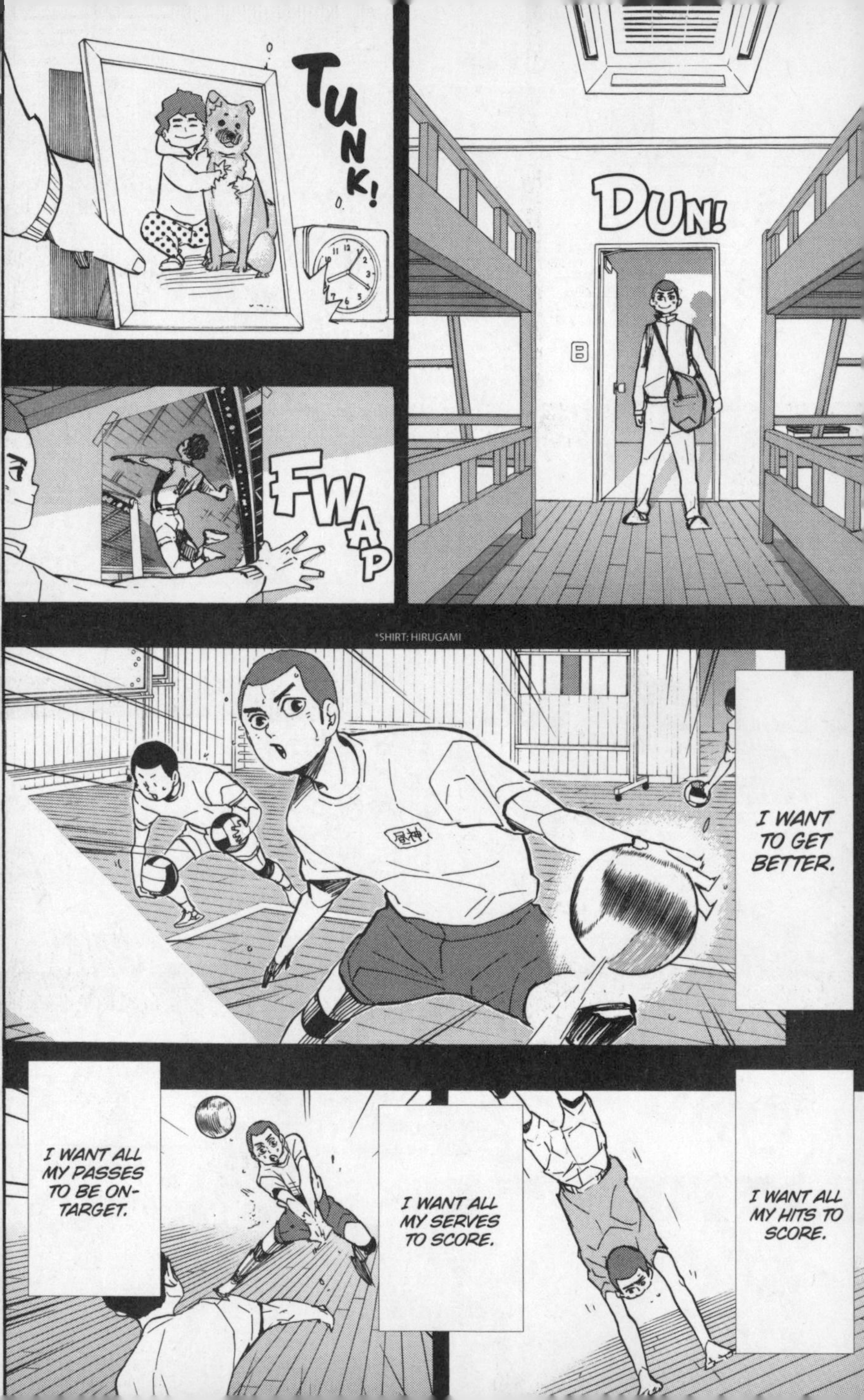
DUN!
TUNK!
FWAP
*SHIRT: HIRUGAMI
I WANT TO GET BETTER.
I WANT ALL MY HITS TO SCORE.
I WANT ALL MY SERVES TO SCORE.
I WANT ALL MY PASSES TO BE ON-TARGET.

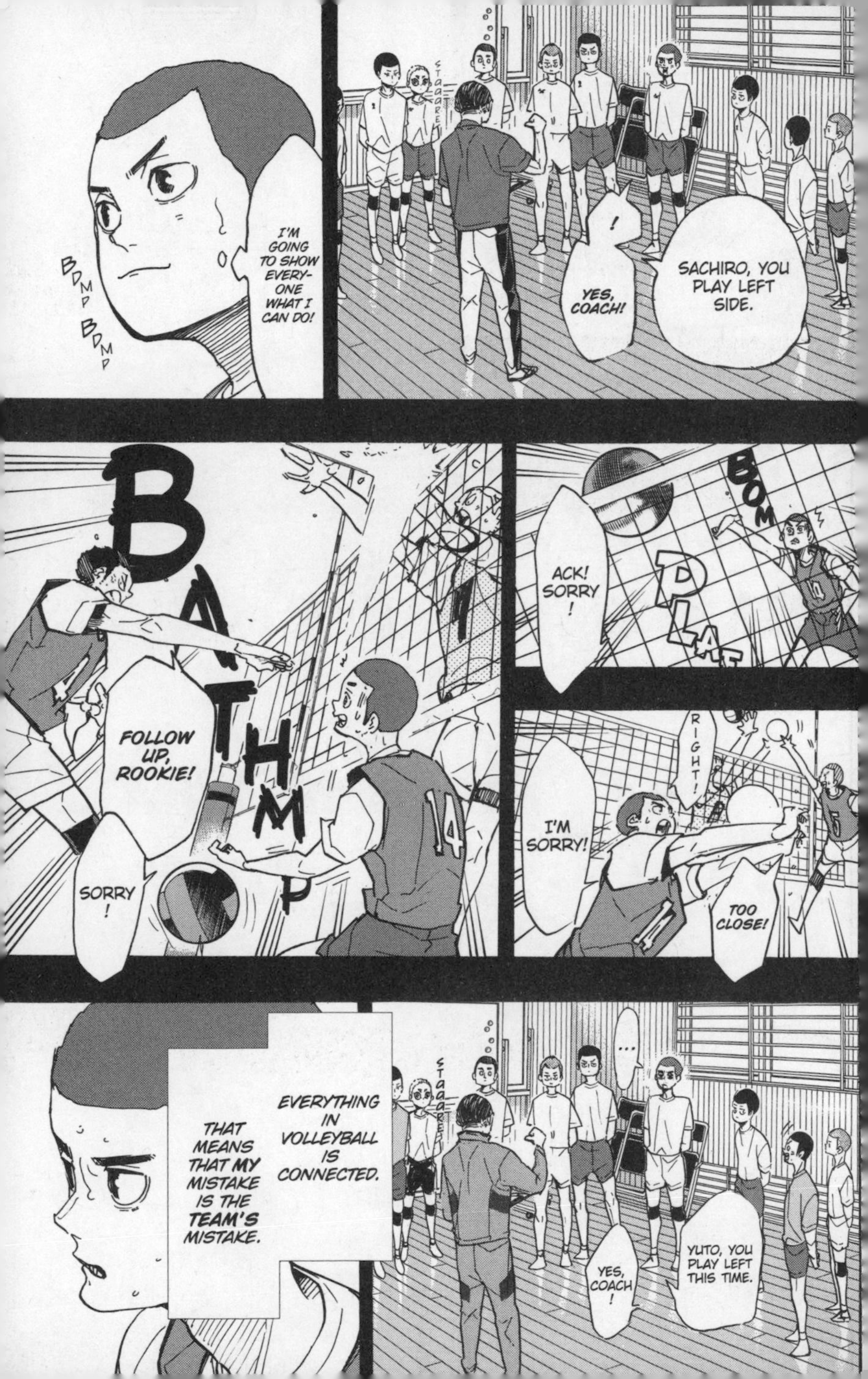
STAAARE
SACHIRO, YOU PLAY LEFT SIDE.
!
YES, COACH!
I'M GOING TO SHOW EVERYONE WHAT I CAN DO!
BDMP BDMP
BOM
ACK! SORRY!
DPLA
RIGHT!
I'M SORRY!
TOO CLOSE!
BATHMP
FOLLOW UP, ROOKIE!
SORRY!
STAAARE
...
YUTO, YOU PLAY LEFT THIS TIME.
YES, COACH!
EVERYTHING IN VOLLEYBALL IS CONNECTED.
THAT MEANS THAT MY MISTAKE IS THE TEAM'S MISTAKE.

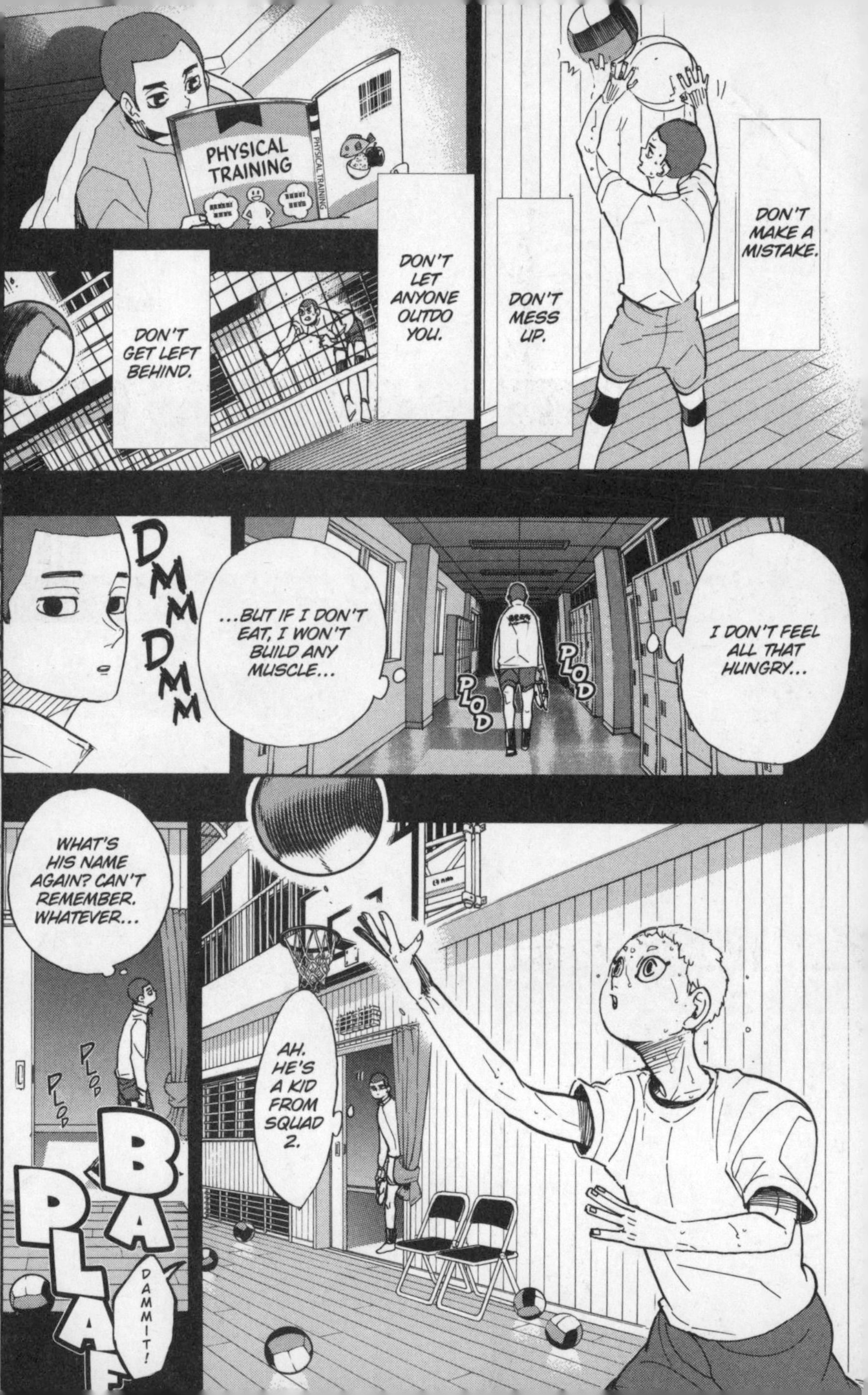
DON'T MAKE A MISTAKE.
DON'T MESS UP.
DON'T LET ANYONE OUTDO YOU.
PHYSICAL TRAINING
PHYSICAL TRAINING
DON'T GET LEFT BEHIND.
I DON'T FEEL ALL THAT HUNGRY...
PLOD PLOD
...BUT IF I DON'T EAT, I WON'T BUILD ANY MUSCLE...
DMMDMM
AH. HE'S A KID FROM SQUAD 2.
WHAT'S HIS NAME AGAIN? CAN'T REMEMBER. WHATEVER...
PLOD PLOD
BA
PLAF
DAMMIT!

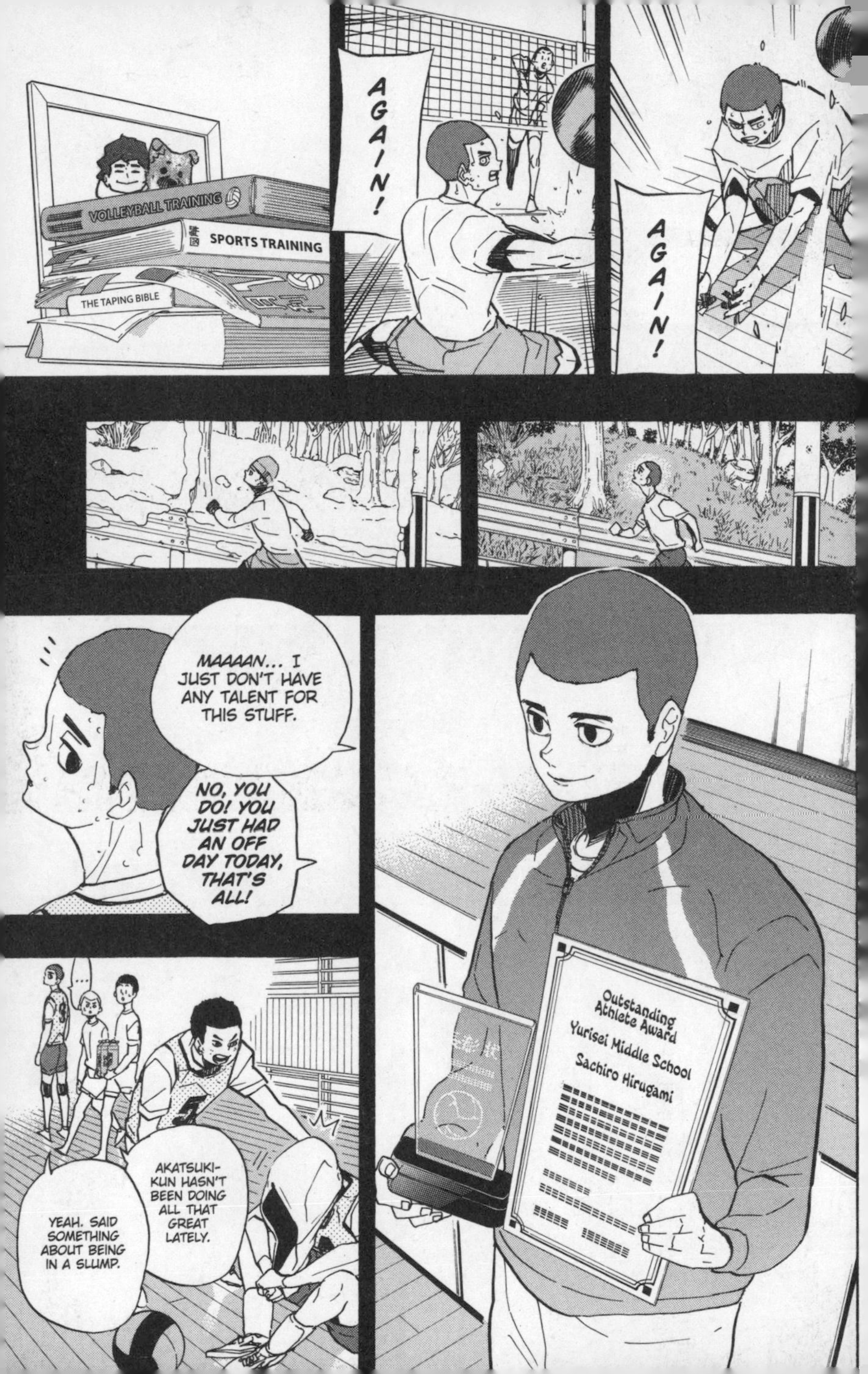
AGAIN!
AGAIN!
VOLLEYBALL TRAINING
SPORTS TRAINING
THE TAPING BIBLE
Outstanding Athlete Award
Yurisei Middle School
Sachiro Hirugami
MAAAAN... I JUST DON'T HAVE ANY TALENT FOR THIS STUFF.
NO, YOU DO! YOU JUST HAD AN OFF DAY TODAY, THAT'S ALL!
...
AKATSUKI-KUN HASN'T BEEN DOING ALL THAT GREAT LATELY.
YEAH. SAID SOMETHING ABOUT BEING IN A SLUMP.

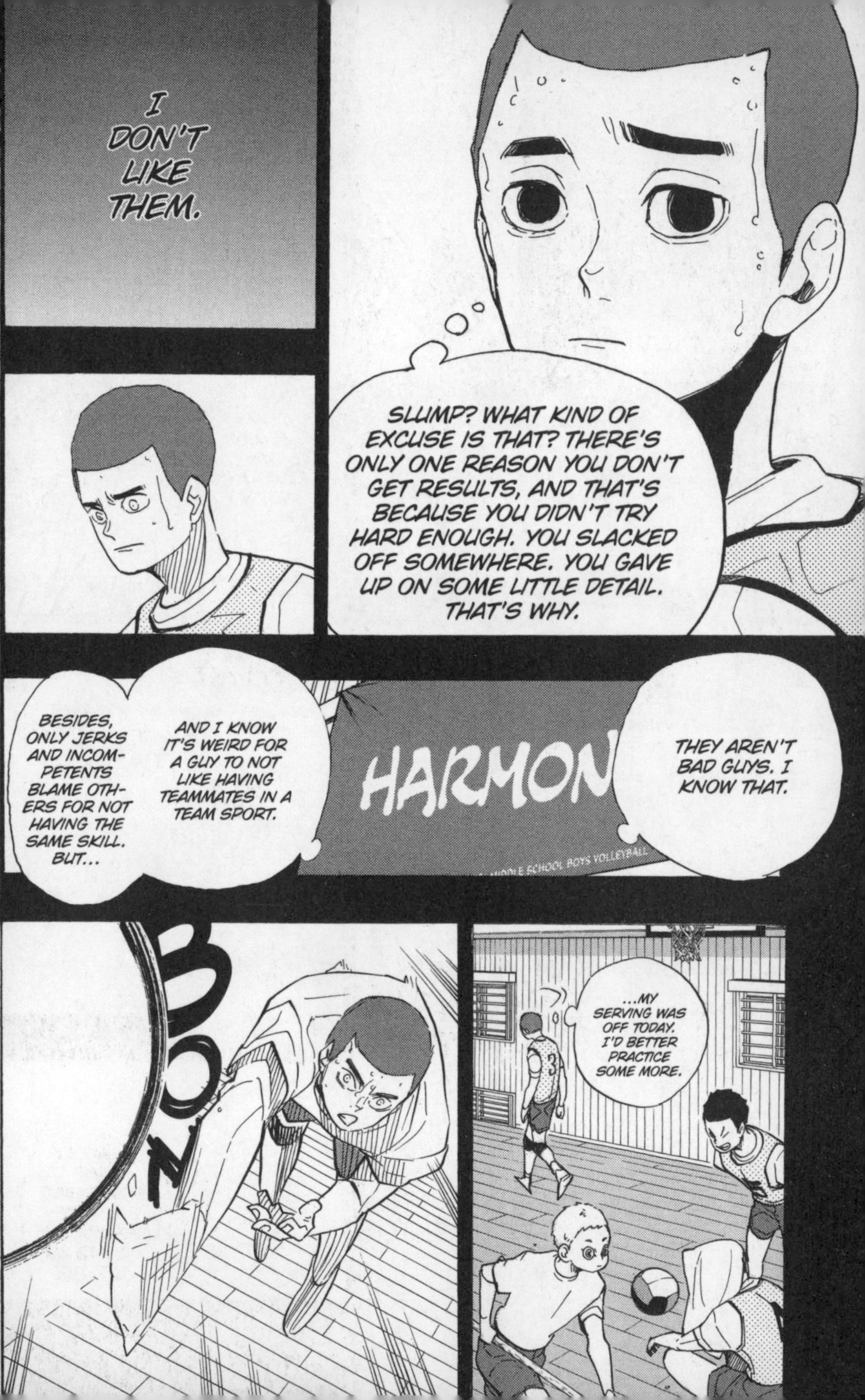
SLUMP? WHAT KIND OF EXCUSE IS THAT? THERE'S ONLY ONE REASON YOU DON'T GET RESULTS, AND THAT'S BECAUSE YOU DIDN'T TRY HARD ENOUGH. YOU SLACKED OFF SOMEWHERE. YOU GAVE UP ON SOME LITTLE DETAIL. THAT'S WHY.
I DON'T LIKE THEM.
THEY AREN'T BAD GUYS. I KNOW THAT.
HARMON
SCHOOL BOYS VOLLEYBALL
AND I KNOW IT'S WEIRD FOR A GUY TO NOT LIKE HAVING TEAMMATES IN A TEAM SPORT.
BESIDES, ONLY JERKS AND INCOMPETENTS BLAME OTHERS FOR NOT HAVING THE SAME SKILL. BUT...
...MY SERVING WAS OFF TODAY. I'D BETTER PRACTICE SOME MORE.

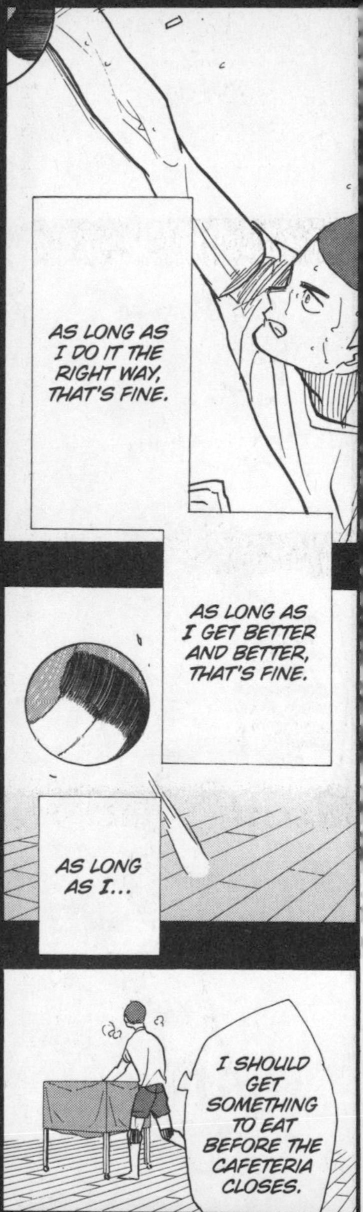
AS LONG AS I DO IT THE RIGHT WAY, THAT'S FINE.
AS LONG AS I GET BETTER AND BETTER, THAT'S FINE.
AS LONG AS I...
I SHOULD GET SOMETHING TO EAT BEFORE THE CAFETERIA CLOSES.

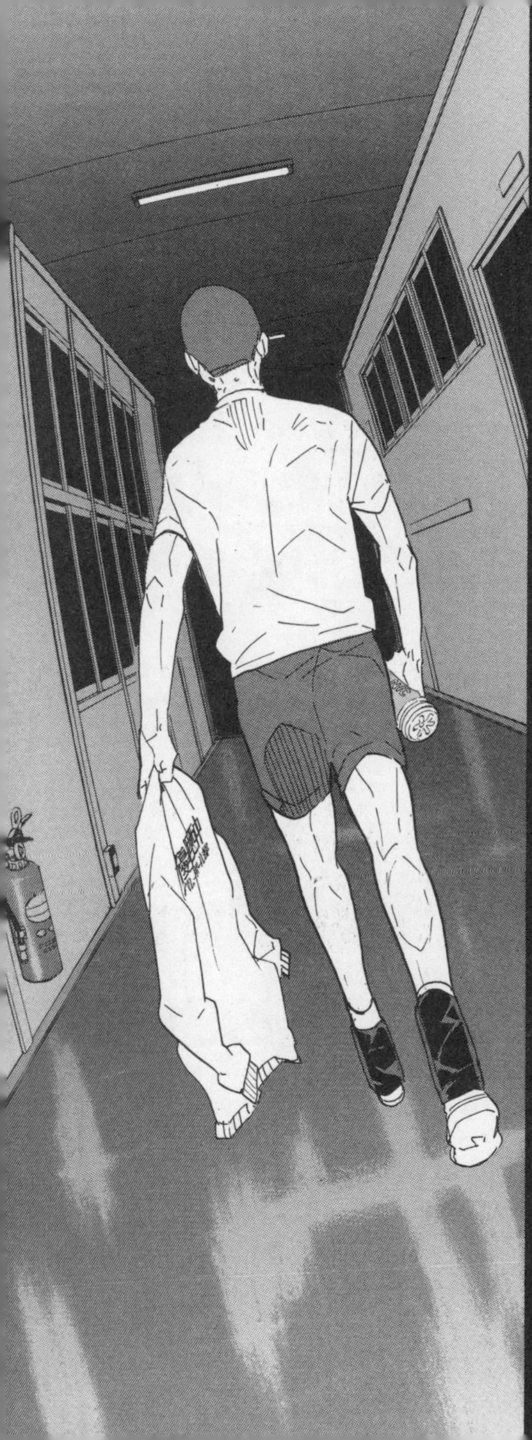

*JACKET: YURISEI MIDDLE SCHOOL VOLLEYBALL CLUB

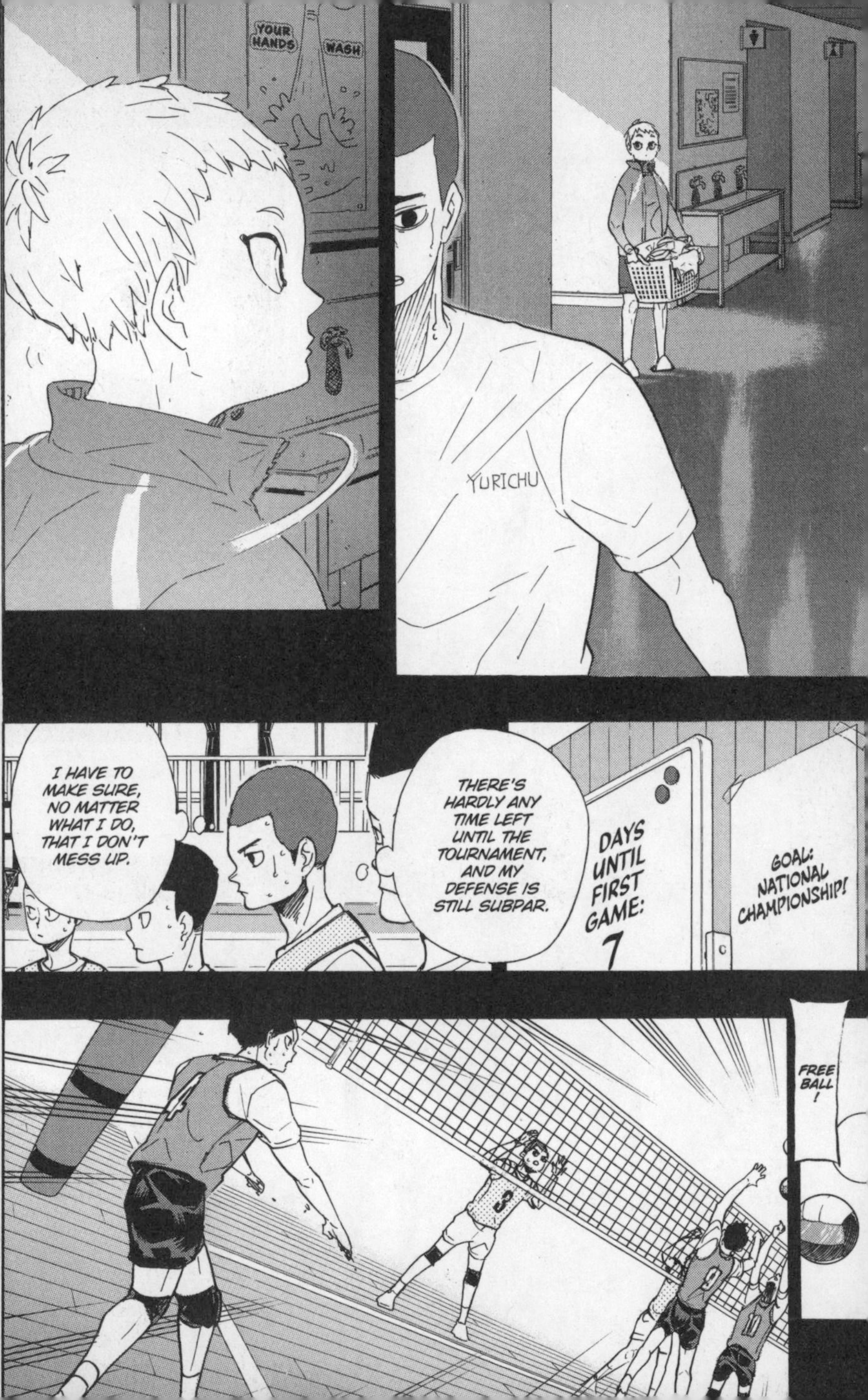
YURICHU
WASH
YOUR HANDS
GOAL: NATIONAL CHAMPIONSHIP!
DAYS UNTIL FIRST GAME: 7
THERE'S HARDLY ANY TIME LEFT UNTIL THE TOURNAMENT, AND MY DEFENSE IS STILL SUBPAR.
I HAVE TO MAKE SURE, NO MATTER WHAT I DO, THAT I DON'T MESS UP.
FREE BALL!

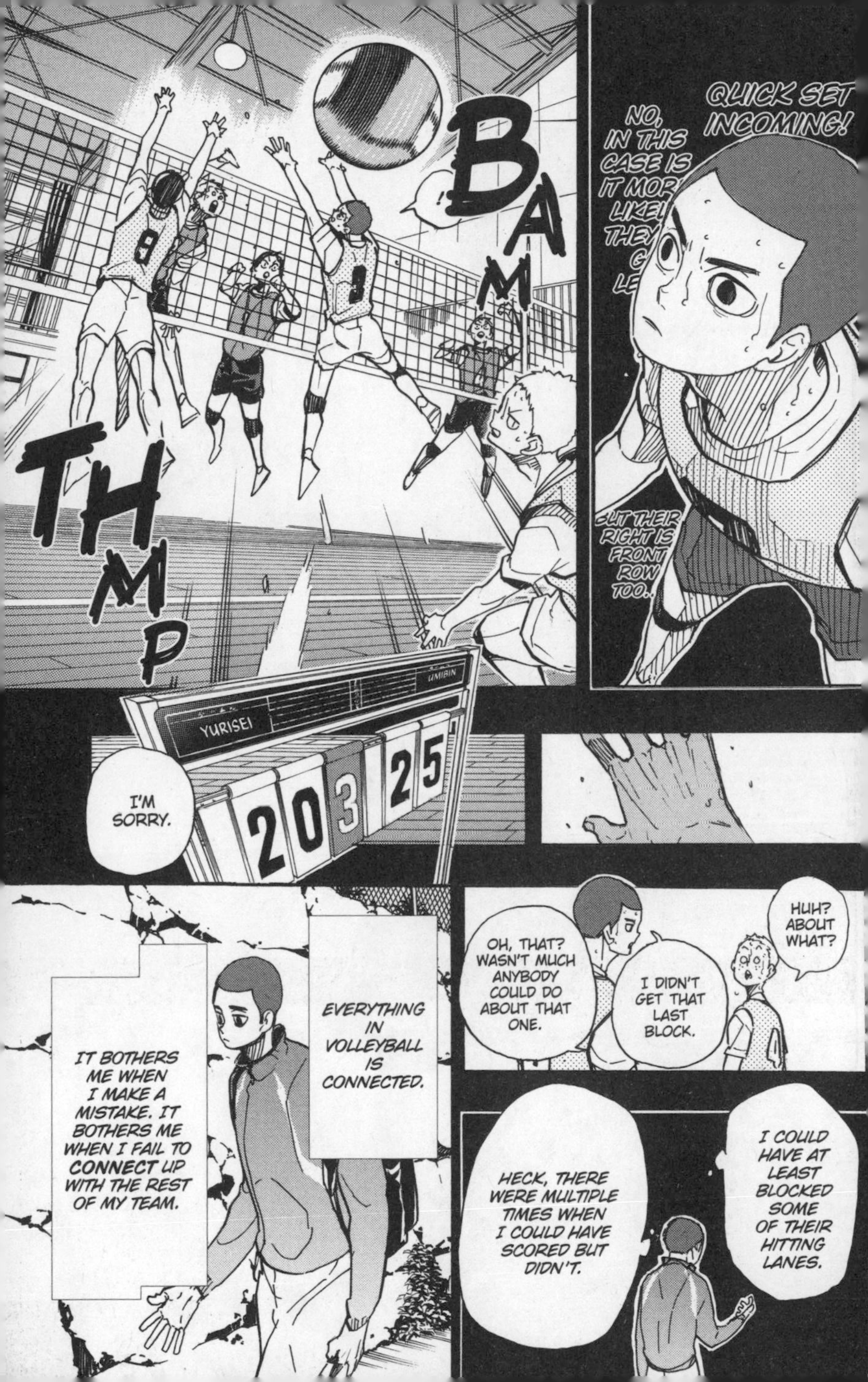
QUICK SET INCOMING!
NO, IN THIS CASE IS IT MOR LIKEL THEY
BUT THEIR RIGHT IS FRONT ROW TOO...
BAM
!
THUMP
YURISEI
UMIBIN
20 3 25
I'M SORRY.
HUH? ABOUT WHAT?
I DIDN'T GET THAT LAST BLOCK.
OH, THAT? WASN'T MUCH ANYBODY COULD DO ABOUT THAT ONE.
I COULD HAVE AT LEAST BLOCKED SOME OF THEIR HITTING LANES.
HECK, THERE WERE MULTIPLE TIMES WHEN I COULD HAVE SCORED BUT DIDN'T.
EVERYTHING IN VOLLEYBALL IS CONNECTED.
IT BOTHERS ME WHEN I MAKE A MISTAKE. IT BOTHERS ME WHEN I FAIL TO CONNECT UP WITH THE REST OF MY TEAM.

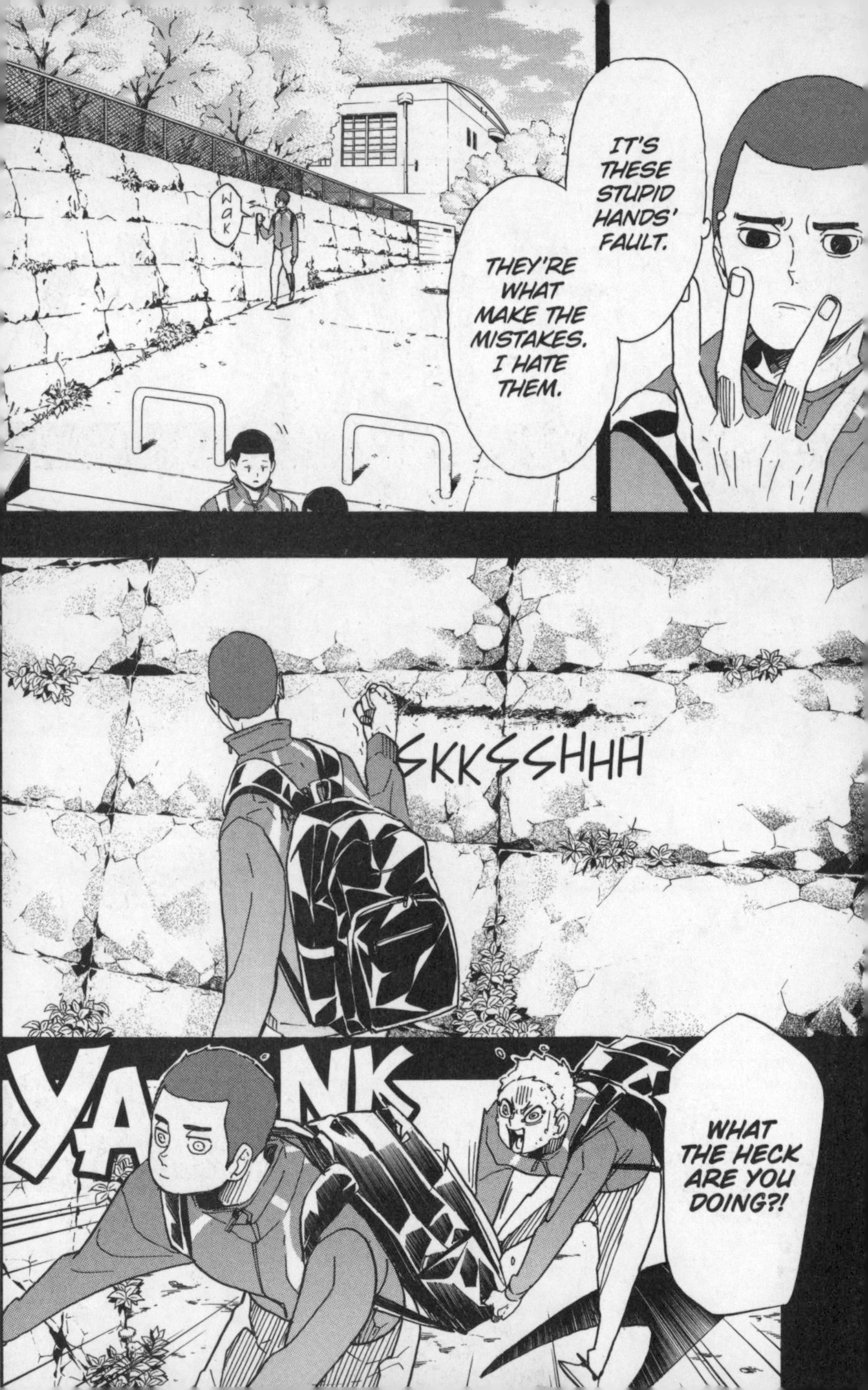
IT'S THESE STUPID HANDS' FAULT.
THEY'RE WHAT MAKE THE MISTAKES. I HATE THEM.
wak
SKKSSHHH
WHAT THE HECK ARE YOU DOING?!
YA NK

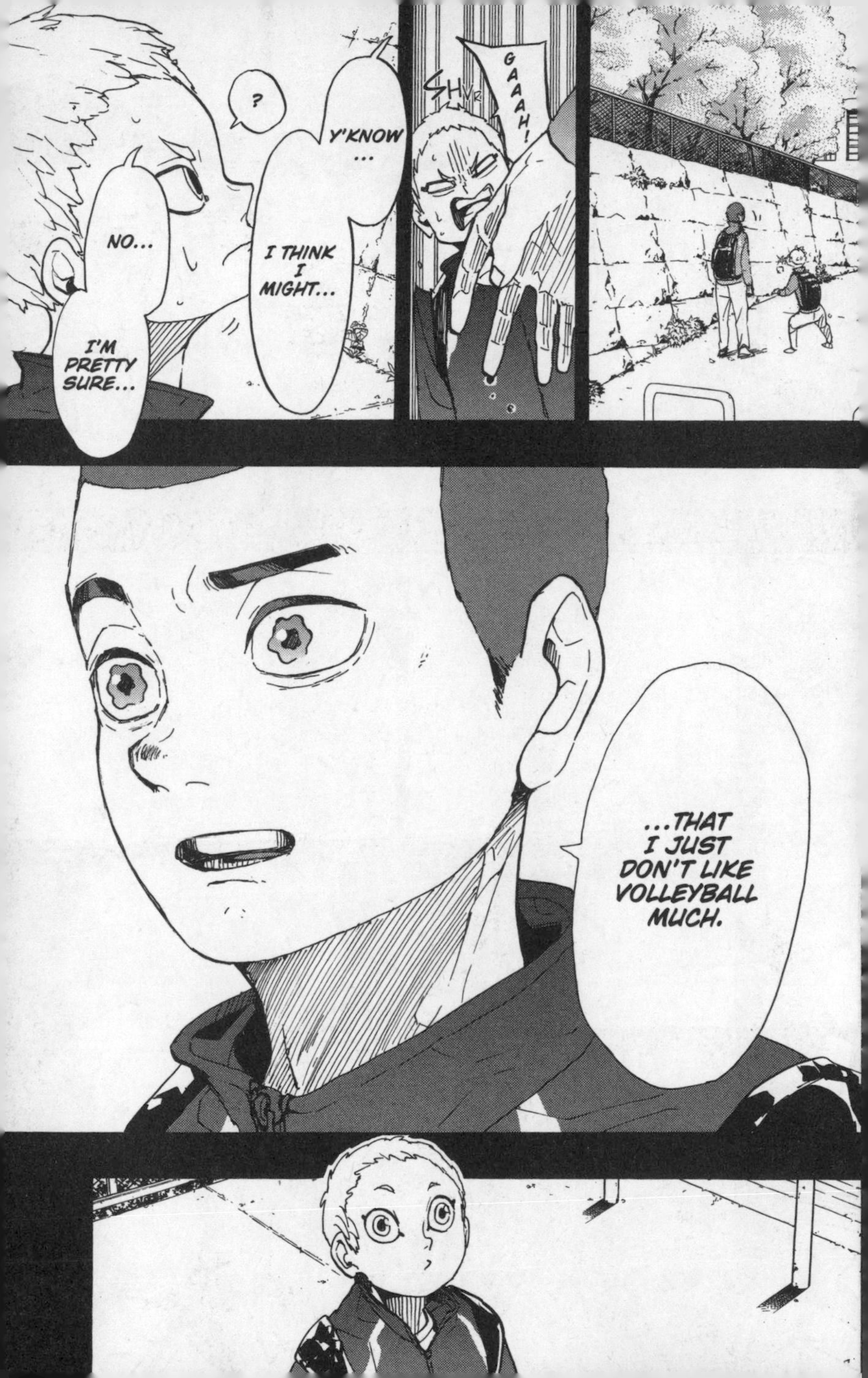
SHVR
GAAAH!
Y'KNOW...
I THINK I MIGHT...
?
NO...
I'M PRETTY SURE...
...THAT I JUST DON'T LIKE VOLLEYBALL MUCH.

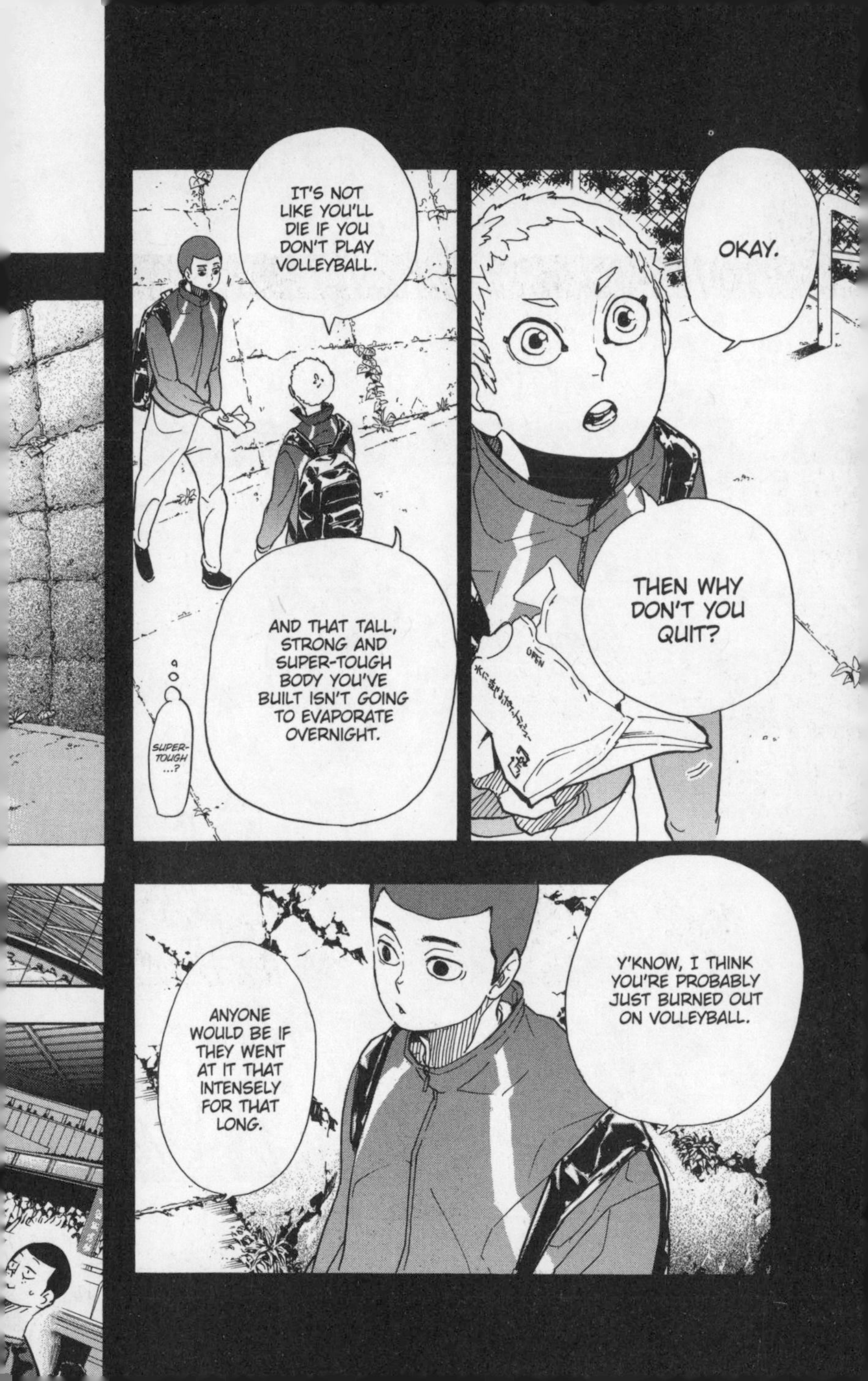
OKAY.
THEN WHY DON'T YOU QUIT?
IT'S NOT LIKE YOU'LL DIE IF YOU DON'T PLAY VOLLEYBALL.
AND THAT TALL, STRONG AND SUPER-TOUGH BODY YOU'VE BUILT ISN'T GOING TO EVAPORATE OVERNIGHT.
SUPER-TOUGH ...?
Y'KNOW, I THINK YOU'RE PROBABLY JUST BURNED OUT ON VOLLEYBALL.
ANYONE WOULD BE IF THEY WENT AT IT THAT INTENSELY FOR THAT LONG.

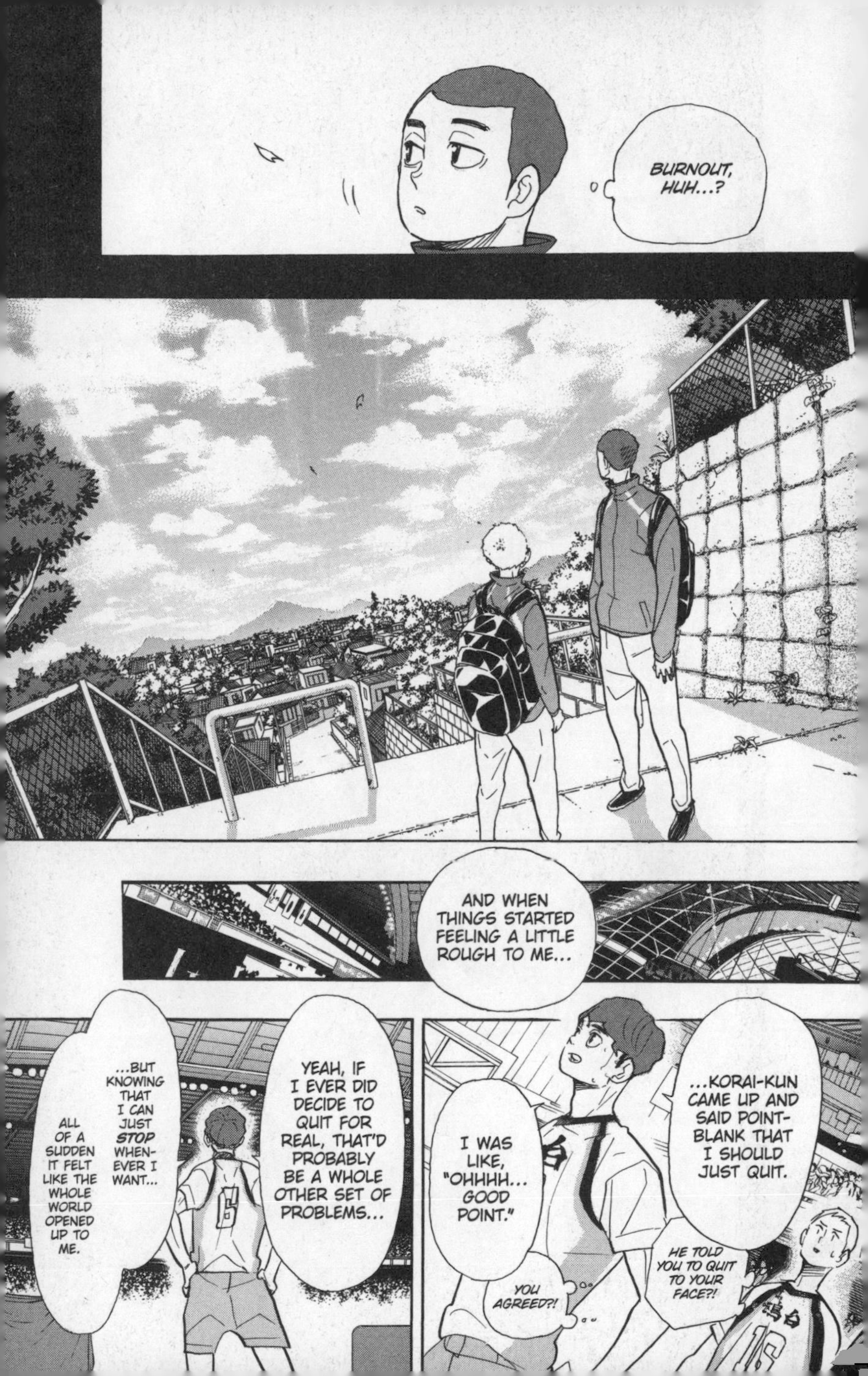
BURNOUT, HUH...?
AND WHEN THINGS STARTED FEELING A LITTLE ROUGH TO ME...
...KORAI-KUN CAME UP AND SAID POINT-BLANK THAT I SHOULD JUST QUIT.
HE TOLD YOU TO QUIT TO YOUR FACE?!
I WAS LIKE, "OHHHH... GOOD POINT."
YOU AGREED?!
YEAH, IF I EVER DID DECIDE TO QUIT FOR REAL, THAT'D PROBABLY BE A WHOLE OTHER SET OF PROBLEMS...
...BUT KNOWING THAT I CAN JUST *STOP* WHENEVER I WANT...
ALL OF A SUDDEN IT FELT LIKE THE WHOLE WORLD OPENED UP TO ME.

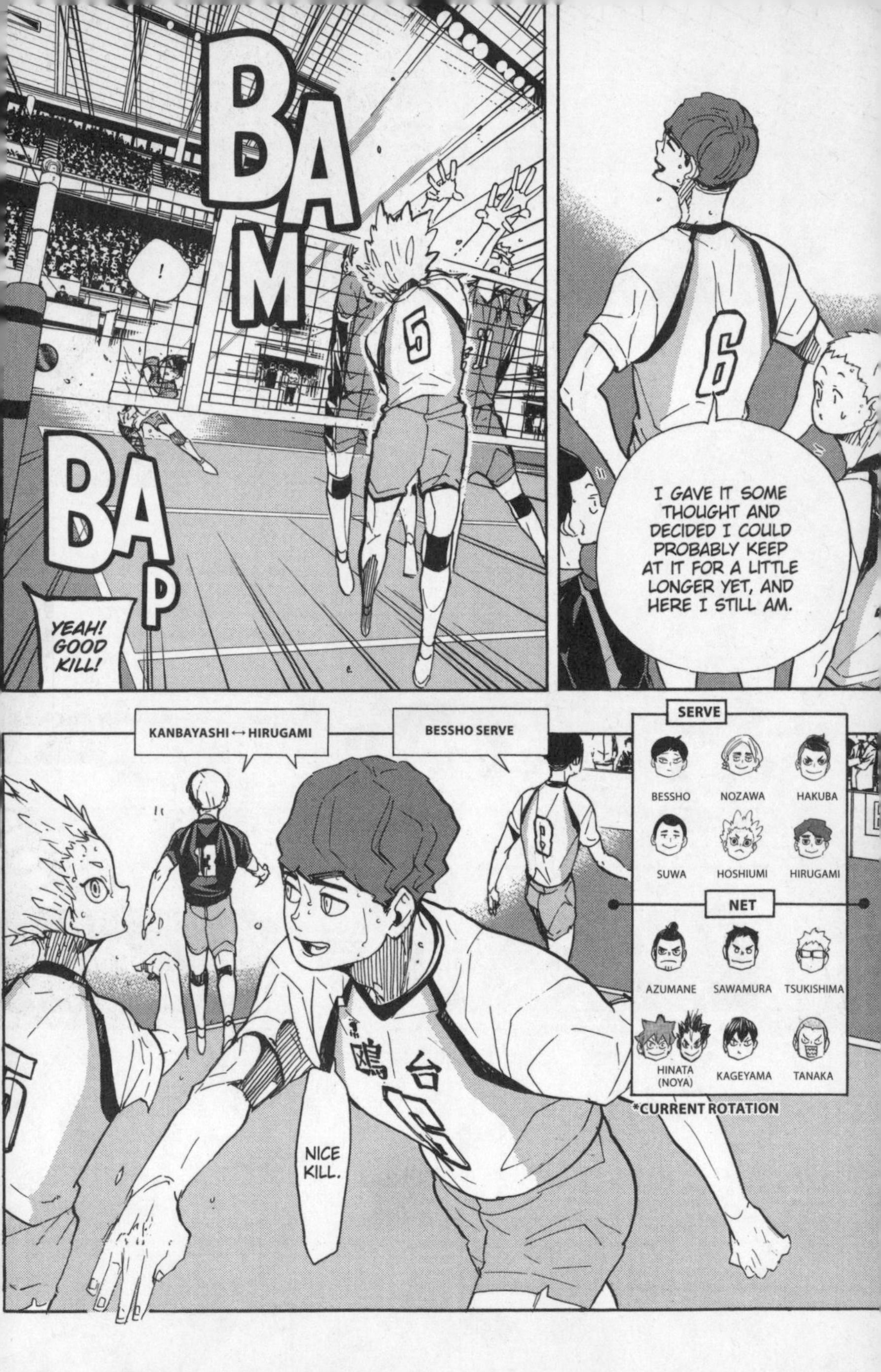
I GAVE IT SOME THOUGHT AND DECIDED I COULD PROBABLY KEEP AT IT FOR A LITTLE LONGER YET, AND HERE I STILL AM.
BAM
!
BAP
YEAH! GOOD KILL!
SERVE
BESSHO
NOZAWA
HAKUBA
SUWA
HOSHIUMI
HIRUGAMI
NET
AZUMANE
SAWAMURA
TSUKISHIMA
HINATA (NOYA)
KAGEYAMA
TANAKA
*CURRENT ROTATION
BESSHO SERVE
KANBAYASHI ↔ HIRUGAMI
NICE KILL.

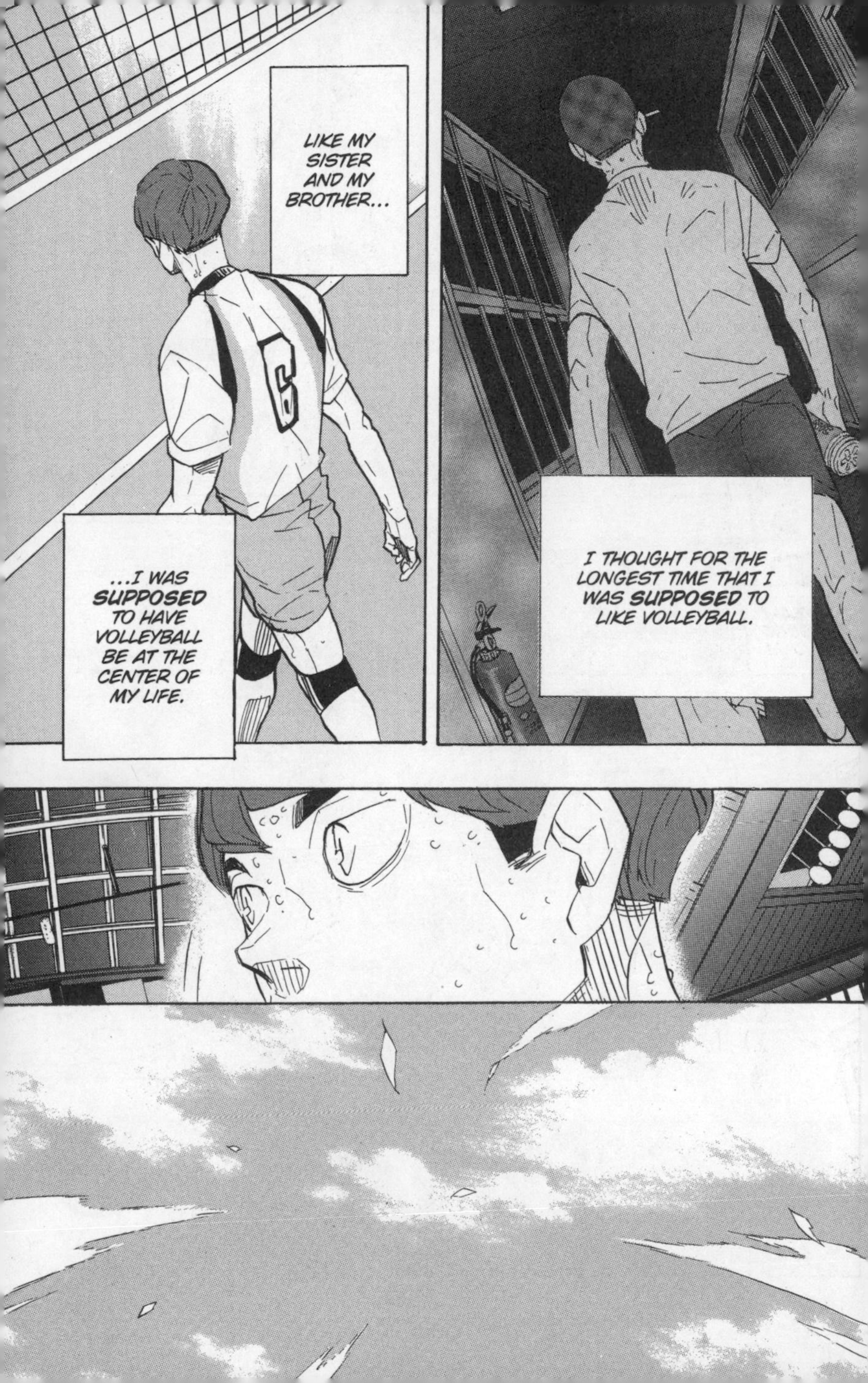
I THOUGHT FOR THE LONGEST TIME THAT I WAS **SUPPOSED** TO LIKE VOLLEYBALL.
LIKE MY SISTER AND MY BROTHER...
...I WAS **SUPPOSED** TO HAVE VOLLEYBALL BE AT THE CENTER OF MY LIFE.

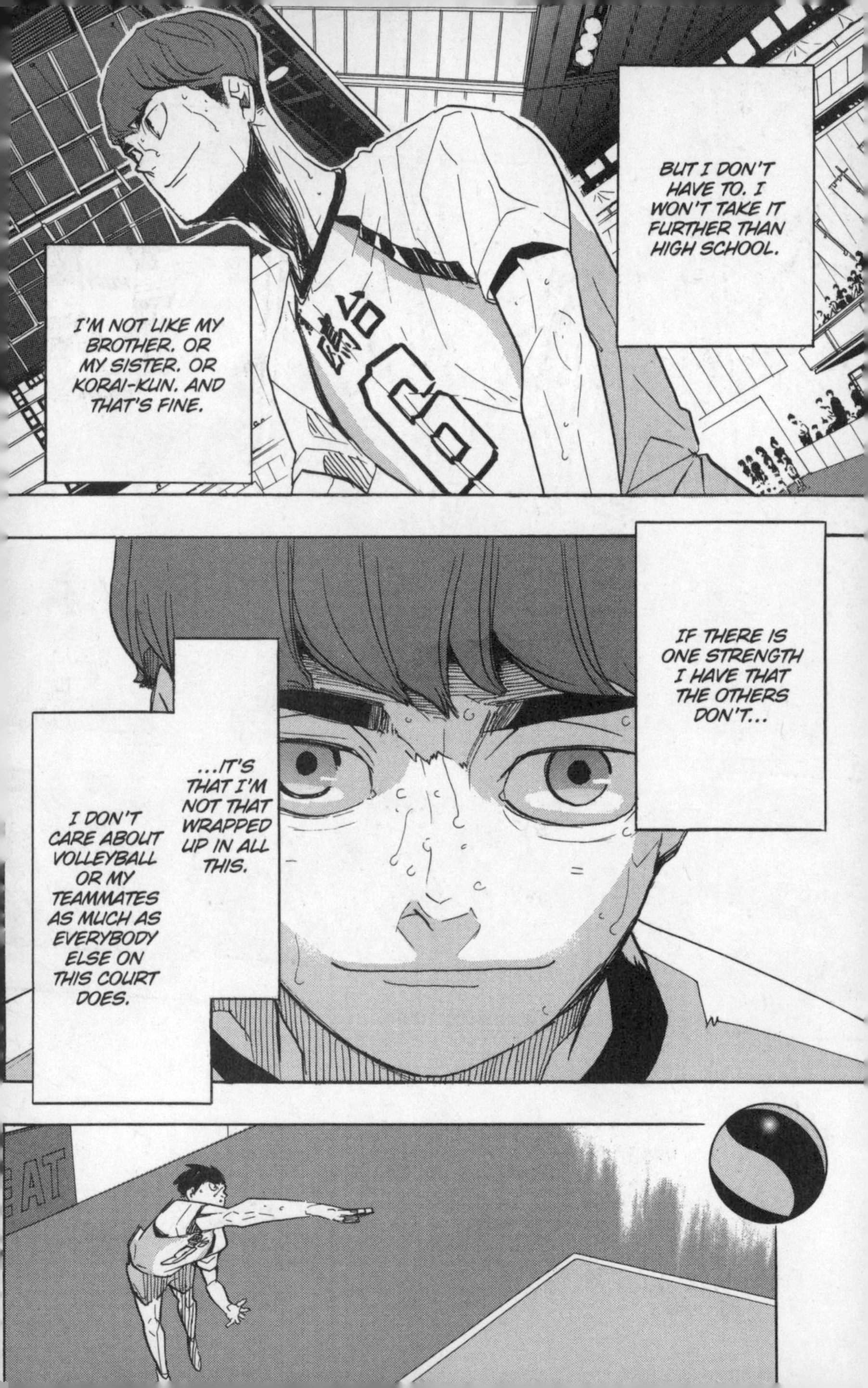
BUT I DON'T HAVE TO. I WON'T TAKE IT FURTHER THAN HIGH SCHOOL.
I'M NOT LIKE MY BROTHER. OR MY SISTER. OR KORAI-KUN. AND THAT'S FINE.
IF THERE IS ONE STRENGTH I HAVE THAT THE OTHERS DON'T...
...IT'S THAT I'M NOT THAT WRAPPED UP IN ALL THIS.
I DON'T CARE ABOUT VOLLEYBALL OR MY TEAMMATES AS MUCH AS EVERYBODY ELSE ON THIS COURT DOES.

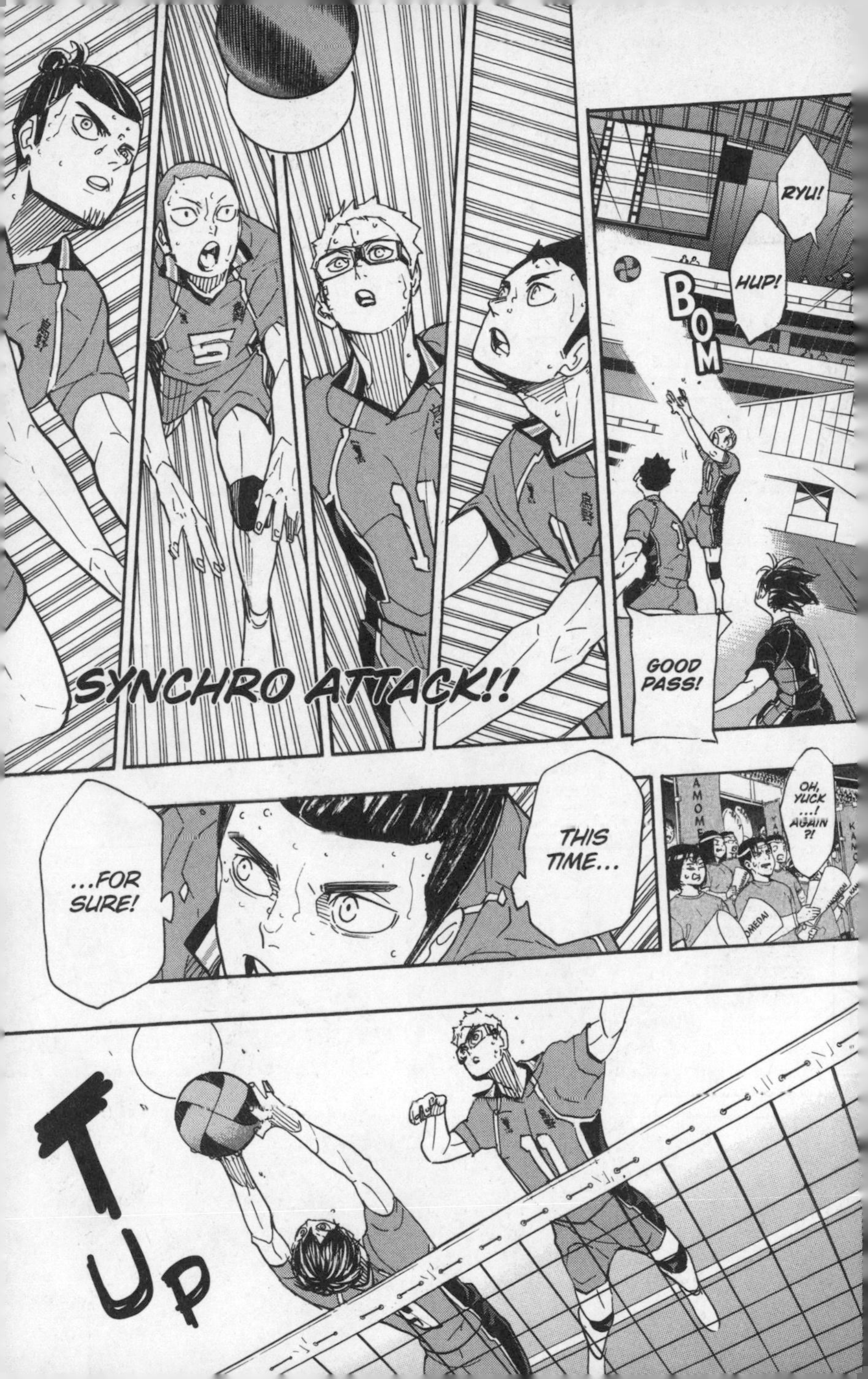
RYU!
HUP!
BOM
GOOD PASS!
SYNCHRO ATTACK!!
OH, YUCK ...! AGAIN ?!
THIS TIME...
...FOR SURE!
TUP

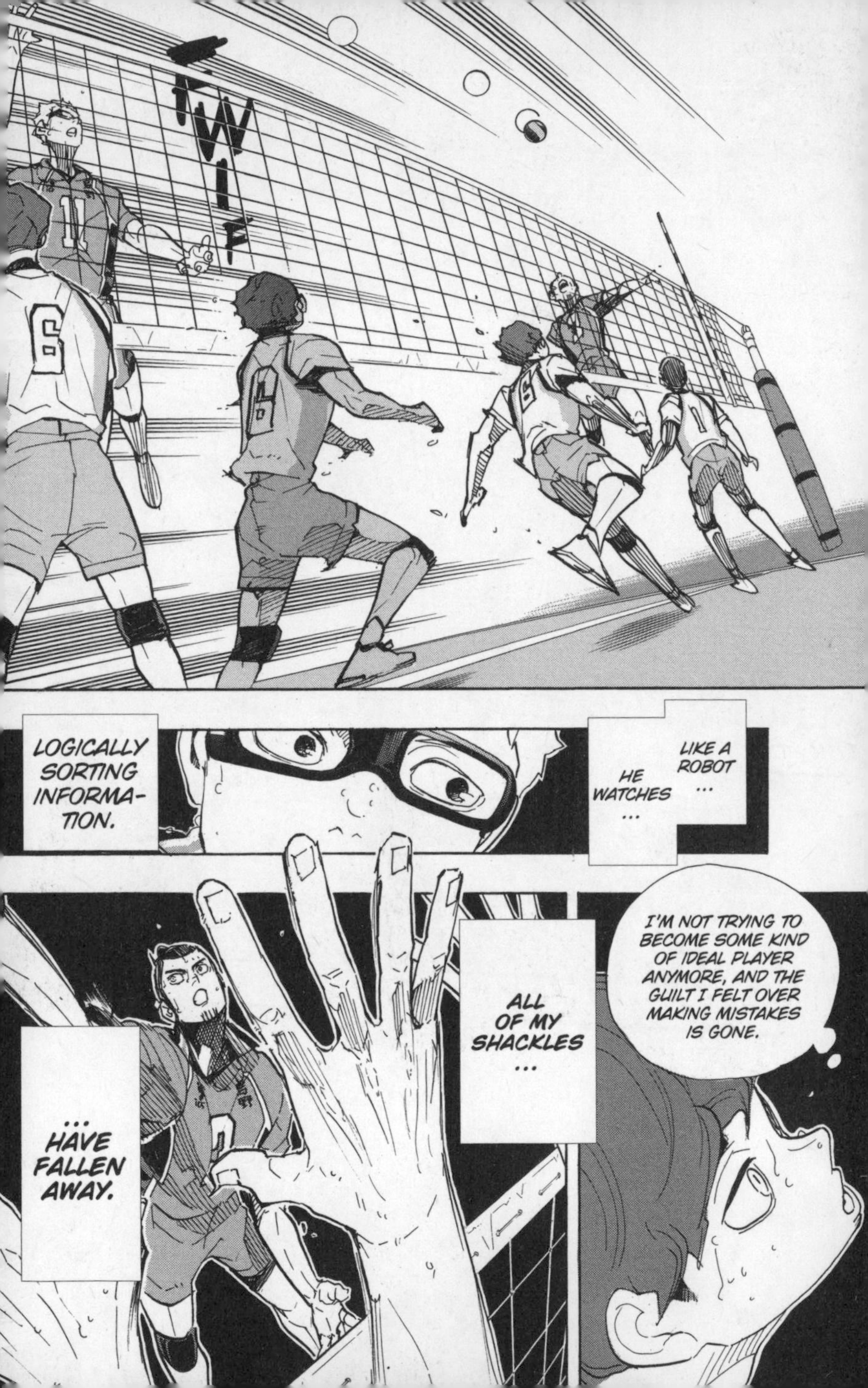
FWIF
HE WATCHES ... LIKE A ROBOT ...
LOGICALLY SORTING INFORMATION.
I'M NOT TRYING TO BECOME SOME KIND OF IDEAL PLAYER ANYMORE, AND THE GUILT I FELT OVER MAKING MISTAKES IS GONE.
ALL OF MY SHACKLES ...
... HAVE FALLEN AWAY.

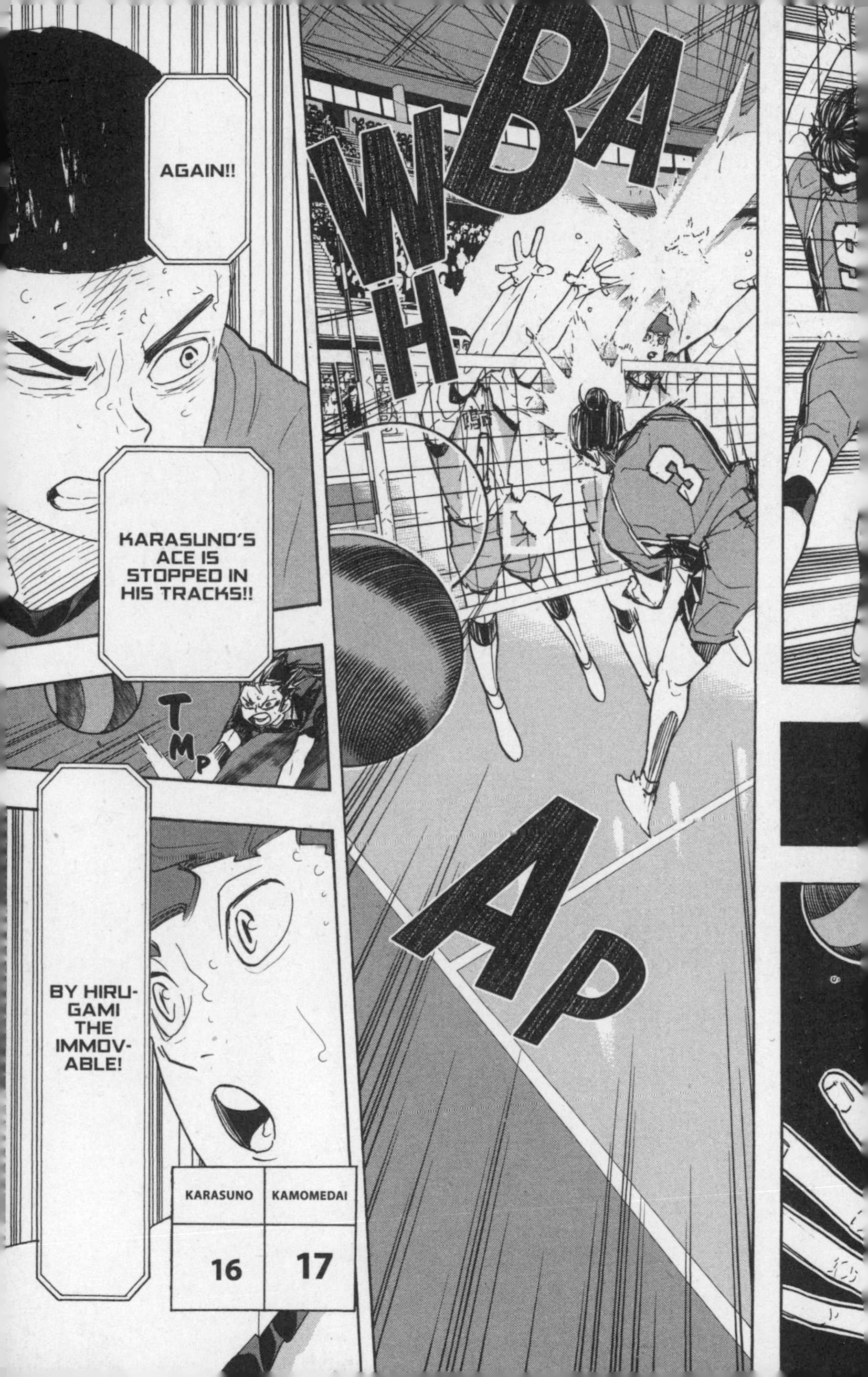
WHBA
AP
AGAIN!!
KARASUNO'S ACE IS STOPPED IN HIS TRACKS!!
TMP
BY HIRU-GAMI THE IMMOV-ABLE!
KARASUNO KAMOMEDAI
16 17

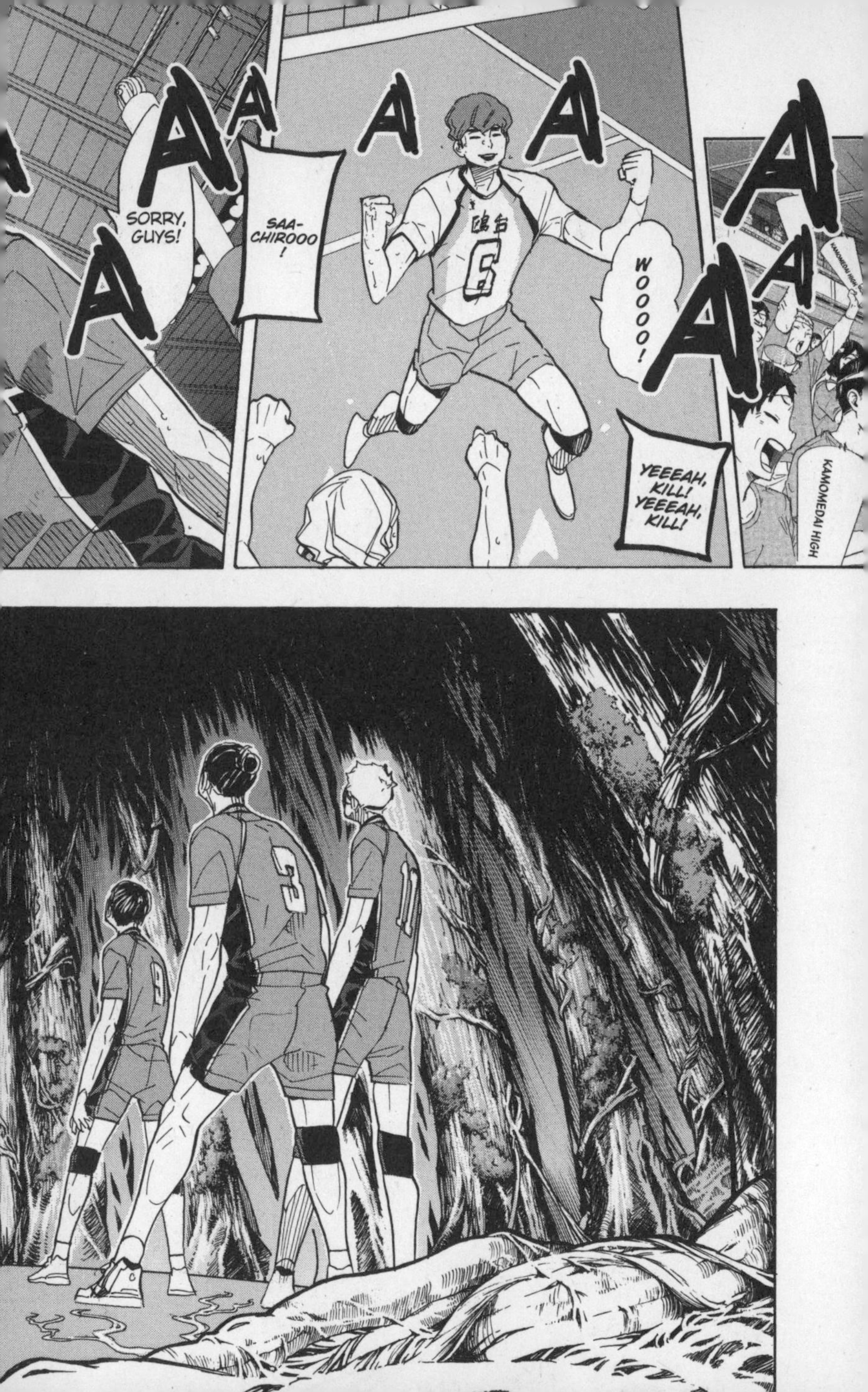
AAAA
KAMOMEDAI HIGH
KAMOMEDAI HIGH
YEEEAH, KILL! YEEEAH, KILL!
WOOOOO!
AAA
SAA-CHIROOO!
SORRY, GUYS!
AAAA

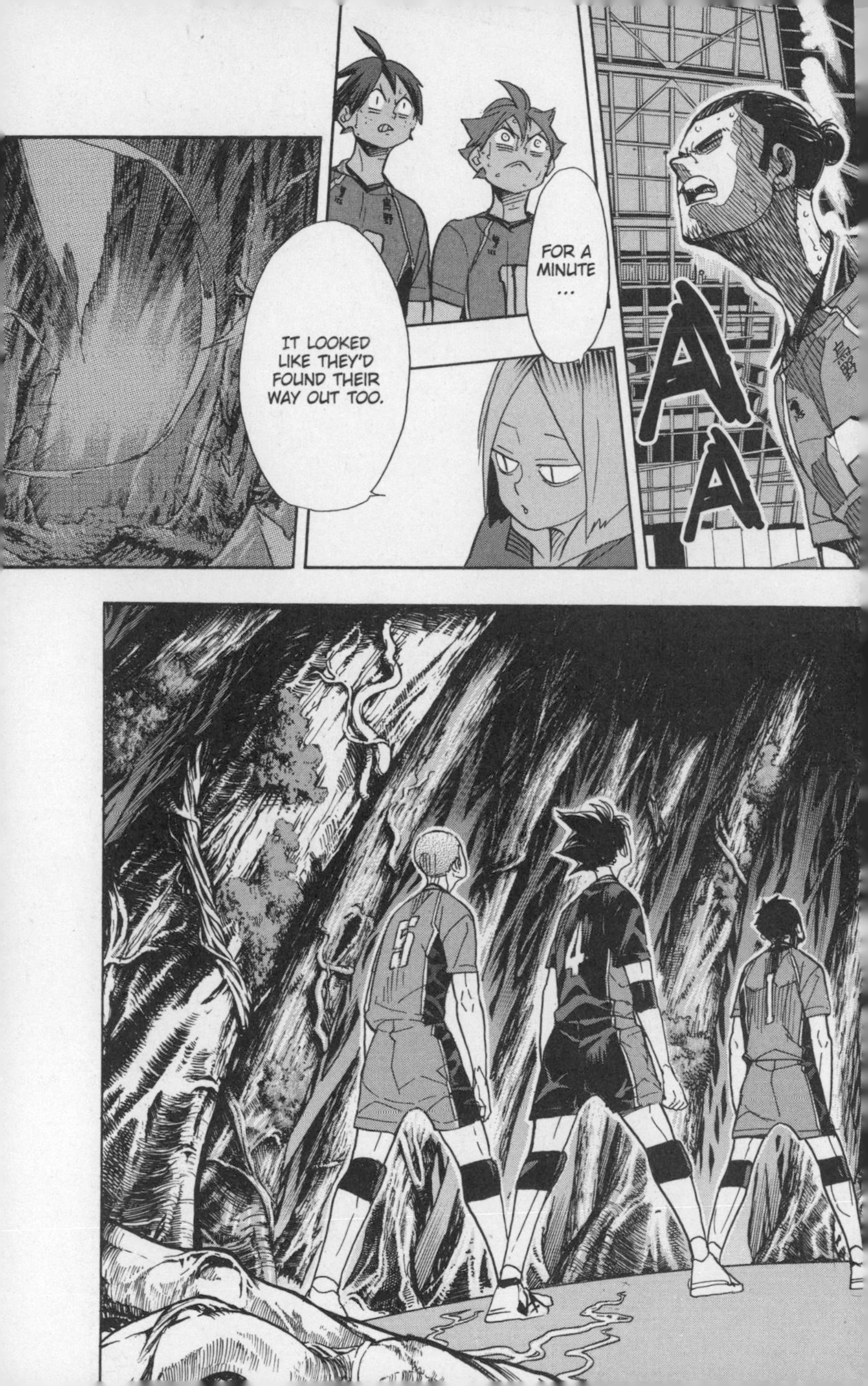
AA
FOR A MINUTE ...
IT LOOKED LIKE THEY'D FOUND THEIR WAY OUT TOO.

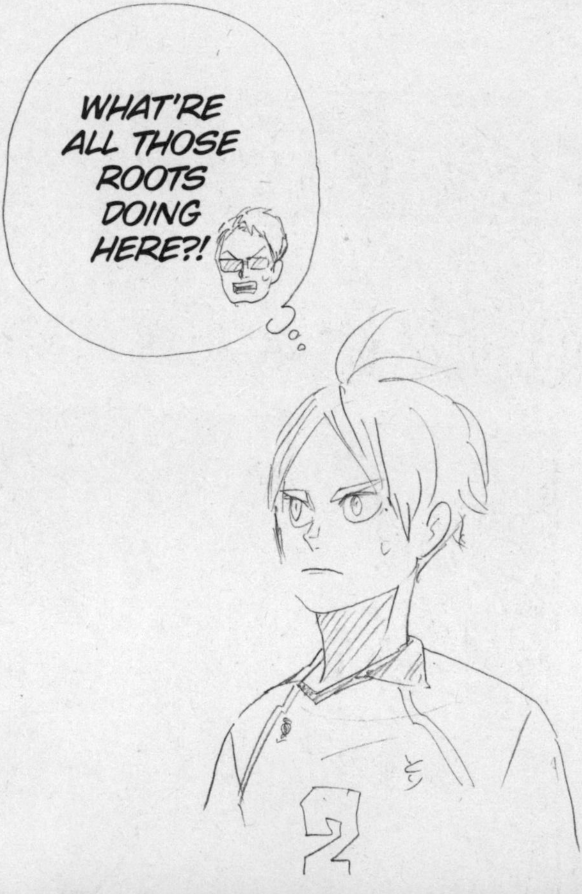
WHAT'RE ALL THOSE ROOTS DOING HERE?!

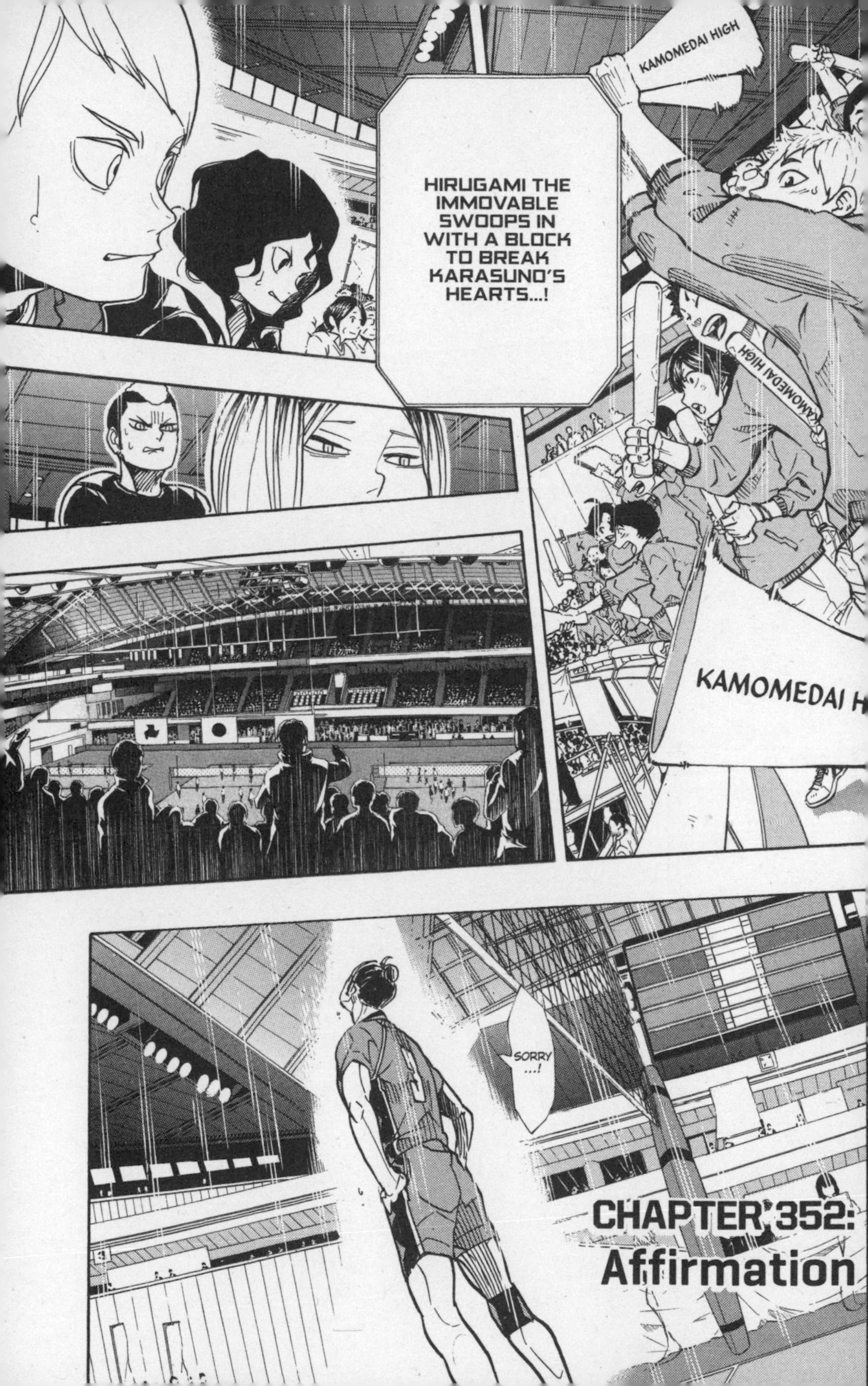
KAMOMEDAI HIGH
KAMOMEDAI HIGH
KAMOMEDAI HIGH
HIRUGAMI THE IMMOVABLE SWOOPS IN WITH A BLOCK TO BREAK KARASUNO'S HEARTS...!
SORRY ...!
CHAPTER 352:
Affirmation

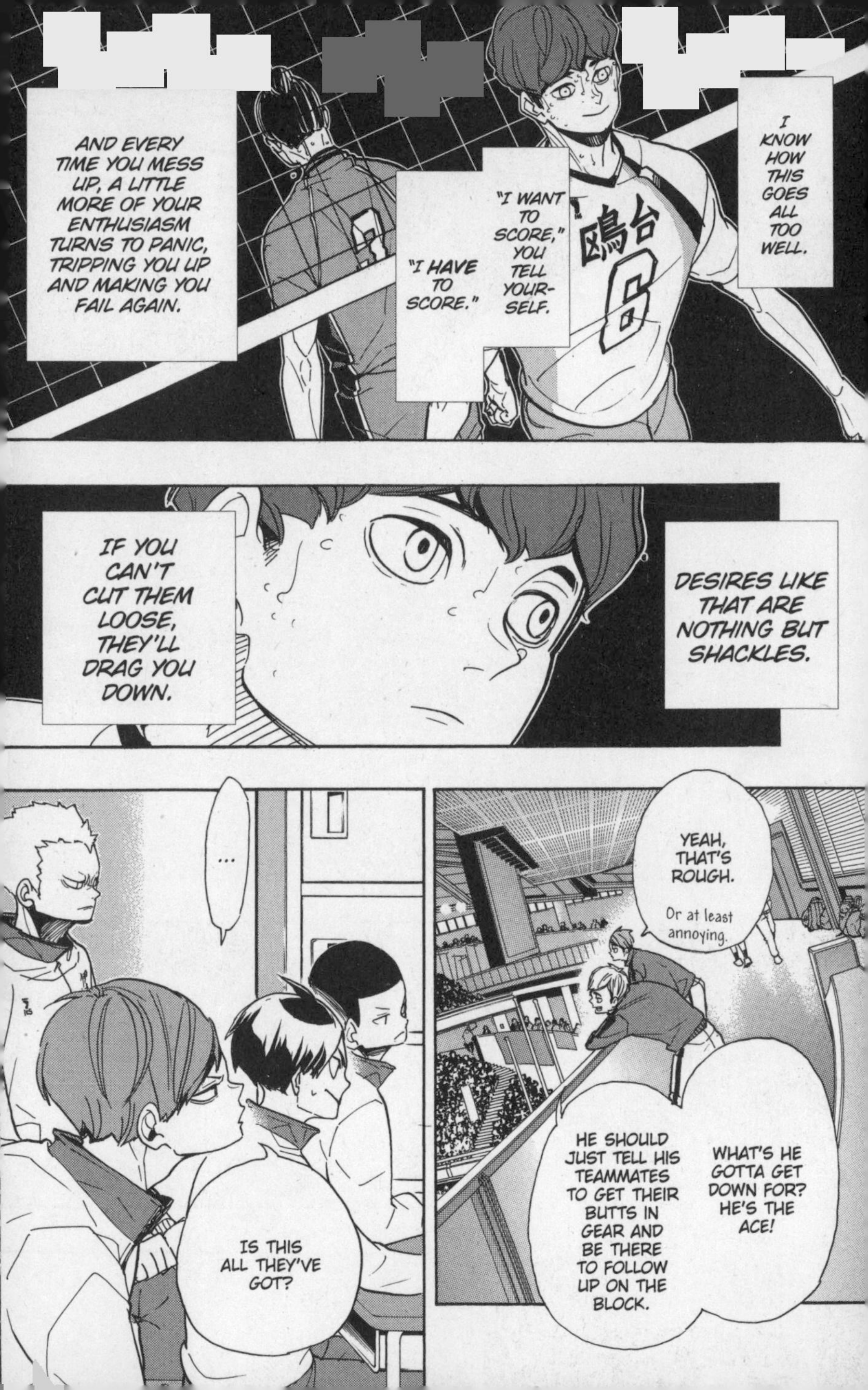
I KNOW HOW THIS GOES ALL TOO WELL.
"I WANT TO SCORE," YOU TELL YOURSELF.
"I HAVE TO SCORE."
AND EVERY TIME YOU MESS UP, A LITTLE MORE OF YOUR ENTHUSIASM TURNS TO PANIC, TRIPPING YOU UP AND MAKING YOU FAIL AGAIN.
鴎台
8
DESIRES LIKE THAT ARE NOTHING BUT SHACKLES.
IF YOU CAN'T CUT THEM LOOSE, THEY'LL DRAG YOU DOWN.
YEAH, THAT'S ROUGH.
Or at least annoying.
WHAT'S HE GOTTA GET DOWN FOR? HE'S THE ACE!
HE SHOULD JUST TELL HIS TEAMMATES TO GET THEIR BUTTS IN GEAR AND BE THERE TO FOLLOW UP ON THE BLOCK.
...
IS THIS ALL THEY'VE GOT?

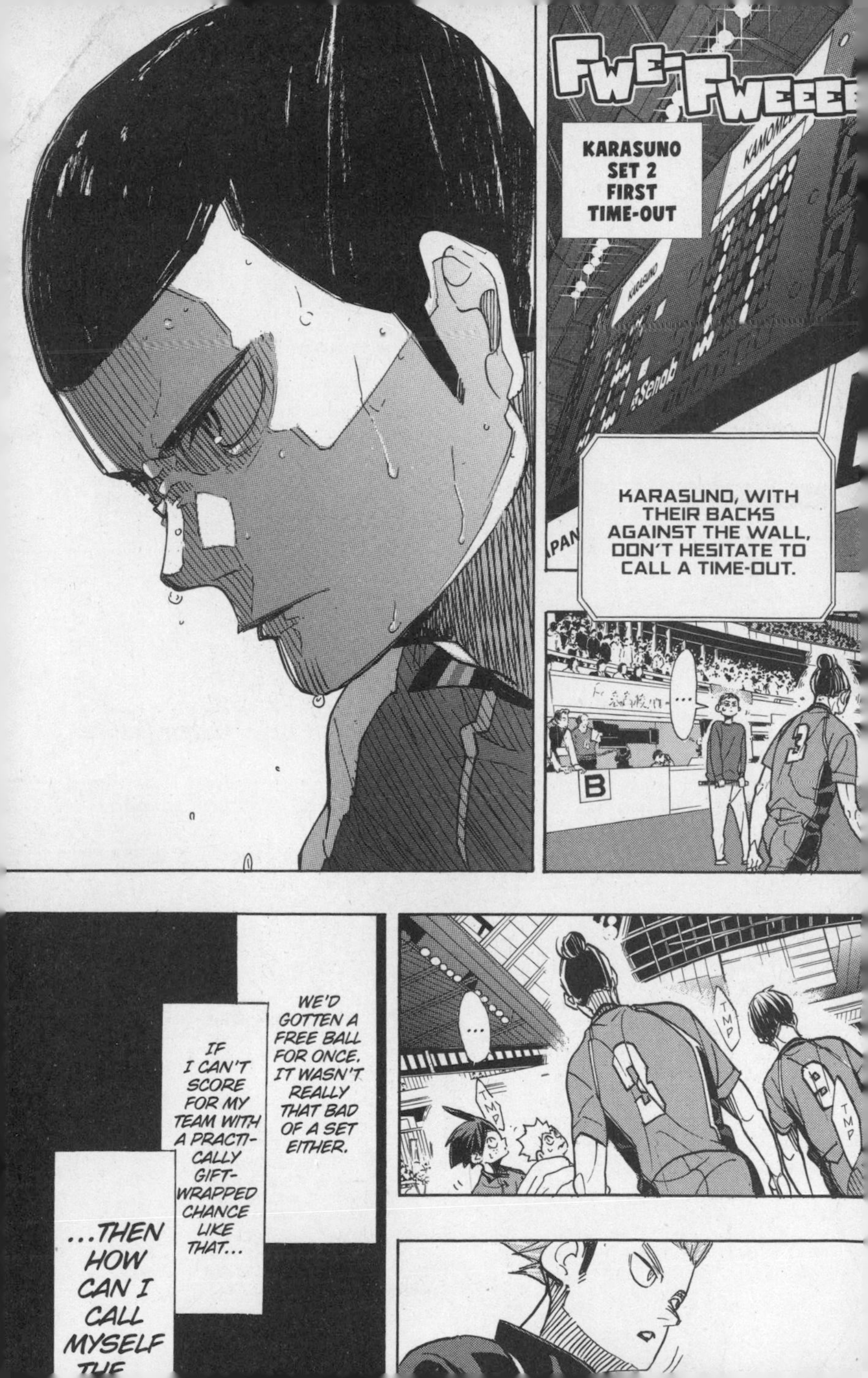
FWE-FWEEEE
KARASUNO SET 2 FIRST TIME-OUT
KARASUNO, WITH THEIR BACKS AGAINST THE WALL, DON'T HESITATE TO CALL A TIME-OUT.
...
...
TMP
TMP
TMP
WE'D GOTTEN A FREE BALL FOR ONCE. IT WASN'T REALLY THAT BAD OF A SET EITHER.
IF I CAN'T SCORE FOR MY TEAM WITH A PRACTICALLY GIFT-WRAPPED CHANCE LIKE THAT...
...THEN HOW CAN I CALL MYSELF

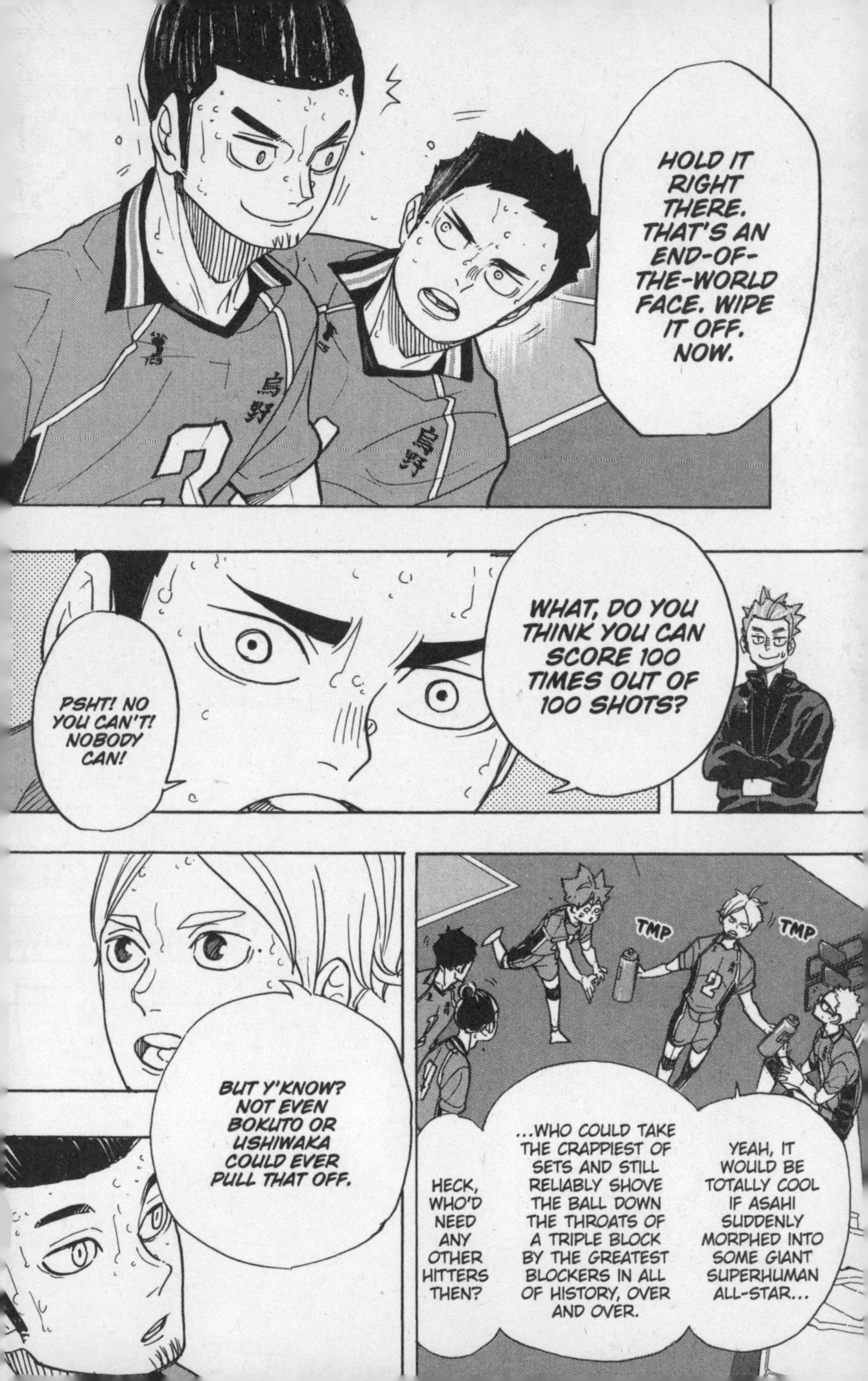
HOLD IT RIGHT THERE. THAT'S AN END-OF-THE-WORLD FACE. WIPE IT OFF. NOW.
WHAT, DO YOU THINK YOU CAN SCORE 100 TIMES OUT OF 100 SHOTS?
PSHT! NO YOU CAN'T! NOBODY CAN!
TMP
TMP
YEAH, IT WOULD BE TOTALLY COOL IF ASAHI SUDDENLY MORPHED INTO SOME GIANT SUPERHUMAN ALL-STAR...
...WHO COULD TAKE THE CRAPPIEST OF SETS AND STILL RELIABLY SHOVE THE BALL DOWN THE THROATS OF A TRIPLE BLOCK BY THE GREATEST BLOCKERS IN ALL OF HISTORY, OVER AND OVER.
HECK, WHO'D NEED ANY OTHER HITTERS THEN?
BUT Y'KNOW? NOT EVEN BOKUTO OR USHIWAKA COULD EVER PULL THAT OFF.

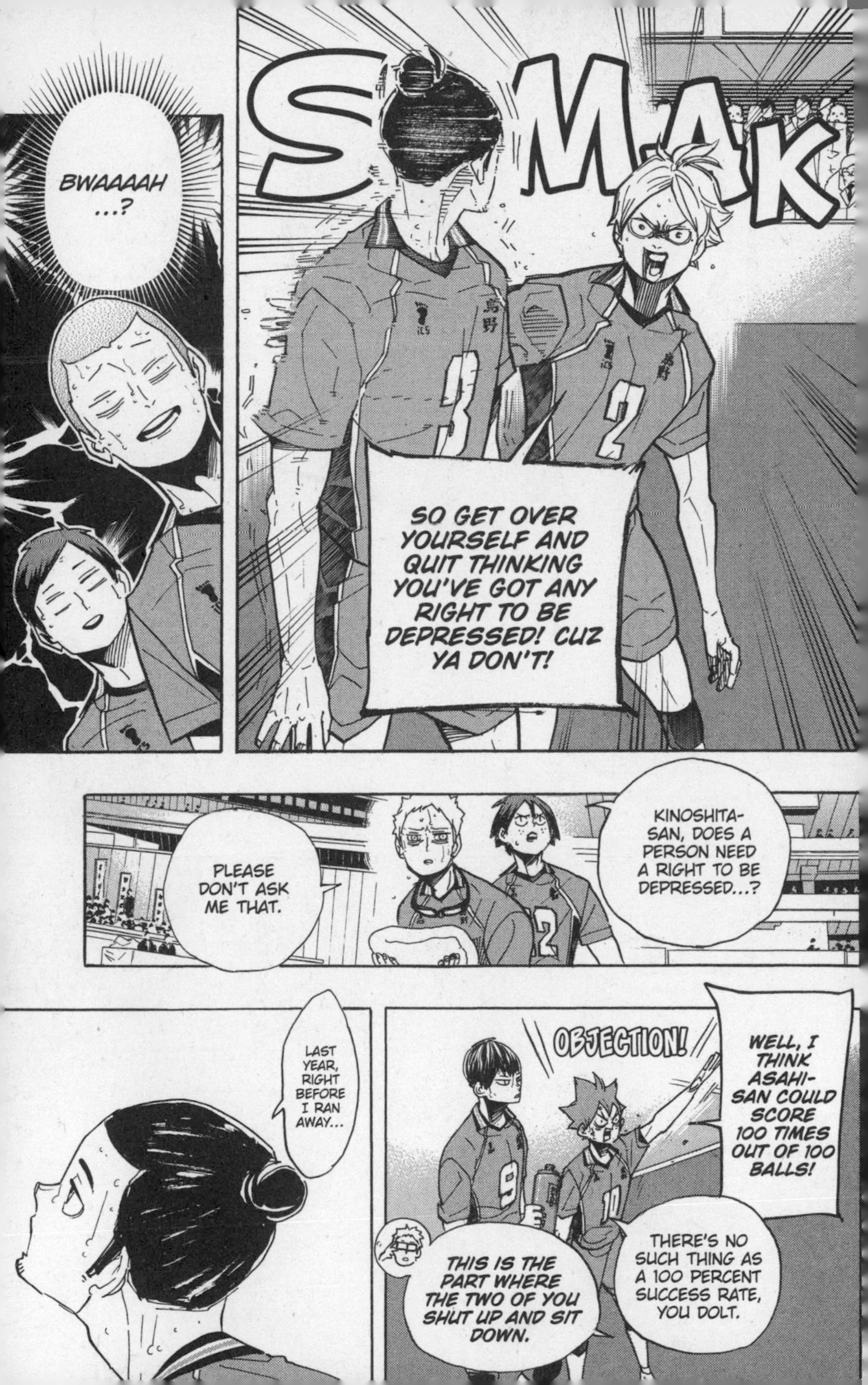
SMAK
SO GET OVER YOURSELF AND QUIT THINKING YOU'VE GOT ANY RIGHT TO BE DEPRESSED! CUZ YA DON'T!
BWAAAAH ...?
KINOSHITA-SAN, DOES A PERSON NEED A RIGHT TO BE DEPRESSED...?
PLEASE DON'T ASK ME THAT.
OBJECTION!
WELL, I THINK ASAHI-SAN COULD SCORE 100 TIMES OUT OF 100 BALLS!
THERE'S NO SUCH THING AS A 100 PERCENT SUCCESS RATE, YOU DOLT.
THIS IS THE PART WHERE THE TWO OF YOU SHUT UP AND SIT DOWN.
LAST YEAR, RIGHT BEFORE I RAN AWAY...

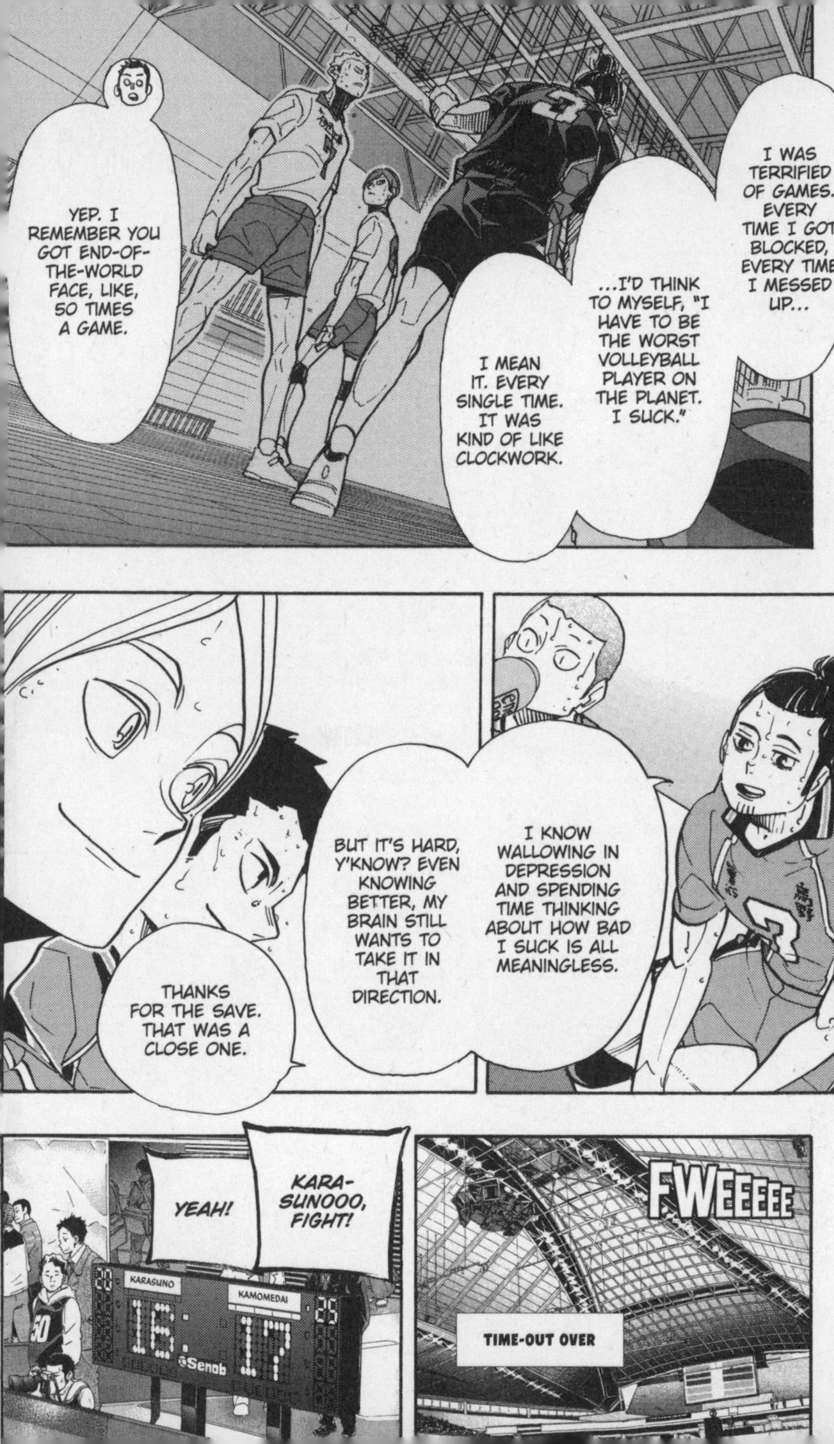
I WAS TERRIFIED OF GAMES. EVERY TIME I GOT BLOCKED, EVERY TIME I MESSED UP...
...I'D THINK TO MYSELF, "I HAVE TO BE THE WORST VOLLEYBALL PLAYER ON THE PLANET. I SUCK."
I MEAN IT. EVERY SINGLE TIME. IT WAS KIND OF LIKE CLOCKWORK.
YEP. I REMEMBER YOU GOT END-OF-THE-WORLD FACE, LIKE, 50 TIMES A GAME.
I KNOW WALLOWING IN DEPRESSION AND SPENDING TIME THINKING ABOUT HOW BAD I SUCK IS ALL MEANINGLESS.
BUT IT'S HARD, Y'KNOW? EVEN KNOWING BETTER, MY BRAIN STILL WANTS TO TAKE IT IN THAT DIRECTION.
THANKS FOR THE SAVE. THAT WAS A CLOSE ONE.
FWEEEEE
TIME-OUT OVER
KARA-SUNOOO, FIGHT!
YEAH!
KARASUNO
KAMOMEDAI
16
17
Senob

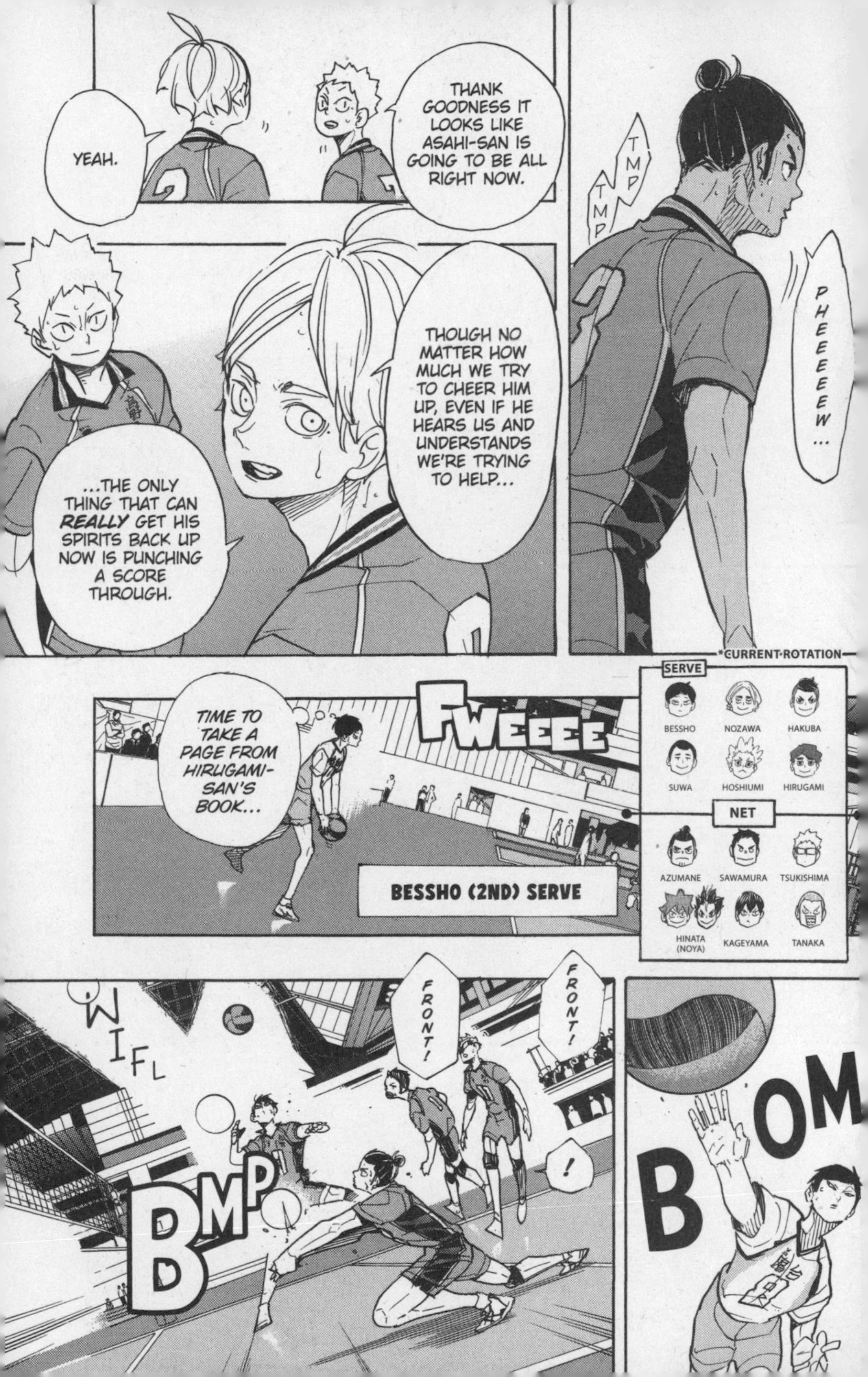

TMP
TMP
PHEEEEEW...
THANK GOODNESS IT LOOKS LIKE ASAHI-SAN IS GOING TO BE ALL RIGHT NOW.
YEAH.
THOUGH NO MATTER HOW MUCH WE TRY TO CHEER HIM UP, EVEN IF HE HEARS US AND UNDERSTANDS WE'RE TRYING TO HELP...
...THE ONLY THING THAT CAN *REALLY* GET HIS SPIRITS BACK UP NOW IS PUNCHING A SCORE THROUGH.
*CURRENT ROTATION
SERVE
BESSHO
NOZAWA
HAKUBA
SUWA
HOSHIUMI
HIRUGAMI
NET
AZUMANE
SAWAMURA
TSUKISHIMA
HINATA (NOYA)
KAGEYAMA
TANAKA
FWEEEE
TIME TO TAKE A PAGE FROM HIRUGAMI-SAN'S BOOK...
BESSHO (2ND) SERVE
BOOM
WIFL
FRONT!
FRONT!
!
BMP

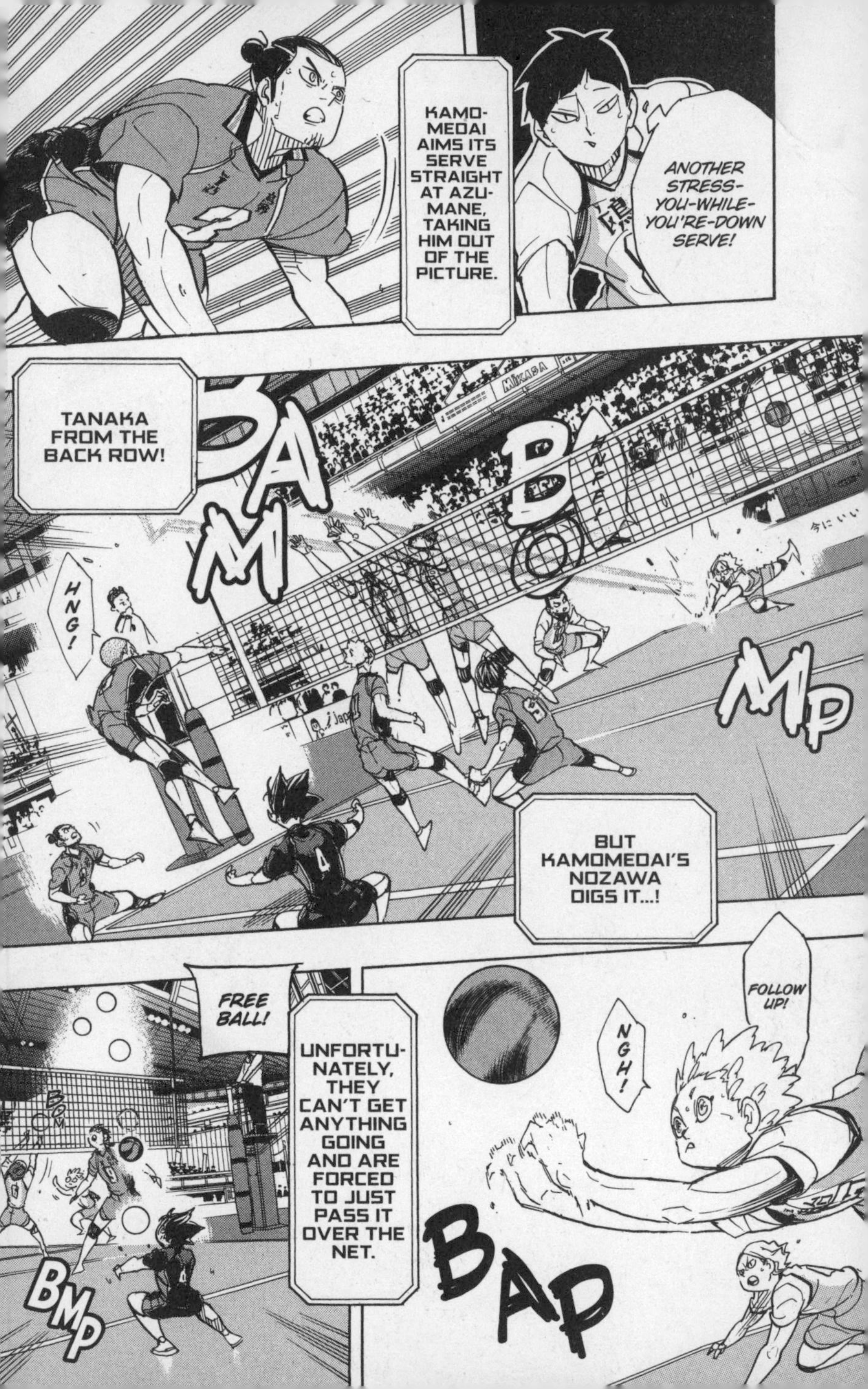
ANOTHER STRESS-YOU-WHILE-YOU'RE-DOWN SERVE!
KAMOMEDAI AIMS ITS SERVE STRAIGHT AT AZUMANE, TAKING HIM OUT OF THE PICTURE.
TANAKA FROM THE BACK ROW!
BAM
MP
HNG!
BUT KAMOMEDAI'S NOZAWA DIGS IT...!
FOLLOW UP!
NGH!
BAP
UNFORTUNATELY, THEY CAN'T GET ANYTHING GOING AND ARE FORCED TO JUST PASS IT OVER THE NET.
FREE BALL!
BOOM
BMP

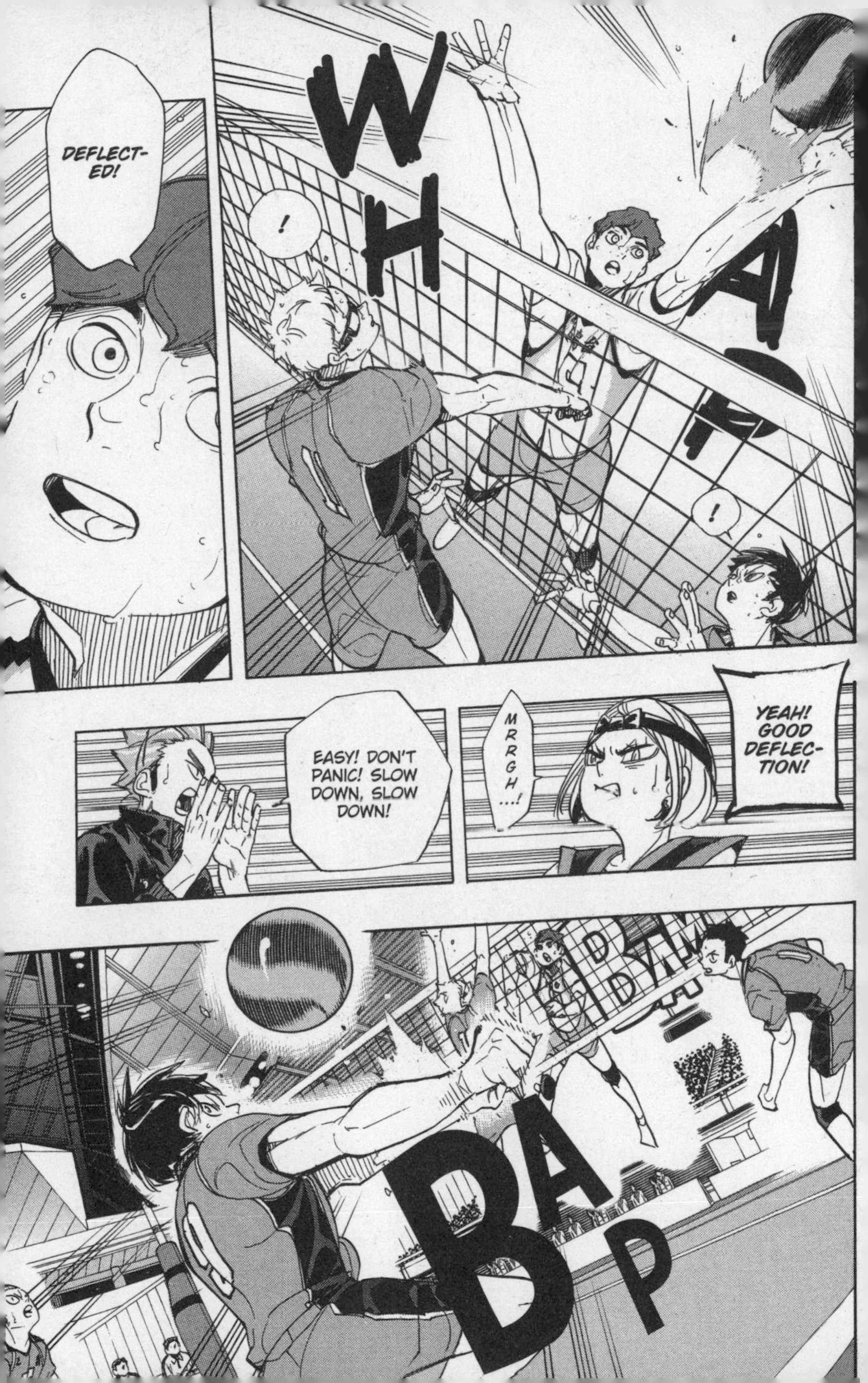
WHAP
!
!
DEFLECTED!
YEAH! GOOD DEFLECTION!
MRRGH ...!
EASY! DON'T PANIC! SLOW DOWN, SLOW DOWN!
BAP

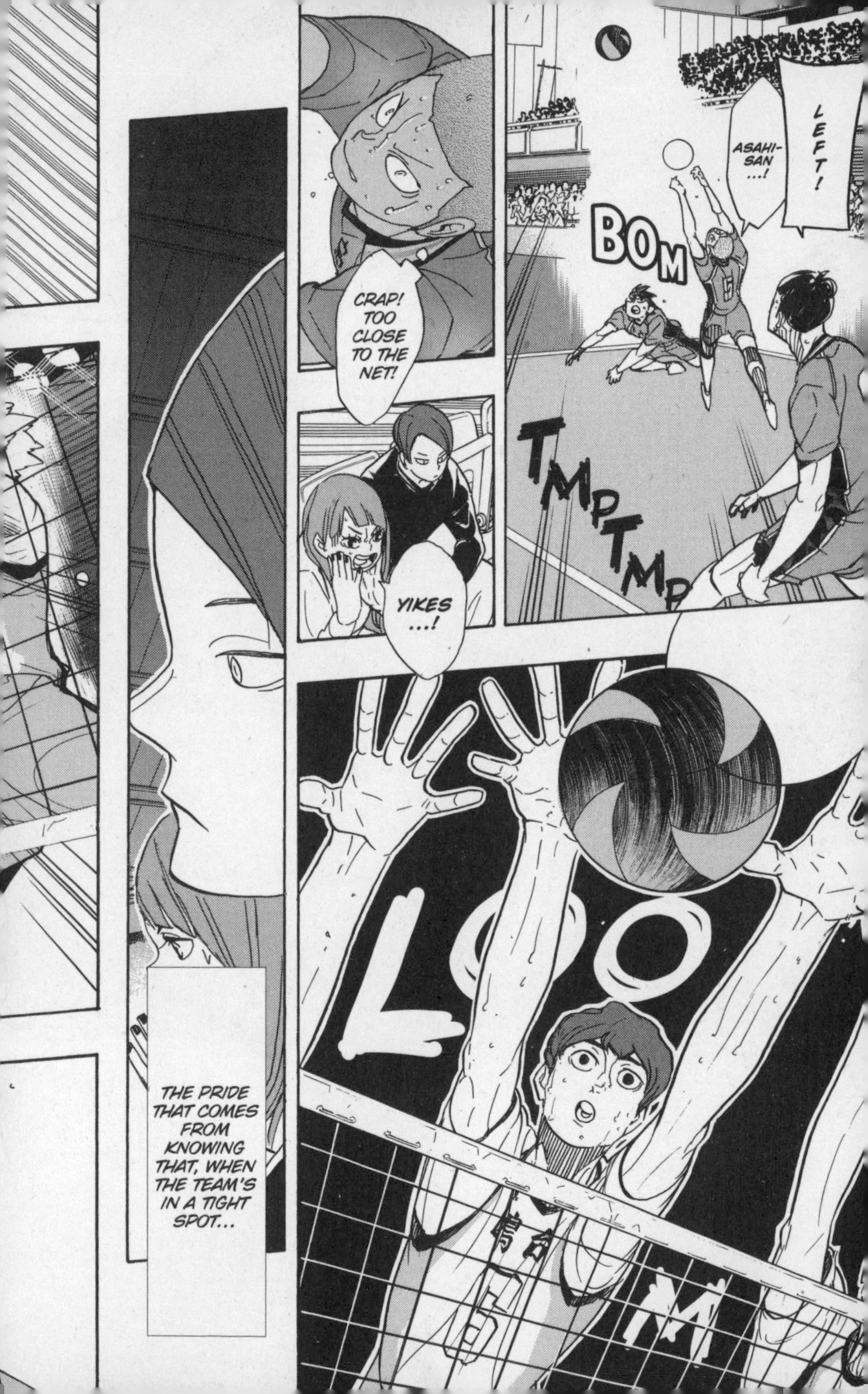
LEFT!
ASAHI-SAN...!
BOM
TMPTMP
CRAP! TOO CLOSE TO THE NET!
YIKES...!
THE PRIDE THAT COMES FROM KNOWING THAT, WHEN THE TEAM'S IN A TIGHT SPOT...

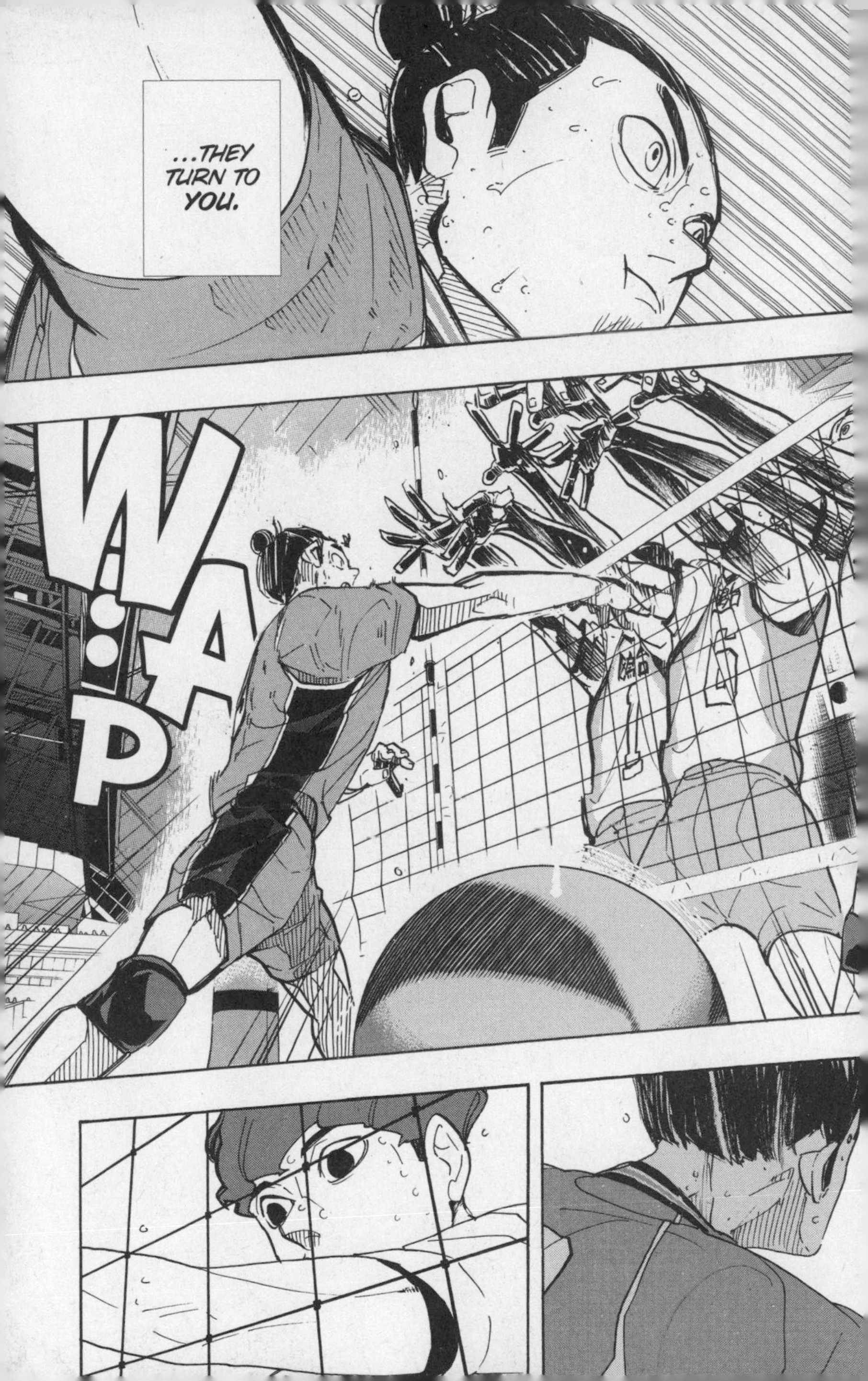
...THEY TURN TO YOU.
WAP

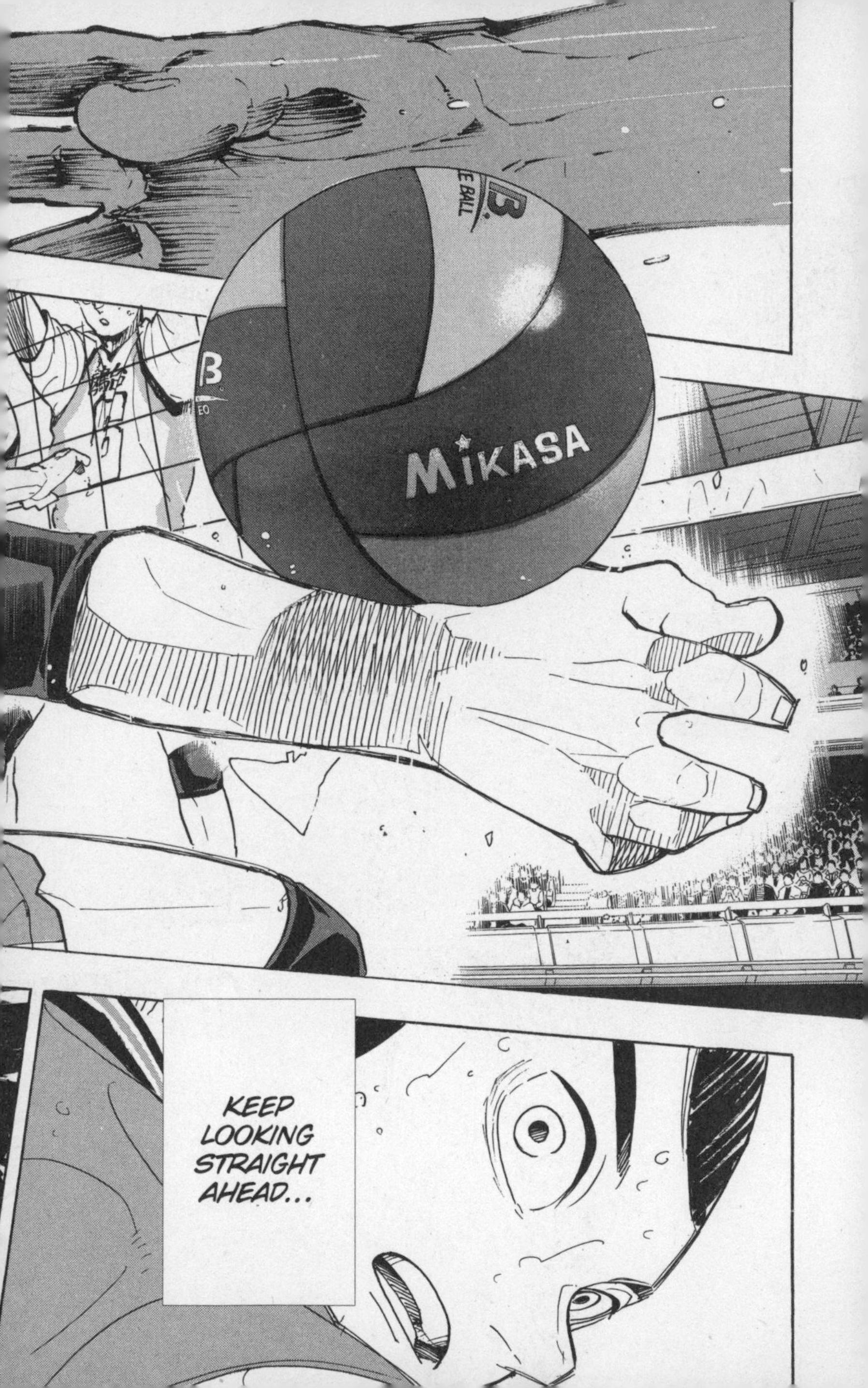
MIKASA
KEEP LOOKING STRAIGHT AHEAD...

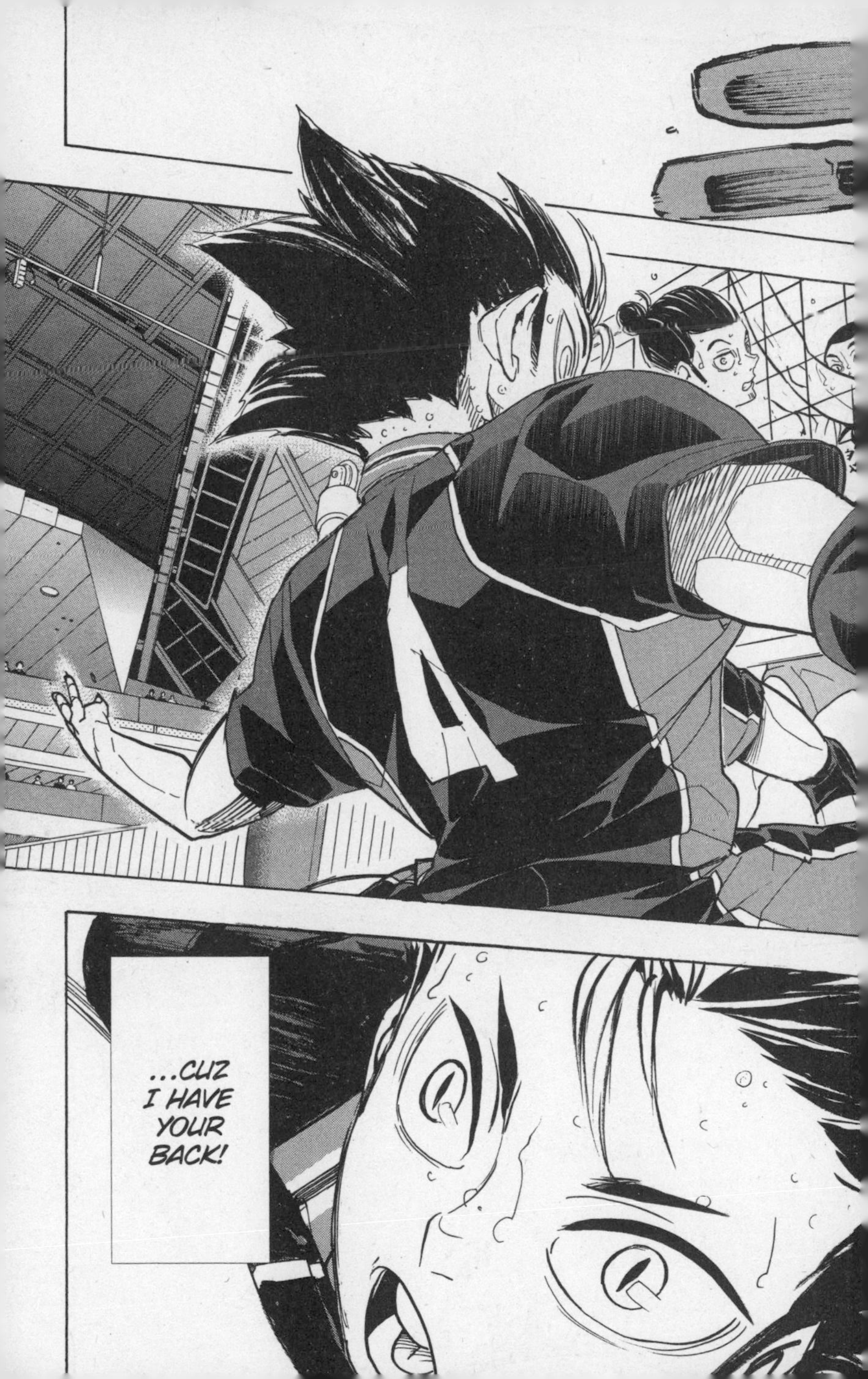
...CUZ I HAVE YOUR BACK!

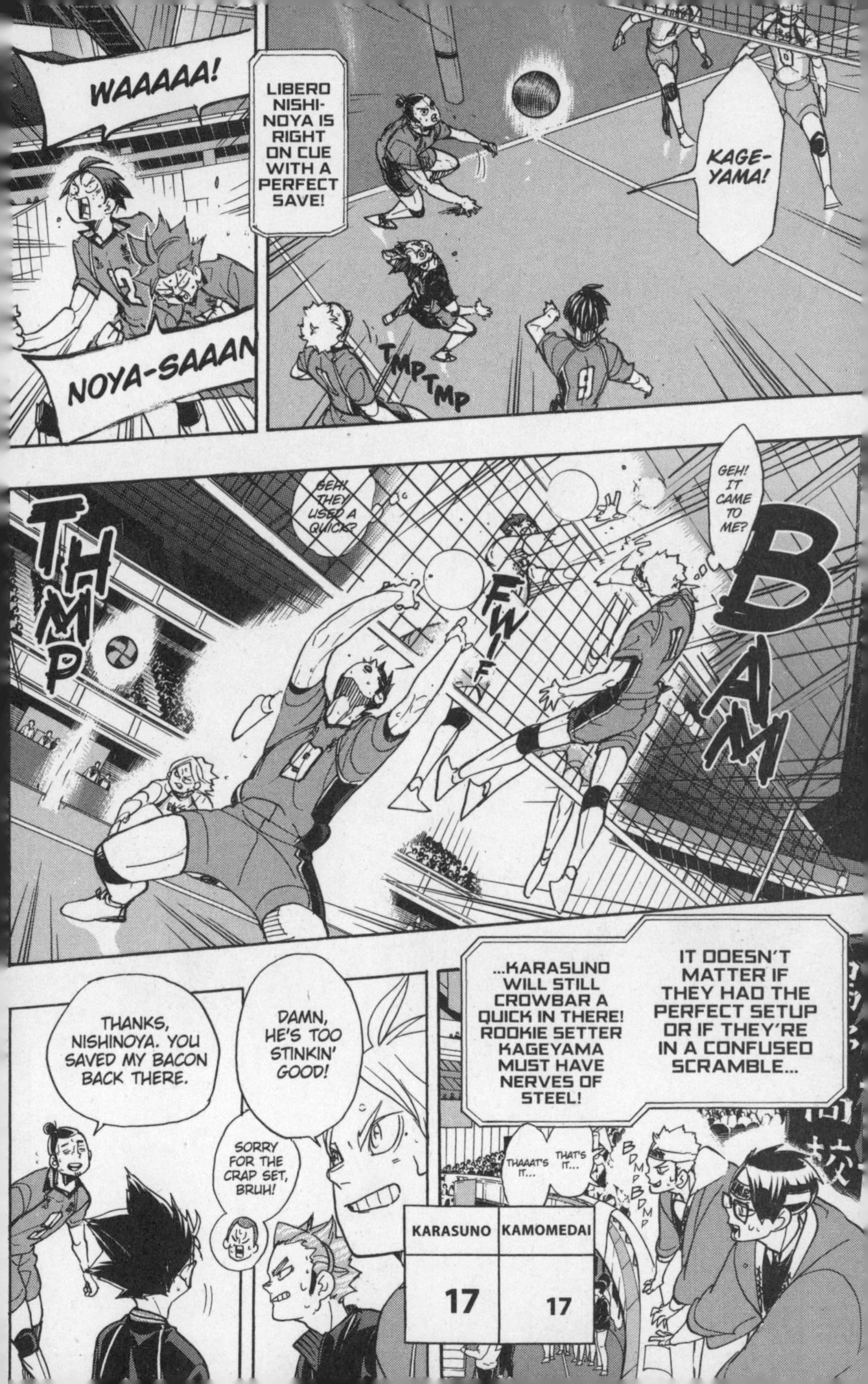
KAGE-YAMA!
LIBERO NISHI-NOYA IS RIGHT ON CUE WITH A PERFECT SAVE!
TMPTMP
WAAAAA!
NOYA-SAAAN
GEH! IT CAME TO ME?
BAM
FWIF
GEH! THEY USED A QUICK?
THMP
IT DOESN'T MATTER IF THEY HAD THE PERFECT SETUP OR IF THEY'RE IN A CONFUSED SCRAMBLE...
...KARASUNO WILL STILL CROWBAR A QUICK IN THERE! ROOKIE SETTER KAGEYAMA MUST HAVE NERVES OF STEEL!
BDMPBDMP
THAT'S IT...
THAAAT'S IT...
KARASUNO 17
KAMOMEDAI 17
DAMN, HE'S TOO STINKIN' GOOD!
THANKS, NISHINOYA. YOU SAVED MY BACON BACK THERE.
SORRY FOR THE CRAP SET, BRUH!

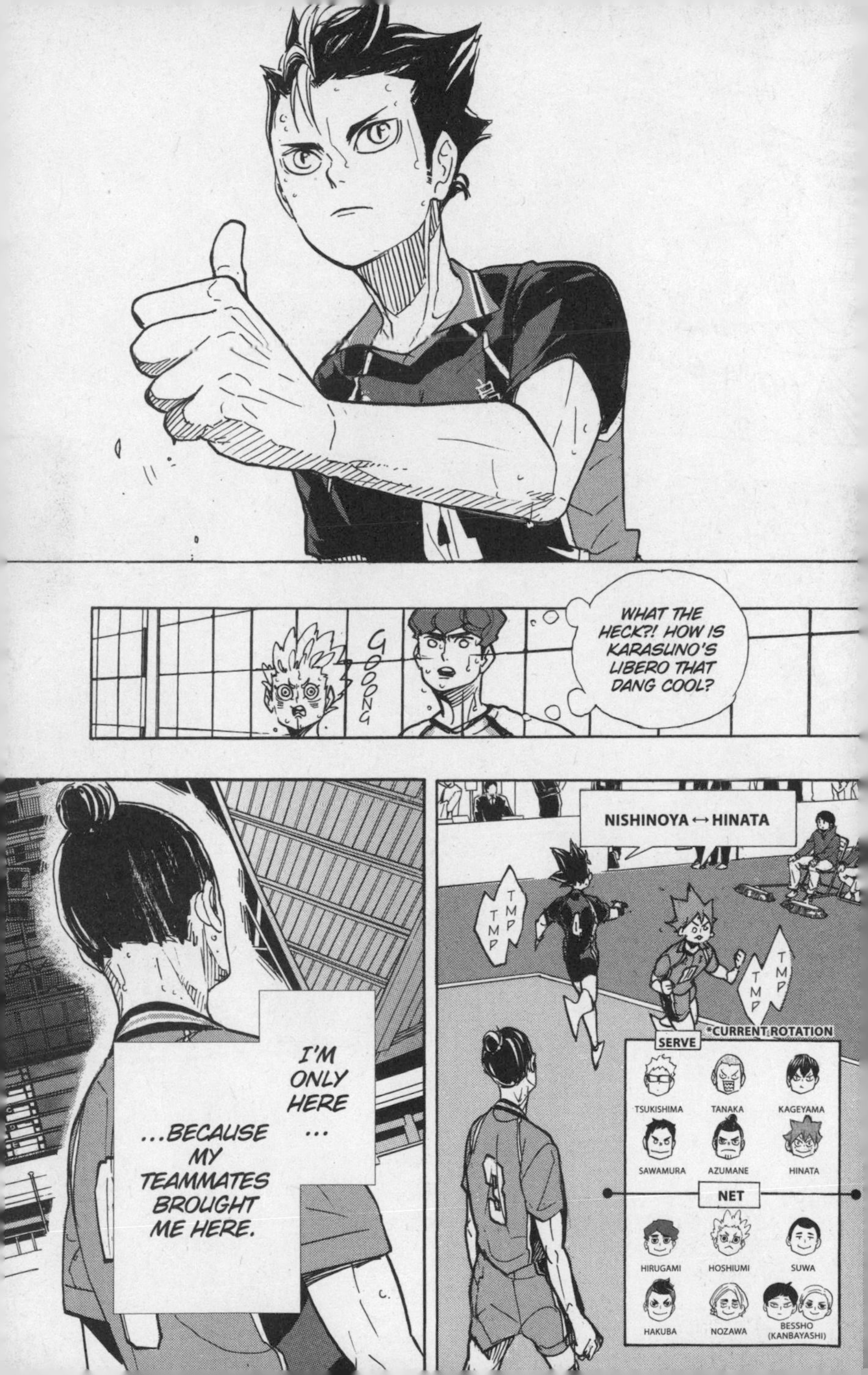
WHAT THE HECK?! HOW IS KARASUNO'S LIBERO THAT DANG COOL?
GOOONG
NISHINOYA ↔ HINATA
TMP TMP
TMP TMP
*CURRENT ROTATION
SERVE
TSUKISHIMA
TANAKA
KAGEYAMA
SAWAMURA
AZUMANE
HINATA
NET
HIRUGAMI
HOSHIUMI
SUWA
HAKUBA
NOZAWA
BESSHO (KANBAYASHI)
I'M ONLY HERE...
...BECAUSE MY TEAMMATES BROUGHT ME HERE.

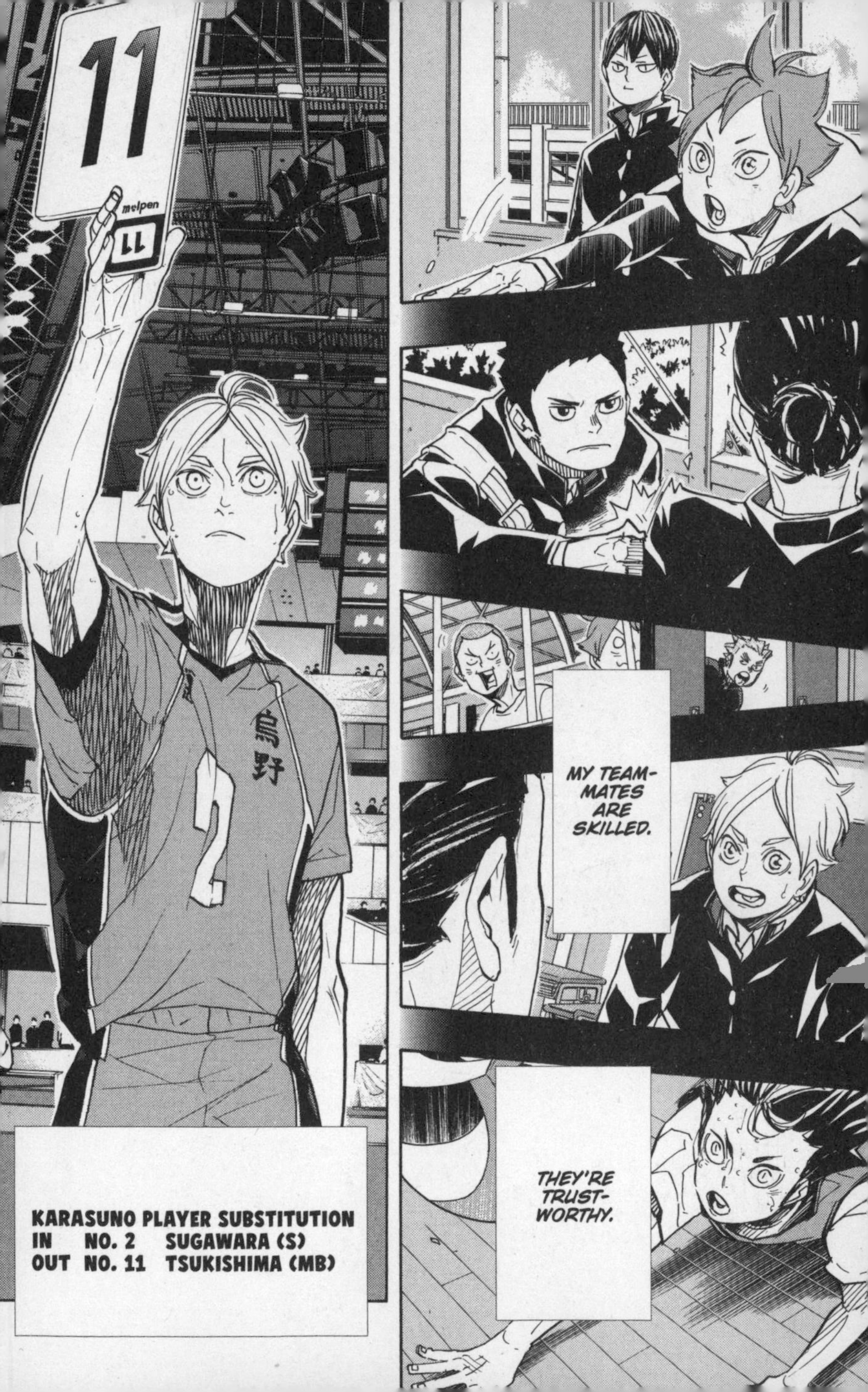
MY TEAM-MATES ARE SKILLED.
THEY'RE TRUST-WORTHY.
11
KARASUNO PLAYER SUBSTITUTION
IN NO. 2 SUGAWARA (S)
OUT NO. 11 TSUKISHIMA (MB)

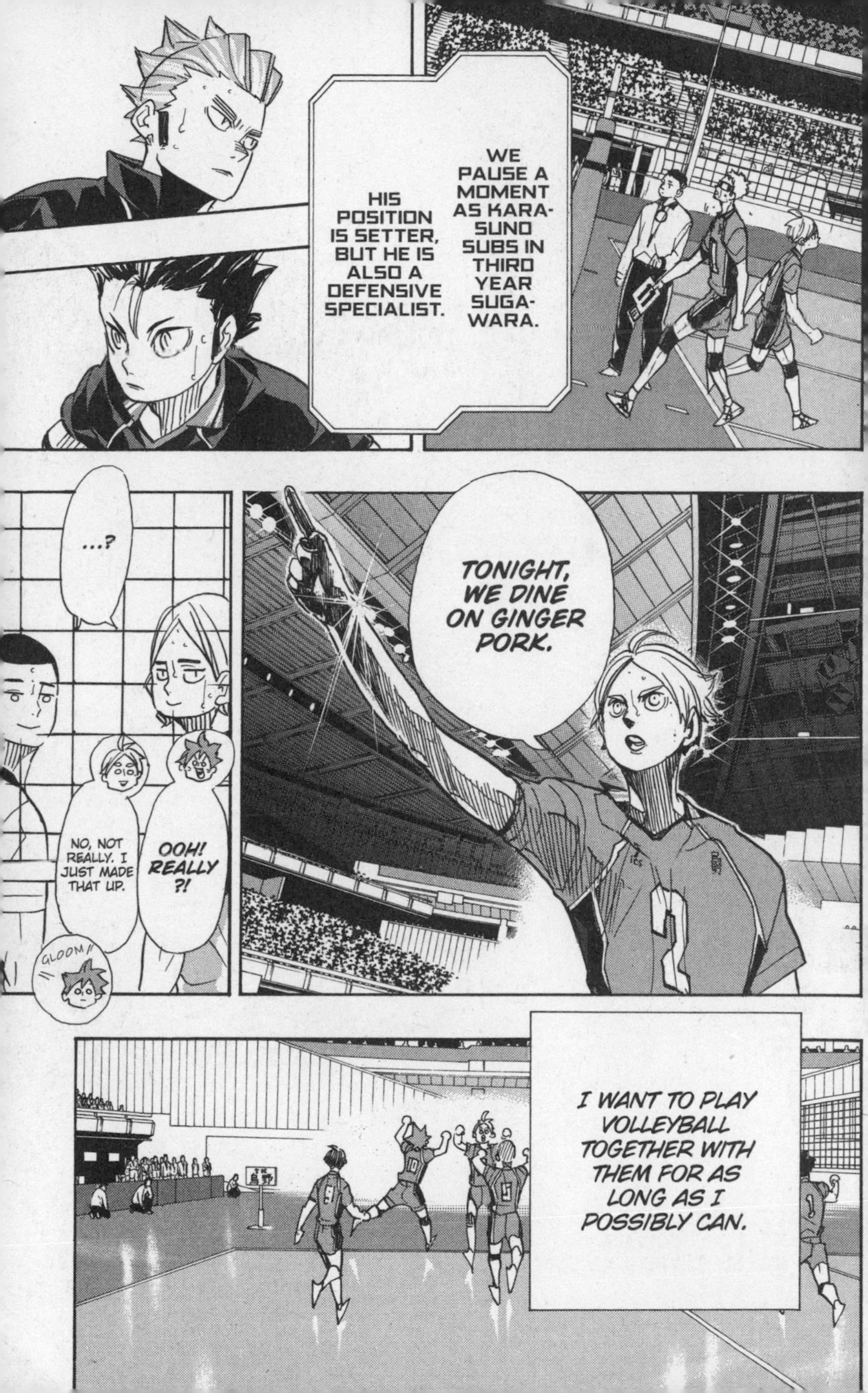
WE PAUSE A MOMENT AS KARASUNO SUBS IN THIRD YEAR SUGAWARA.
HIS POSITION IS SETTER, BUT HE IS ALSO A DEFENSIVE SPECIALIST.
TONIGHT, WE DINE ON GINGER PORK.
...?
OOH! REALLY?!
NO, NOT REALLY. I JUST MADE THAT UP.
GLOOM
I WANT TO PLAY VOLLEYBALL TOGETHER WITH THEM FOR AS LONG AS I POSSIBLY CAN.

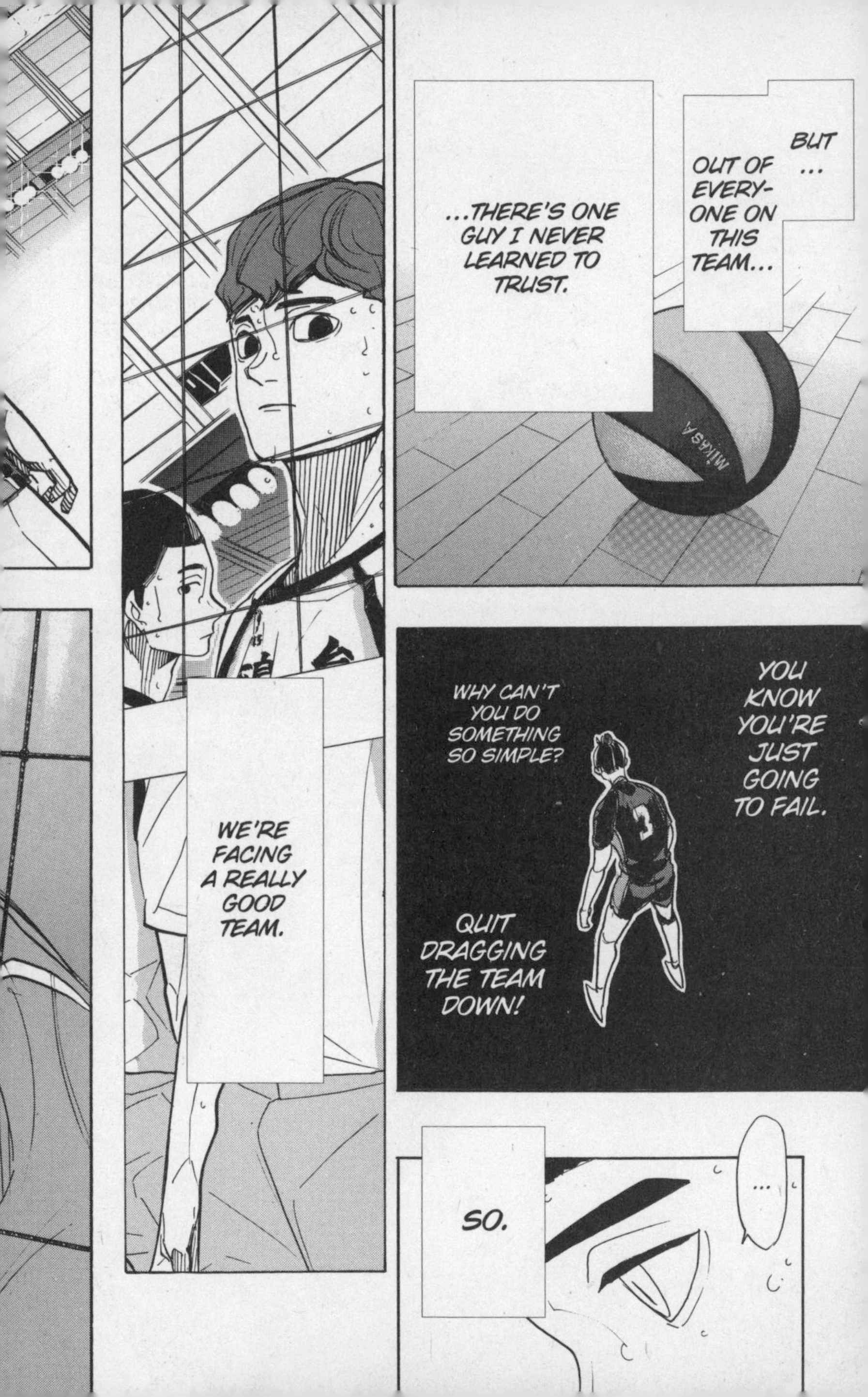
BUT ...
OUT OF EVERYONE ON THIS TEAM...
...THERE'S ONE GUY I NEVER LEARNED TO TRUST.
YOU KNOW YOU'RE JUST GOING TO FAIL.
WHY CAN'T YOU DO SOMETHING SO SIMPLE?
QUIT DRAGGING THE TEAM DOWN!
...
SO.
WE'RE FACING A REALLY GOOD TEAM.

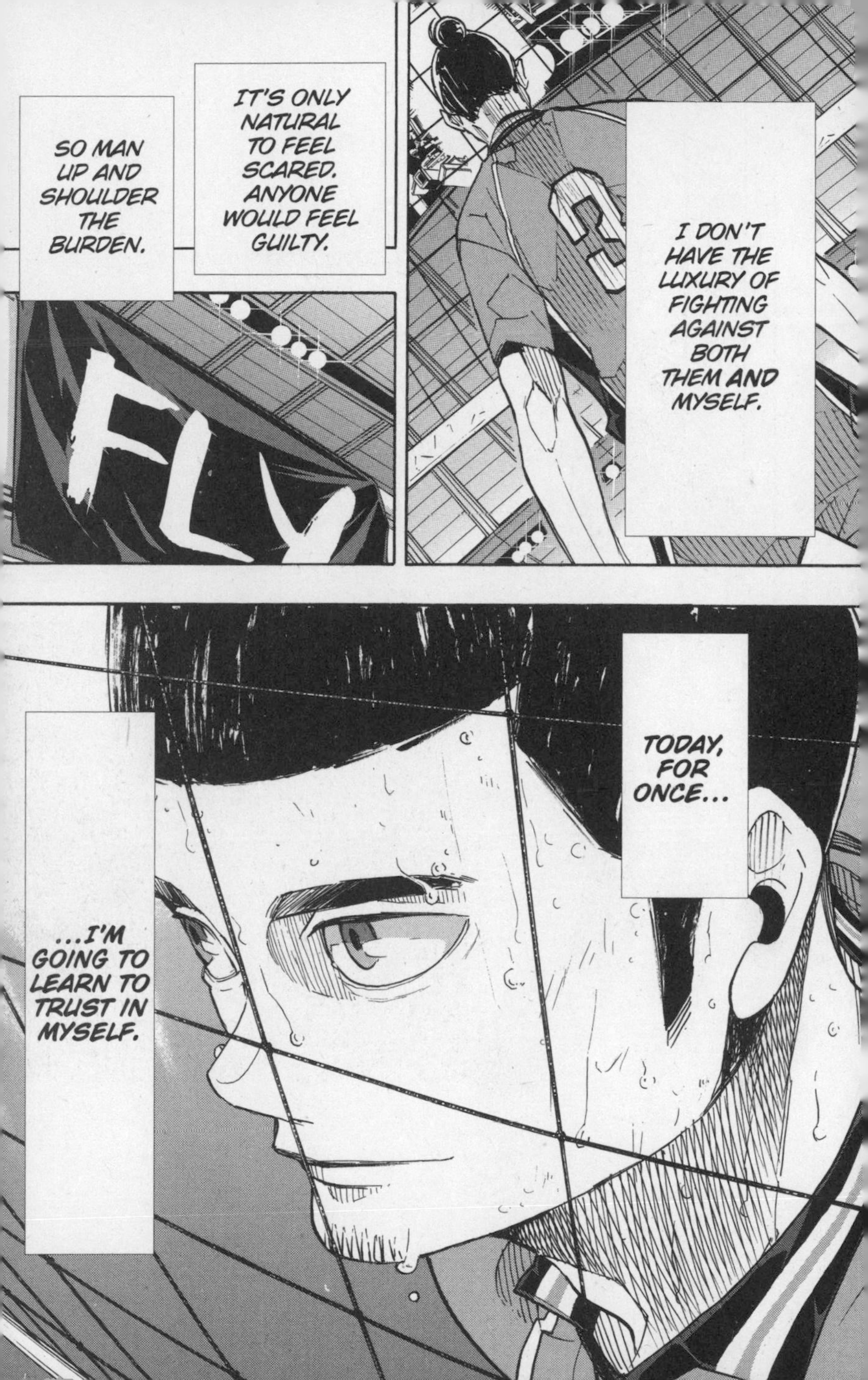
I DON'T HAVE THE LUXURY OF FIGHTING AGAINST BOTH THEM AND MYSELF.
IT'S ONLY NATURAL TO FEEL SCARED. ANYONE WOULD FEEL GUILTY.
SO MAN UP AND SHOULDER THE BURDEN.
FLY
TODAY, FOR ONCE...
...I'M GOING TO LEARN TO TRUST IN MYSELF.

Oh!

KORAI-KUN, COULD YOU GRAB THE TAPE FOR ME?

**THE SILENT THUMBS-UP QUICKLY BECAME A FAD.**

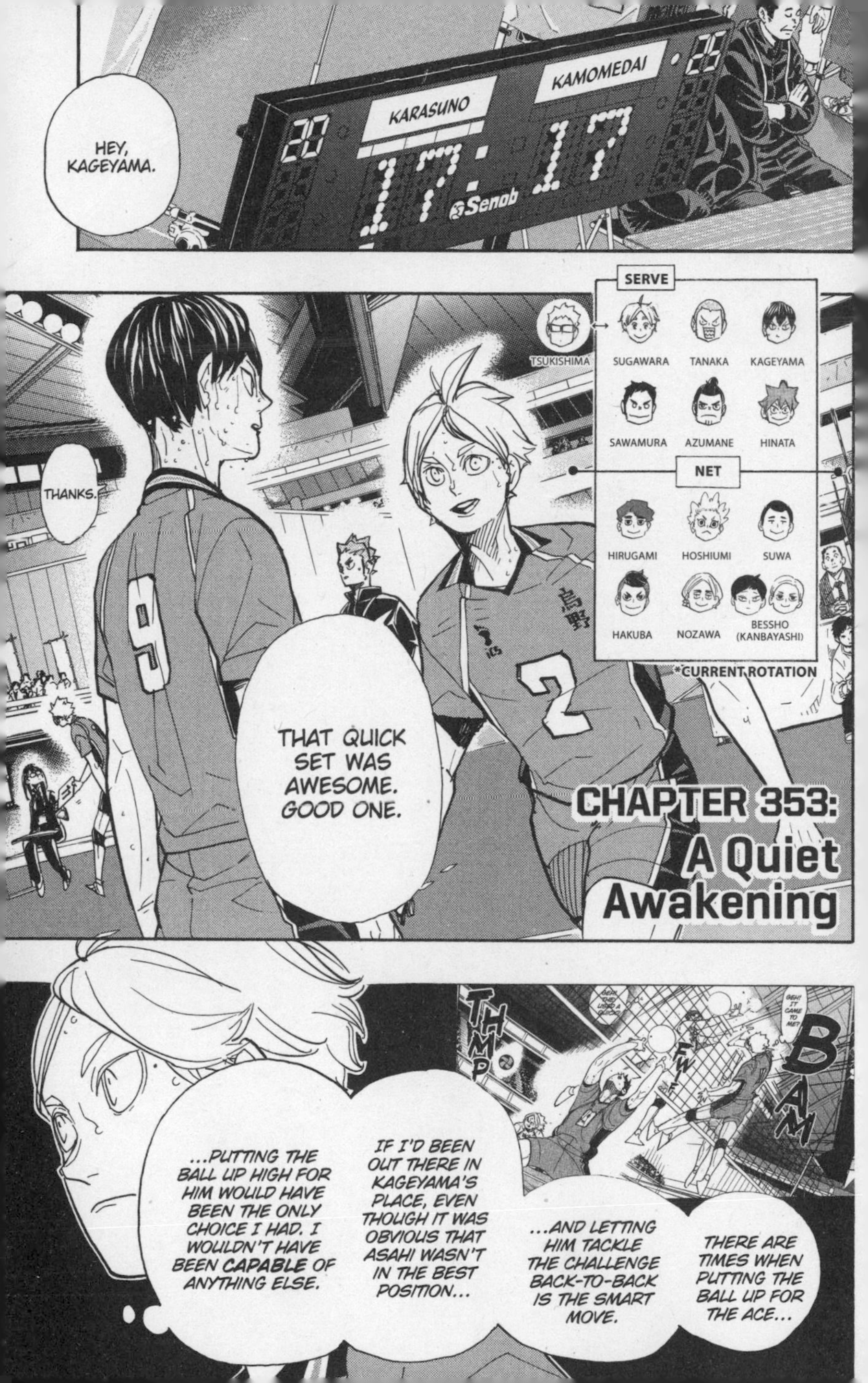
KAMOMEDAI
KARASUNO
17 : 17
Senob
HEY, KAGEYAMA.
SERVE
TSUKISHIMA
SUGAWARA
TANAKA
KAGEYAMA
SAWAMURA
AZUMANE
HINATA
NET
HIRUGAMI
HOSHIUMI
SUWA
HAKUBA
NOZAWA
BESSHO (KANBAYASHI)
*CURRENT ROTATION
CHAPTER 353: A Quiet Awakening
THAT QUICK SET WAS AWESOME. GOOD ONE.
THANKS.
BAM
GEH! IT CAME TO ME?!
FWIF
THMP
THERE ARE TIMES WHEN PUTTING THE BALL UP FOR THE ACE...
...AND LETTING HIM TACKLE THE CHALLENGE BACK-TO-BACK IS THE SMART MOVE.
IF I'D BEEN OUT THERE IN KAGEYAMA'S PLACE, EVEN THOUGH IT WAS OBVIOUS THAT ASAHI WASN'T IN THE BEST POSITION...
...PUTTING THE BALL UP HIGH FOR HIM WOULD HAVE BEEN THE ONLY CHOICE I HAD. I WOULDN'T HAVE BEEN CAPABLE OF ANYTHING ELSE.

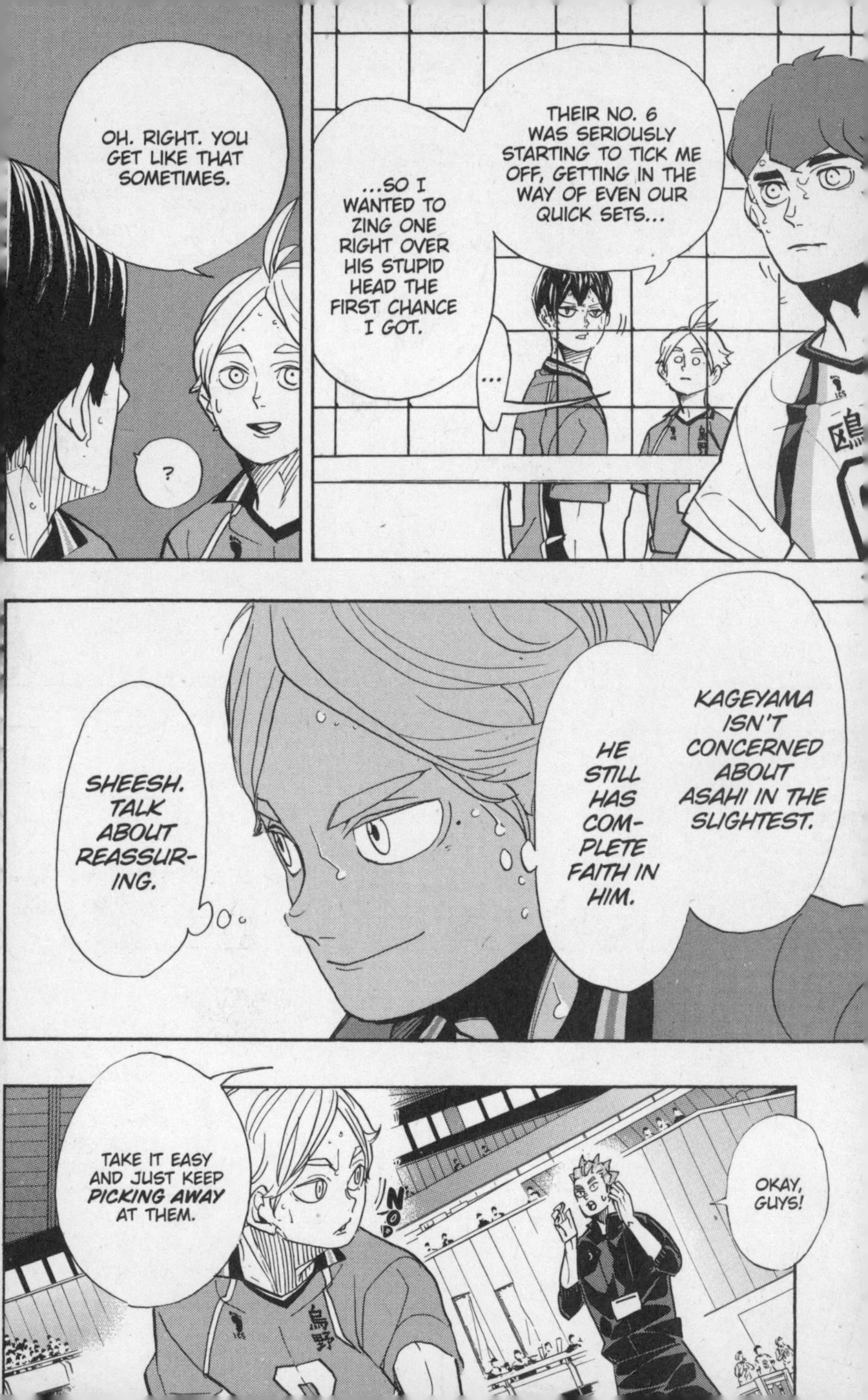
THEIR NO. 6 WAS SERIOUSLY STARTING TO TICK ME OFF, GETTING IN THE WAY OF EVEN OUR QUICK SETS...
...SO I WANTED TO ZING ONE RIGHT OVER HIS STUPID HEAD THE FIRST CHANCE I GOT.
...
OH. RIGHT. YOU GET LIKE THAT SOMETIMES.
?
KAGEYAMA ISN'T CONCERNED ABOUT ASAHI IN THE SLIGHTEST.
HE STILL HAS COMPLETE FAITH IN HIM.
SHEESH. TALK ABOUT REASSURING.
OKAY, GUYS!
NOD
TAKE IT EASY AND JUST KEEP PICKING AWAY AT THEM.

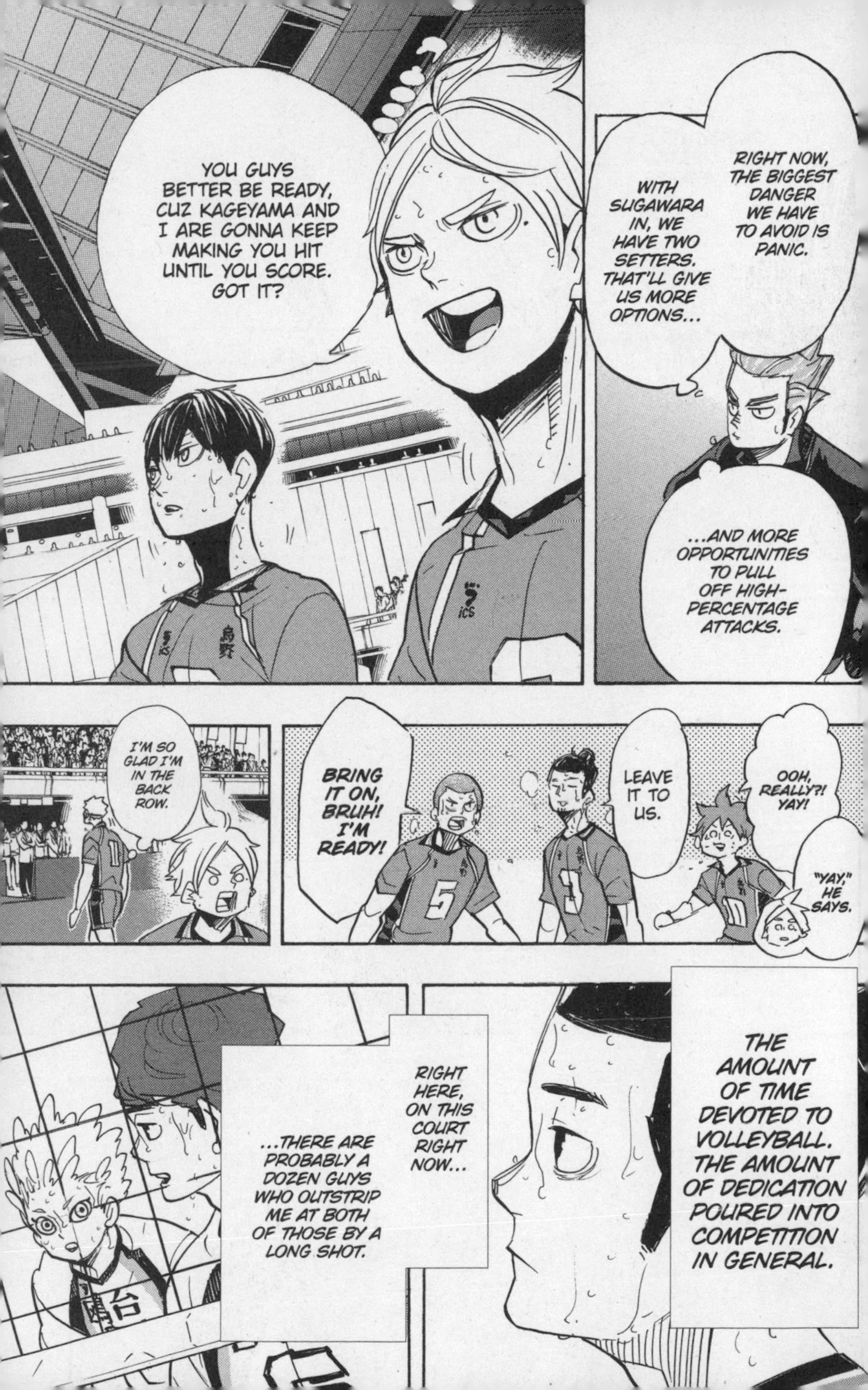
RIGHT NOW, THE BIGGEST DANGER WE HAVE TO AVOID IS PANIC.
WITH SUGAWARA IN, WE HAVE TWO SETTERS. THAT'LL GIVE US MORE OPTIONS...
...AND MORE OPPORTUNITIES TO PULL OFF HIGH-PERCENTAGE ATTACKS.
YOU GUYS BETTER BE READY, CUZ KAGEYAMA AND I ARE GONNA KEEP MAKING YOU HIT UNTIL YOU SCORE. GOT IT?
OOH, REALLY?! YAY!
"YAY," HE SAYS.
LEAVE IT TO US.
BRING IT ON, BRUH! I'M READY!
I'M SO GLAD I'M IN THE BACK ROW.
THE AMOUNT OF TIME DEVOTED TO VOLLEYBALL. THE AMOUNT OF DEDICATION POURED INTO COMPETITION IN GENERAL.
RIGHT HERE, ON THIS COURT RIGHT NOW...
...THERE ARE PROBABLY A DOZEN GUYS WHO OUTSTRIP ME AT BOTH OF THOSE BY A LONG SHOT.

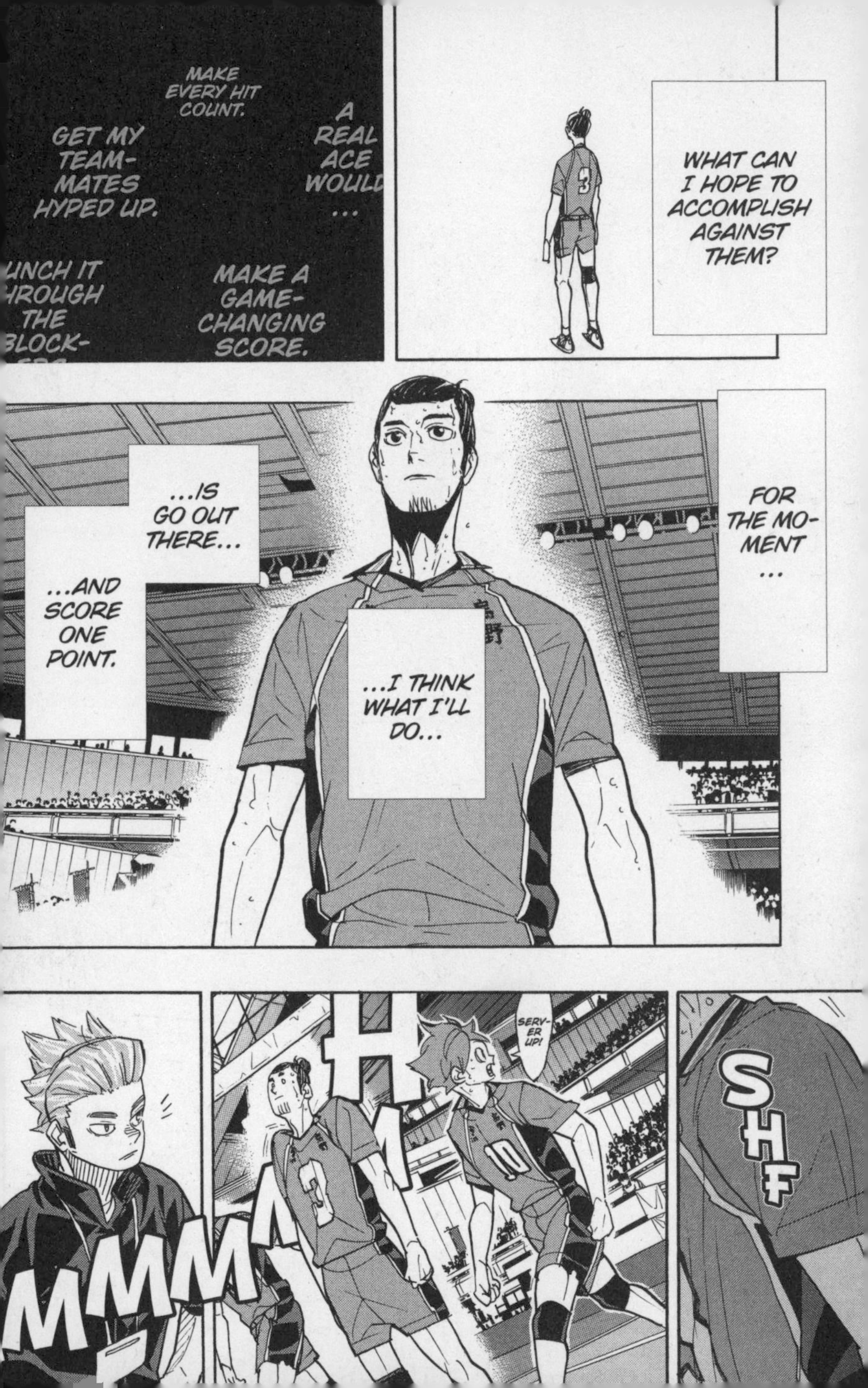
WHAT CAN I HOPE TO ACCOMPLISH AGAINST THEM?
A REAL ACE WOULD...
MAKE EVERY HIT COUNT.
GET MY TEAM-MATES HYPED UP.
MAKE A GAME-CHANGING SCORE.
UNCH IT HROUGH THE BLOCK-
FOR THE MOMENT...
...I THINK WHAT I'LL DO...
...IS GO OUT THERE...
...AND SCORE ONE POINT.
SHF
SERVER UP!
H
MMMM

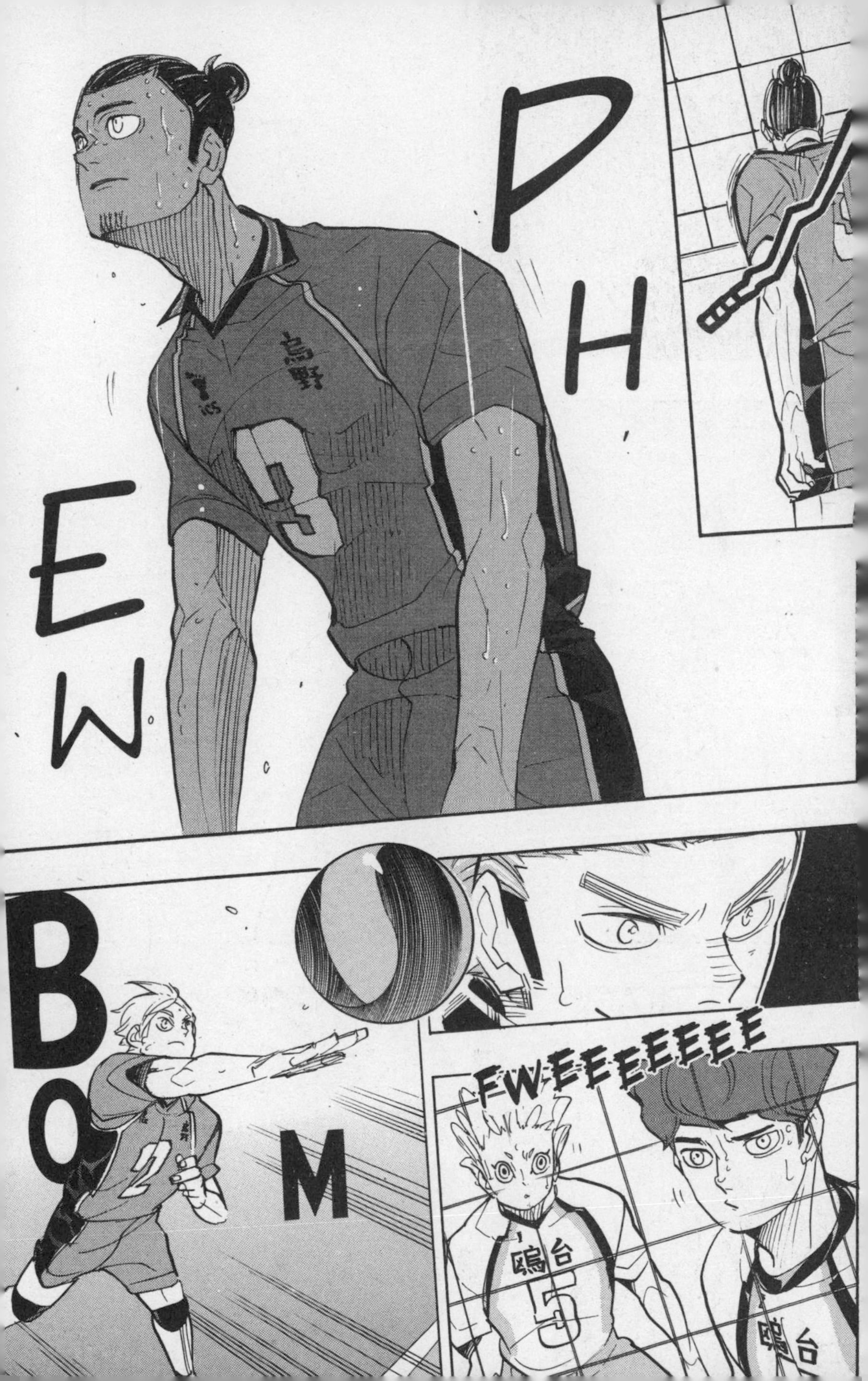
PHEW
FWEEEEEEEE
BOM

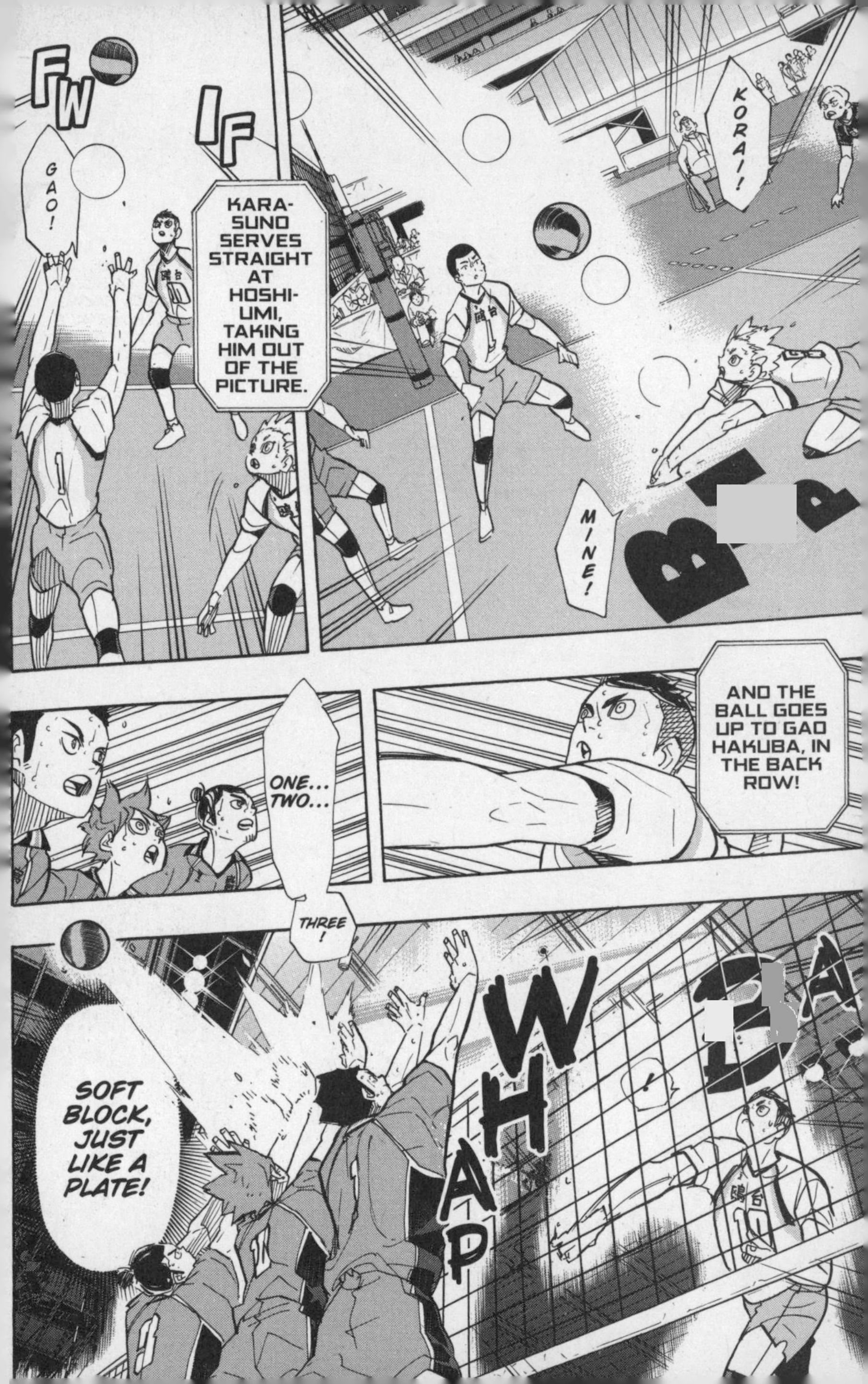
KORAI!
MINE!
FWIF
GAO!
KARA-SUNO SERVES STRAIGHT AT HOSHI-UMI, TAKING HIM OUT OF THE PICTURE.
AND THE BALL GOES UP TO GAO HAKUBA, IN THE BACK ROW!
ONE... TWO...
THREE!
WHAP
SOFT BLOCK, JUST LIKE A PLATE!

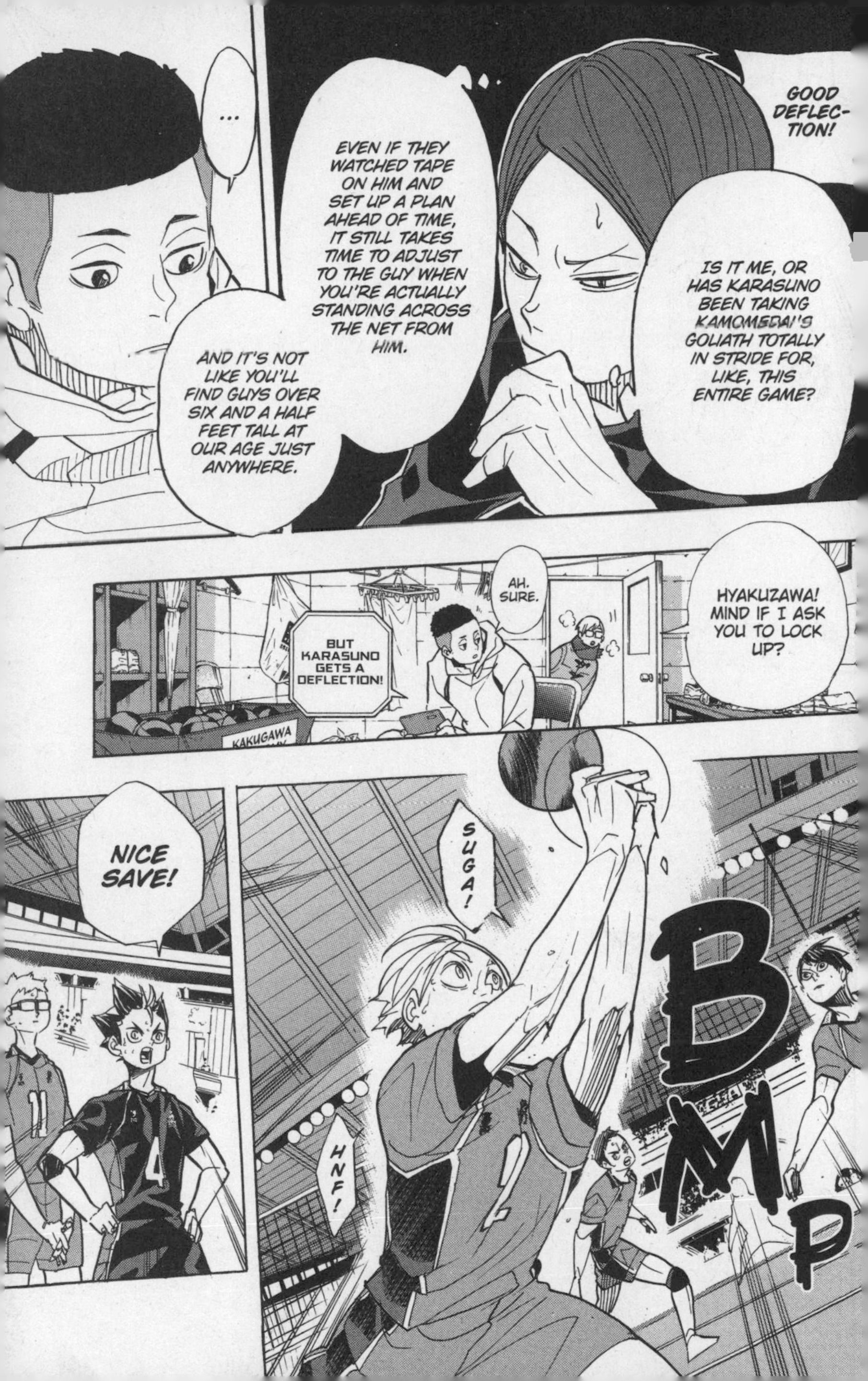
GOOD DEFLECTION!
IS IT ME, OR HAS KARASUNO BEEN TAKING KAMOMEDAI'S GOLIATH TOTALLY IN STRIDE FOR, LIKE, THIS ENTIRE GAME?
EVEN IF THEY WATCHED TAPE ON HIM AND SET UP A PLAN AHEAD OF TIME, IT STILL TAKES TIME TO ADJUST TO THE GUY WHEN YOU'RE ACTUALLY STANDING ACROSS THE NET FROM HIM.
...
AND IT'S NOT LIKE YOU'LL FIND GUYS OVER SIX AND A HALF FEET TALL AT OUR AGE JUST ANYWHERE.
HYAKUZAWA! MIND IF I ASK YOU TO LOCK UP?
AH. SURE.
BUT KARASUNO GETS A DEFLECTION!
KAKUGAWA
BMMP
SUGA!
HNF!
NICE SAVE!

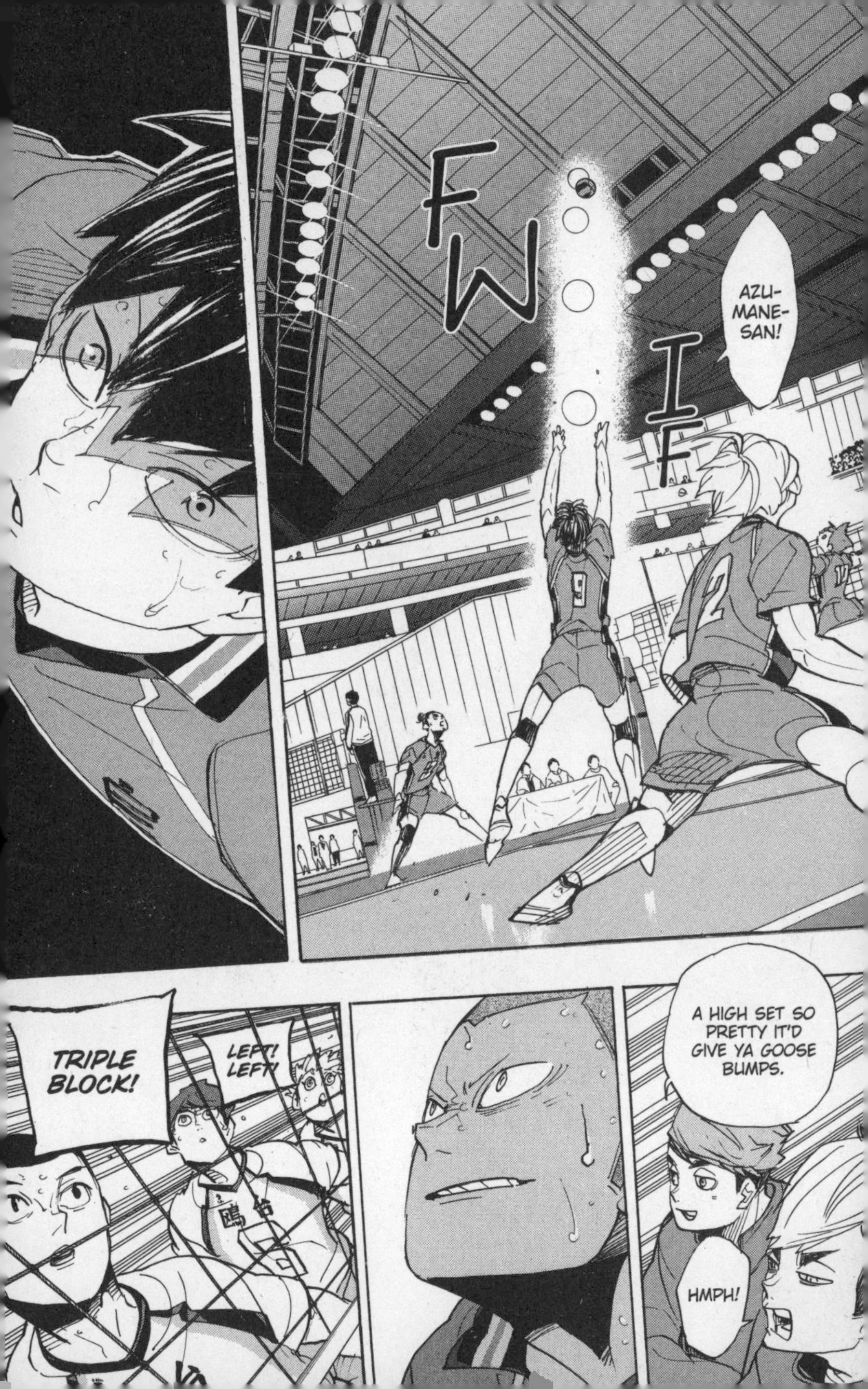
AZUMANE-SAN!
FWIF
A HIGH SET SO PRETTY IT'D GIVE YA GOOSE BUMPS.
HMPH!
LEFT! LEFT!
TRIPLE BLOCK!

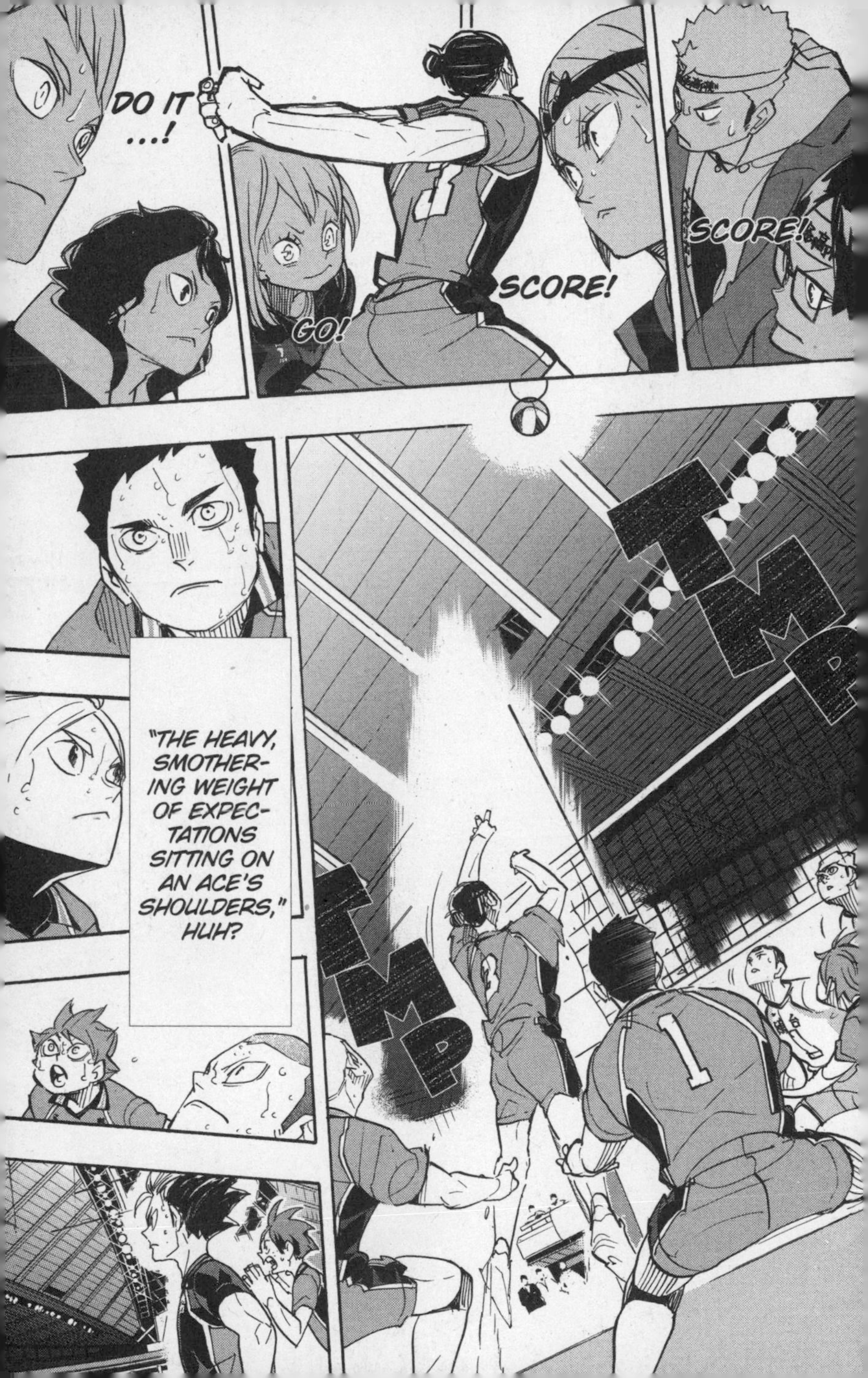
SCORE!
SCORE!
GO!
DO IT ...!
TMP
TMP
"THE HEAVY, SMOTHERING WEIGHT OF EXPECTATIONS SITTING ON AN ACE'S SHOULDERS," HUH?

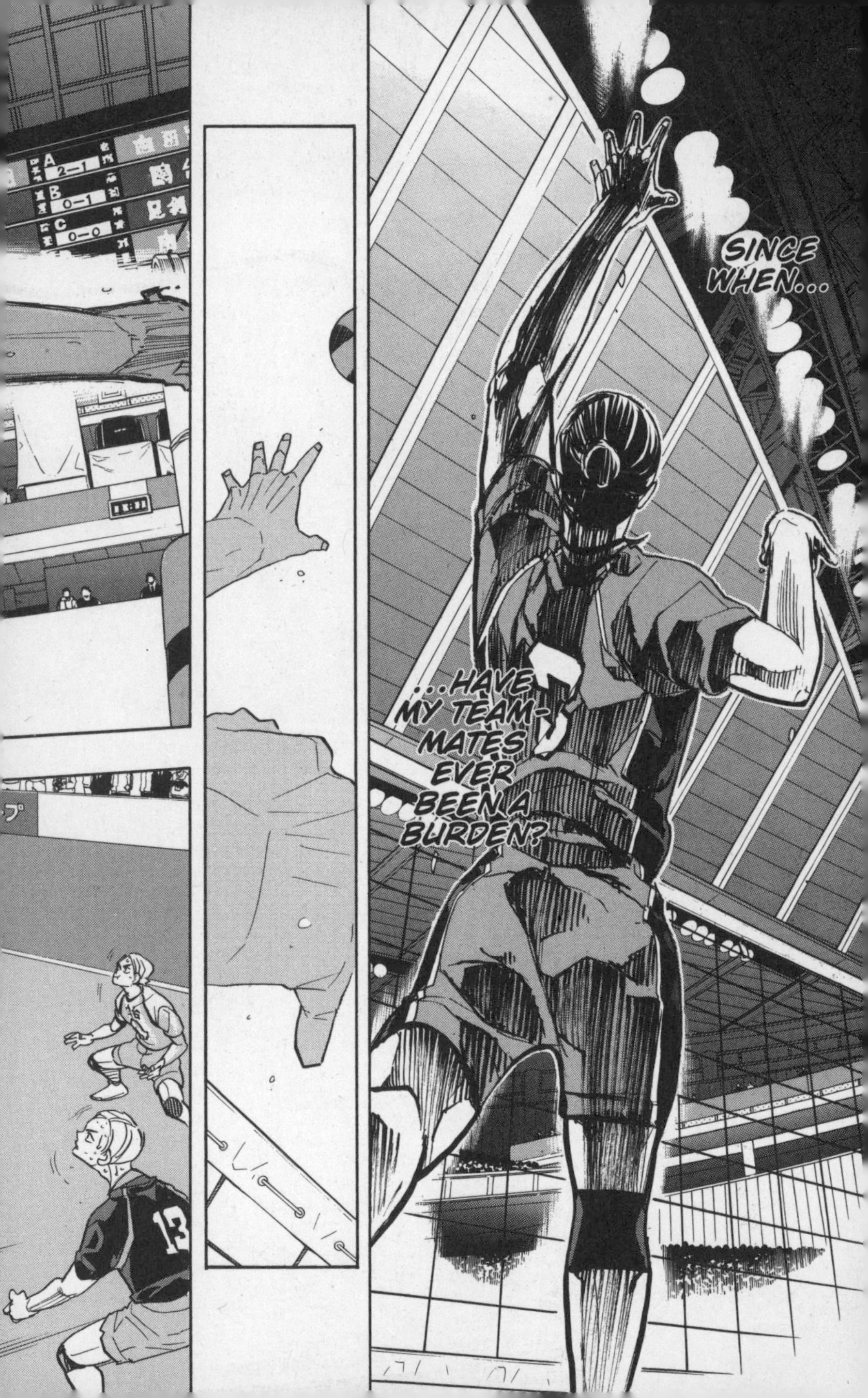
SINCE WHEN...
...HAVE MY TEAM-MATES EVER BEEN A BURDEN?
A
2-1
B
0-1
C
0-0
13

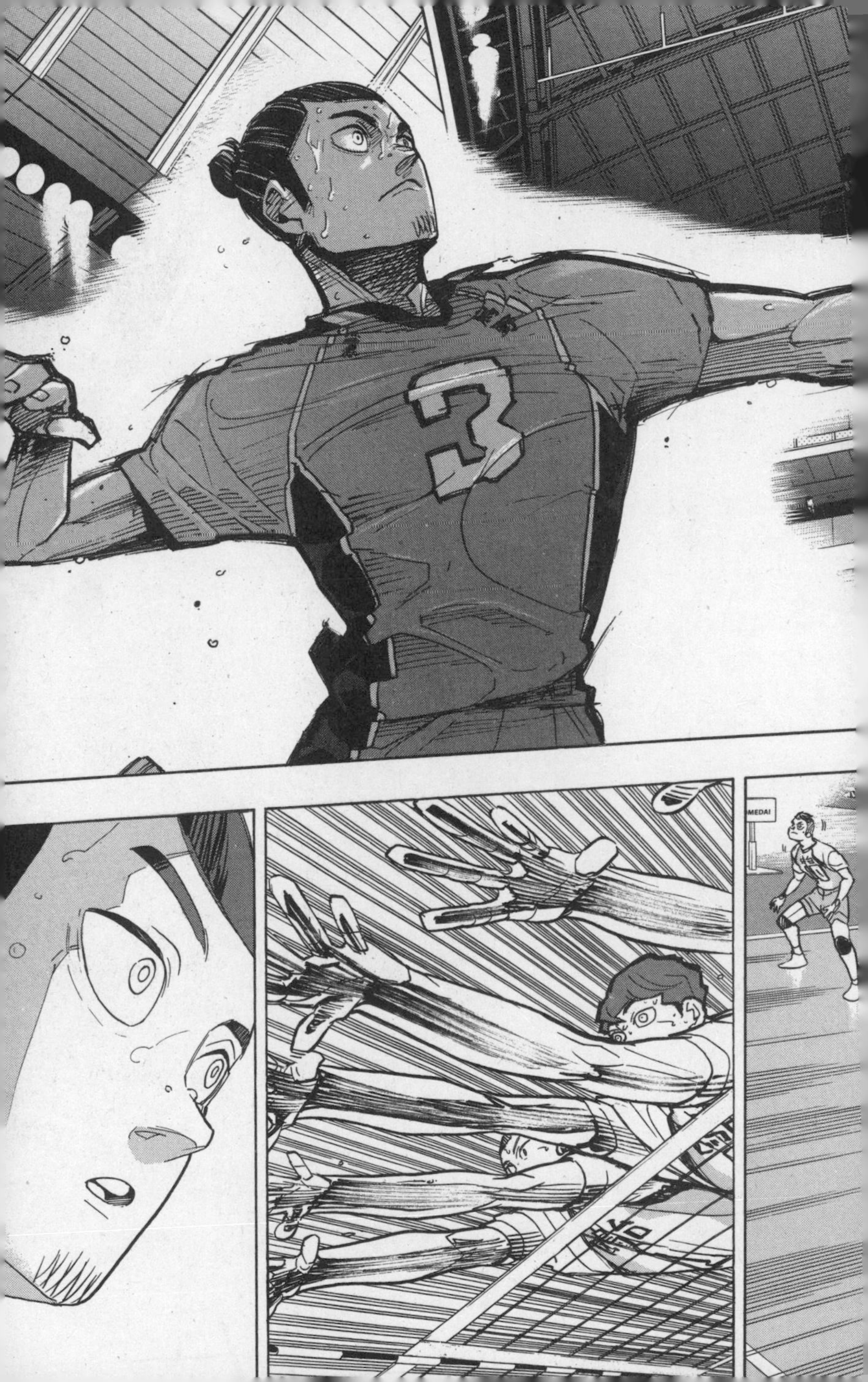
MEDAI

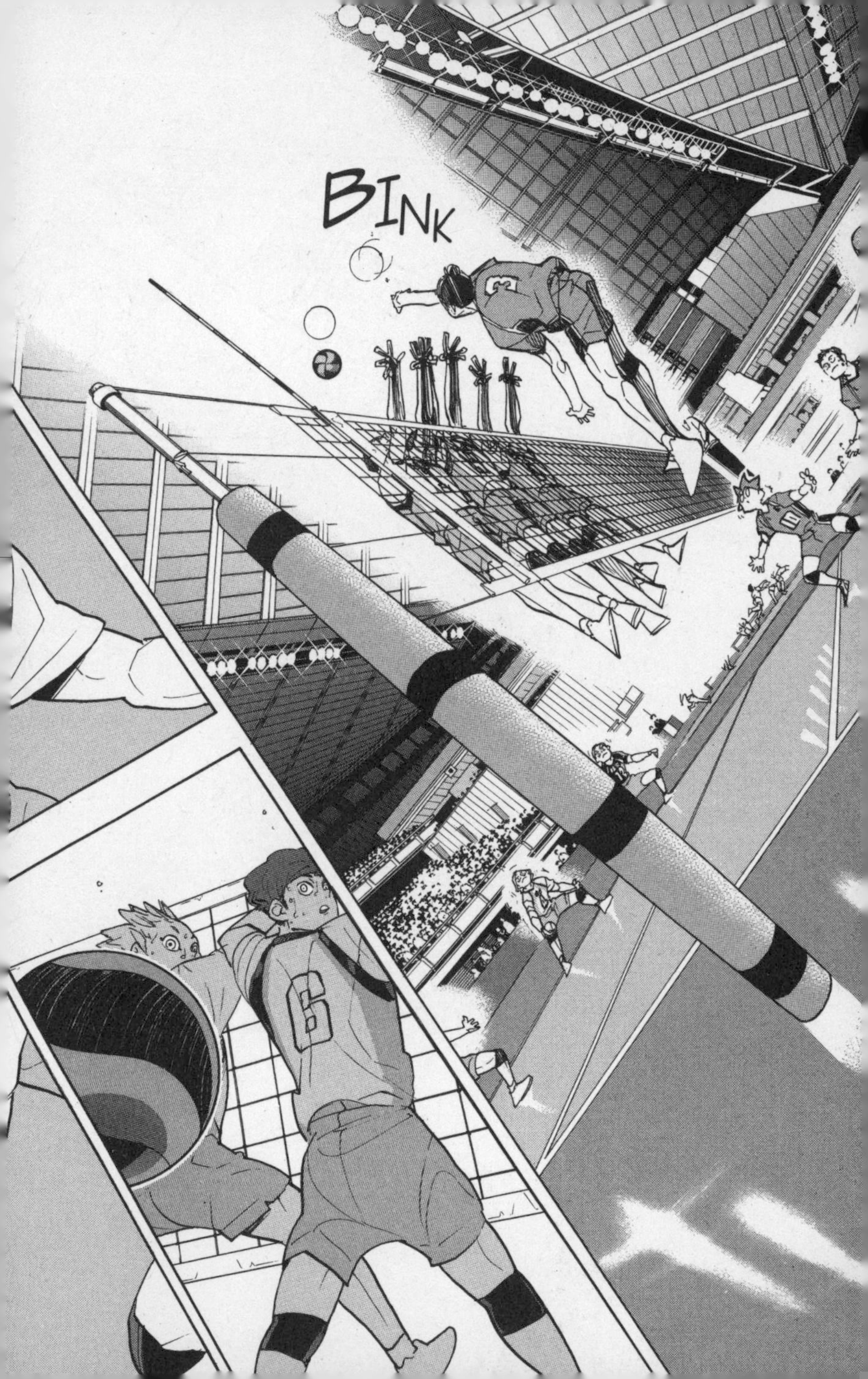
BINK

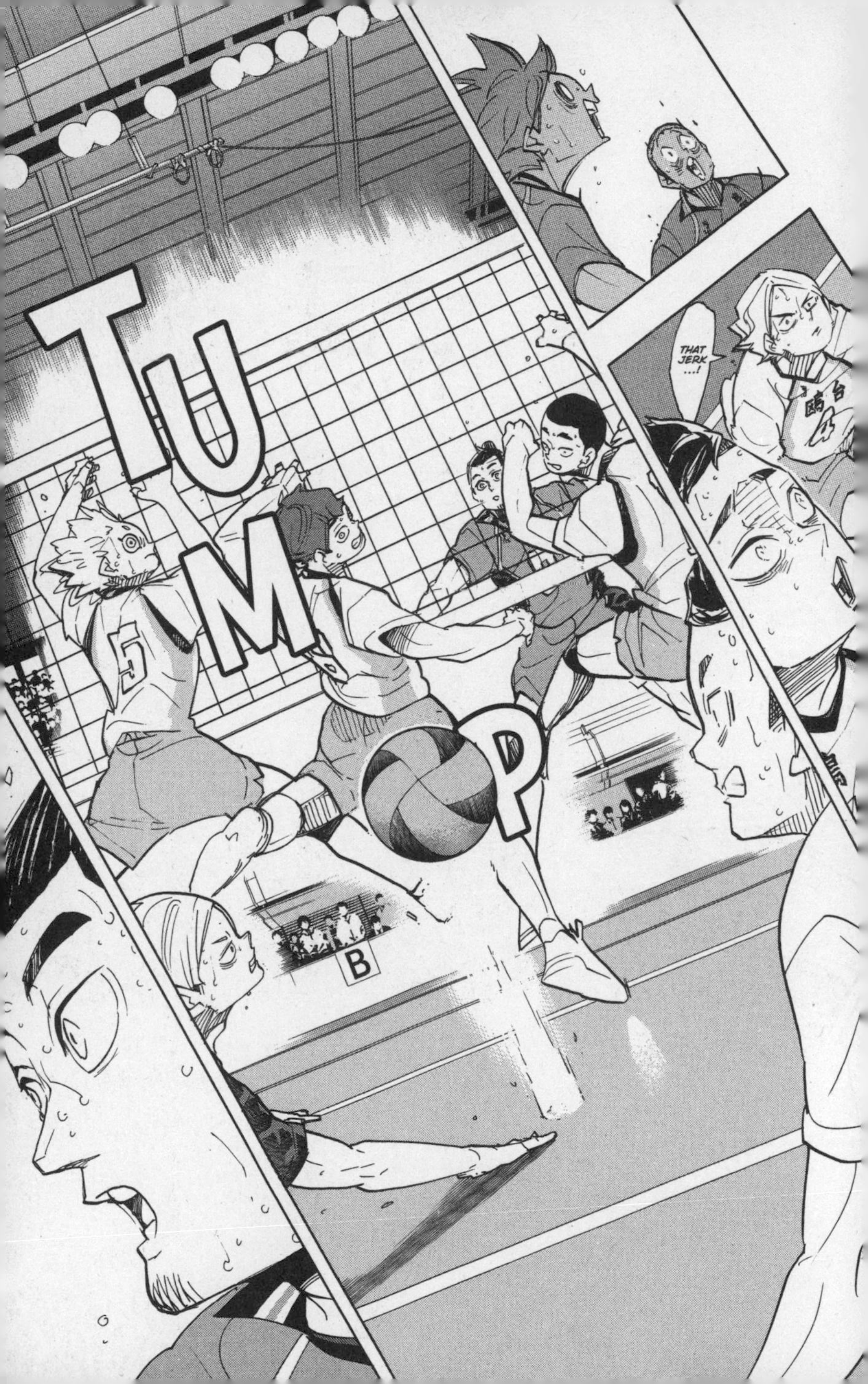
THAT JERK ...!
TUMP
B

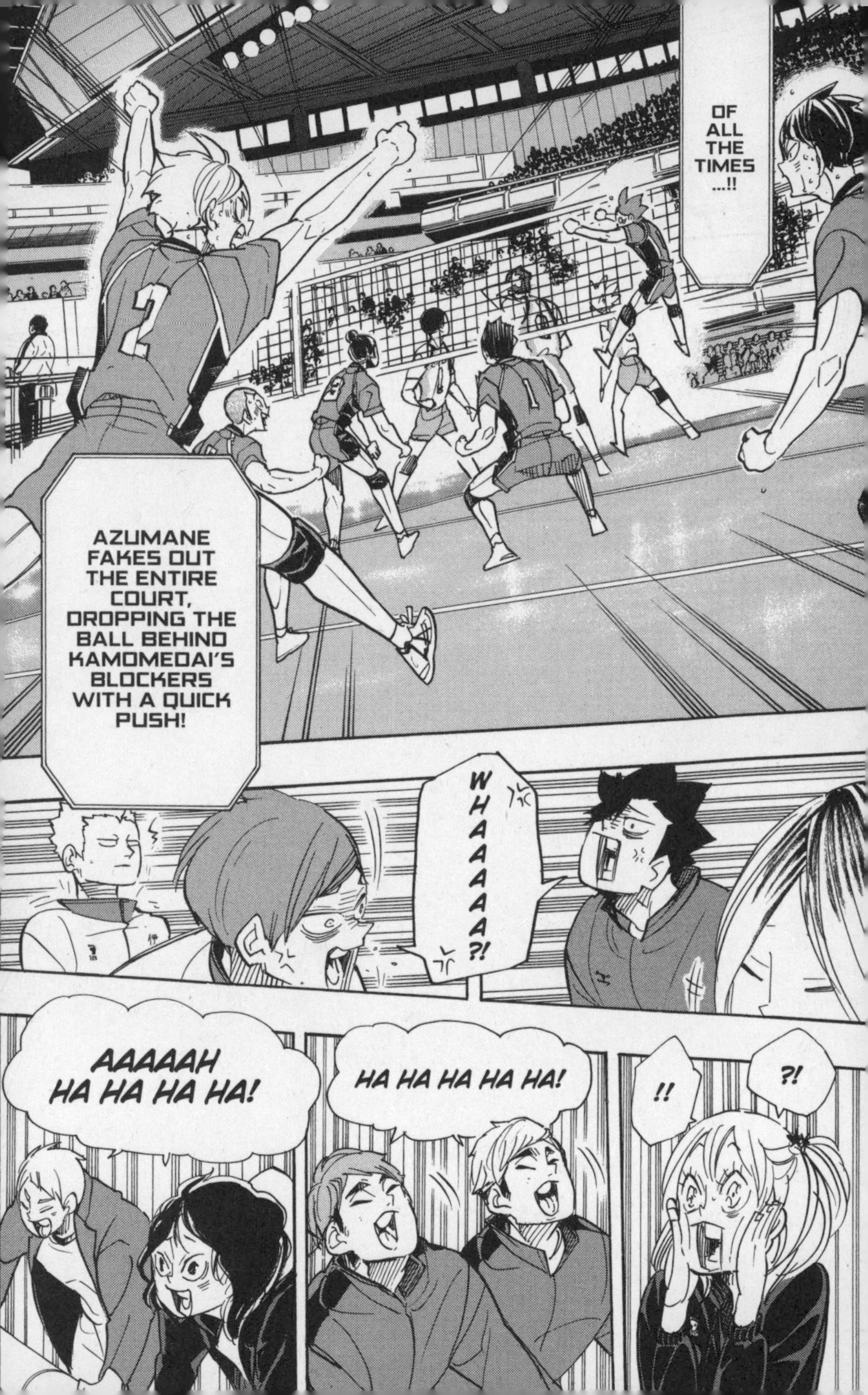

OF ALL THE TIMES ...!!
AZUMANE FAKES OUT THE ENTIRE COURT, DROPPING THE BALL BEHIND KAMOMEDAI'S BLOCKERS WITH A QUICK PUSH!
WHAAAAAAA?!
?!
!!
HA HA HA HA HA HA!
AAAAAH HA HA HA HA!

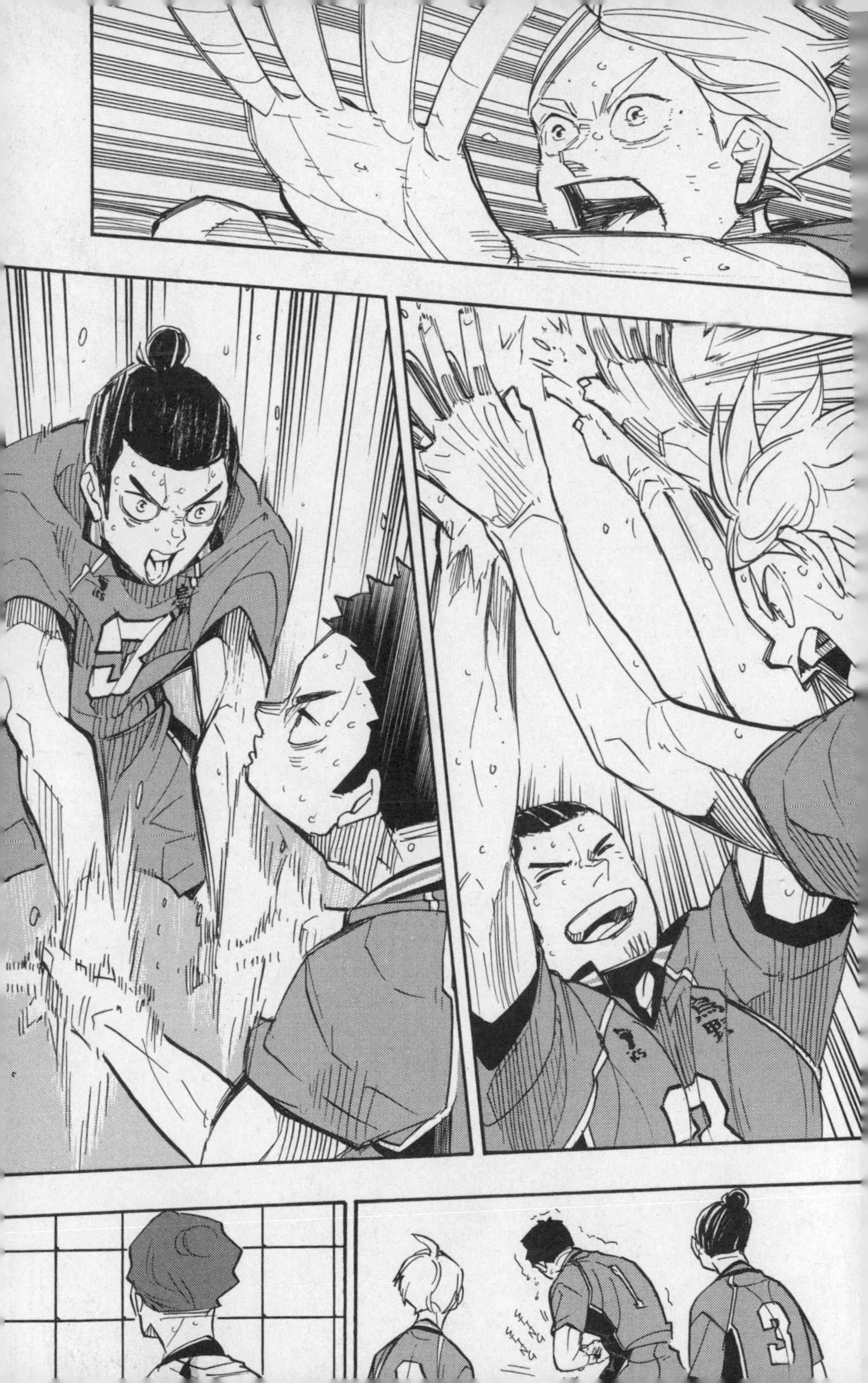

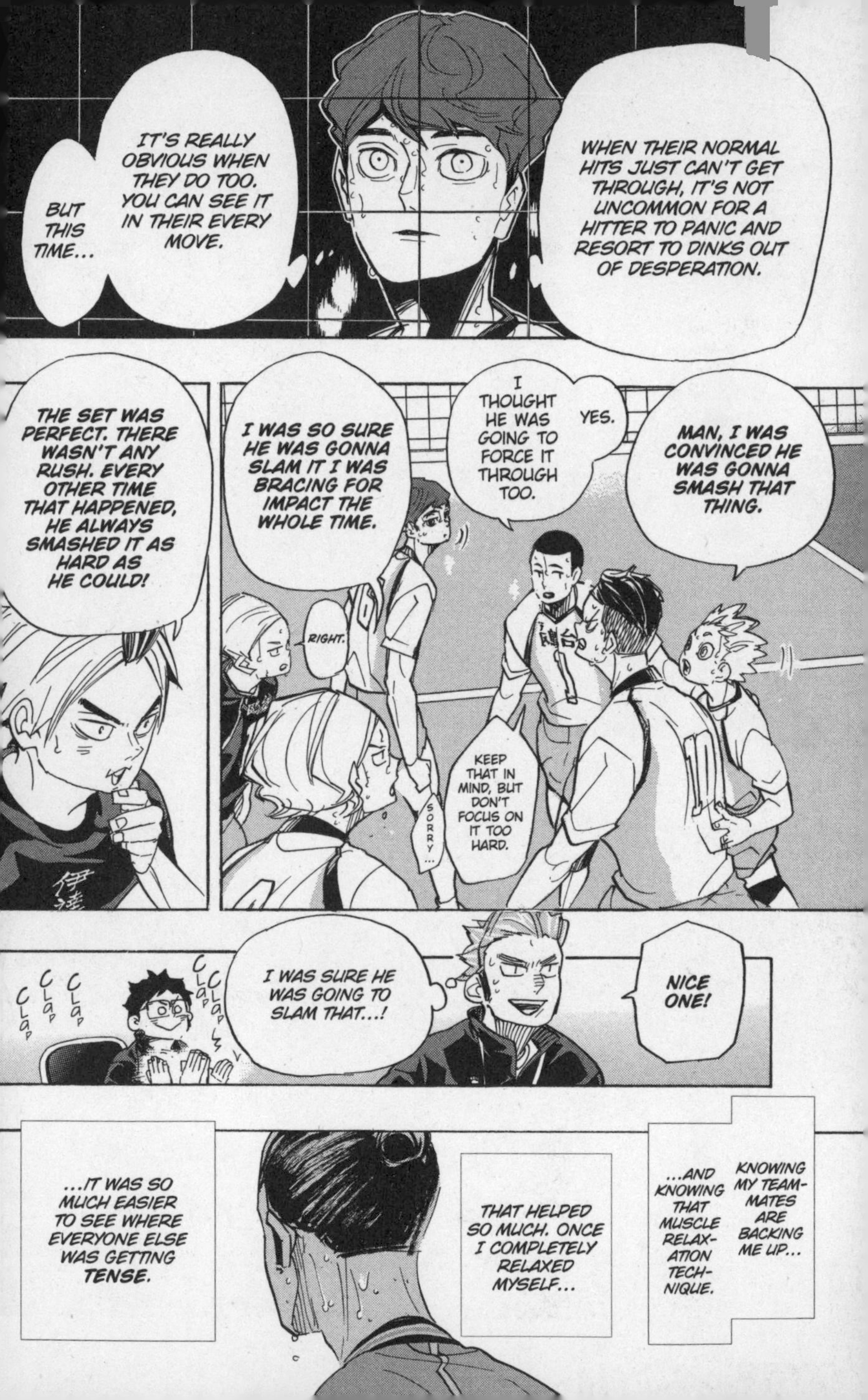
WHEN THEIR NORMAL HITS JUST CAN'T GET THROUGH, IT'S NOT UNCOMMON FOR A HITTER TO PANIC AND RESORT TO DINKS OUT OF DESPERATION.
IT'S REALLY OBVIOUS WHEN THEY DO TOO. YOU CAN SEE IT IN THEIR EVERY MOVE.
BUT THIS TIME...
MAN, I WAS CONVINCED HE WAS GONNA SMASH THAT THING.
YES.
I THOUGHT HE WAS GOING TO FORCE IT THROUGH TOO.
I WAS SO SURE HE WAS GONNA SLAM IT I WAS BRACING FOR IMPACT THE WHOLE TIME.
RIGHT.
KEEP THAT IN MIND, BUT DON'T FOCUS ON IT TOO HARD.
SORRY...
THE SET WAS PERFECT. THERE WASN'T ANY RUSH. EVERY OTHER TIME THAT HAPPENED, HE ALWAYS SMASHED IT AS HARD AS HE COULD!
NICE ONE!
I WAS SURE HE WAS GOING TO SLAM THAT...!
CLAP CLAP CLAP CLAP CLAP
KNOWING MY TEAMMATES ARE BACKING ME UP...
...AND KNOWING THAT MUSCLE RELAXATION TECHNIQUE.
THAT HELPED SO MUCH. ONCE I COMPLETELY RELAXED MYSELF...
...IT WAS SO MUCH EASIER TO SEE WHERE EVERYONE ELSE WAS GETTING TENSE.

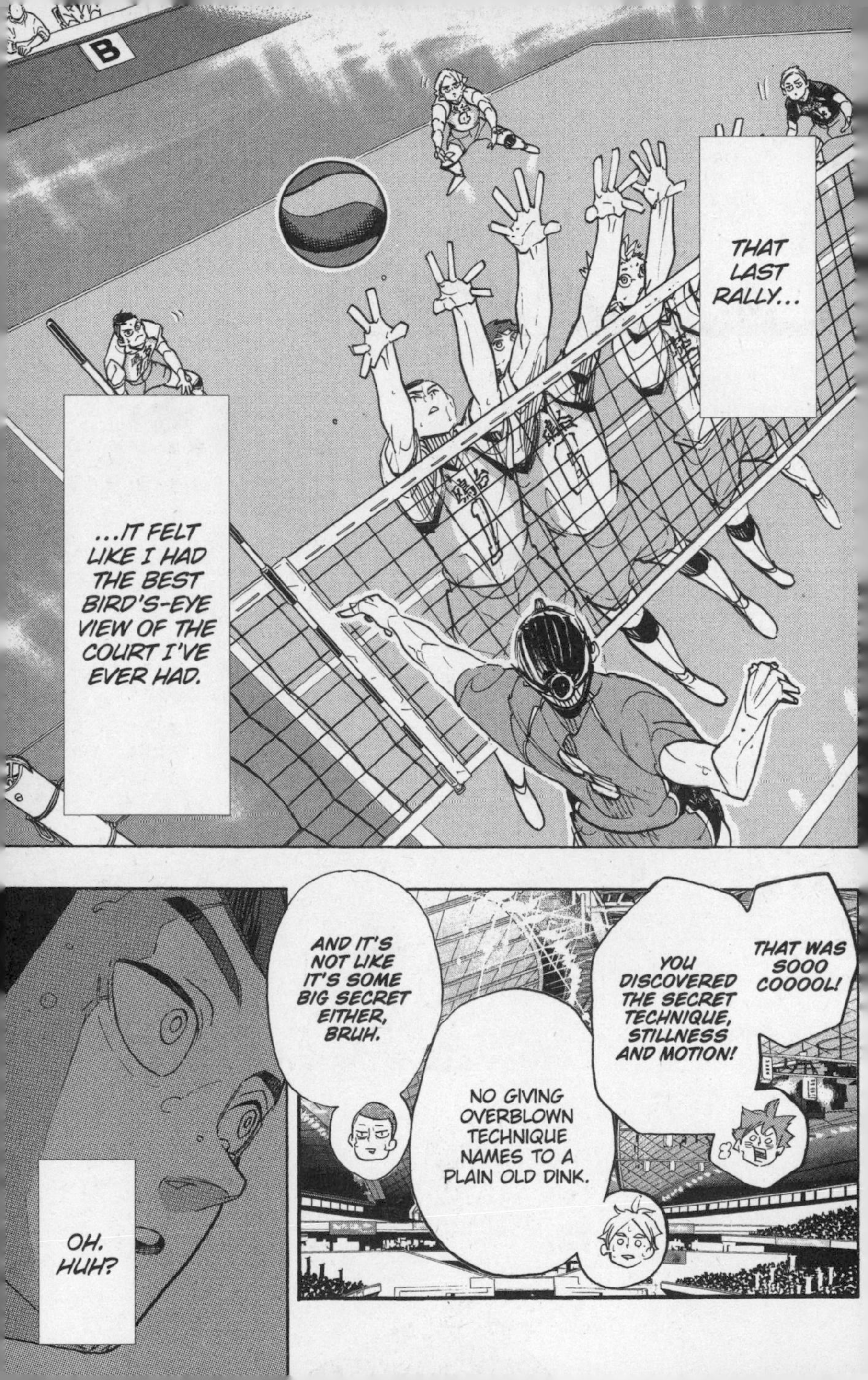
THAT LAST RALLY...
...IT FELT LIKE I HAD THE BEST BIRD'S-EYE VIEW OF THE COURT I'VE EVER HAD.
B
THAT WAS SOOO COOOOL!
YOU DISCOVERED THE SECRET TECHNIQUE, STILLNESS AND MOTION!
NO GIVING OVERBLOWN TECHNIQUE NAMES TO A PLAIN OLD DINK.
AND IT'S NOT LIKE IT'S SOME BIG SECRET EITHER, BRUH.
OH. HUH?

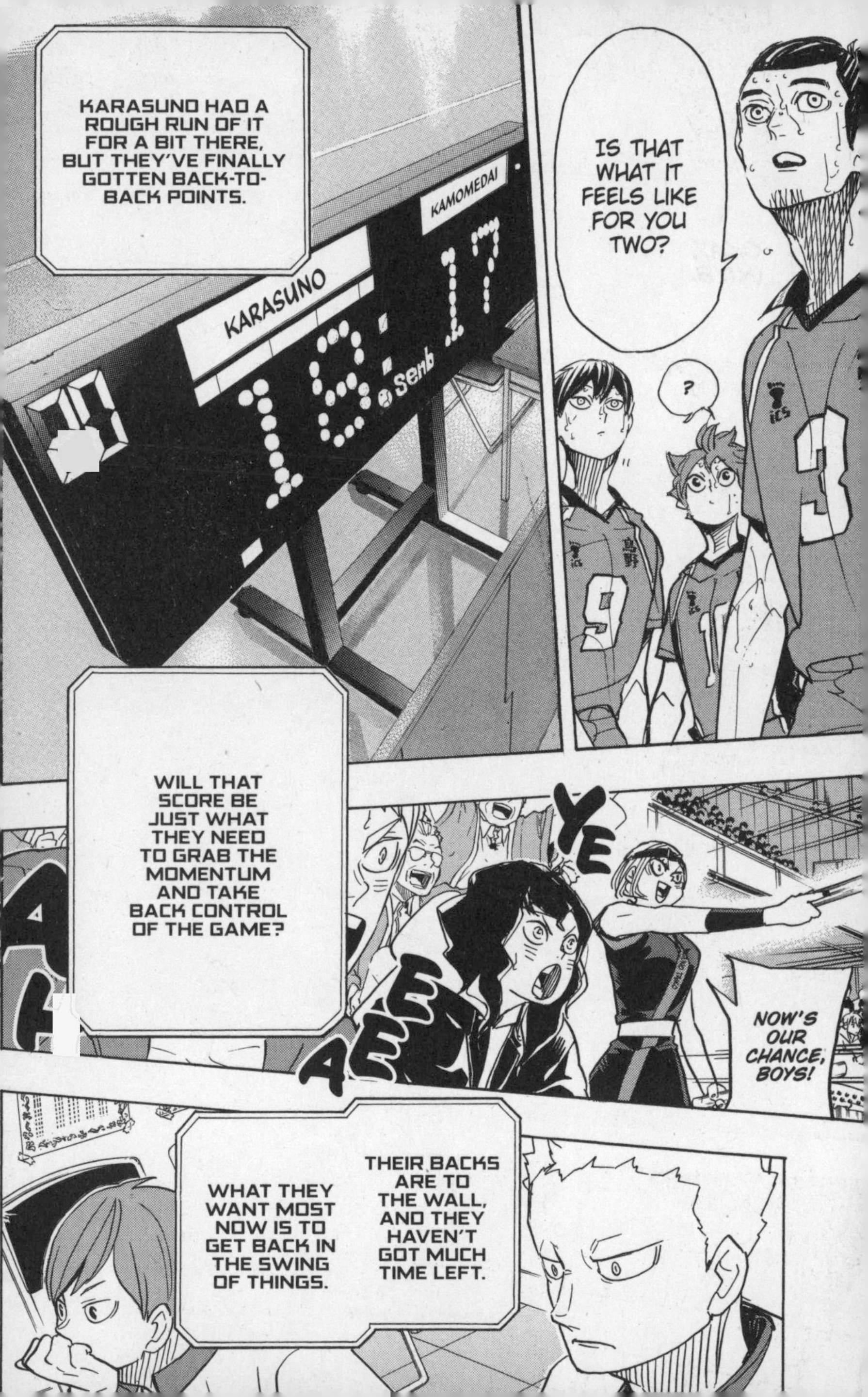
IS THAT WHAT IT FEELS LIKE FOR YOU TWO?
?
KARASUNO HAD A ROUGH RUN OF IT FOR A BIT THERE, BUT THEY'VE FINALLY GOTTEN BACK-TO-BACK POINTS.
KAMOMEDAI
KARASUNO
NOW'S OUR CHANCE, BOYS!
WILL THAT SCORE BE JUST WHAT THEY NEED TO GRAB THE MOMENTUM AND TAKE BACK CONTROL OF THE GAME?
THEIR BACKS ARE TO THE WALL, AND THEY HAVEN'T GOT MUCH TIME LEFT.
WHAT THEY WANT MOST NOW IS TO GET BACK IN THE SWING OF THINGS.

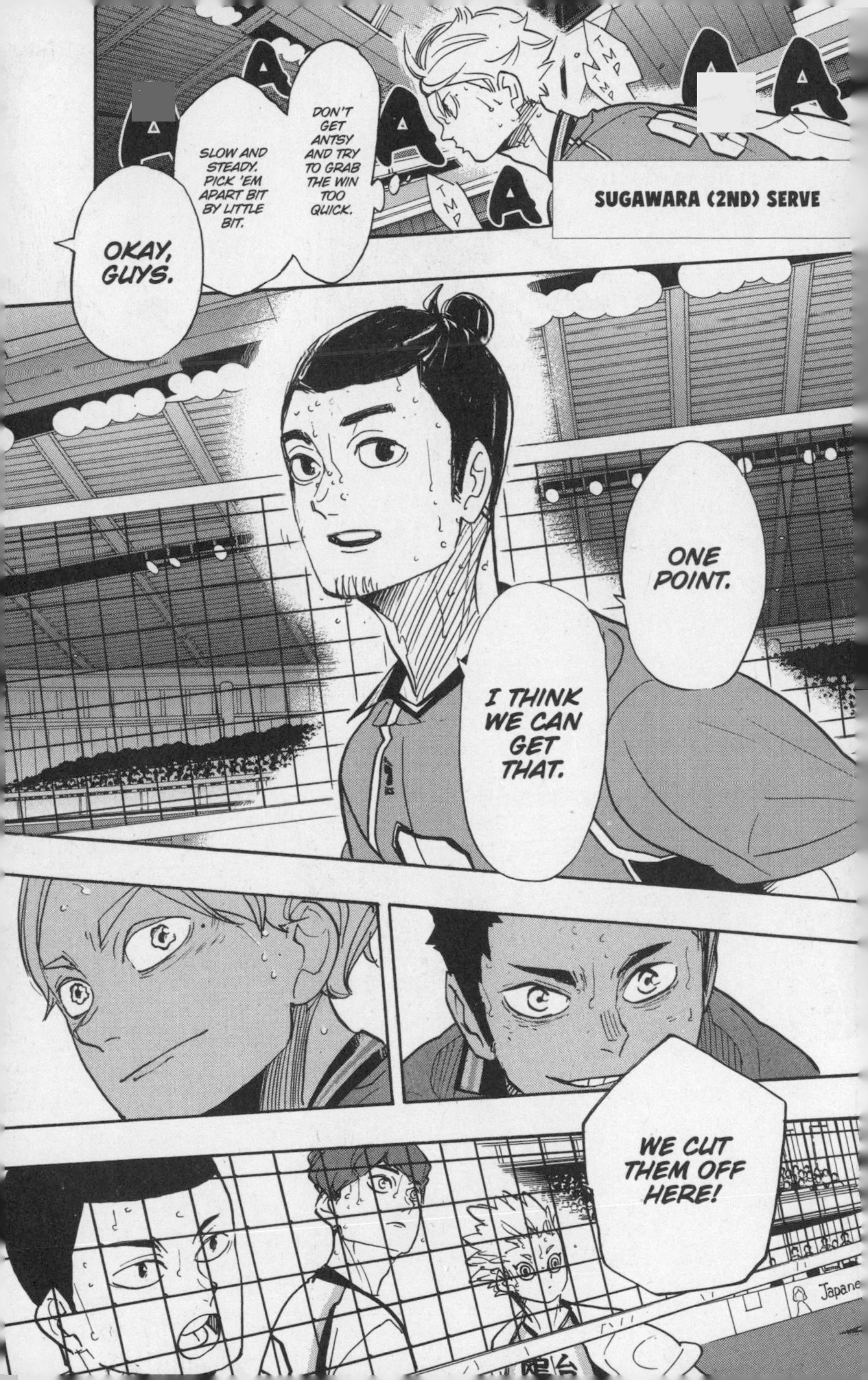
SUGAWARA (2ND) SERVE
A A A A A A
TMP TMP
TMP
DON'T GET ANTSY AND TRY TO GRAB THE WIN TOO QUICK.
SLOW AND STEADY. PICK 'EM APART BIT BY LITTLE BIT.
OKAY, GUYS.
ONE POINT.
I THINK WE CAN GET THAT.
WE CUT THEM OFF HERE!

*LATELY, HYAKUZAWA HAS BEEN WATCHING A LOT OF GAMES REALLY INTENTLY!*

KWEEN

**YUZURU KOMAKI**
**KAKUGAWA ACADEMY**
**VOLLEYBALL CLUB**
**CAPTAIN**

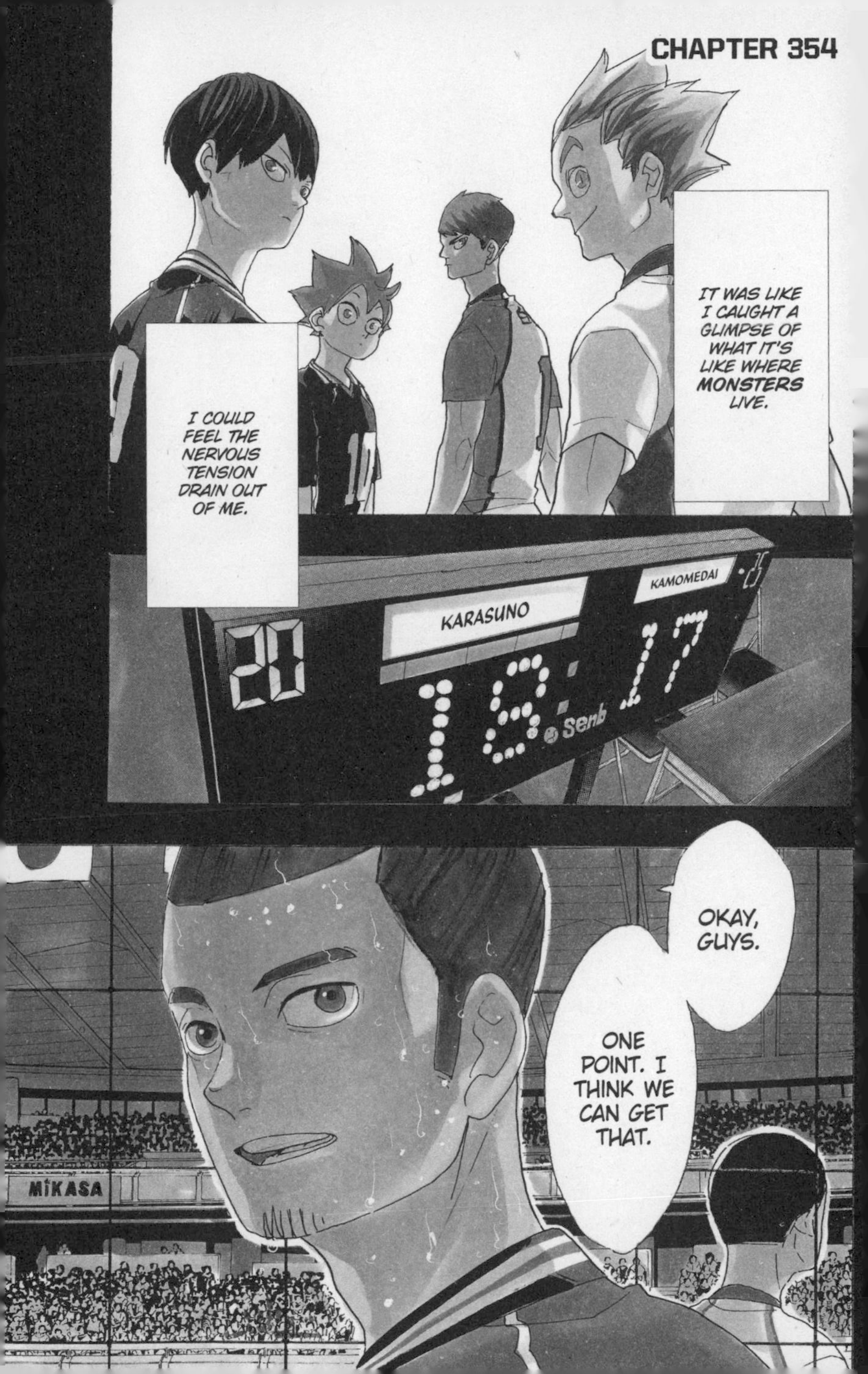
CHAPTER 354
IT WAS LIKE I CAUGHT A GLIMPSE OF WHAT IT'S LIKE WHERE MONSTERS LIVE.
I COULD FEEL THE NERVOUS TENSION DRAIN OUT OF ME.
KAMOMEDAI
KARASUNO
20
18
17
OKAY, GUYS.
ONE POINT. I THINK WE CAN GET THAT.
MIKASA

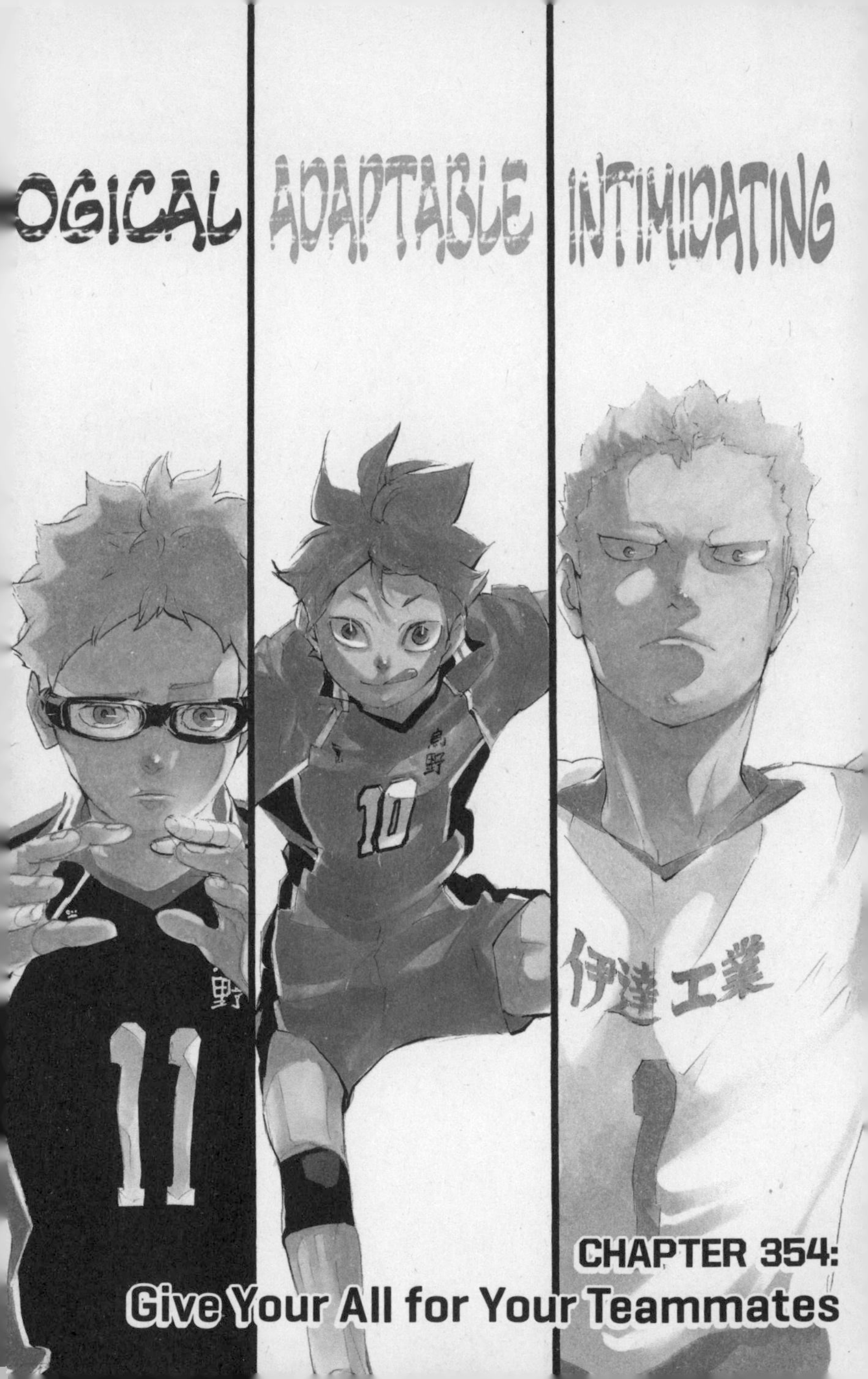
INTIMIDATING
伊達工業
ADAPTABLE
OGICAL

## CHAPTER 354:
## Give Your All for Your Teammates

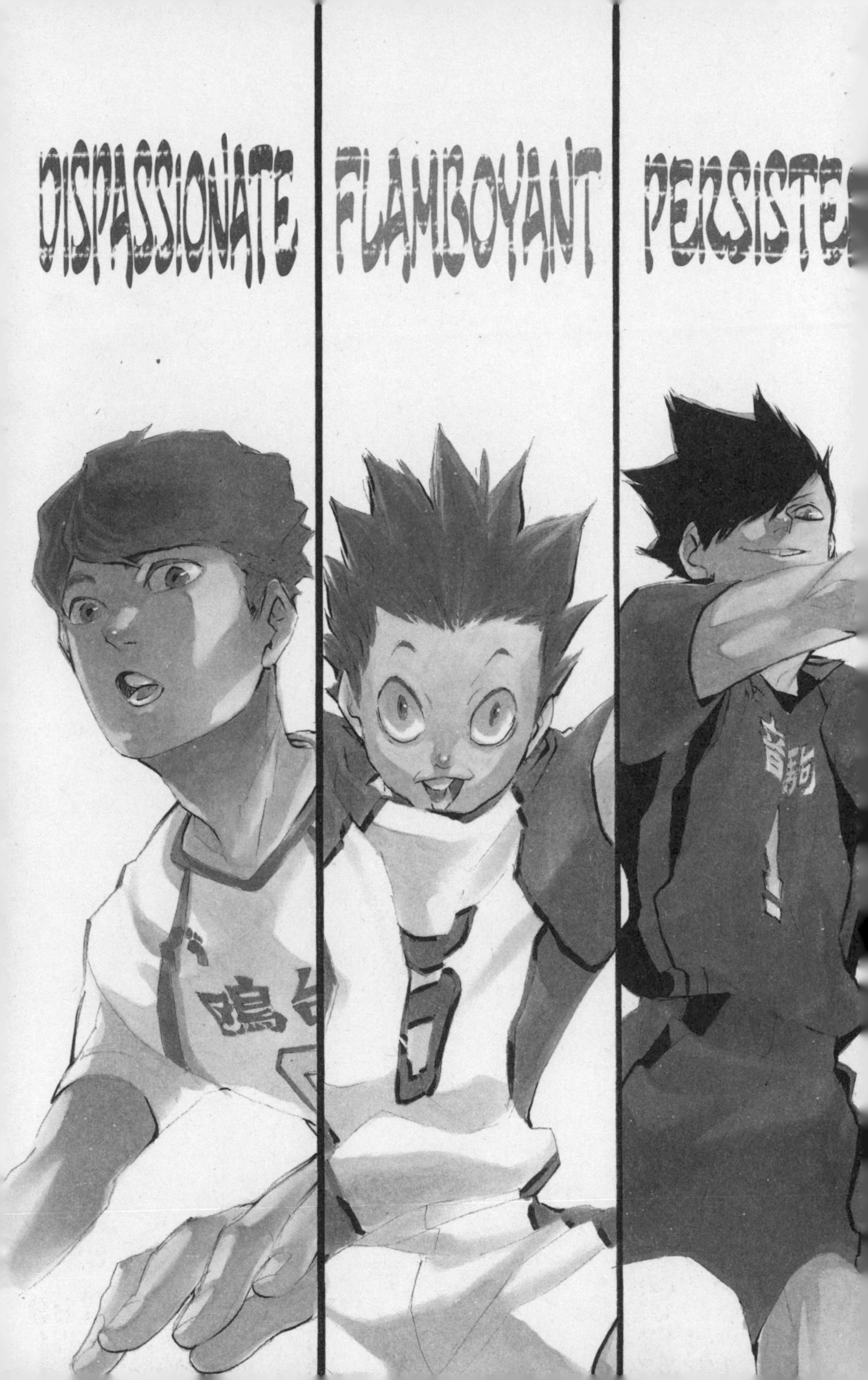
PERSISTE
FLAMBOYANT
DISPASSIONATE

HAIKYU!!

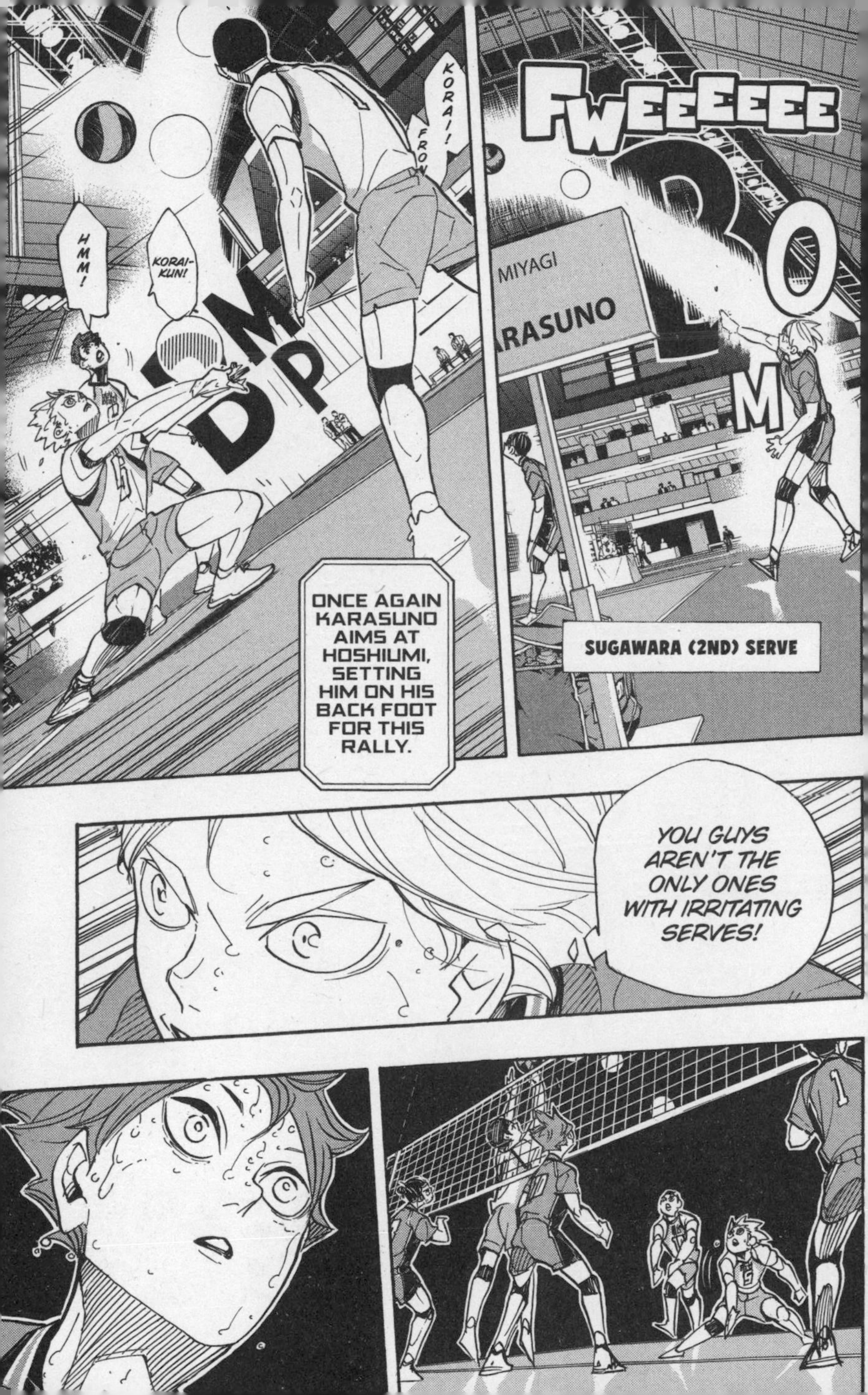
FWEEEEEE
DOM
MIYAGI
ARASUNO
SUGAWARA (2ND) SERVE
KORAI!
HMM!
KORAI-KUN!
DOMP
ONCE AGAIN KARASUNO AIMS AT HOSHIUMI, SETTING HIM ON HIS BACK FOOT FOR THIS RALLY.
YOU GUYS AREN'T THE ONLY ONES WITH IRRITATING SERVES!

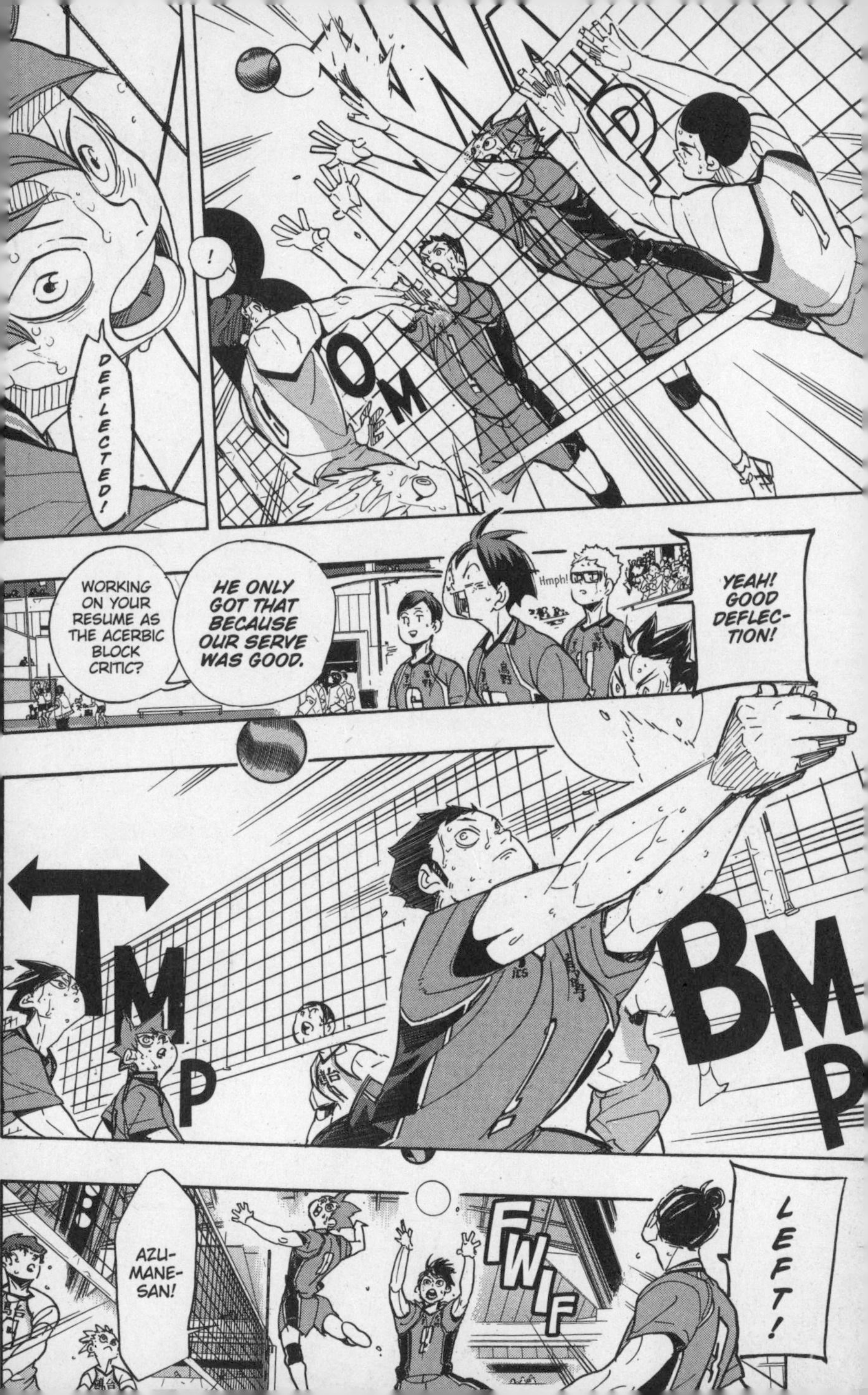

!
DEFLECTED!
YEAH! GOOD DEFLECTION!
Hmph!
HE ONLY GOT THAT BECAUSE OUR SERVE WAS GOOD.
WORKING ON YOUR RESUME AS THE ACERBIC BLOCK CRITIC?
BMP
TMP
LEFT!
FWIF
AZUMANE-SAN!

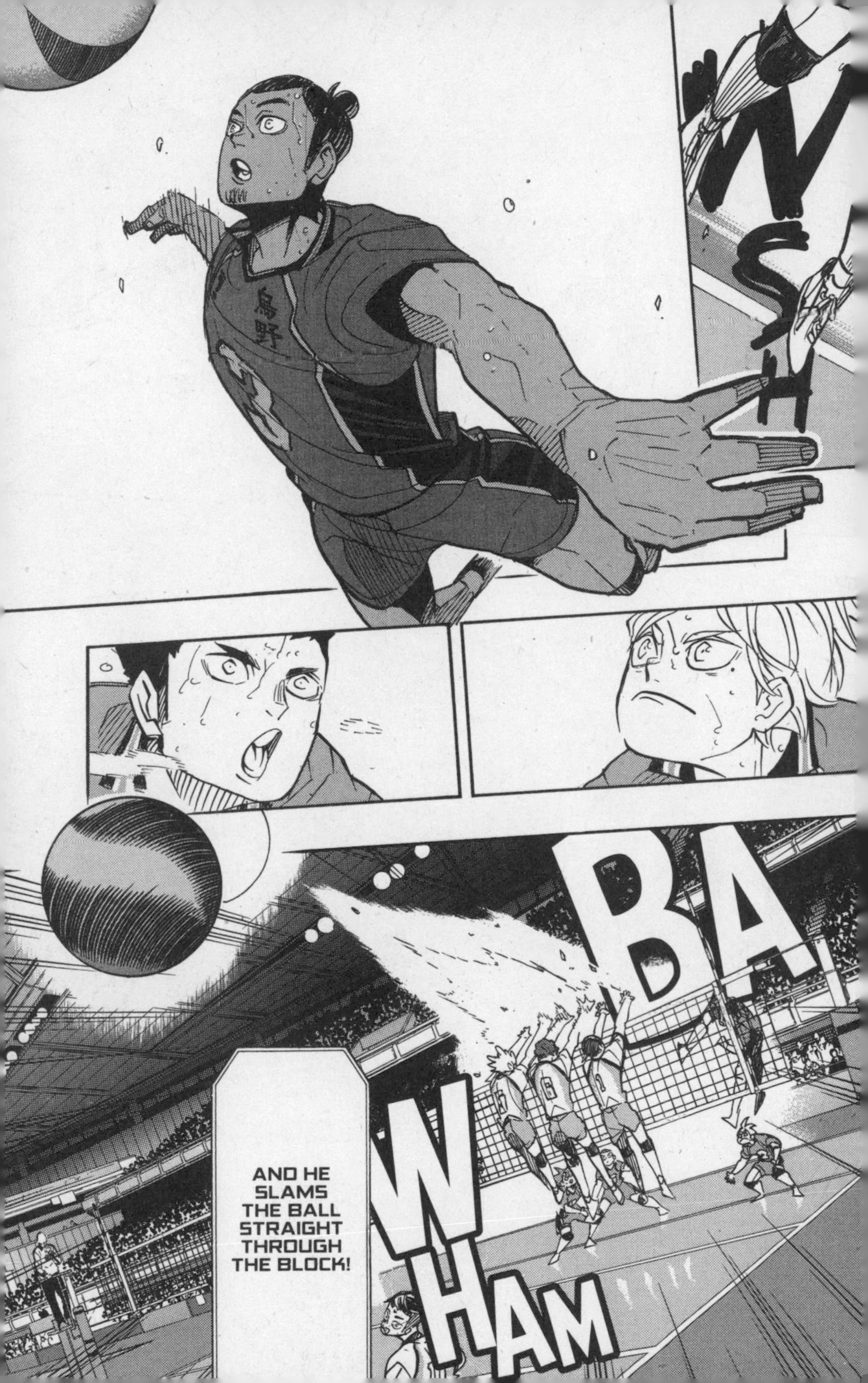
WHSH
BA
AND HE SLAMS THE BALL STRAIGHT THROUGH THE BLOCK!
WHAM

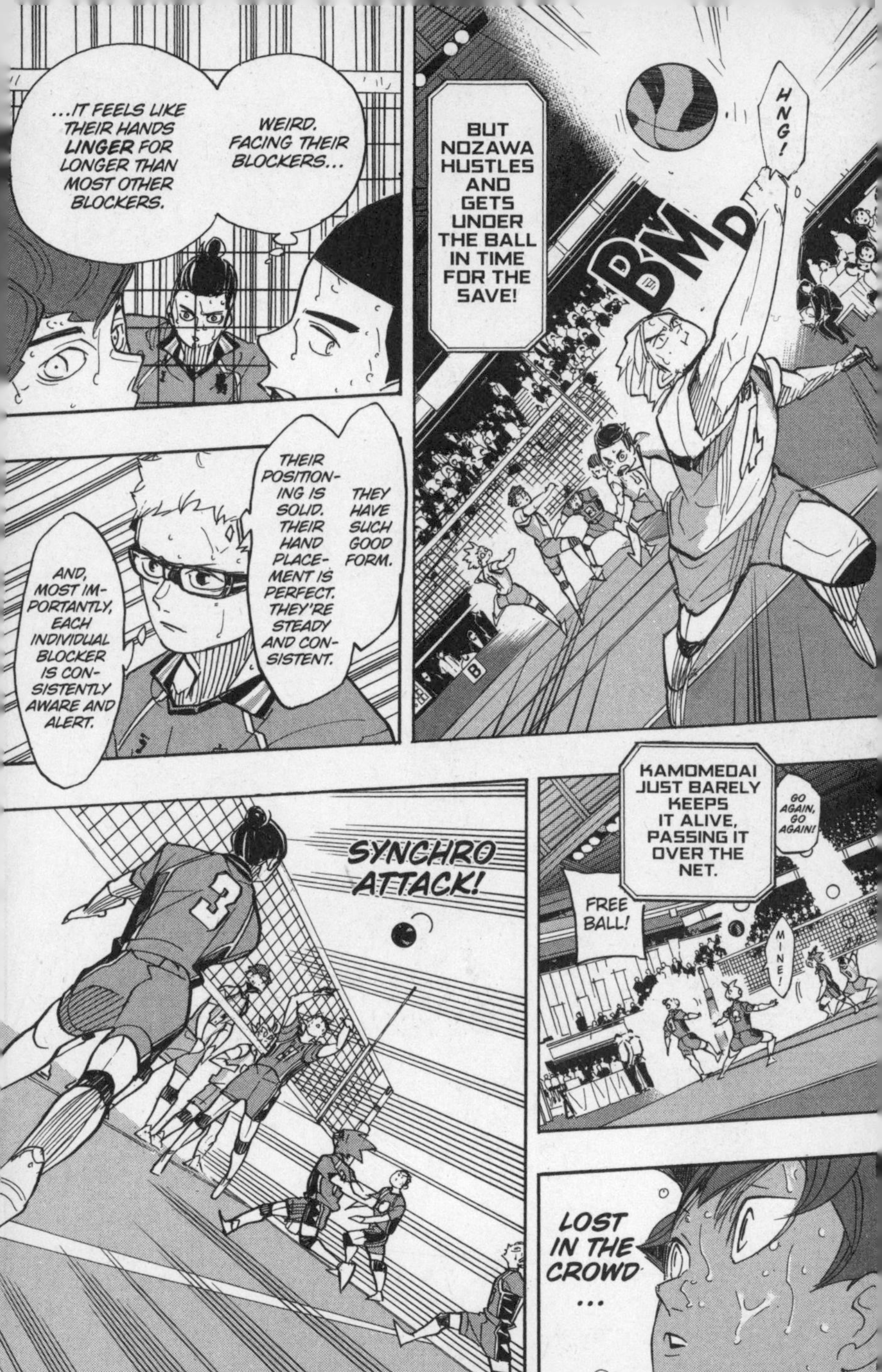
BUT NOZAWA HUSTLES AND GETS UNDER THE BALL IN TIME FOR THE SAVE!
HNG!
WEIRD. FACING THEIR BLOCKERS...
...IT FEELS LIKE THEIR HANDS LINGER FOR LONGER THAN MOST OTHER BLOCKERS.
THEY HAVE SUCH GOOD FORM.
THEIR POSITIONING IS SOLID. THEIR HAND PLACEMENT IS PERFECT. THEY'RE STEADY AND CONSISTENT.
AND, MOST IMPORTANTLY, EACH INDIVIDUAL BLOCKER IS CONSISTENTLY AWARE AND ALERT.
GO AGAIN, GO AGAIN!
KAMOMEDAI JUST BARELY KEEPS IT ALIVE, PASSING IT OVER THE NET.
MINE!
FREE BALL!
LOST IN THE CROWD...
SYNCHRO ATTACK!

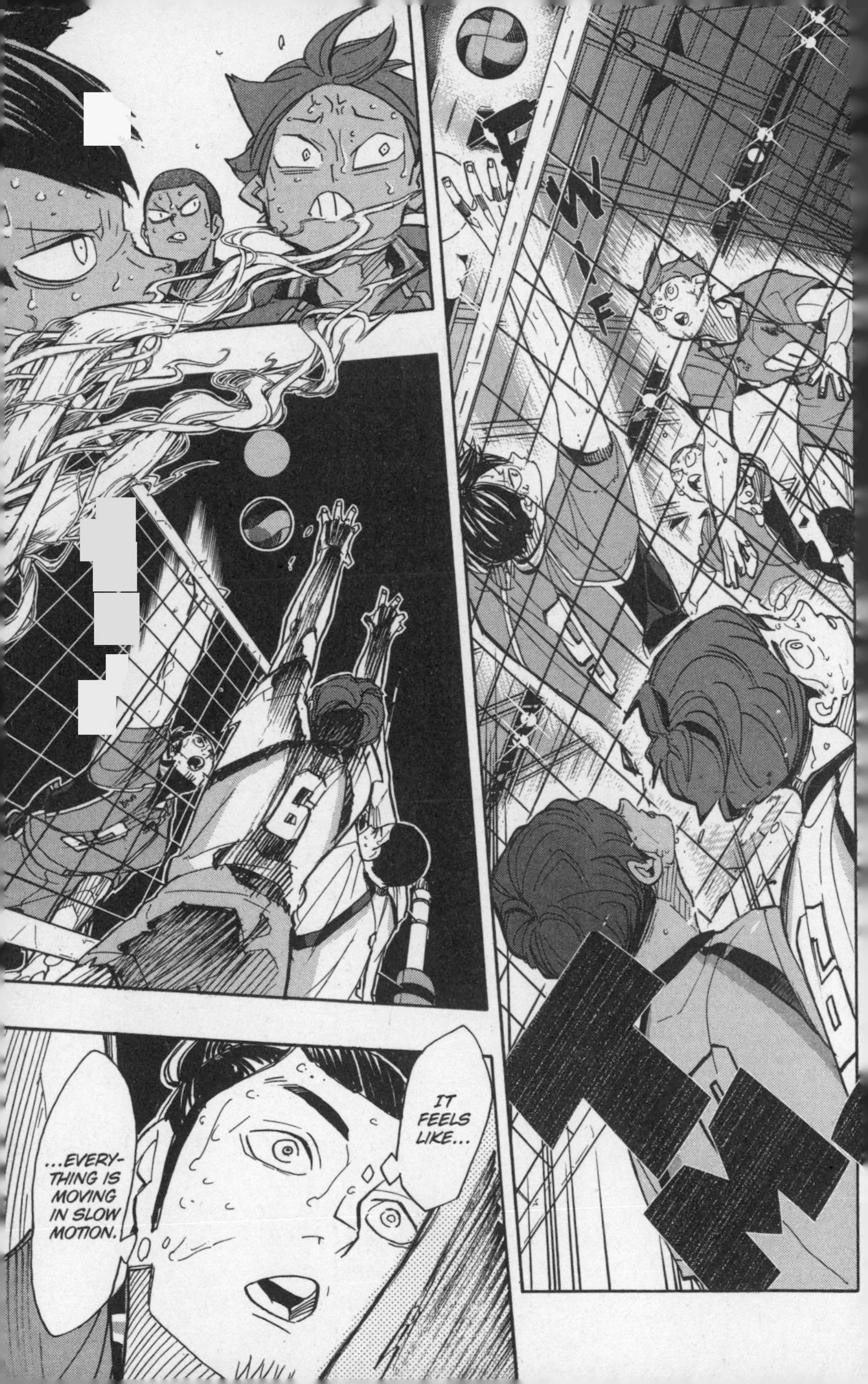
IT FEELS LIKE...
...EVERY-THING IS MOVING IN SLOW MOTION.

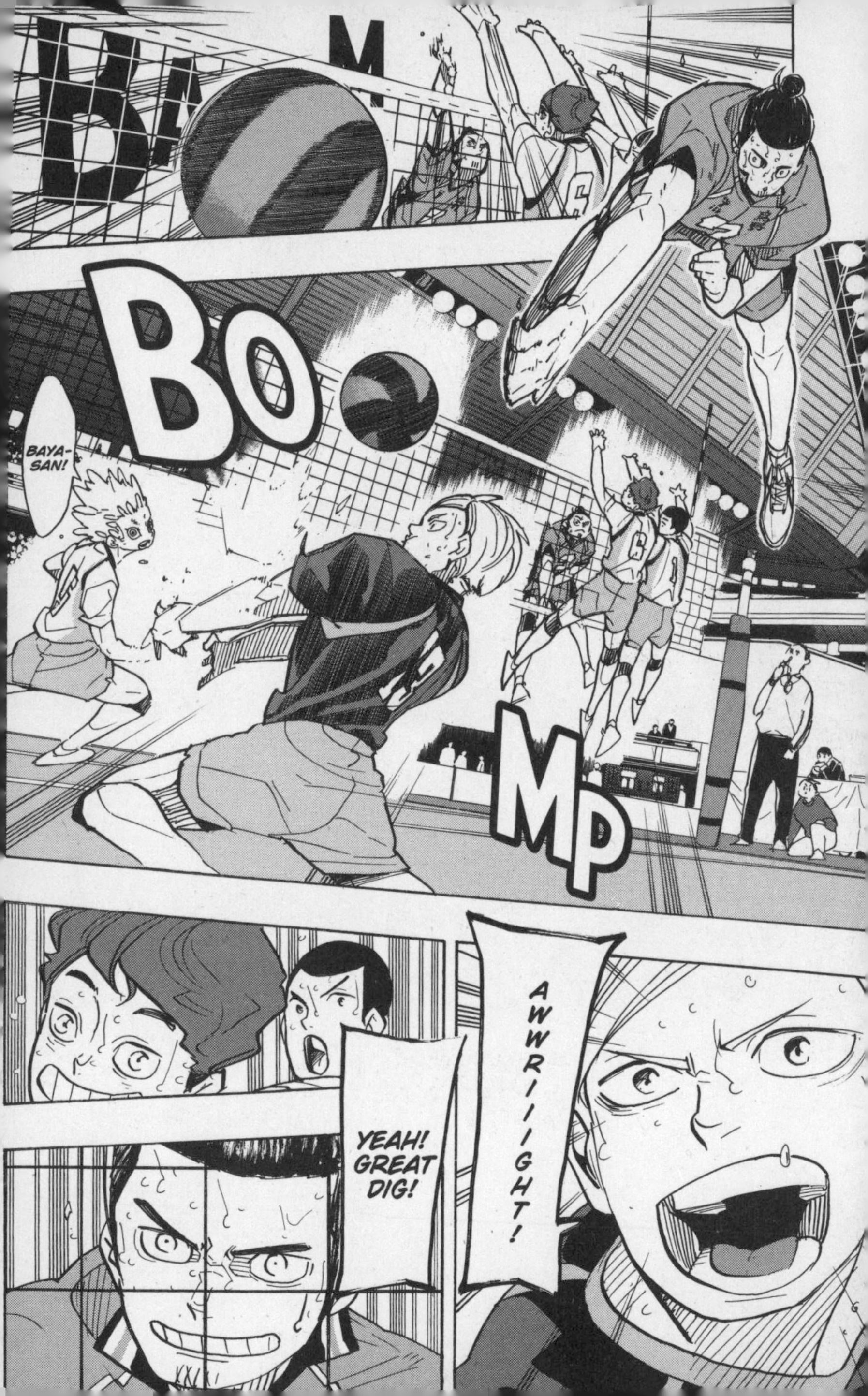

BA
M
BO
MP
BAYA-SAN!
AWWRIIIIGHT!
YEAH! GREAT DIG!

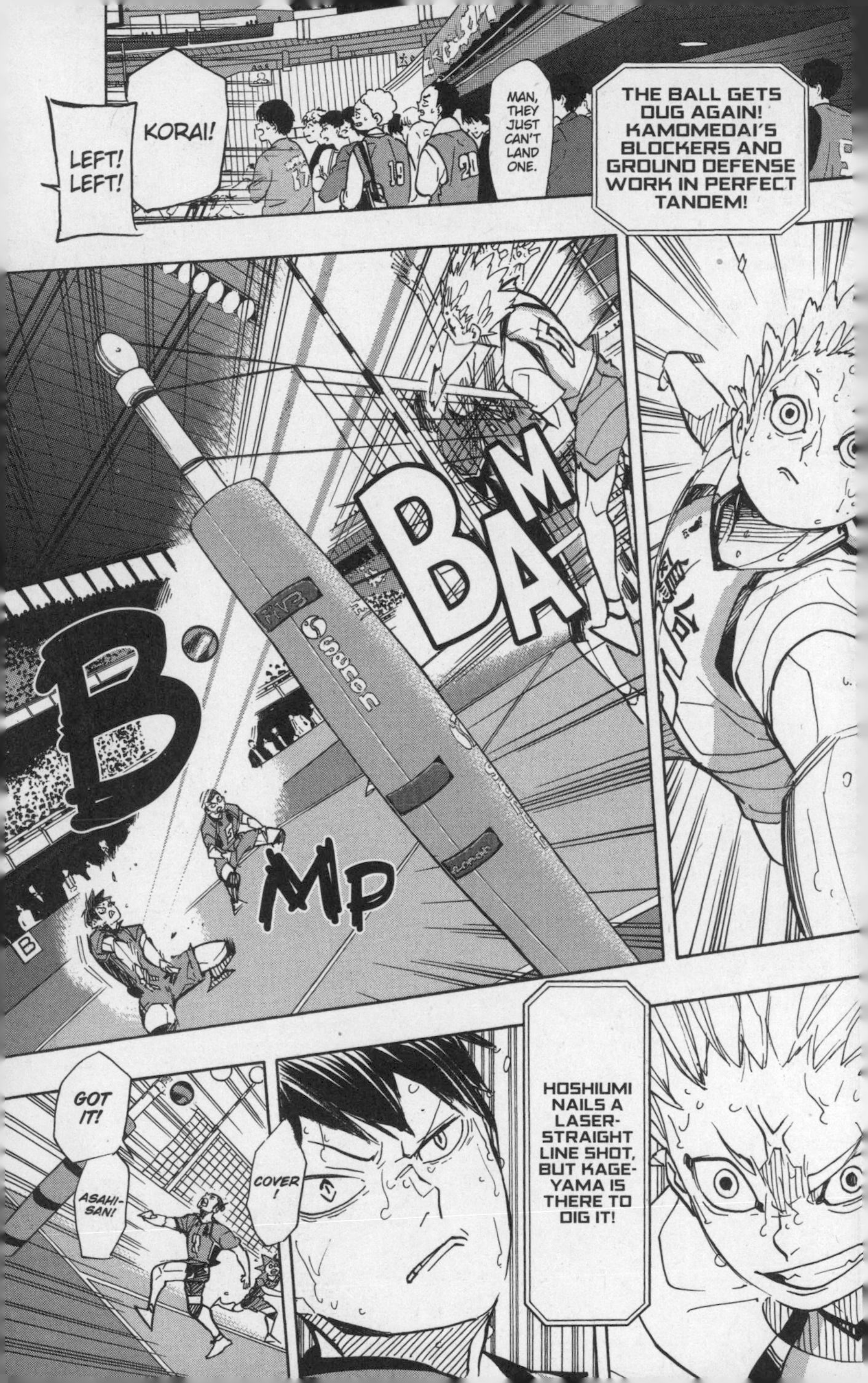
THE BALL GETS DUG AGAIN! KAMOMEDAI'S BLOCKERS AND GROUND DEFENSE WORK IN PERFECT TANDEM!
MAN, THEY JUST CAN'T LAND ONE.
KORAI!
LEFT! LEFT!
BAM
B
MP
HOSHIUMI NAILS A LASER-STRAIGHT LINE SHOT, BUT KAGE-YAMA IS THERE TO DIG IT!
COVER!
GOT IT!
ASAHI-SAN!

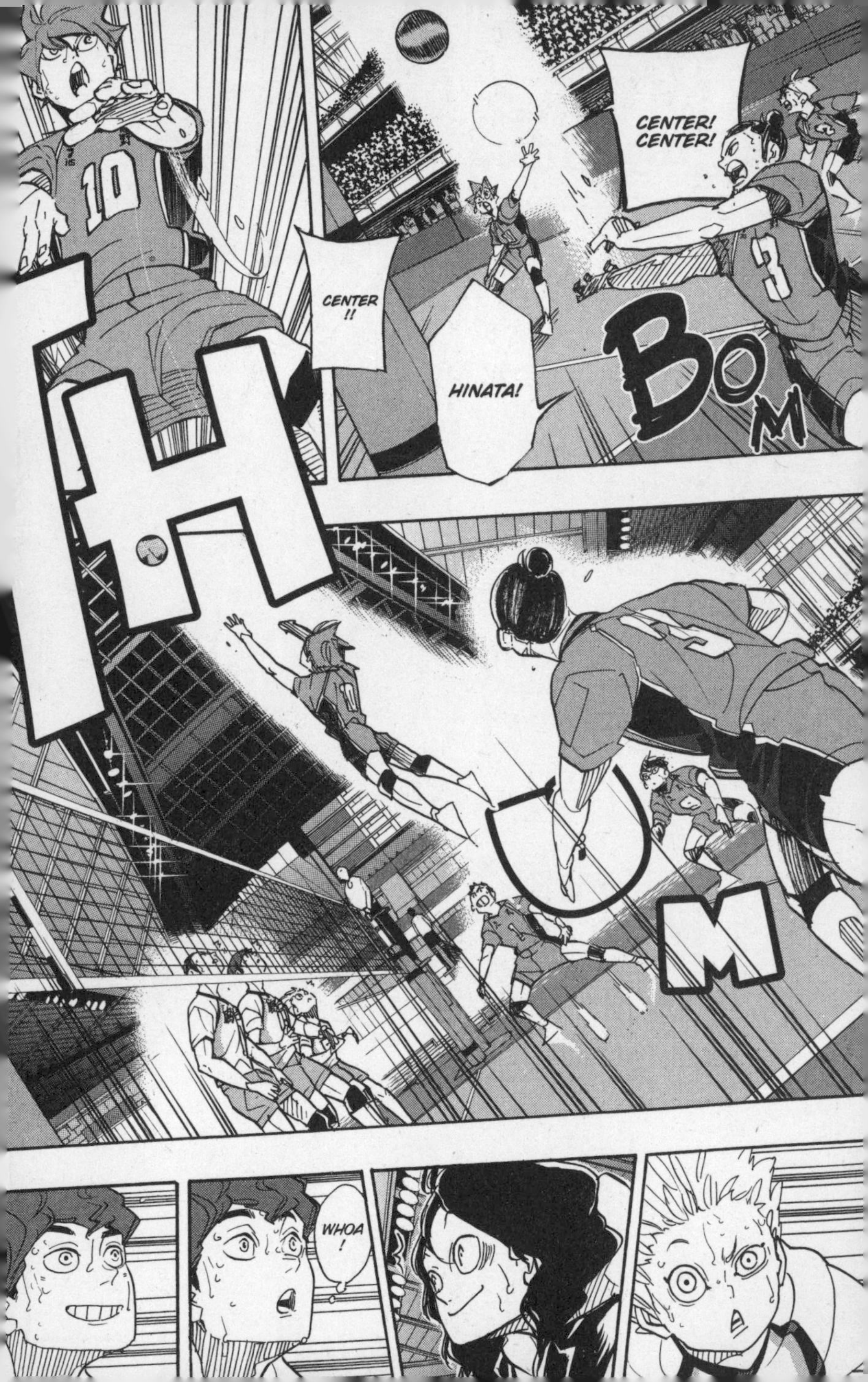
CENTER! CENTER!
CENTER !!
HINATA!
WHOA !

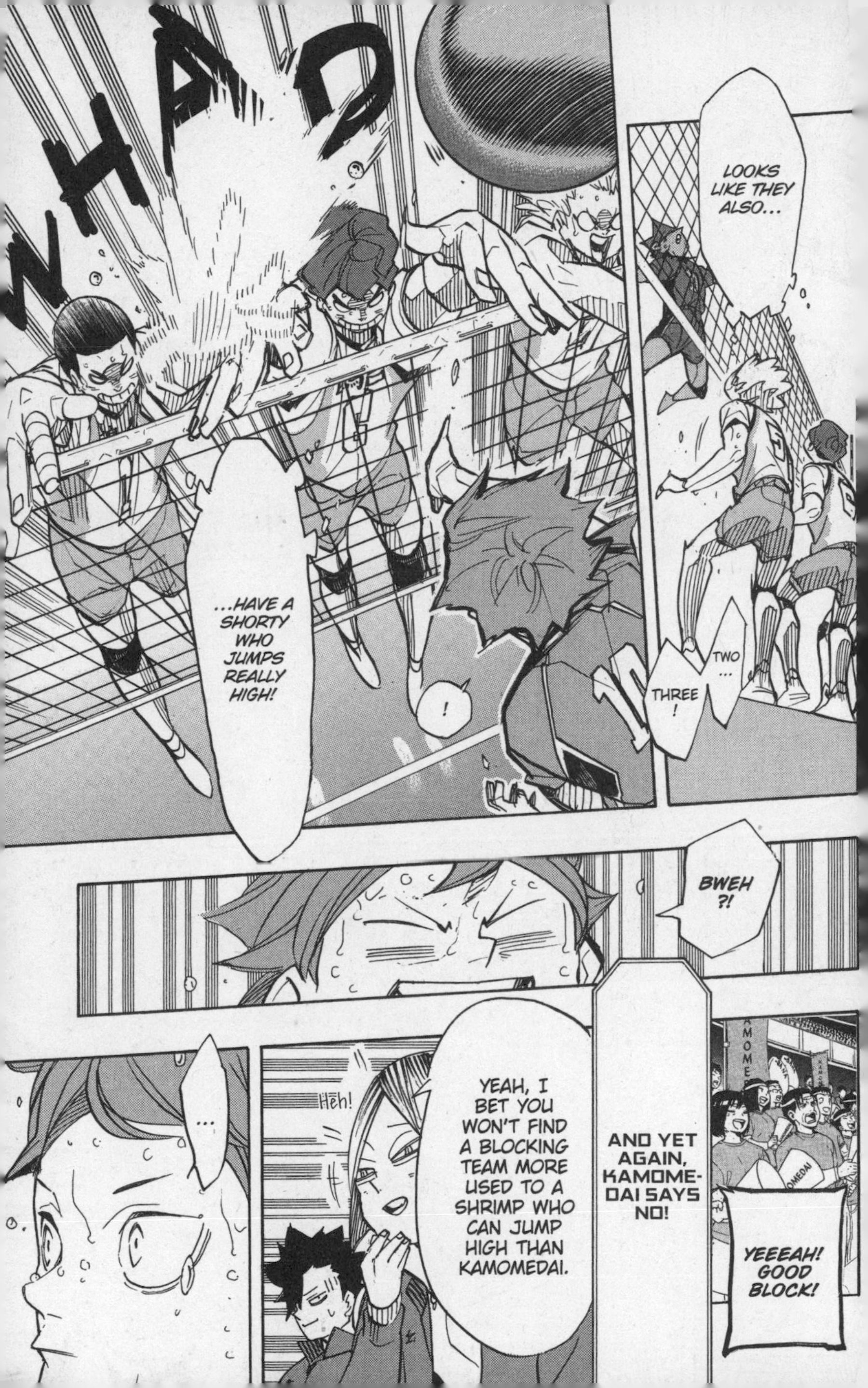
LOOKS LIKE THEY ALSO...
TWO...
THREE!
...HAVE A SHORTY WHO JUMPS REALLY HIGH!
!
BWEH ?!
YEEEAH! GOOD BLOCK!
AND YET AGAIN, KAMOMEDAI SAYS NO!
YEAH, I BET YOU WON'T FIND A BLOCKING TEAM MORE USED TO A SHRIMP WHO CAN JUMP HIGH THAN KAMOMEDAI.
Heh!
...

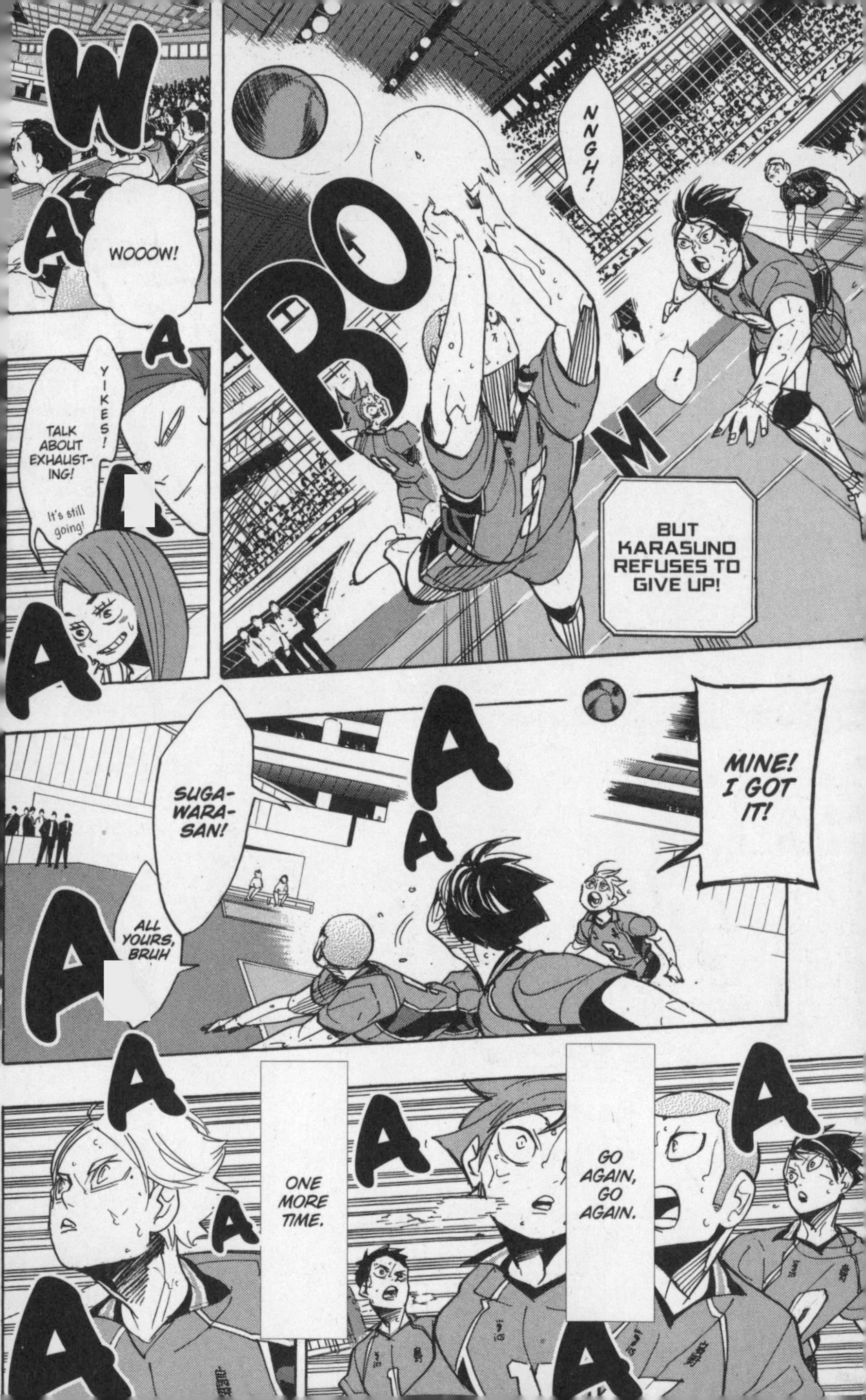
BOOM
NNGH!
!
BUT KARASUNO REFUSES TO GIVE UP!
WOOOW!
YIKES!
TALK ABOUT EXHAUSTING!
It's still going!
MINE! I GOT IT!
SUGAWARA-SAN!
ALL YOURS, BRUH
GO AGAIN, GO AGAIN.
ONE MORE TIME.

...IS THE SOUND OF MY OWN BREATHING.

ALL I CAN HEAR...

A BLOCK M!!

GOOOO!

KAMOMEDAI

ASK THAT PLEASE AIN FROM G FLASH TOGRA-PHY...

YEAH! KI

FWEE

TUM TUM TUM

LEFT!

LEFT!

LEEEEFT!

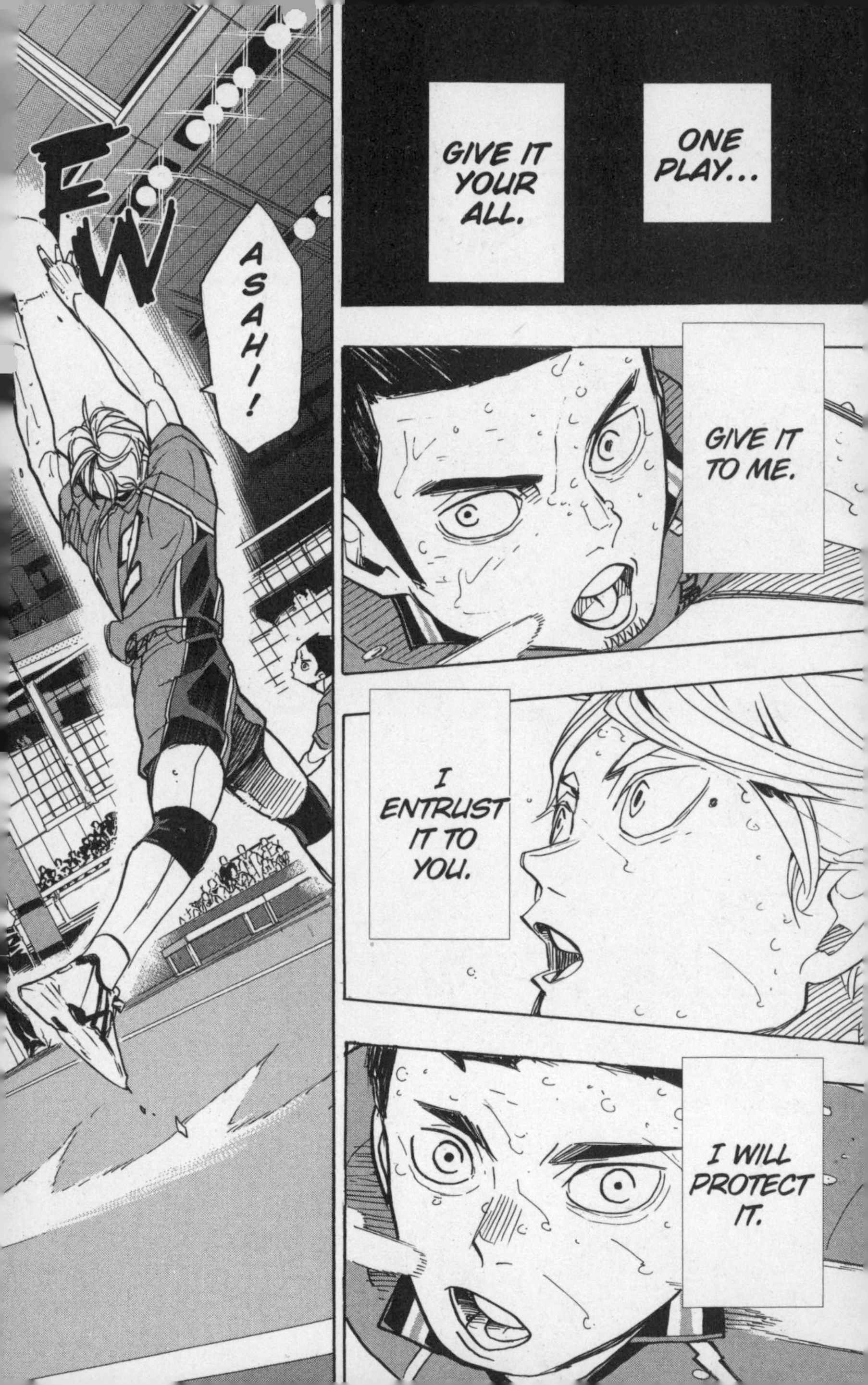
ONE PLAY...
GIVE IT YOUR ALL.
GIVE IT TO ME.
I ENTRUST IT TO YOU.
I WILL PROTECT IT.
ASAHI!
FW

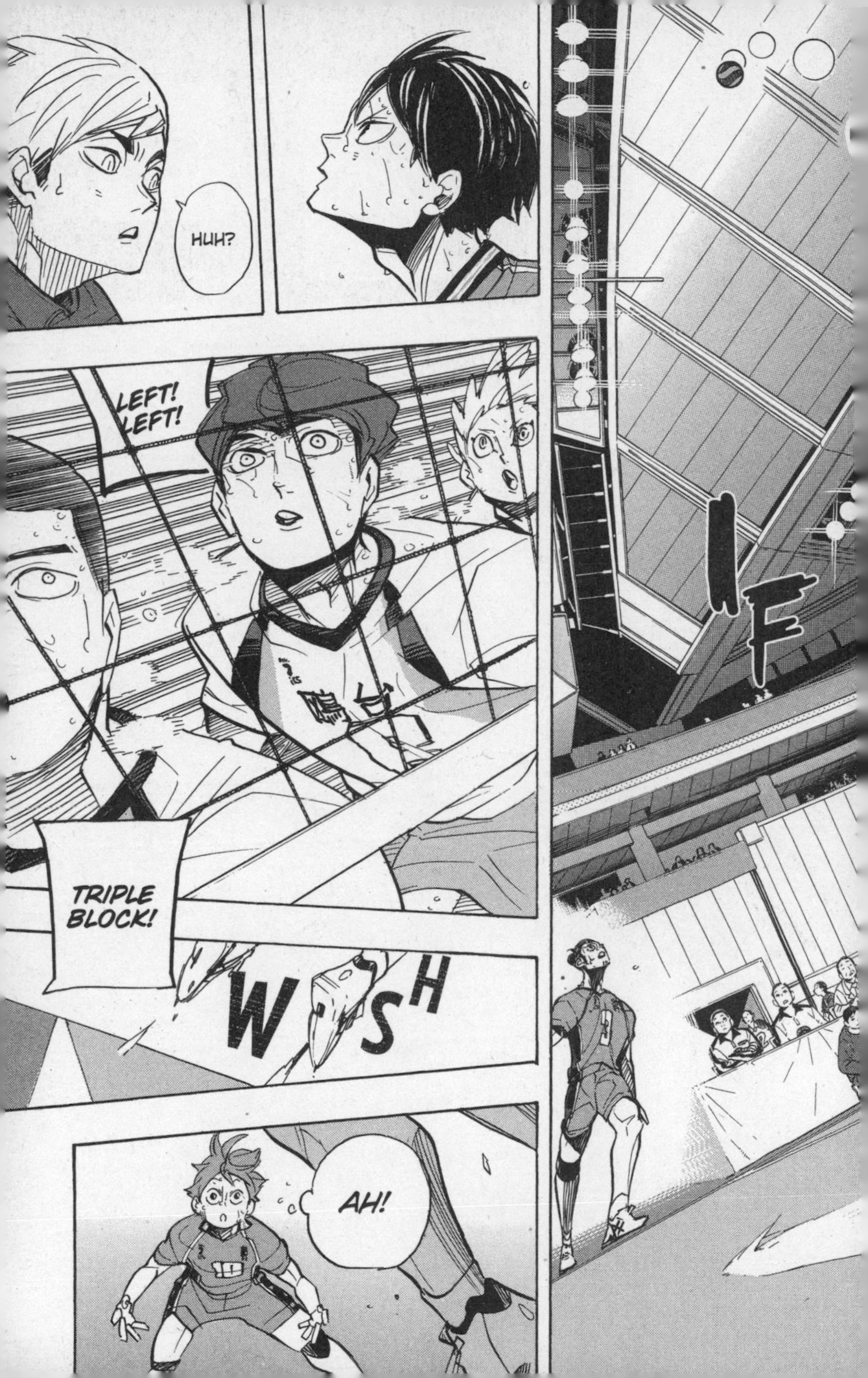
HUH?
LEFT! LEFT!
TRIPLE BLOCK!
WSH
AH!

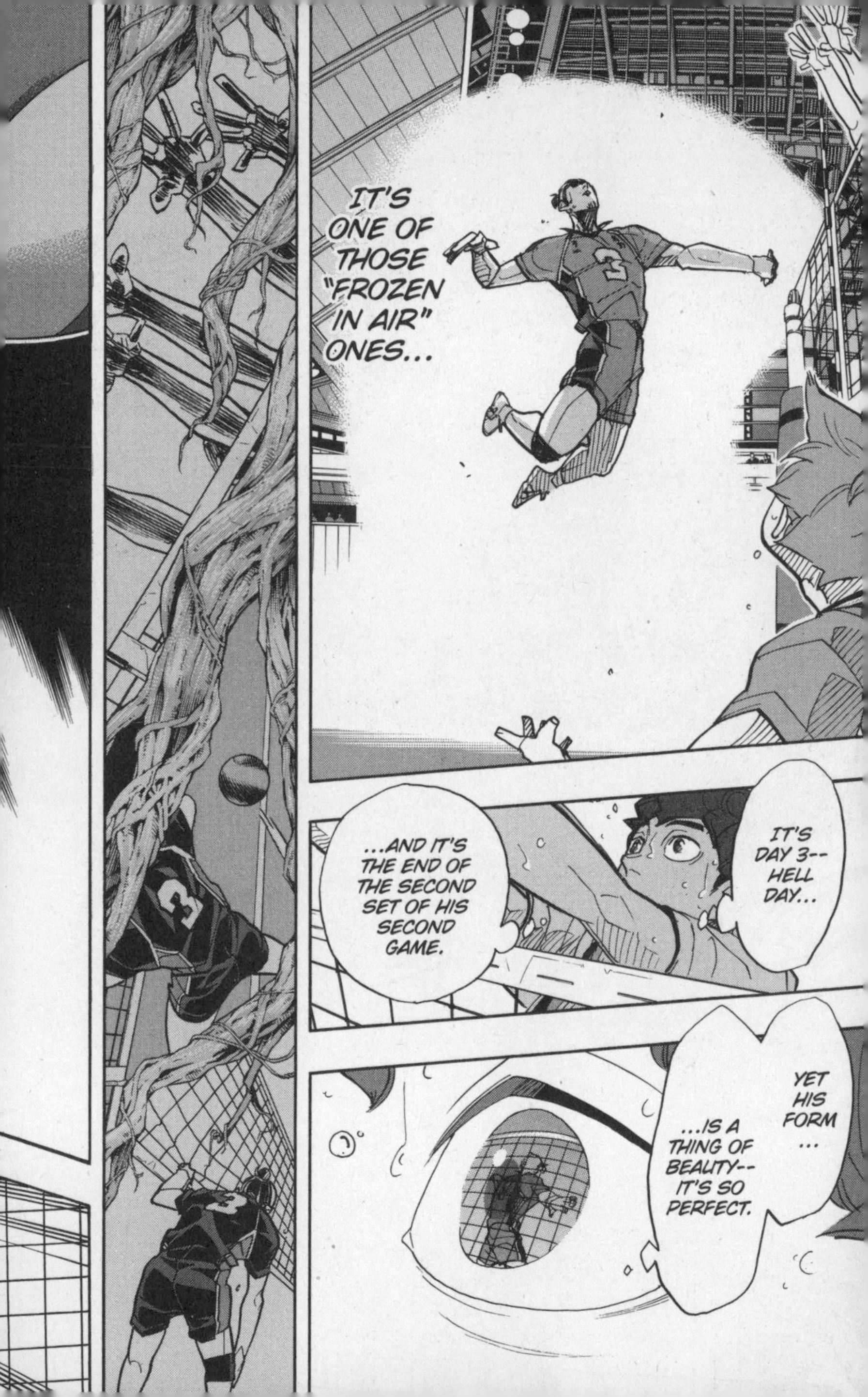
IT'S ONE OF THOSE "FROZEN IN AIR" ONES...
IT'S DAY 3-- HELL DAY...
...AND IT'S THE END OF THE SECOND SET OF HIS SECOND GAME.
YET HIS FORM ...
...IS A THING OF BEAUTY-- IT'S SO PERFECT.

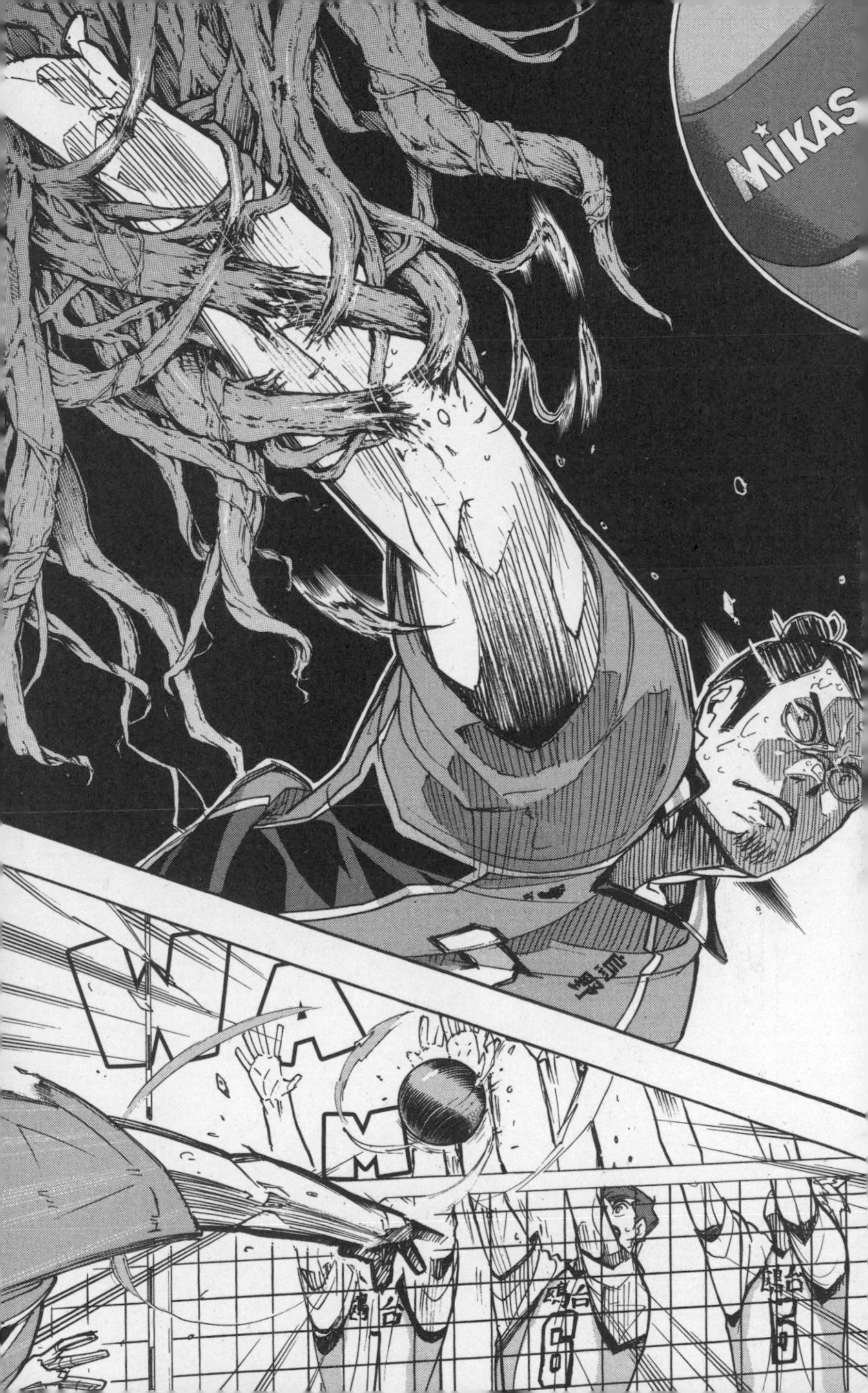
MIKAS

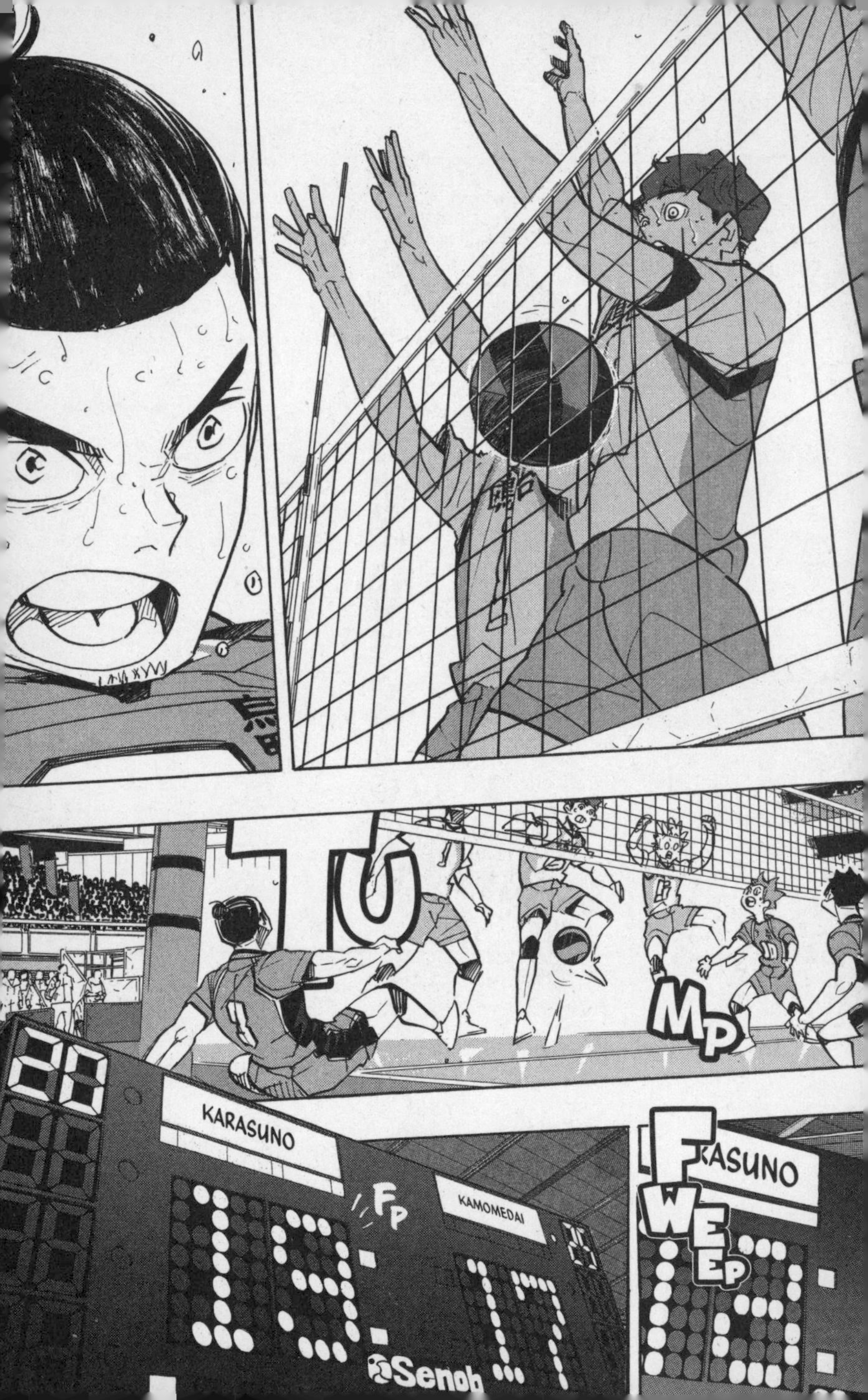
TU
MP
FWEEP
ASUNO
KARASUNO
FP
KAMOMEDAI
Senoh

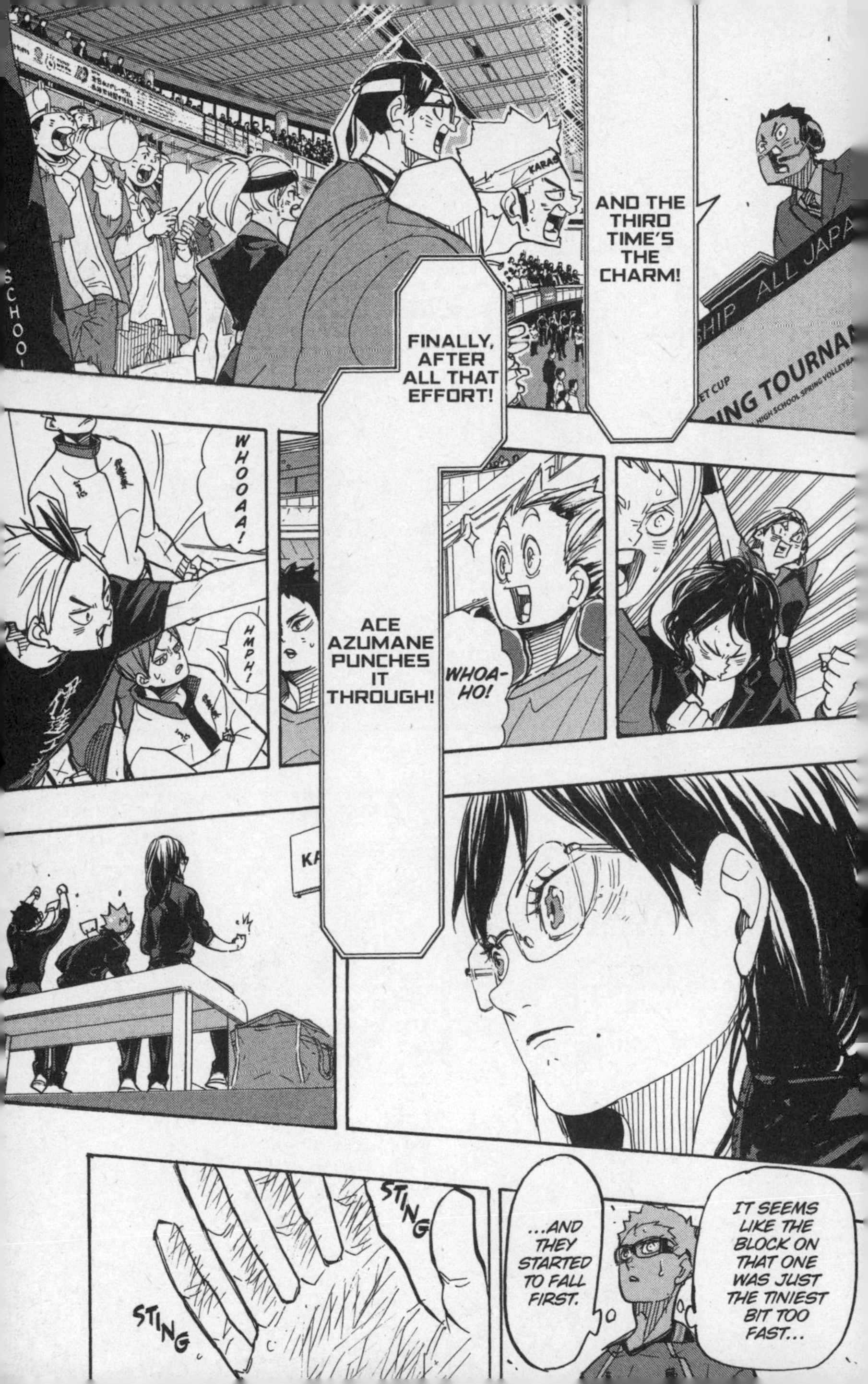
AND THE THIRD TIME'S THE CHARM!
FINALLY, AFTER ALL THAT EFFORT!
ACE AZUMANE PUNCHES IT THROUGH!
WHOA-HO!
HMPH!
WHOOOAA!
IT SEEMS LIKE THE BLOCK ON THAT ONE WAS JUST THE TINIEST BIT TOO FAST...
...AND THEY STARTED TO FALL FIRST.
STING
STING

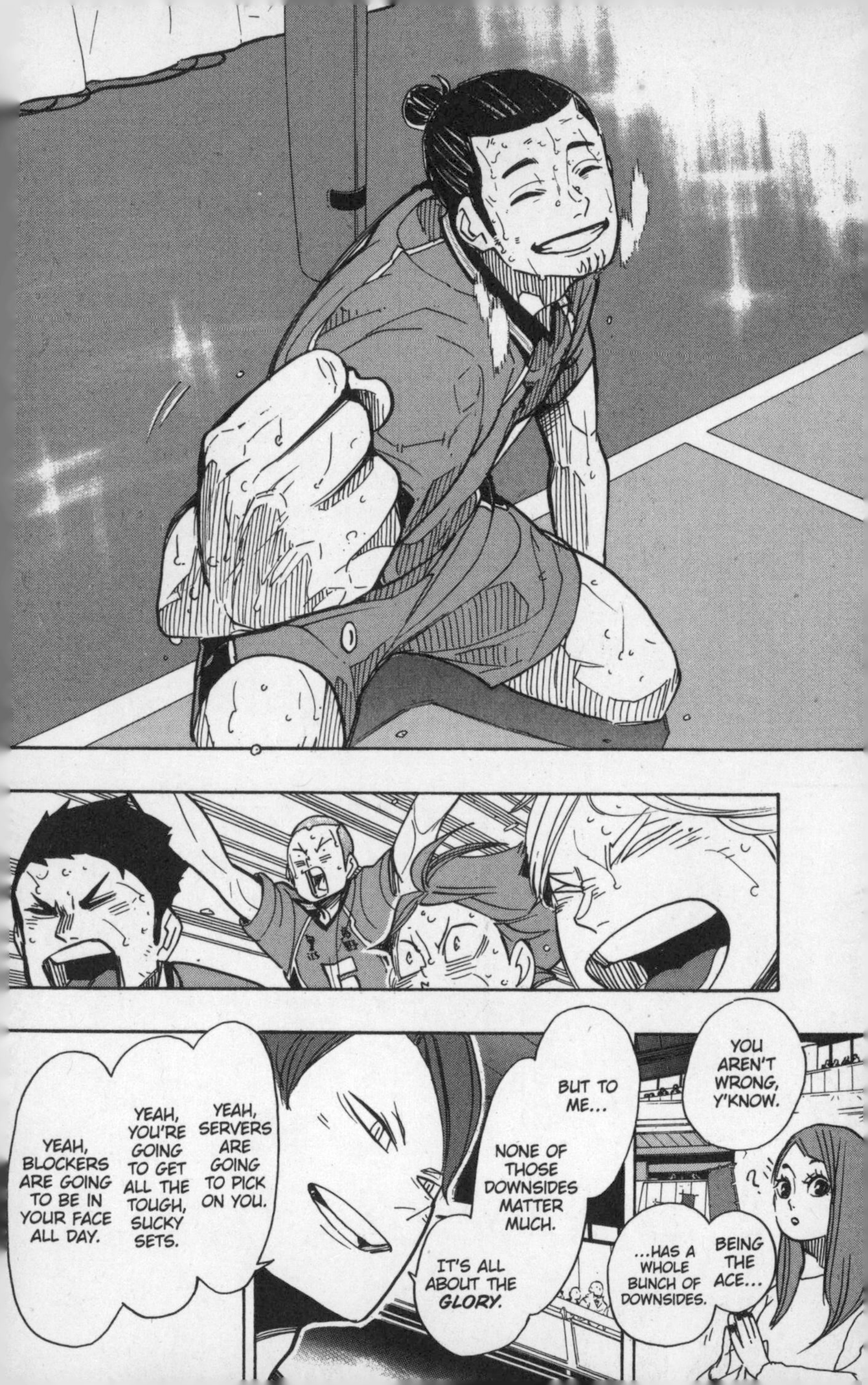
YOU AREN'T WRONG, Y'KNOW.
BEING THE ACE...
...HAS A WHOLE BUNCH OF DOWNSIDES.
BUT TO ME...
NONE OF THOSE DOWNSIDES MATTER MUCH.
IT'S ALL ABOUT THE *GLORY.*
YEAH, SERVERS ARE GOING TO PICK ON YOU.
YEAH, YOU'RE GOING TO GET ALL THE TOUGH, SUCKY SETS.
YEAH, BLOCKERS ARE GOING TO BE IN YOUR FACE ALL DAY.

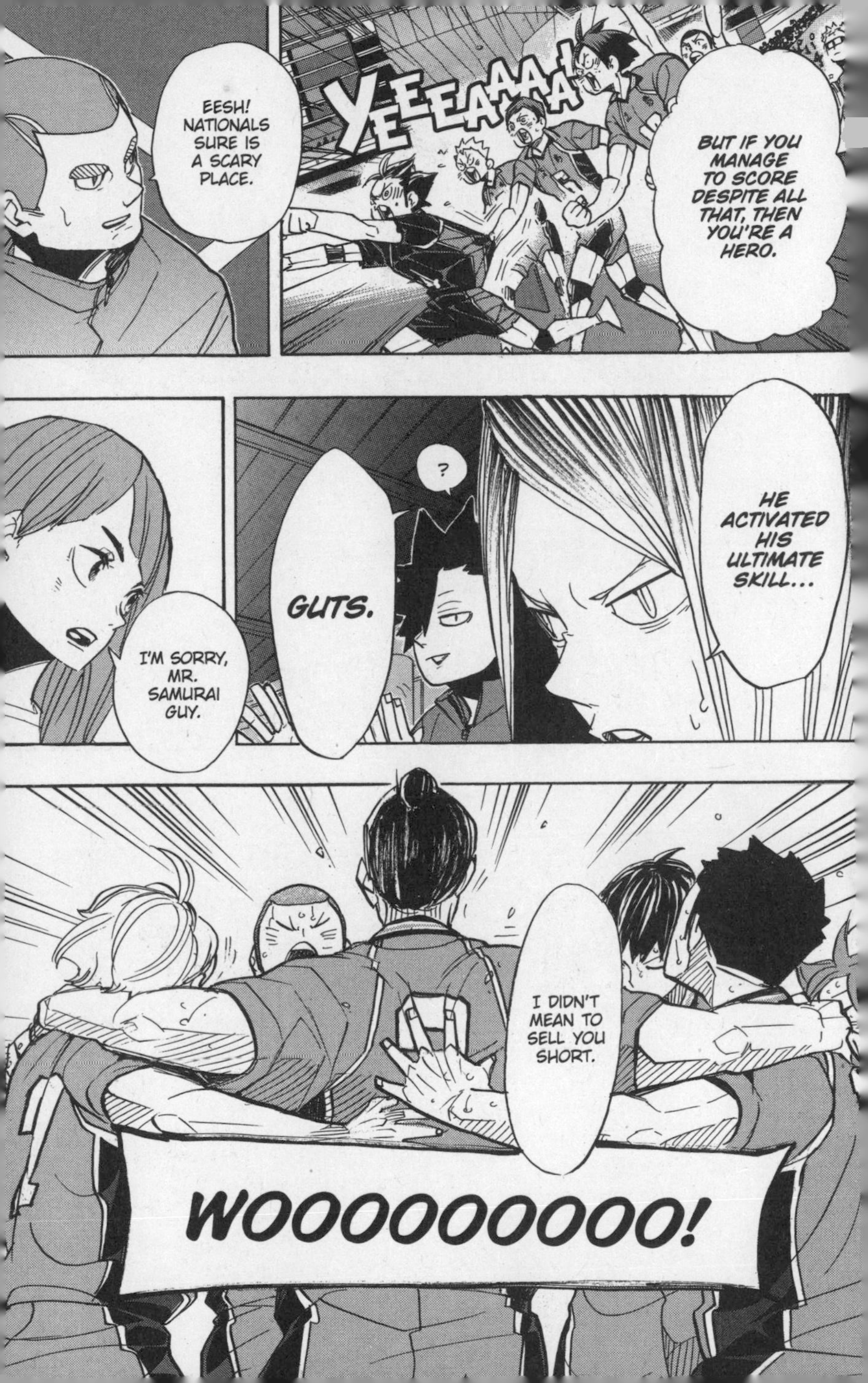
YEEAAAA!
BUT IF YOU MANAGE TO SCORE DESPITE ALL THAT, THEN YOU'RE A HERO.
EESH! NATIONALS SURE IS A SCARY PLACE.
HE ACTIVATED HIS ULTIMATE SKILL...
?
GUTS.
I'M SORRY, MR. SAMURAI GUY.
I DIDN'T MEAN TO SELL YOU SHORT.
WOOOOOOOOO!

HELLO FROM BEYOND THE (PAGE) EDGE!!
GUESS WHICH PANEL THIS IS!!

**FROM CHAPTER 354**

**GETTING PETS...**

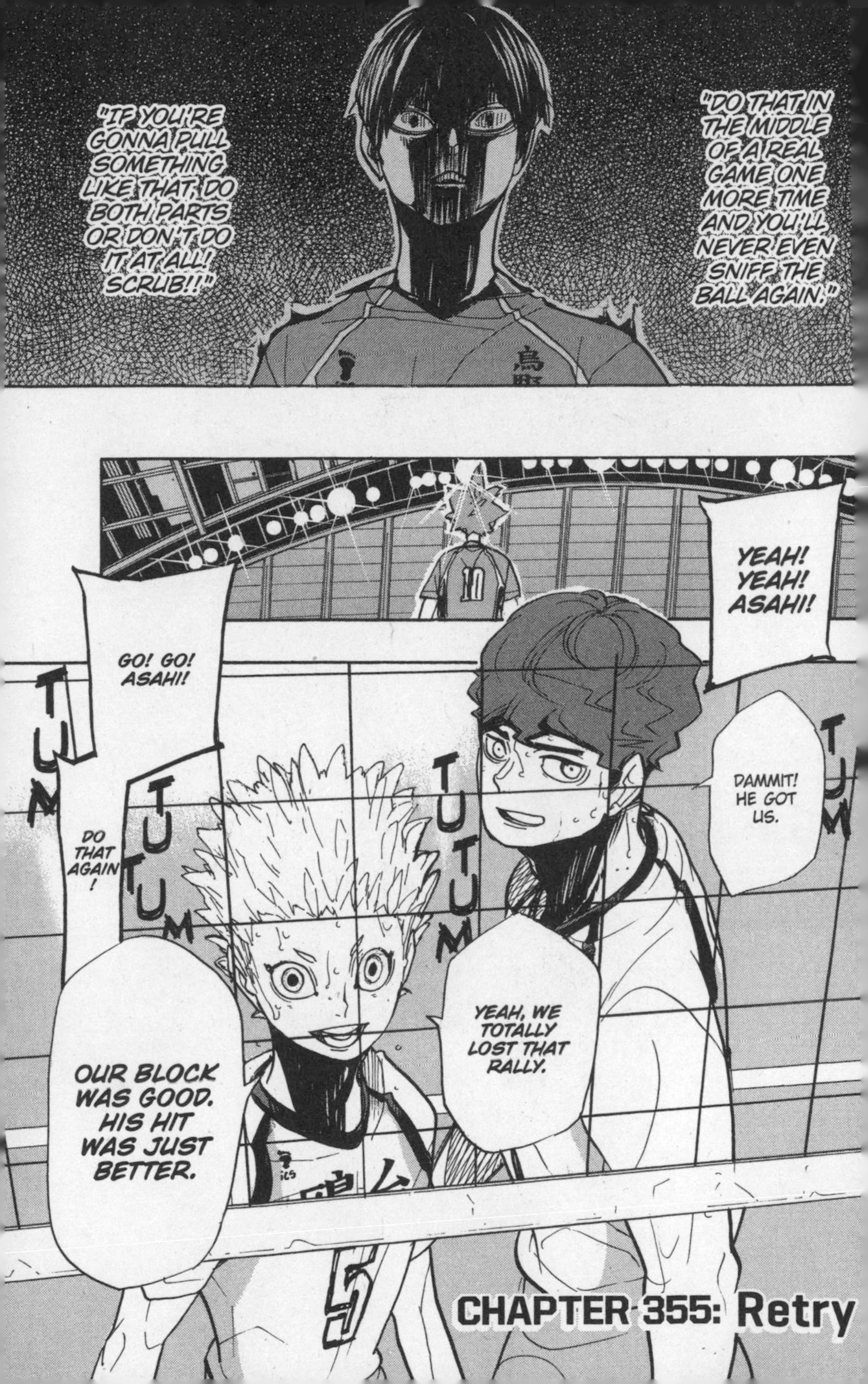
"DO THAT IN THE MIDDLE OF A REAL GAME ONE MORE TIME AND YOU'LL NEVER EVEN SNIFF THE BALL AGAIN."
"IF YOU'RE GONNA PULL SOMETHING LIKE THAT, DO BOTH PARTS OR DON'T DO IT AT ALL! SCRUB!!"
YEAH! YEAH! ASAHI!
GO! GO! ASAHI!
TUM
TUM
DAMMIT! HE GOT US.
TUTUM
TUTUM
DO THAT AGAIN!
YEAH, WE TOTALLY LOST THAT RALLY.
OUR BLOCK WAS GOOD. HIS HIT WAS JUST BETTER.
CHAPTER 355: Retry

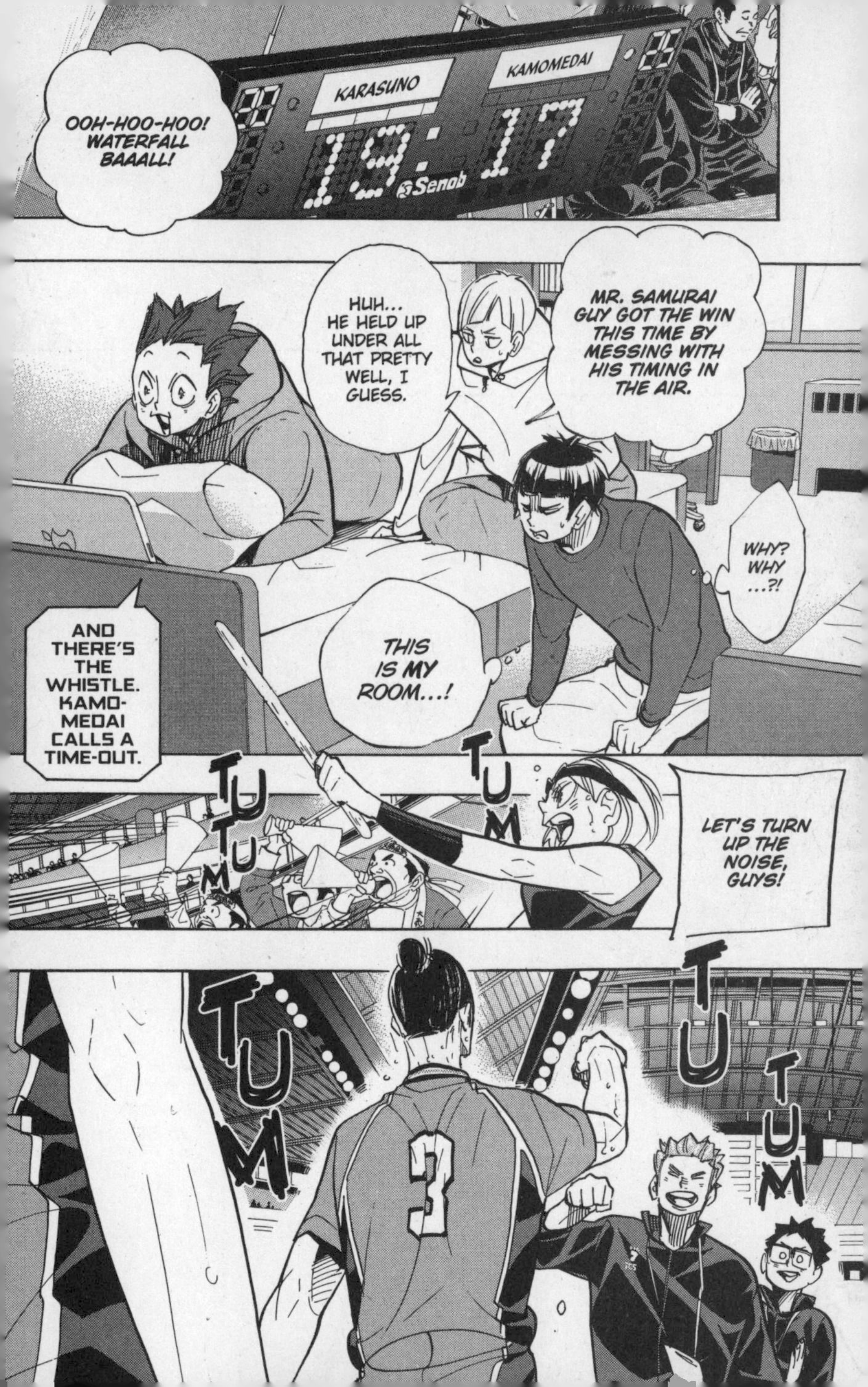
KARASUNO
KAMOMEDAI
19:17
Senob
OOH-HOO-HOO! WATERFALL BAAALL!
MR. SAMURAI GUY GOT THE WIN THIS TIME BY MESSING WITH HIS TIMING IN THE AIR.
HUH... HE HELD UP UNDER ALL THAT PRETTY WELL, I GUESS.
WHY? WHY ...?!
THIS IS MY ROOM...!
AND THERE'S THE WHISTLE. KAMOMEDAI CALLS A TIME-OUT.
LET'S TURN UP THE NOISE, GUYS!
TUM
TUM
TUM
TUM
TUM
TUM

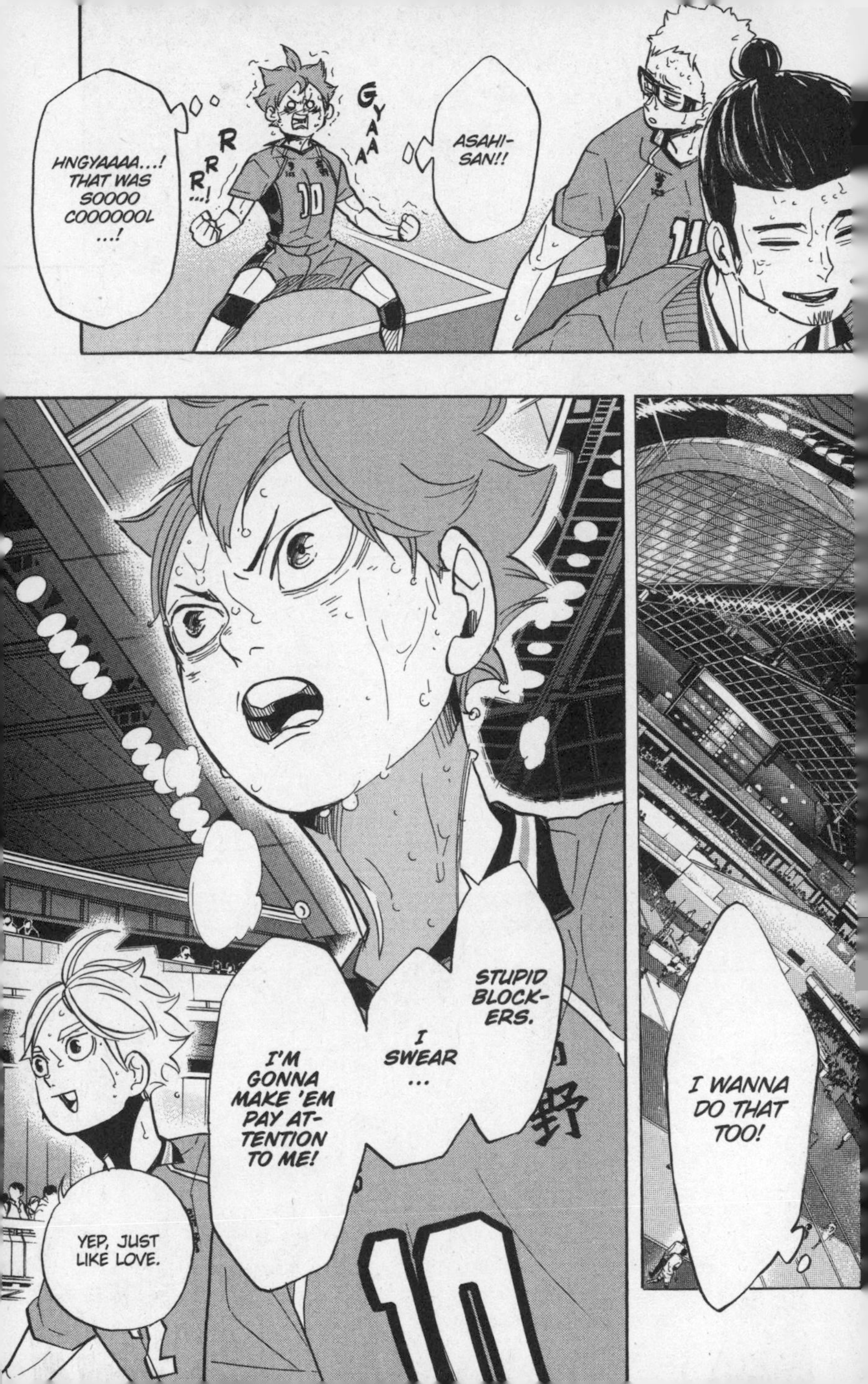
ASAHI-SAN!!
GYAAA
HNGYAAAA...! THAT WAS SOOOO COOOOOOL ...!
RRR...!
I WANNA DO THAT TOO!
STUPID BLOCKERS.
I SWEAR ...
I'M GONNA MAKE 'EM PAY ATTENTION TO ME!
YEP, JUST LIKE LOVE.

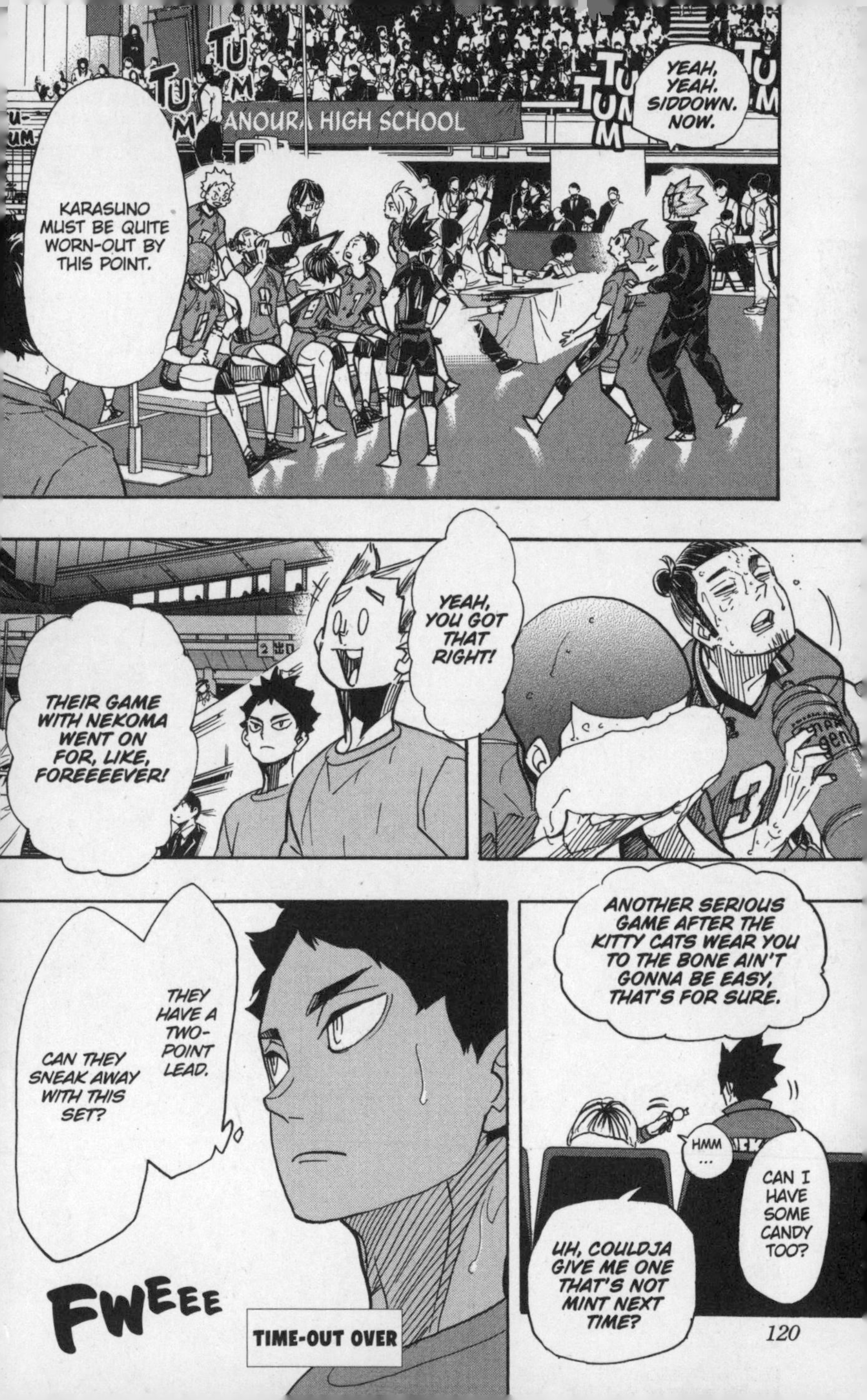
TU M
YEAH, YEAH. SIDDOWN. NOW.
TU TUM
TU M
ANOURA HIGH SCHOOL
KARASUNO MUST BE QUITE WORN-OUT BY THIS POINT.
YEAH, YOU GOT THAT RIGHT!
THEIR GAME WITH NEKOMA WENT ON FOR, LIKE, FOREEEEVER!
ANOTHER SERIOUS GAME AFTER THE KITTY CATS WEAR YOU TO THE BONE AIN'T GONNA BE EASY, THAT'S FOR SURE.
CAN I HAVE SOME CANDY TOO?
HMM ...
UH, COULDJA GIVE ME ONE THAT'S NOT MINT NEXT TIME?
THEY HAVE A TWO-POINT LEAD.
CAN THEY SNEAK AWAY WITH THIS SET?
FWEEE
TIME-OUT OVER

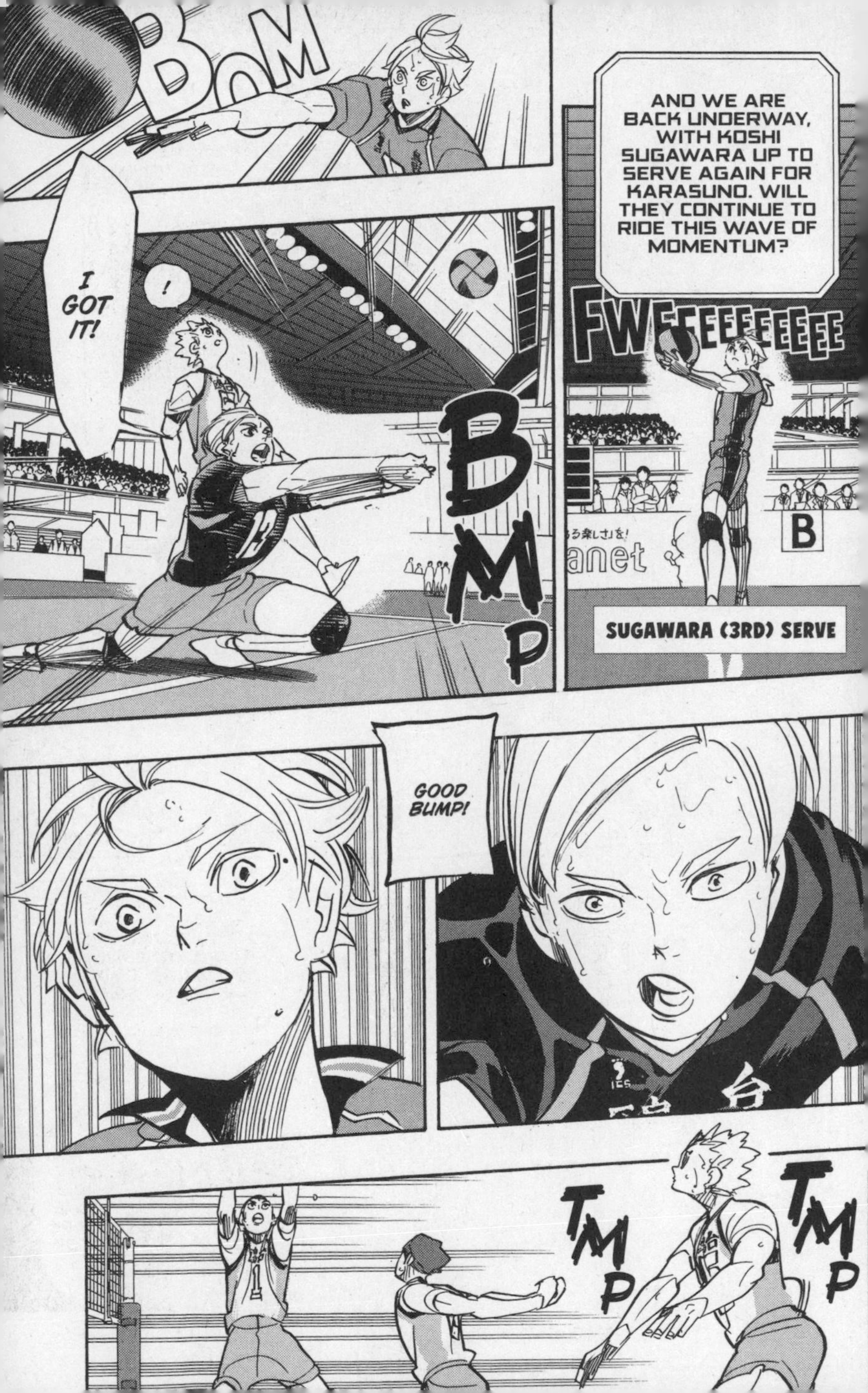
AND WE ARE BACK UNDERWAY, WITH KOSHI SUGAWARA UP TO SERVE AGAIN FOR KARASUNO. WILL THEY CONTINUE TO RIDE THIS WAVE OF MOMENTUM?
FWEEEEEEEEE
B
SUGAWARA (3RD) SERVE
BOM
!
I GOT IT!
BMP
GOOD BUMP!
TMP
TMP

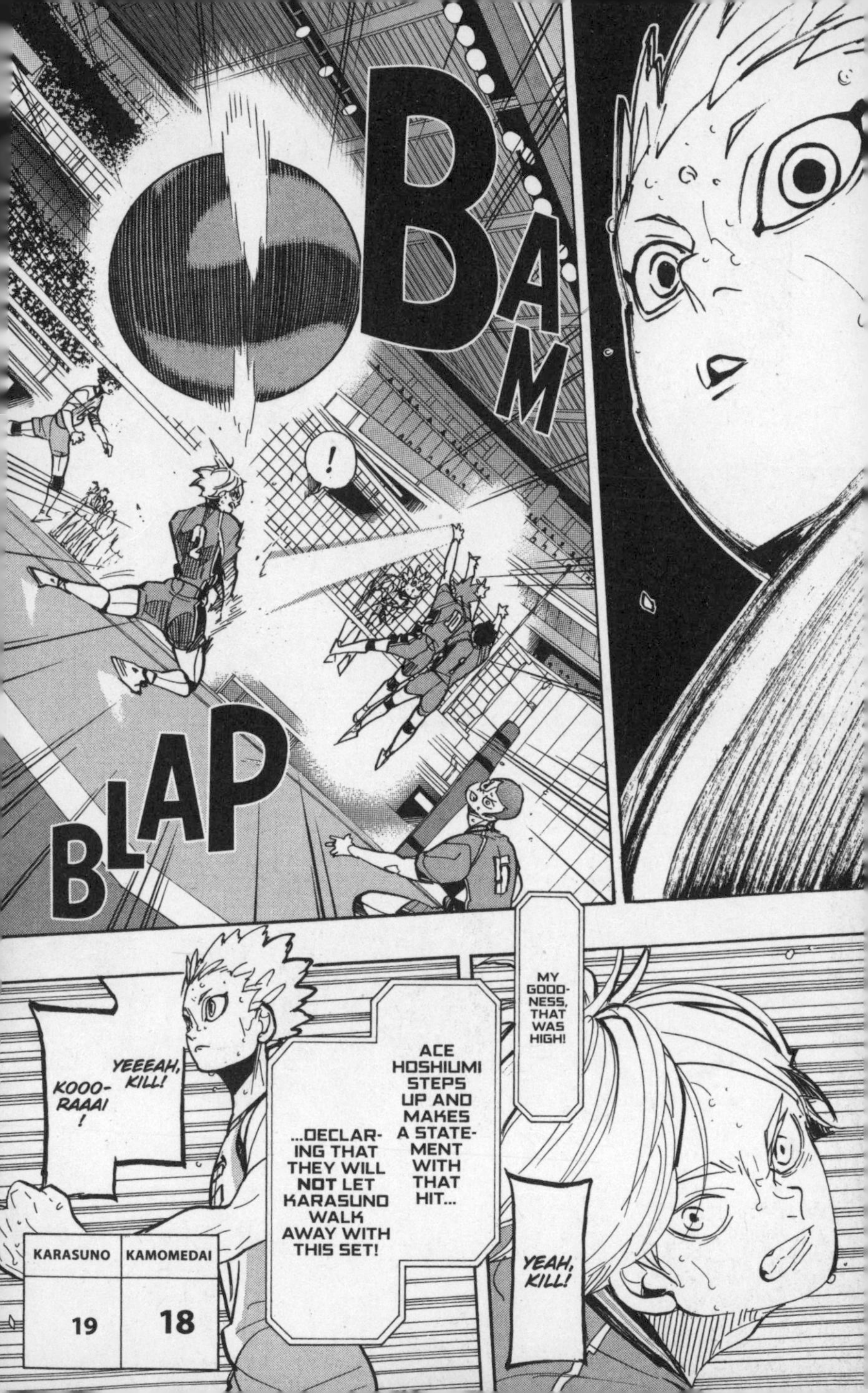
BAM
!
BLAP
MY GOODNESS, THAT WAS HIGH!
ACE HOSHIUMI STEPS UP AND MAKES A STATEMENT WITH THAT HIT...
...DECLARING THAT THEY WILL NOT LET KARASUNO WALK AWAY WITH THIS SET!
YEAH, KILL!
YEEEAH, KILL!
KOOO-RAAAI!
KARASUNO 19
KAMOMEDAI 18

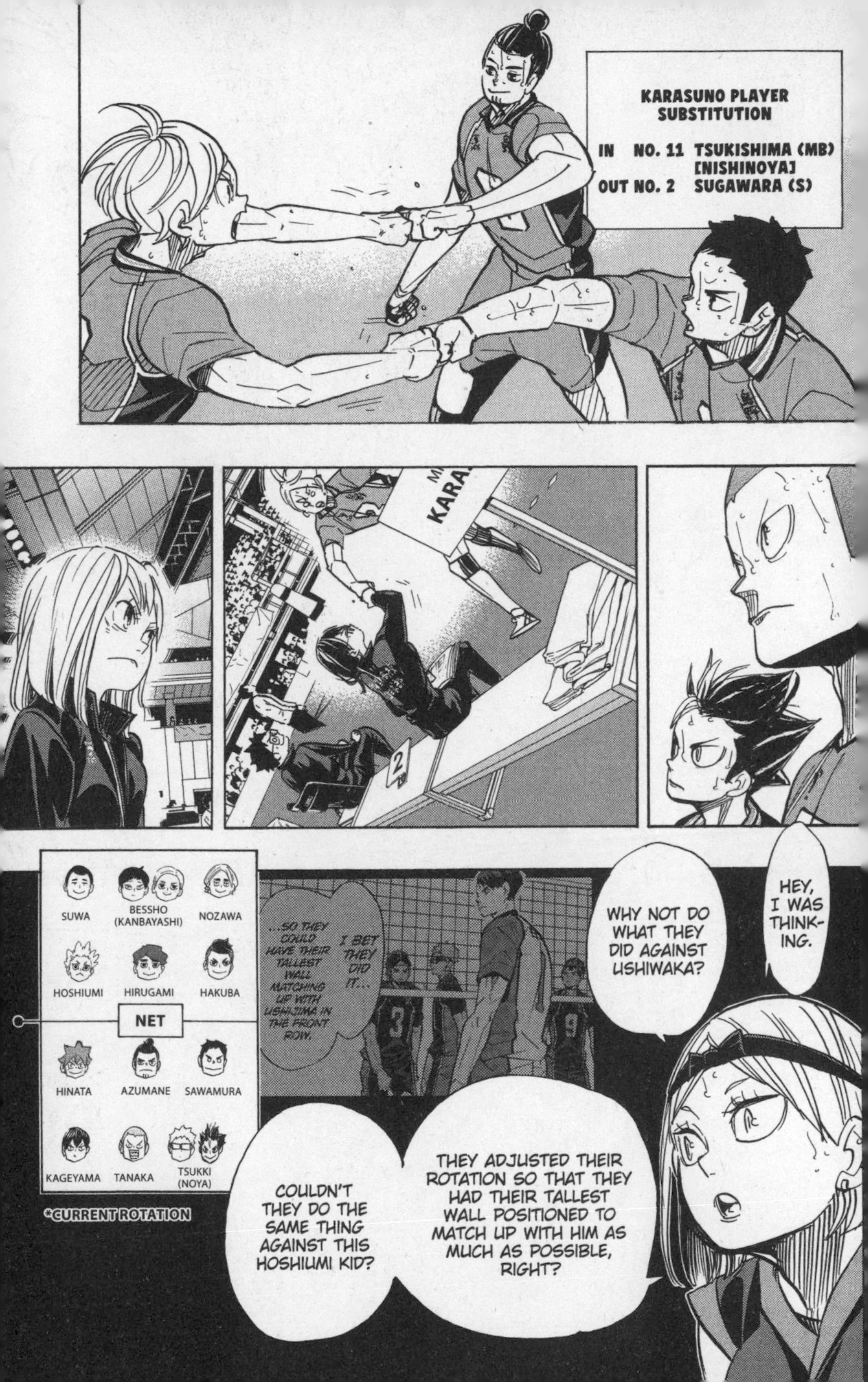
KARASUNO PLAYER SUBSTITUTION
IN NO. 11 TSUKISHIMA (MB) [NISHINOYA]
OUT NO. 2 SUGAWARA (S)
HEY, I WAS THINKING.
WHY NOT DO WHAT THEY DID AGAINST USHIWAKA?
THEY ADJUSTED THEIR ROTATION SO THAT THEY HAD THEIR TALLEST WALL POSITIONED TO MATCH UP WITH HIM AS MUCH AS POSSIBLE, RIGHT?
COULDN'T THEY DO THE SAME THING AGAINST THIS HOSHIUMI KID?
I BET THEY DID IT...
...SO THEY COULD HAVE THEIR TALLEST WALL MATCHING UP WITH USHIJIMA IN THE FRONT ROW.
SUWA
BESSHO (KANBAYASHI)
NOZAWA
HOSHIUMI
HIRUGAMI
HAKUBA
NET
HINATA
AZUMANE
SAWAMURA
KAGEYAMA
TANAKA
TSUKKI (NOYA)
*CURRENT ROTATION

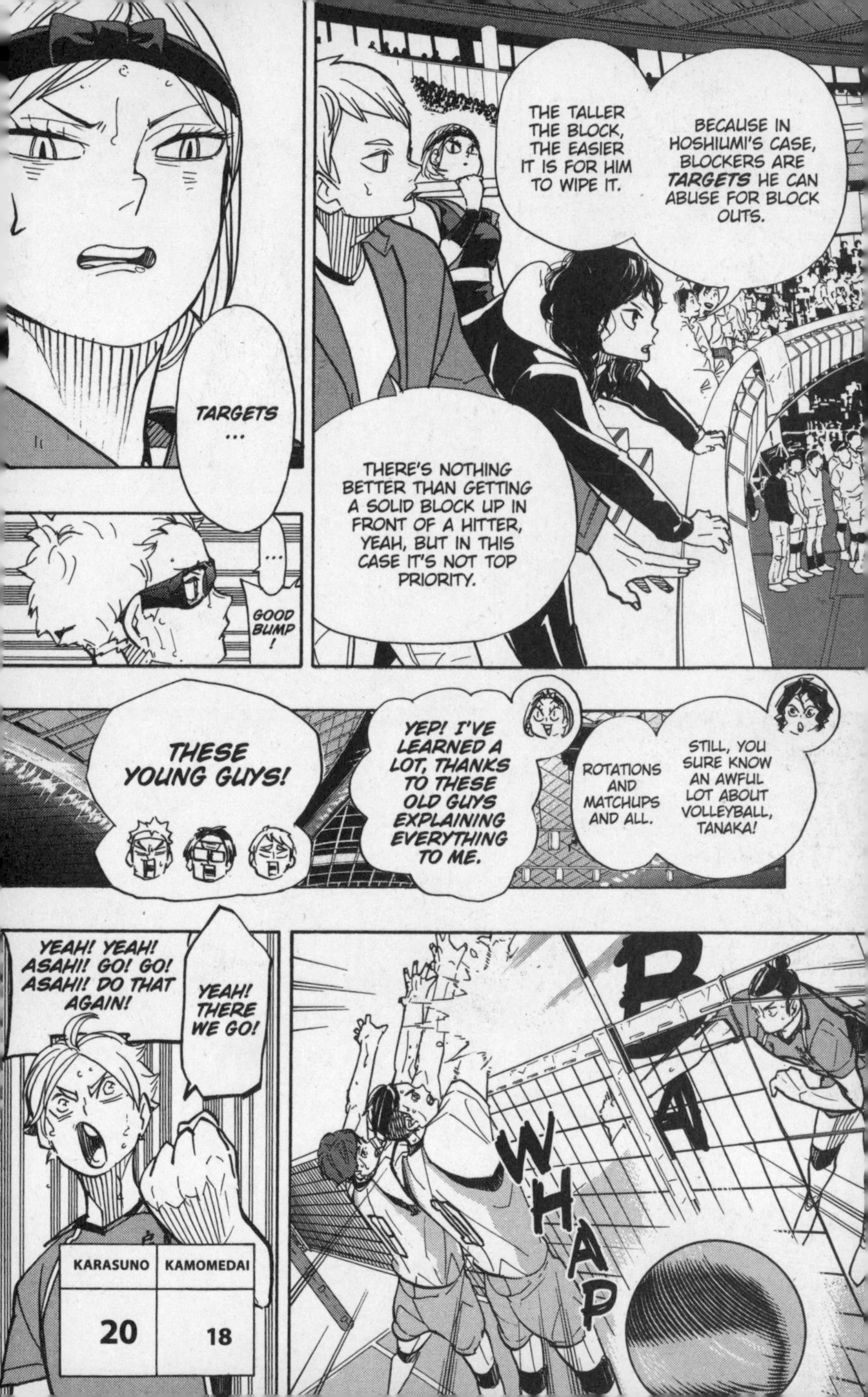
BECAUSE IN HOSHIUMI'S CASE, BLOCKERS ARE **TARGETS** HE CAN ABUSE FOR BLOCK OUTS.
THE TALLER THE BLOCK, THE EASIER IT IS FOR HIM TO WIPE IT.
THERE'S NOTHING BETTER THAN GETTING A SOLID BLOCK UP IN FRONT OF A HITTER, YEAH, BUT IN THIS CASE IT'S NOT TOP PRIORITY.
TARGETS ...
...
GOOD BUMP!
STILL, YOU SURE KNOW AN AWFUL LOT ABOUT VOLLEYBALL, TANAKA!
ROTATIONS AND MATCHUPS AND ALL.
YEP! I'VE LEARNED A LOT, THANKS TO THESE OLD GUYS EXPLAINING EVERYTHING TO ME.
THESE YOUNG GUYS!
BA
WHAP
YEAH! THERE WE GO!
YEAH! YEAH! ASAHI! GO! GO! ASAHI! DO THAT AGAIN!
KARASUNO
KAMOMEDAI
20
18

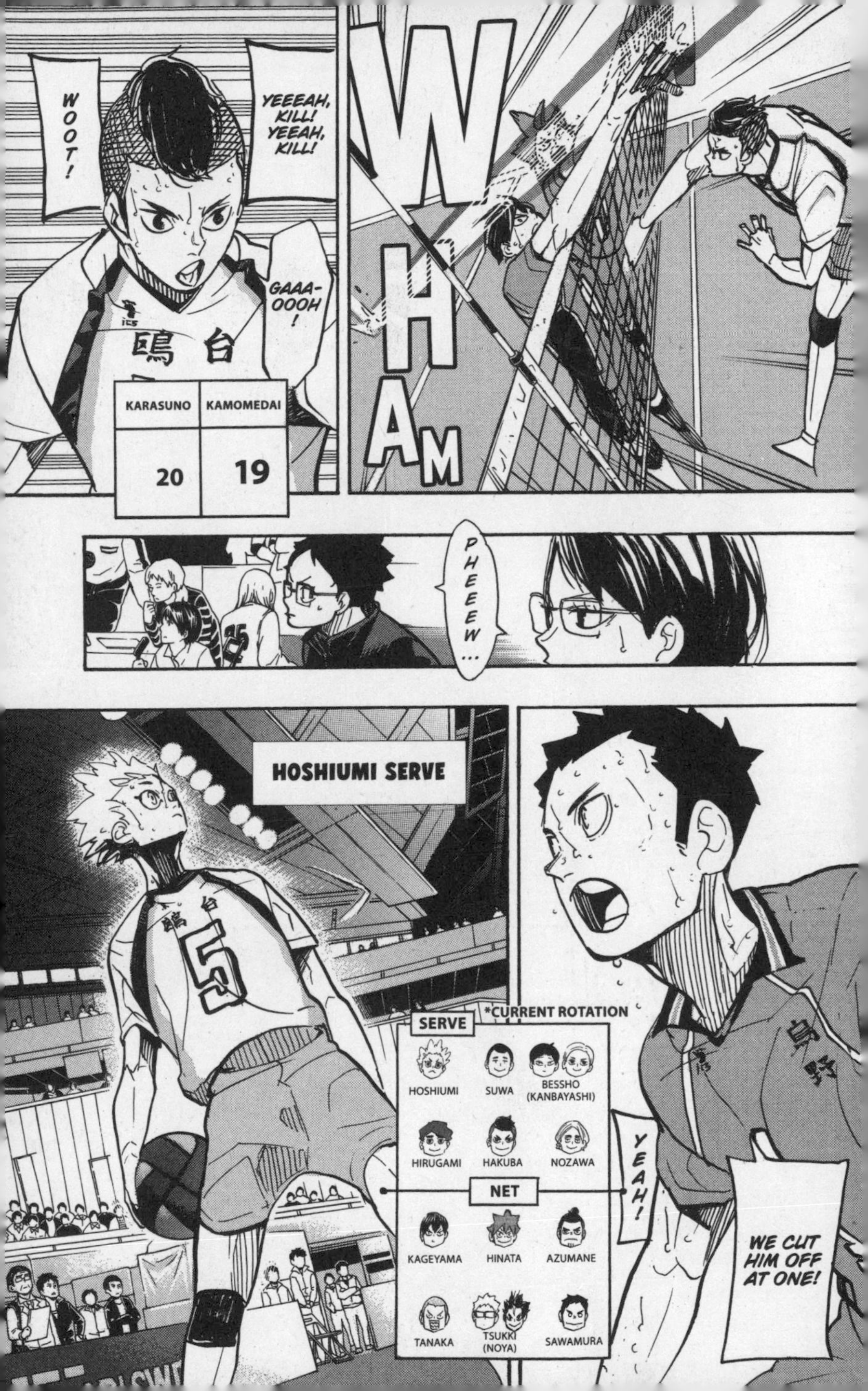
WHAM
YEEEAH, KILL! YEEAH, KILL!
WOOT!
GAAA-OOOH!
KARASUNO 20
KAMOMEDAI 19
PHEEEW...
YEAH!
WE CUT HIM OFF AT ONE!
HOSHIUMI SERVE
*CURRENT ROTATION
SERVE
HOSHIUMI
SUWA
BESSHO (KANBAYASHI)
HIRUGAMI
HAKUBA
NOZAWA
NET
KAGEYAMA
HINATA
AZUMANE
TANAKA
TSUKKI (NOYA)
SAWAMURA

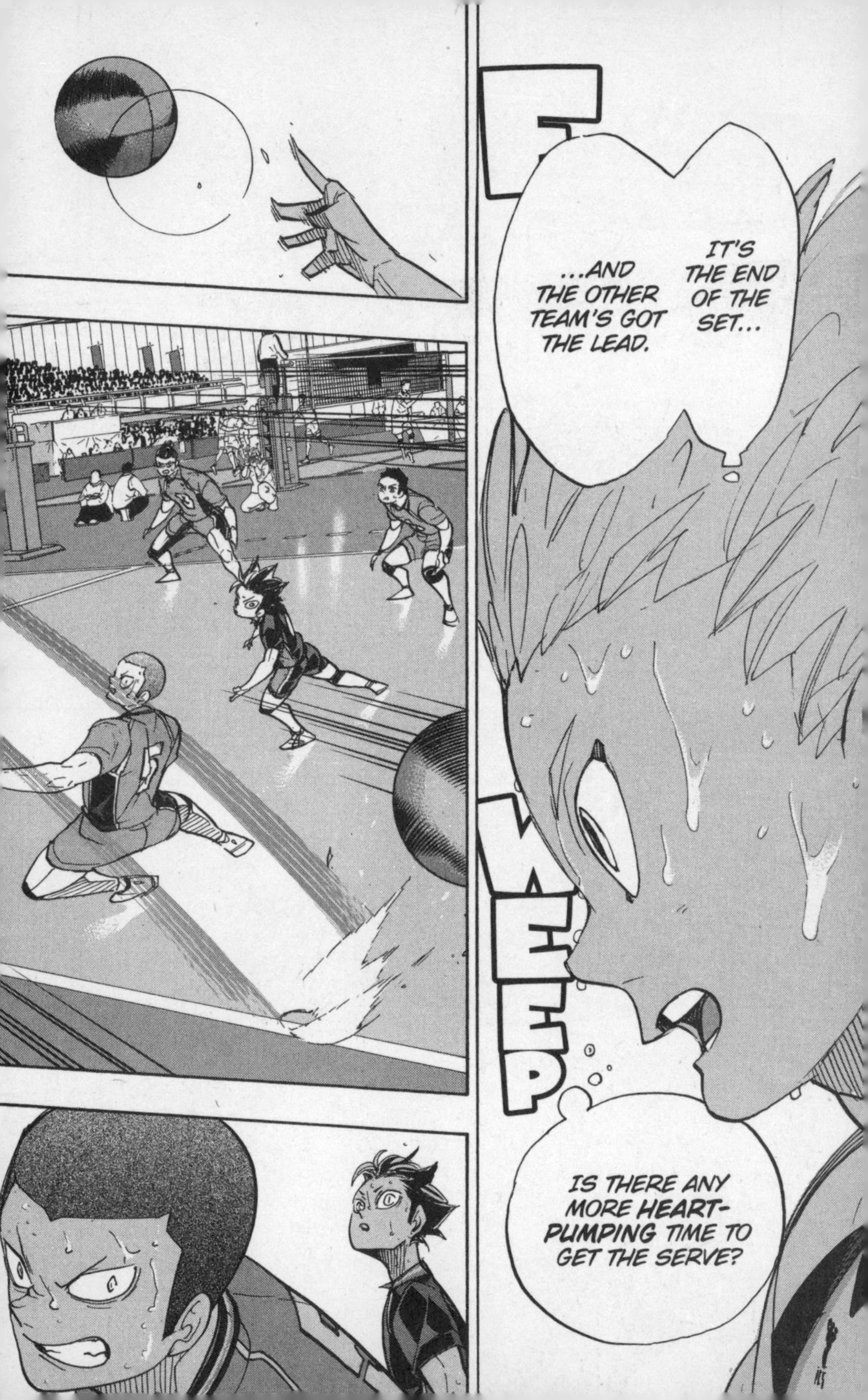
IT'S THE END OF THE SET...
...AND THE OTHER TEAM'S GOT THE LEAD.
FWEEP
IS THERE ANY MORE HEART-PUMPING TIME TO GET THE SERVE?

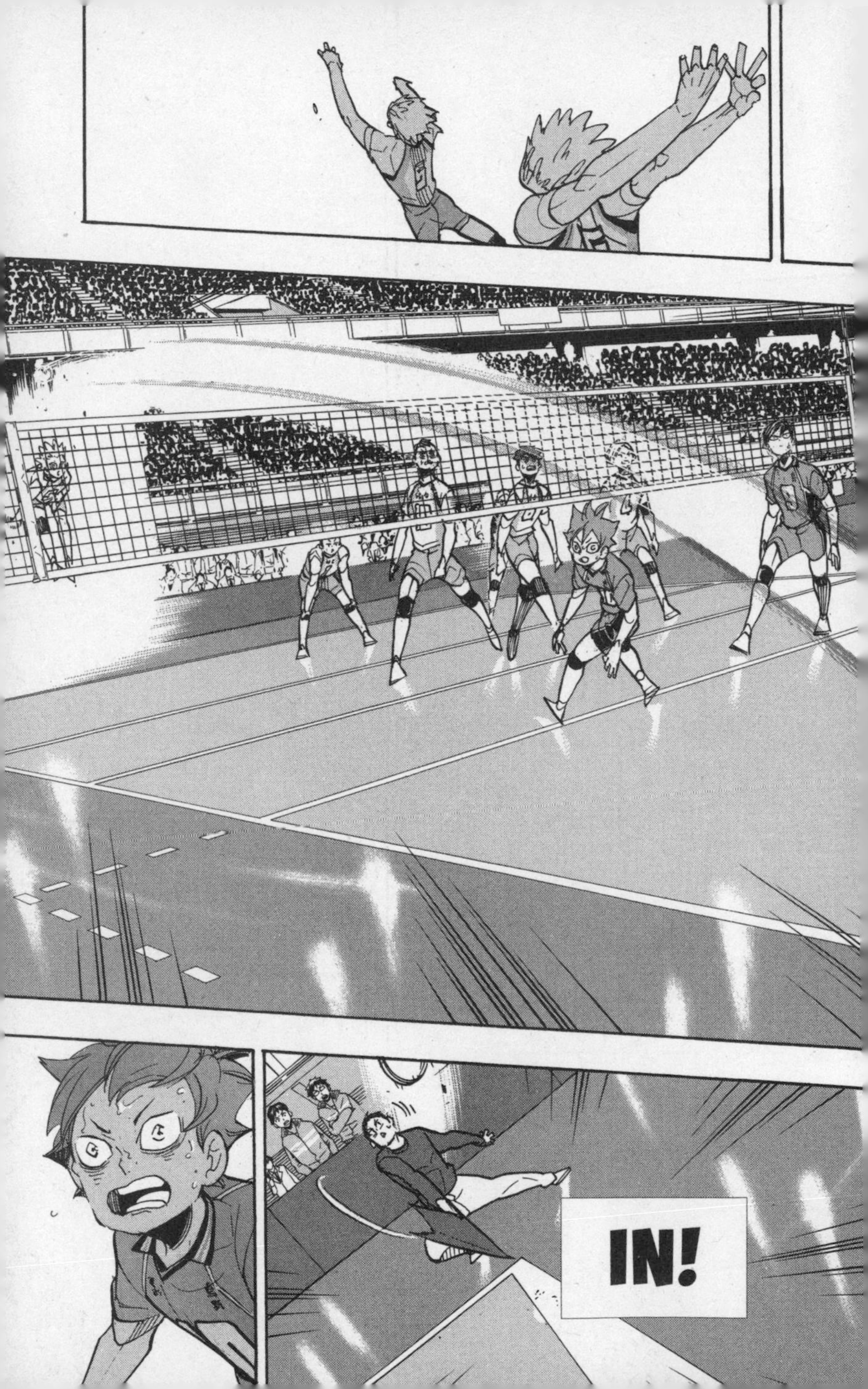
IN!

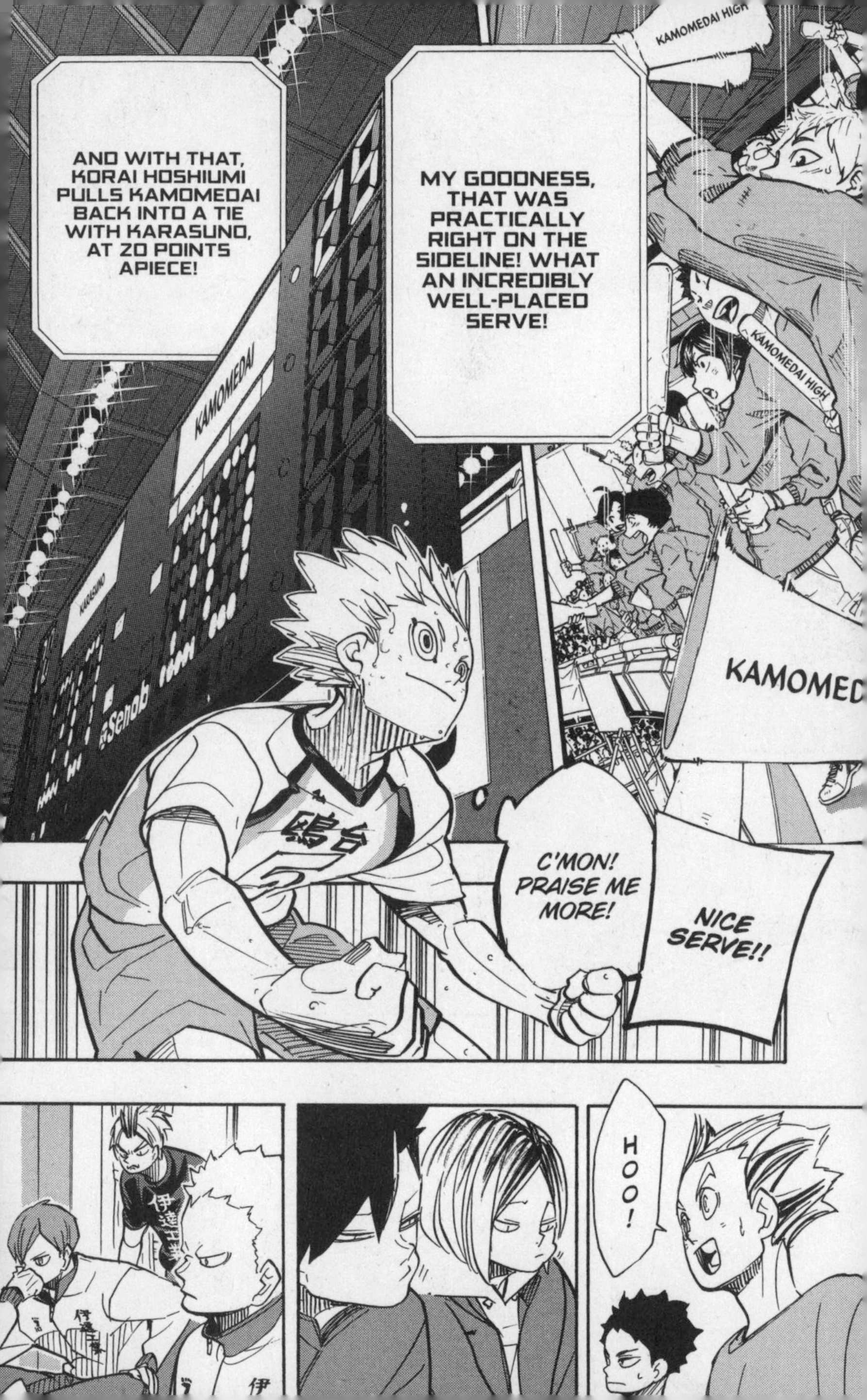
KAMOMEDAI HIGH
MY GOODNESS, THAT WAS PRACTICALLY RIGHT ON THE SIDELINE! WHAT AN INCREDIBLY WELL-PLACED SERVE!
AND WITH THAT, KORAI HOSHIUMI PULLS KAMOMEDAI BACK INTO A TIE WITH KARASUNO, AT 20 POINTS APIECE!
KAMOMEDAI HIGH
KAMOMEDAI
KARASUNO
KAMOMED
NICE SERVE!!
C'MON! PRAISE ME MORE!
HOO!

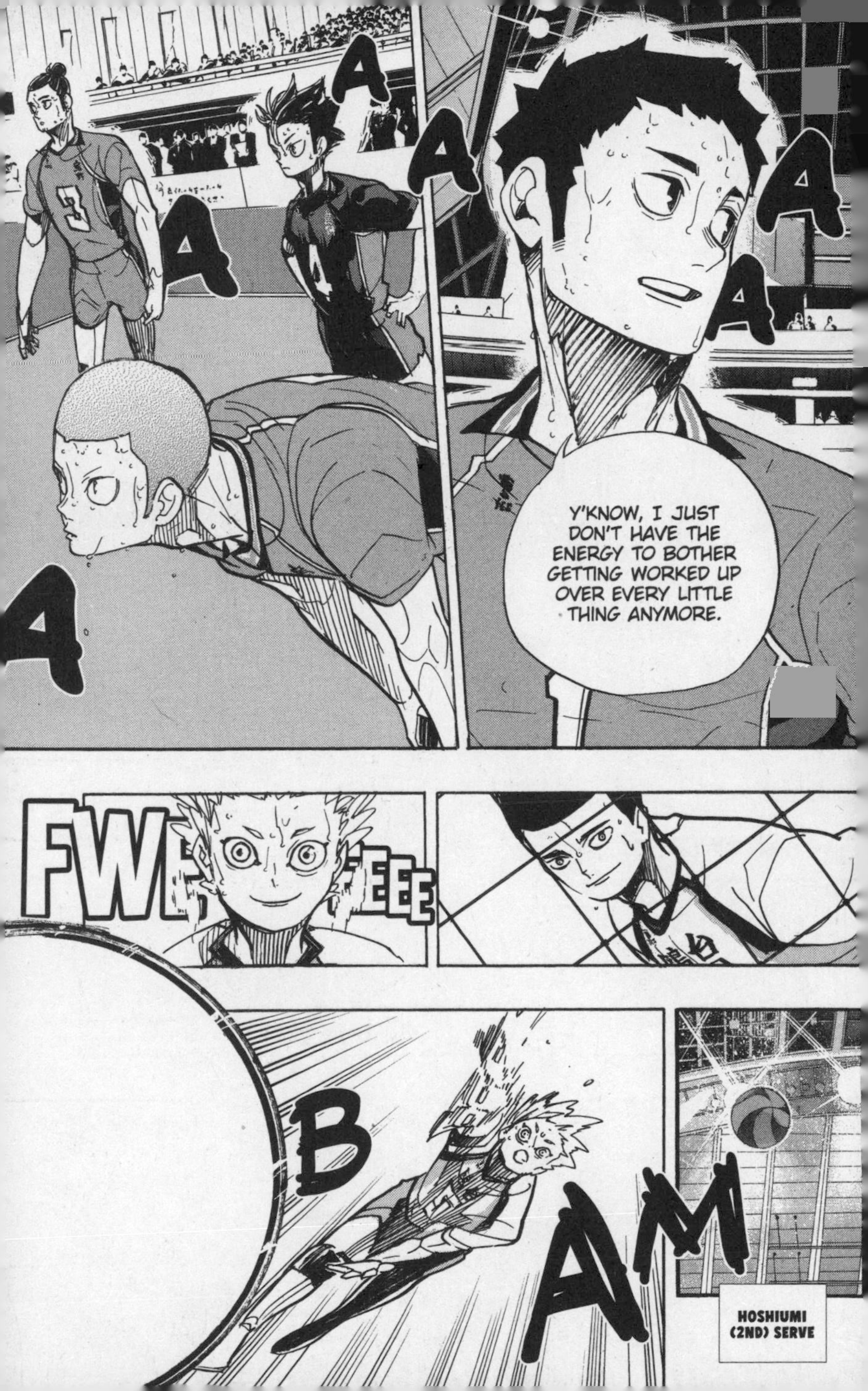
AAAA
Y'KNOW, I JUST DON'T HAVE THE ENERGY TO BOTHER GETTING WORKED UP OVER EVERY LITTLE THING ANYMORE.
AAAA
FWEEEE
HOSHIUMI (2ND) SERVE
BAM

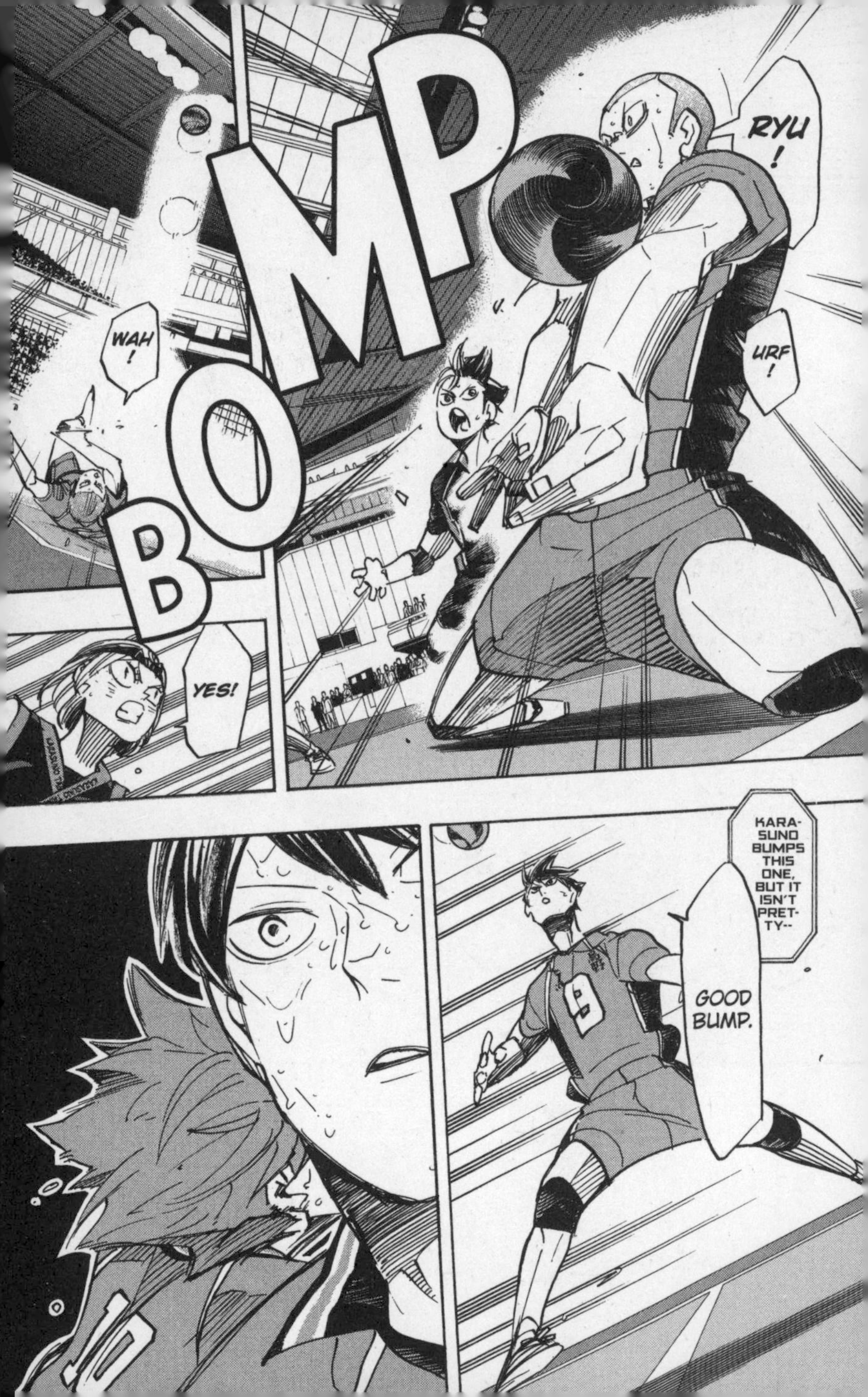
RYU!
BOMP
URF!
WAH!
YES!
KARASUNO BUMPS THIS ONE, BUT IT ISN'T PRETTY--
GOOD BUMP.

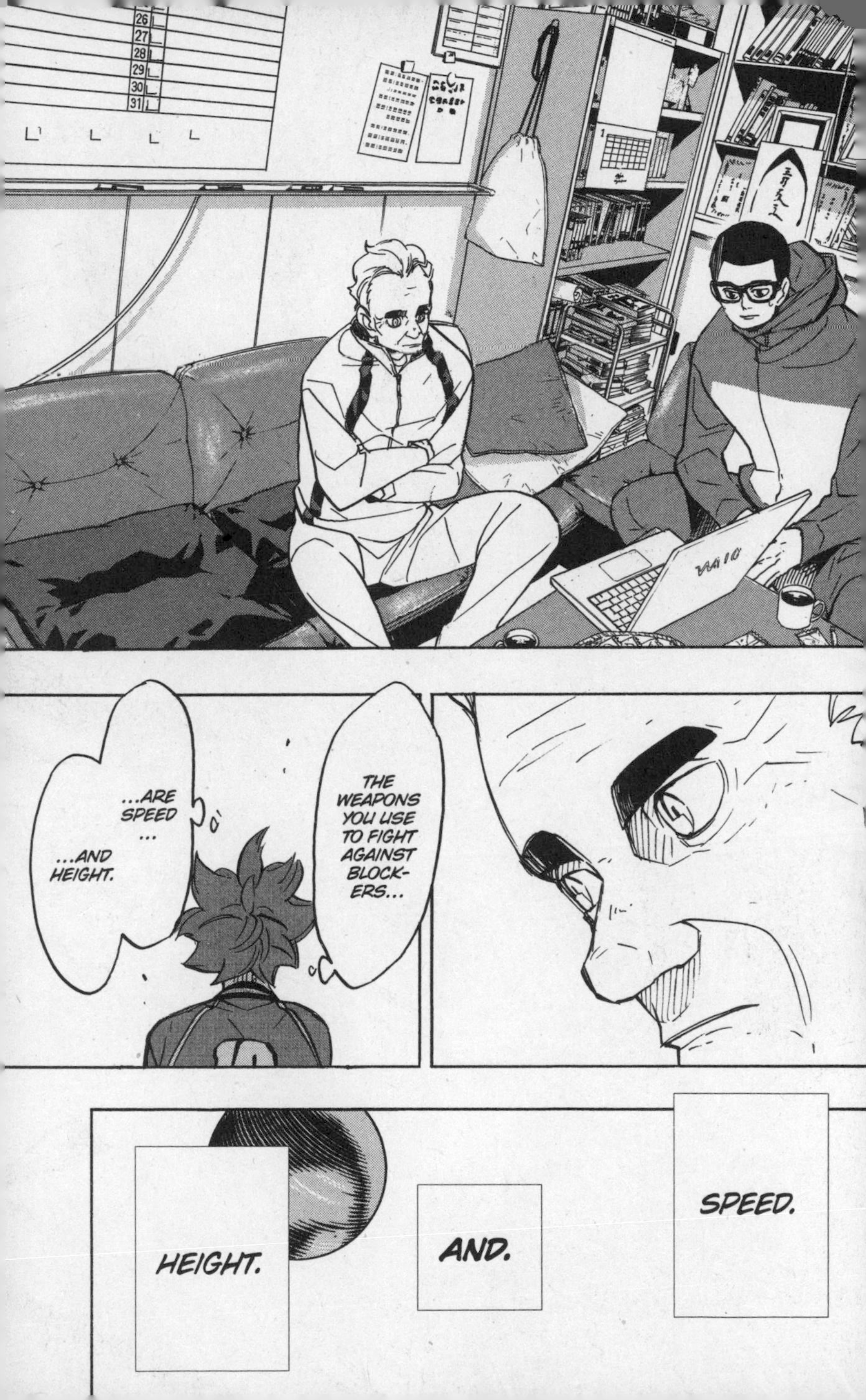
THE WEAPONS YOU USE TO FIGHT AGAINST BLOCKERS...
...ARE SPEED ... ...AND HEIGHT.
SPEED.
AND.
HEIGHT.

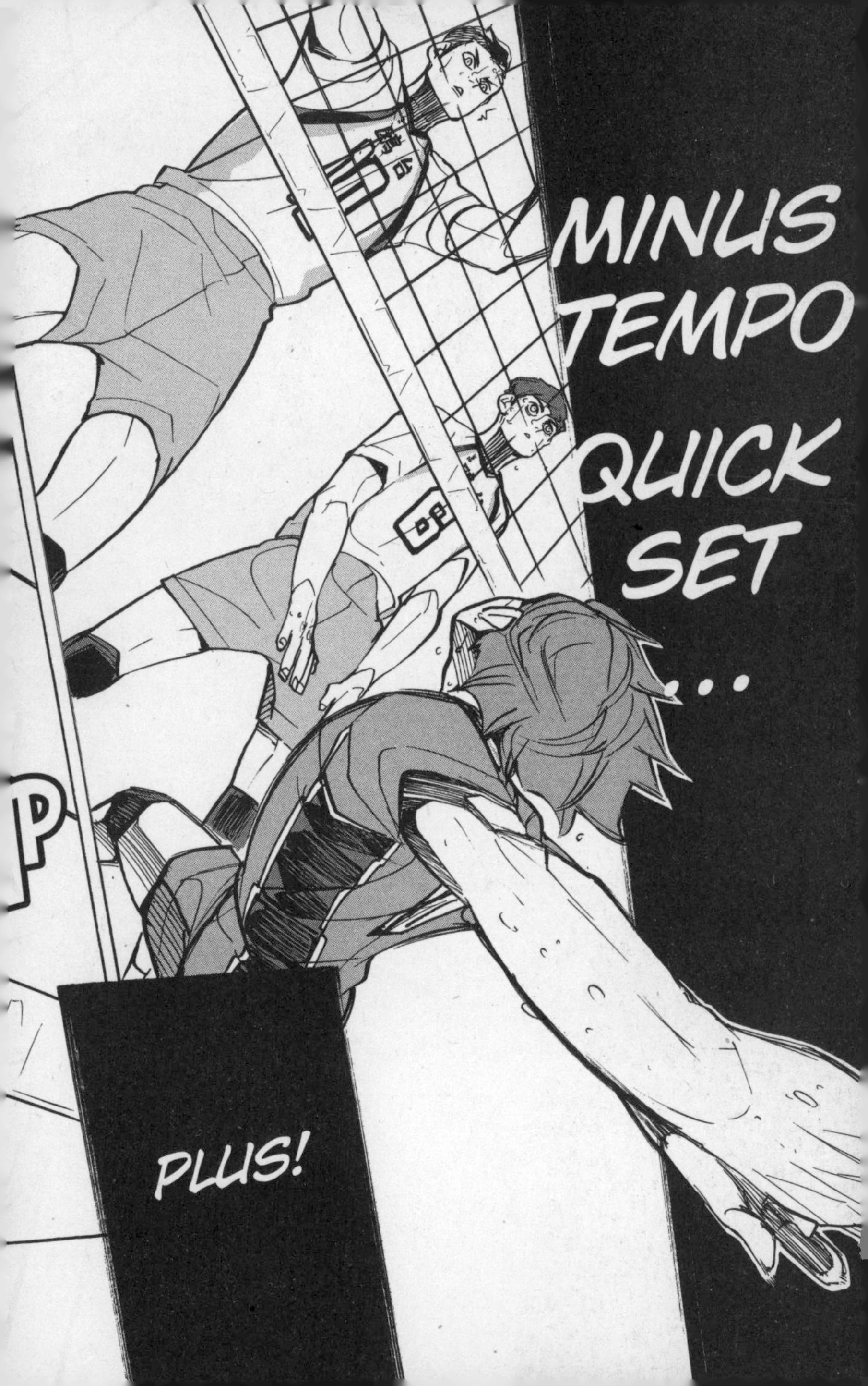
MINUS TEMPO QUICK SET...
PLUS!

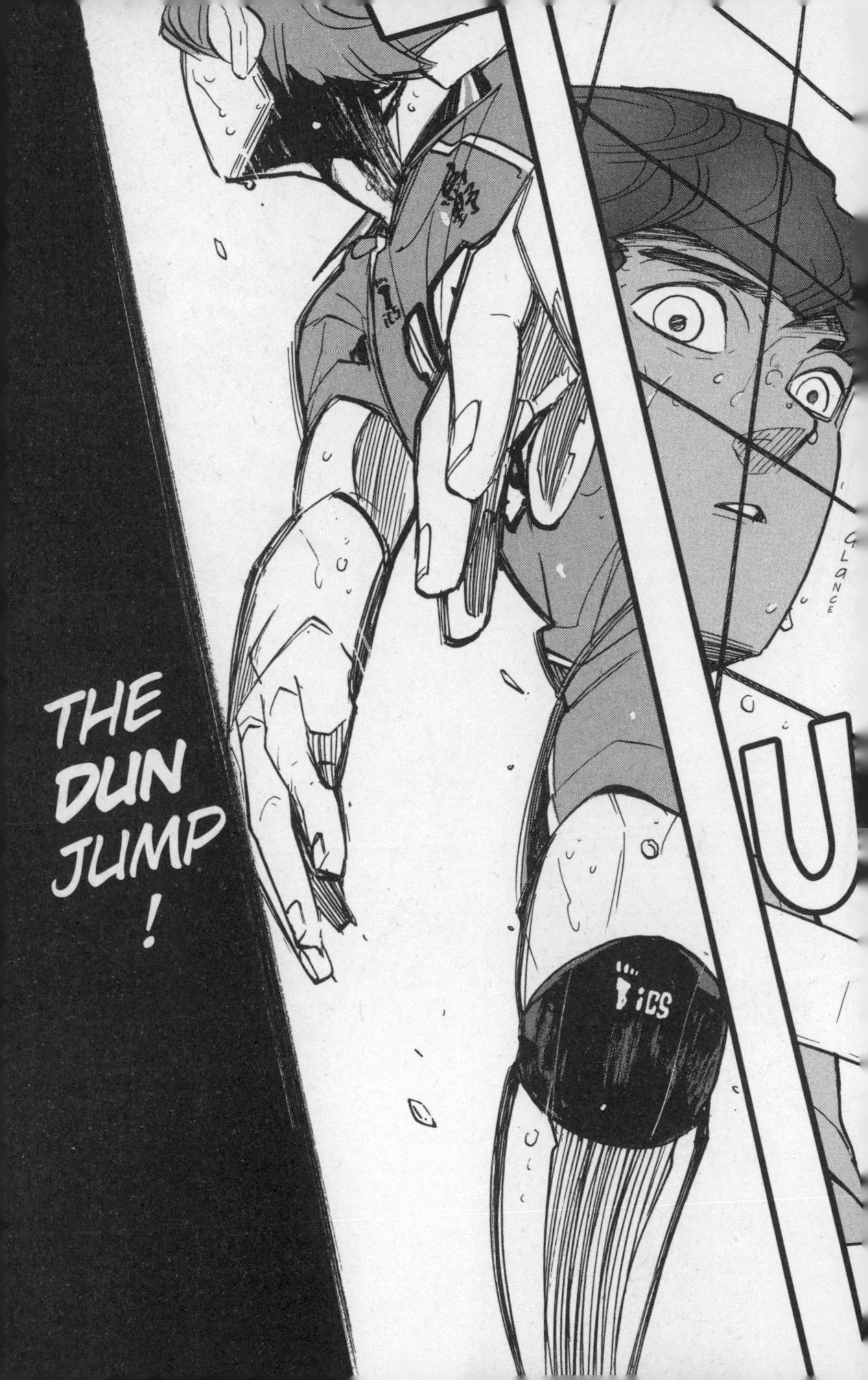
THE DUN JUMP!
GLANCE

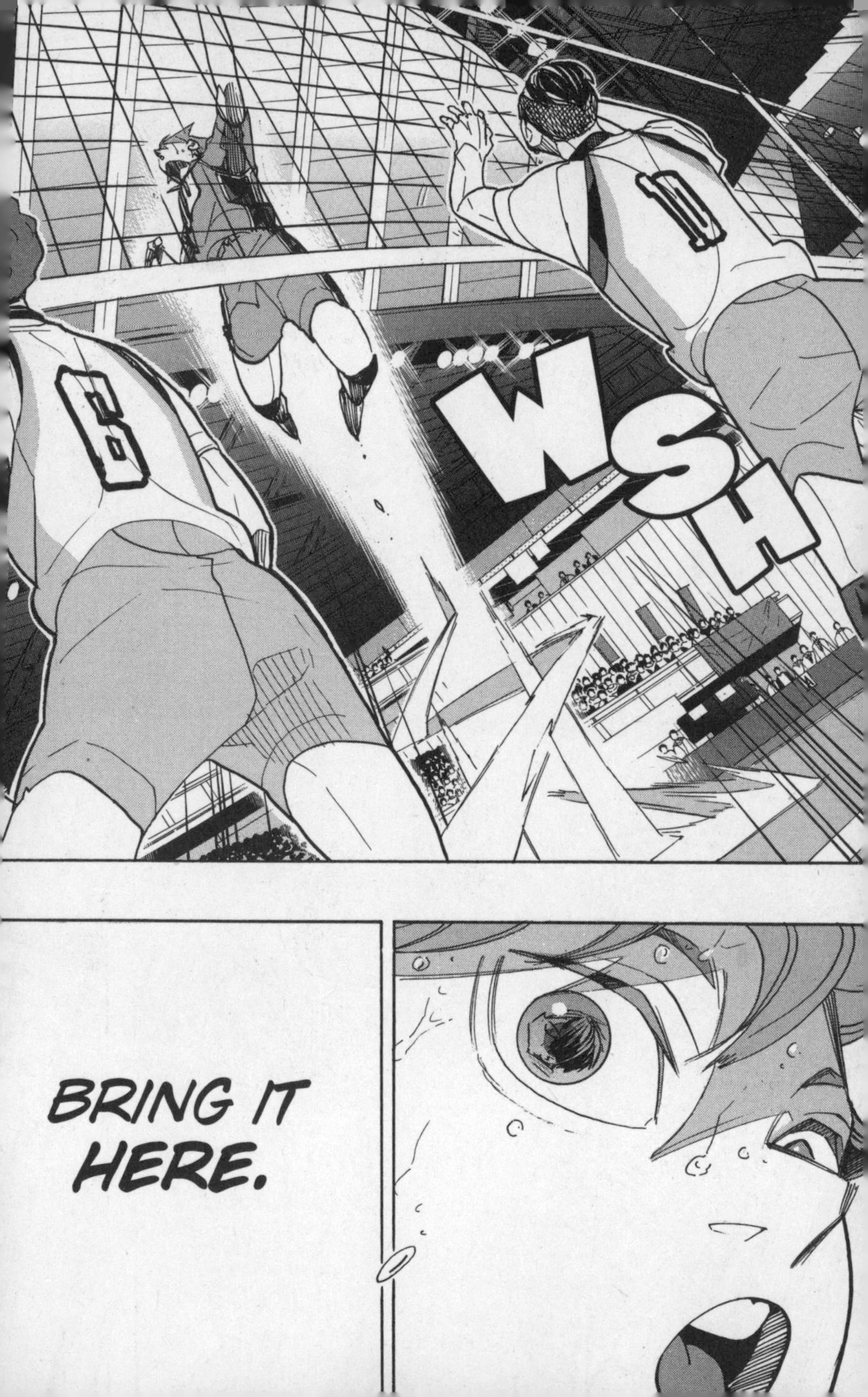
WSH
BRING IT HERE.

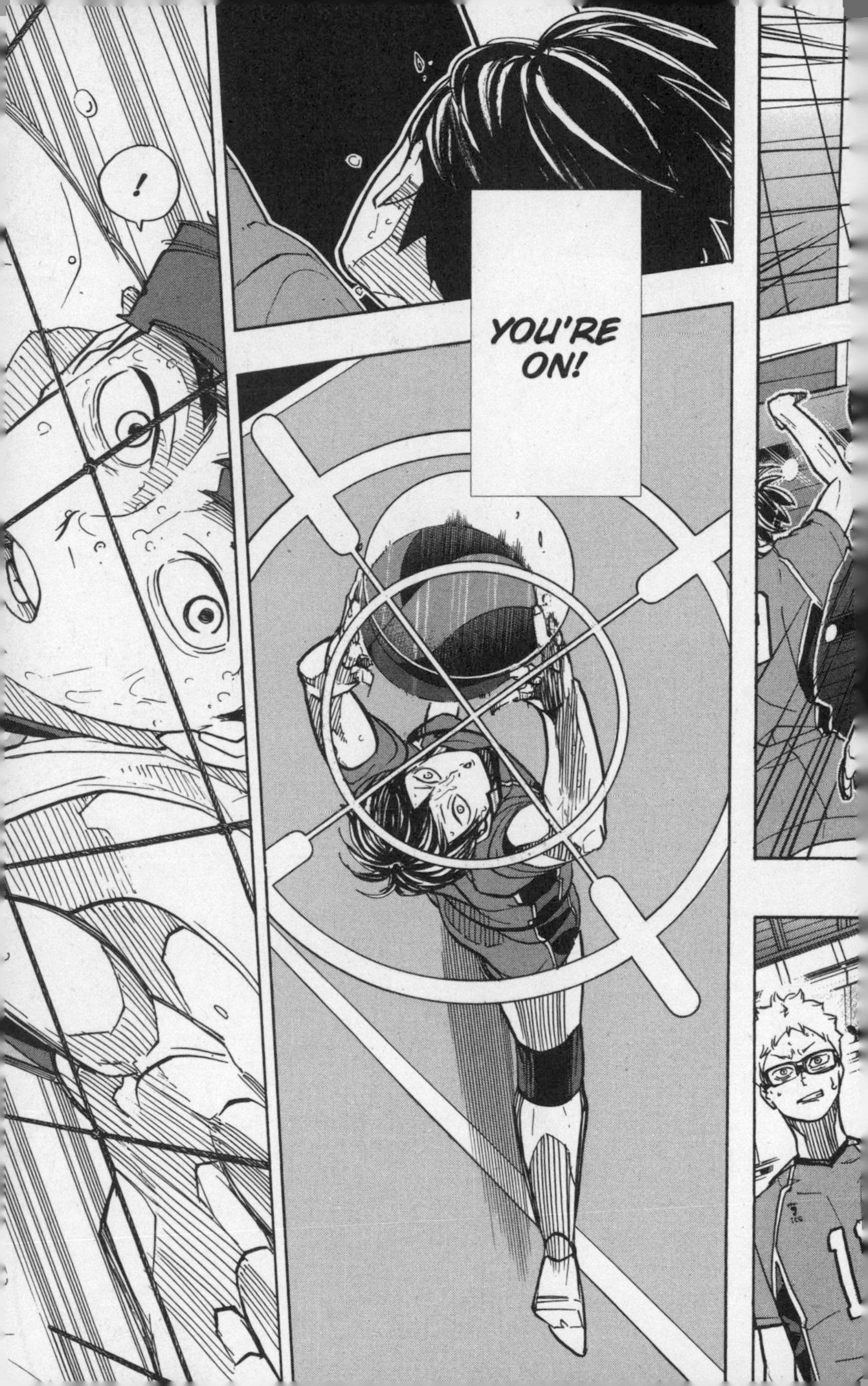
YOU'RE ON!
!

**HERE'S ANOTHER LITTLE MISTAKE NOTICED ON THE FINAL PROOFREADING PASS BEFORE THE SCRIPT WAS SENT TO THE PRINTERS.**

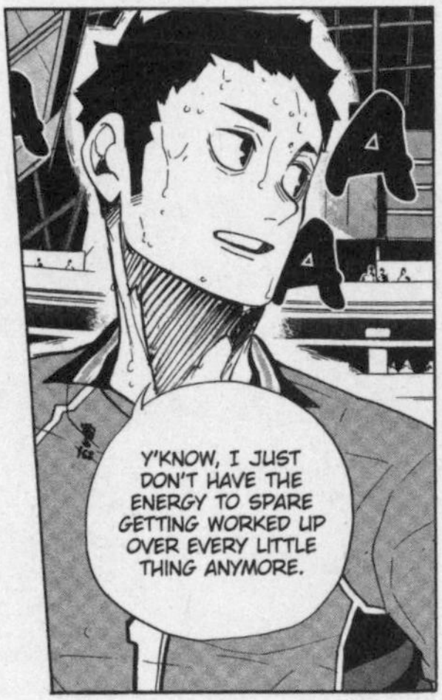
Y'KNOW, I JUST DON'T HAVE THE ENERGY TO SPARE GETTING WORKED UP OVER EVERY LITTLE THING ANYMORE.

**BEFORE REVISION**

→

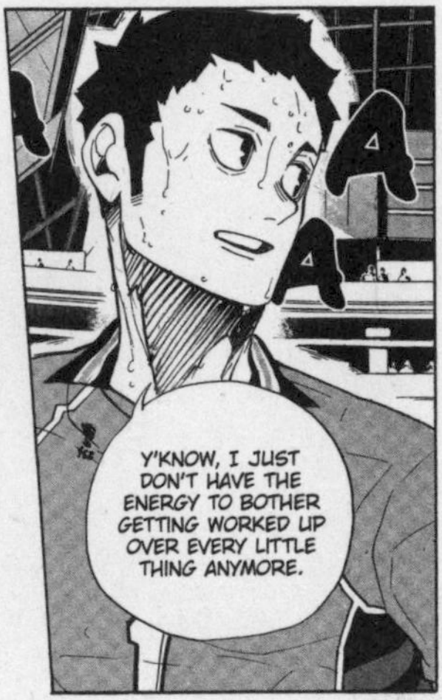
Y'KNOW, I JUST DON'T HAVE THE ENERGY TO BOTHER GETTING WORKED UP OVER EVERY LITTLE THING ANYMORE.

**AFTER REVISION**

**CHANGE JUST A WORD AND SUDDENLY DAICHI TURNS INTO SUCH A NASTY JERK.**

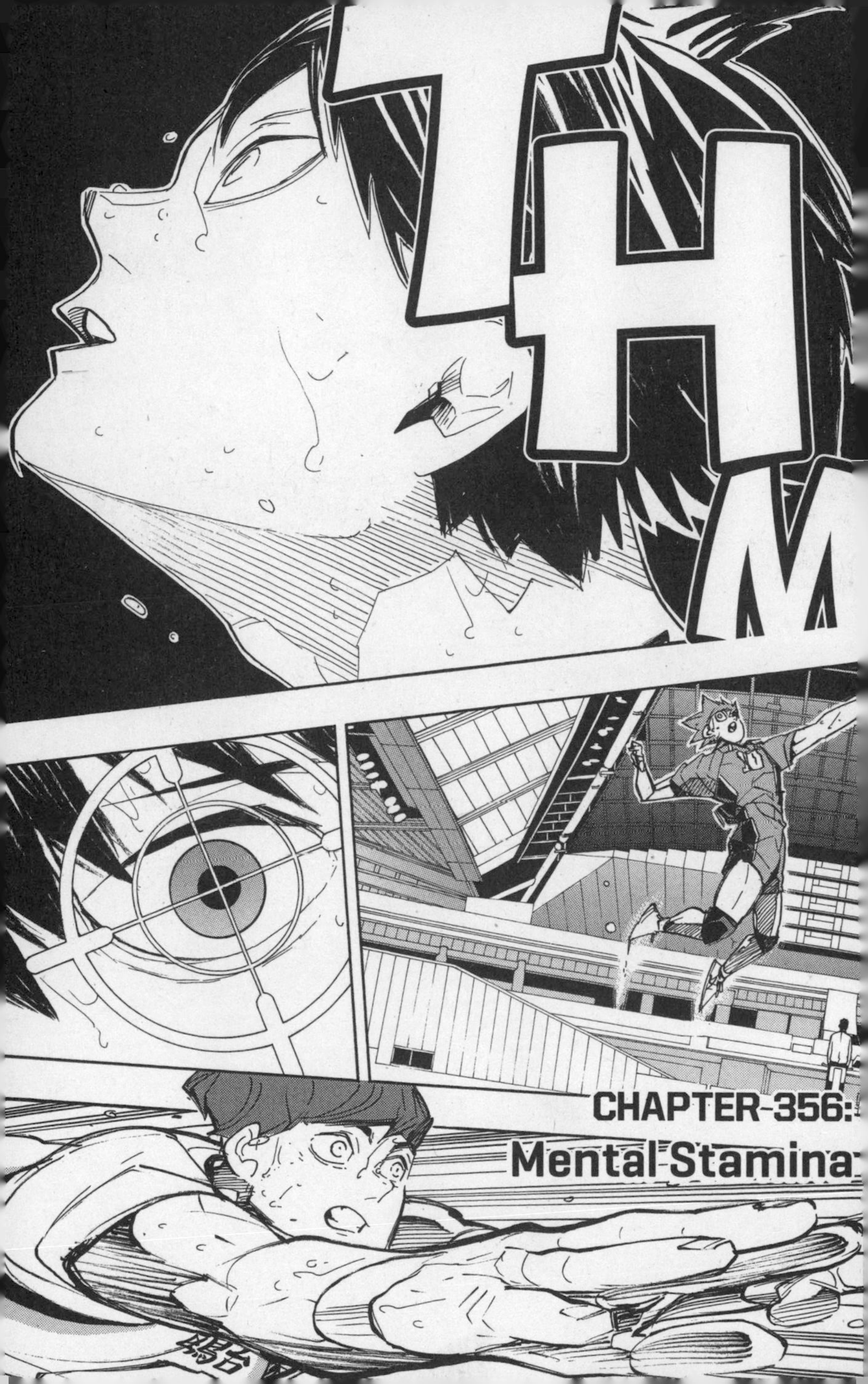
THM
CHAPTER 356:
Mental Stamina

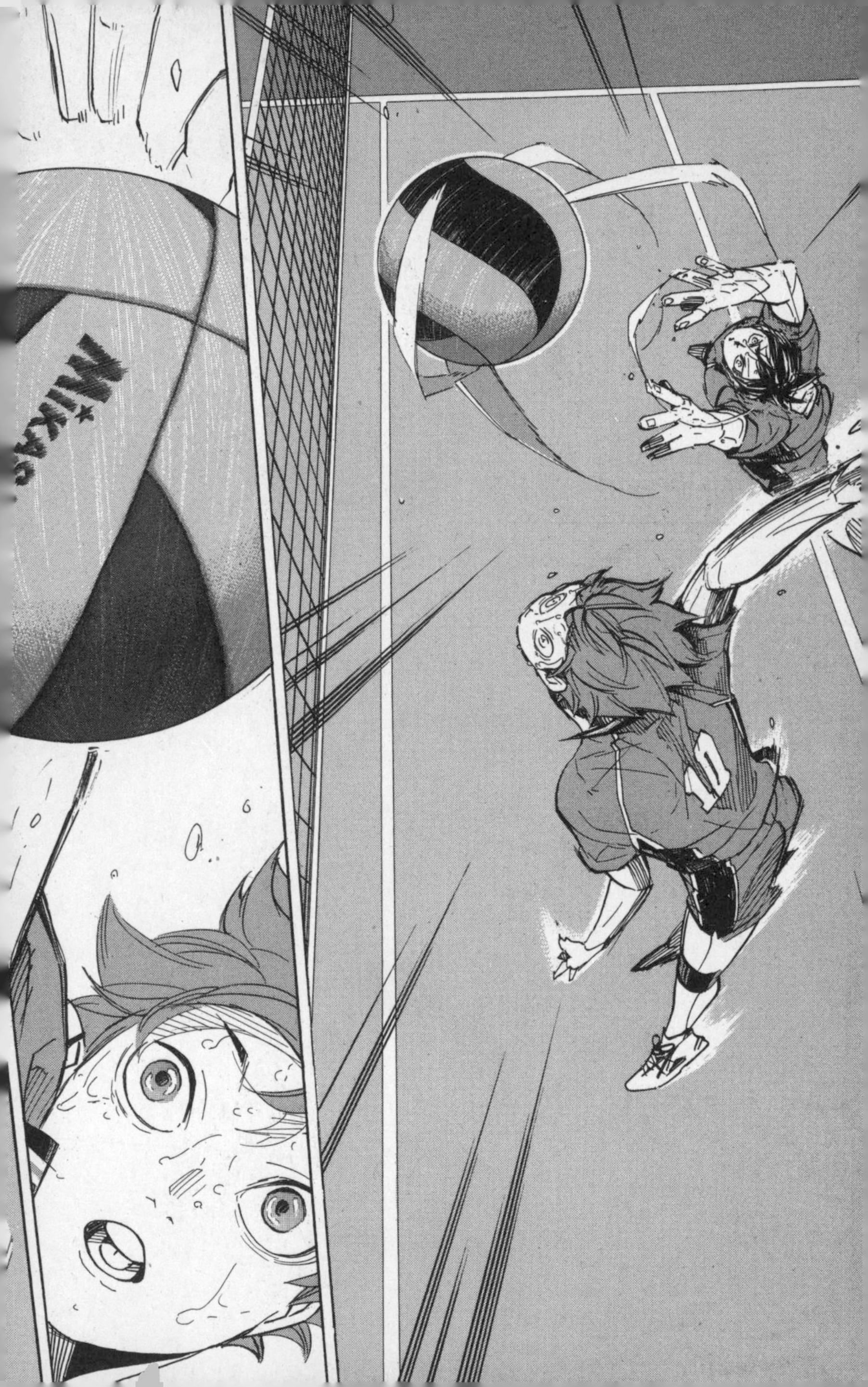

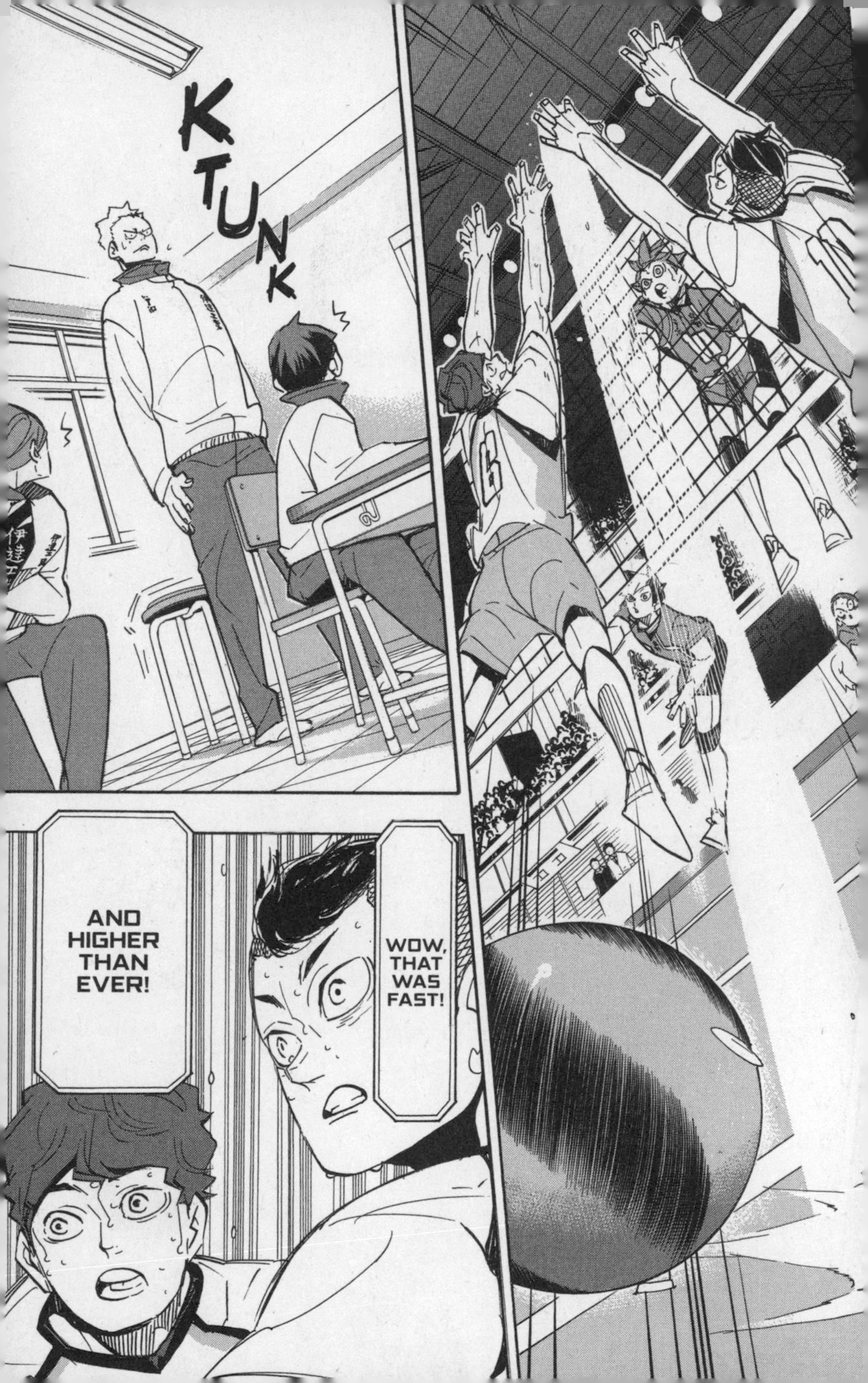
KTUNK
WOW, THAT WAS FAST!
AND HIGHER THAN EVER!

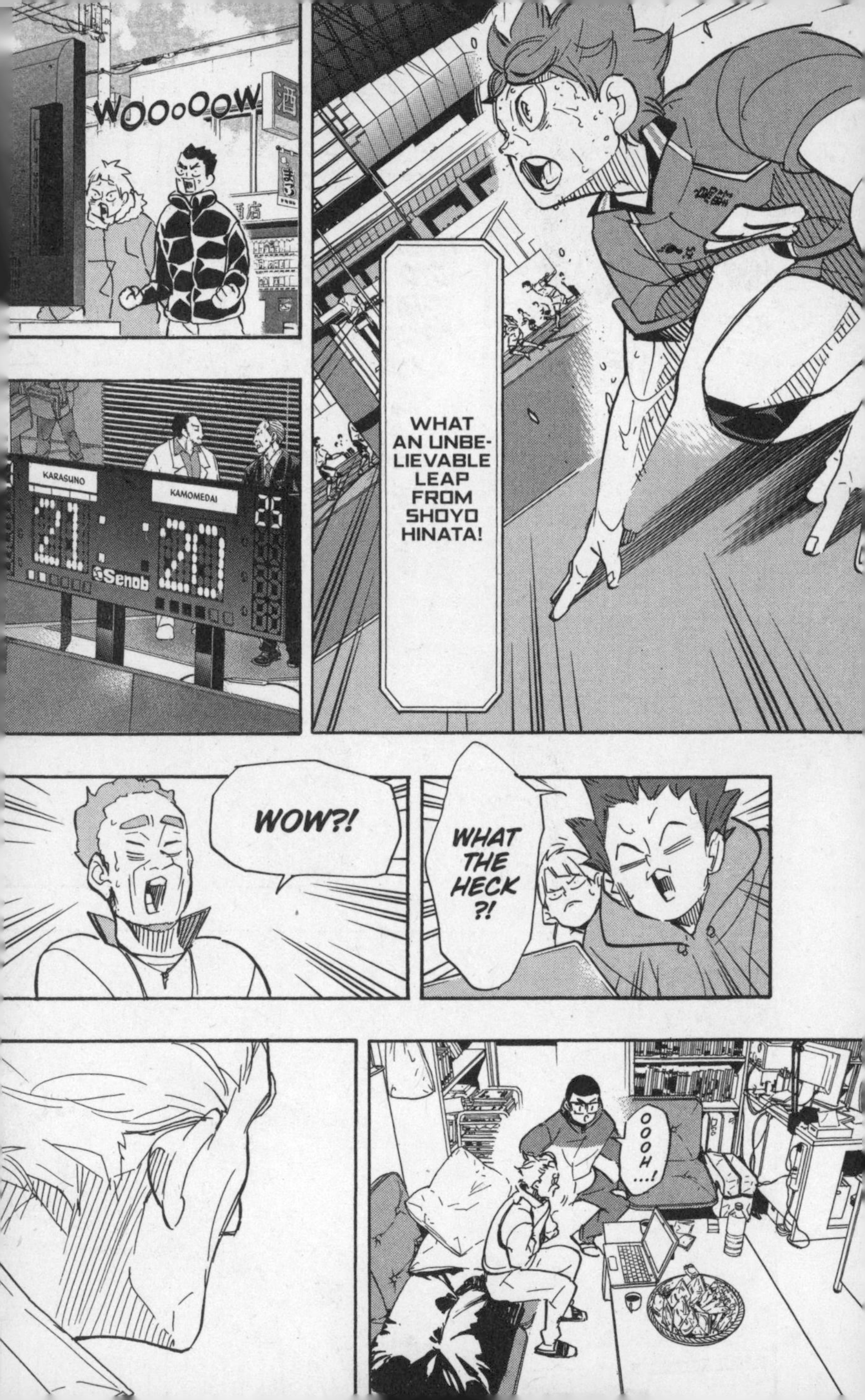
WHAT AN UNBE-LIEVABLE LEAP FROM SHOYO HINATA!
WOOoOOW
酒
KARASUNO
KAMOMEDAI
21
20
Senob
WHAT THE HECK?!
WOW?!
OOOH...!

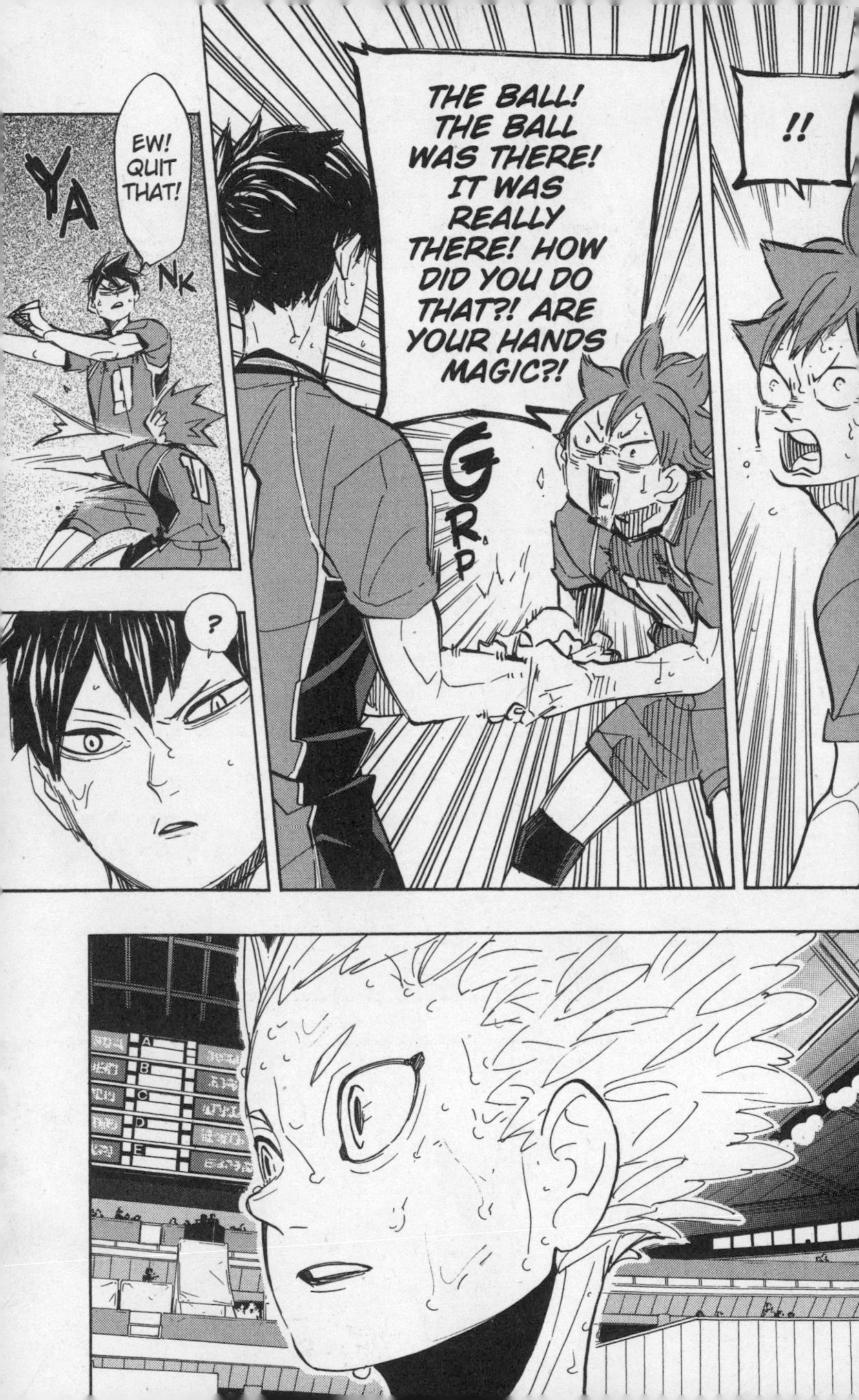
!!
THE BALL! THE BALL WAS THERE! IT WAS REALLY THERE! HOW DID YOU DO THAT?! ARE YOUR HANDS MAGIC?!
GRP
EW! QUIT THAT!
YANK
?

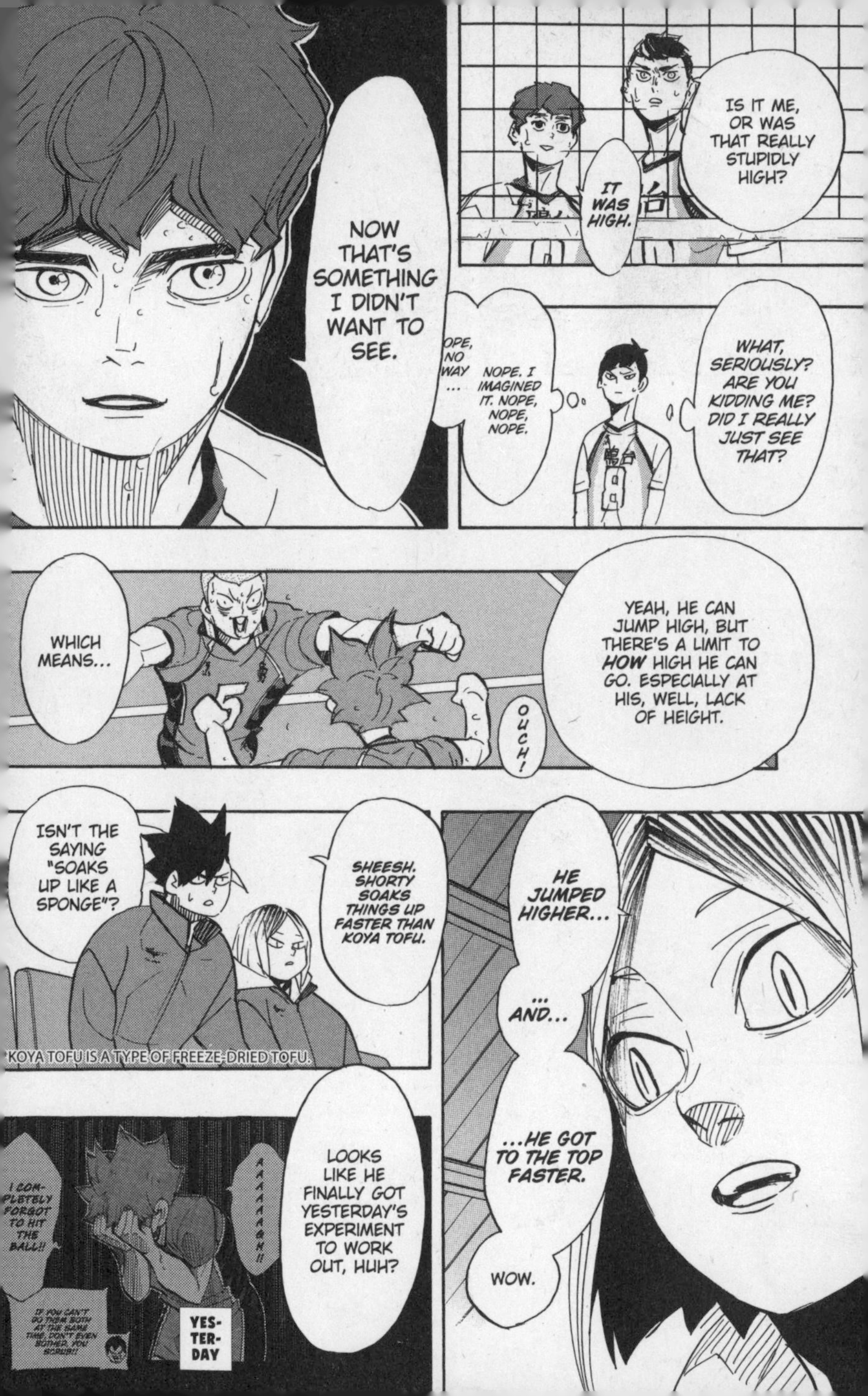
IS IT ME, OR WAS THAT REALLY STUPIDLY HIGH?
IT WAS HIGH.
WHAT, SERIOUSLY? ARE YOU KIDDING ME? DID I REALLY JUST SEE THAT?
NOPE. I IMAGINED IT. NOPE, NOPE, NOPE.
OPE, NO WAY ...
NOW THAT'S SOMETHING I DIDN'T WANT TO SEE.
YEAH, HE CAN JUMP HIGH, BUT THERE'S A LIMIT TO HOW HIGH HE CAN GO. ESPECIALLY AT HIS, WELL, LACK OF HEIGHT.
OUCH!
WHICH MEANS...
HE JUMPED HIGHER...
... AND...
...HE GOT TO THE TOP FASTER.
WOW.
SHEESH. SHORTY SOAKS THINGS UP FASTER THAN KOYA TOFU.
ISN'T THE SAYING "SOAKS UP LIKE A SPONGE"?
KOYA TOFU IS A TYPE OF FREEZE-DRIED TOFU.
LOOKS LIKE HE FINALLY GOT YESTERDAY'S EXPERIMENT TO WORK OUT, HUH?
AAAAAAAAAGH!!
I COMPLETELY FORGOT TO HIT THE BALL!!
YESTERDAY
IF YOU CAN'T DO THEM BOTH AT THE SAME TIME, DON'T EVEN BOTHER, YOU SCRUB!!

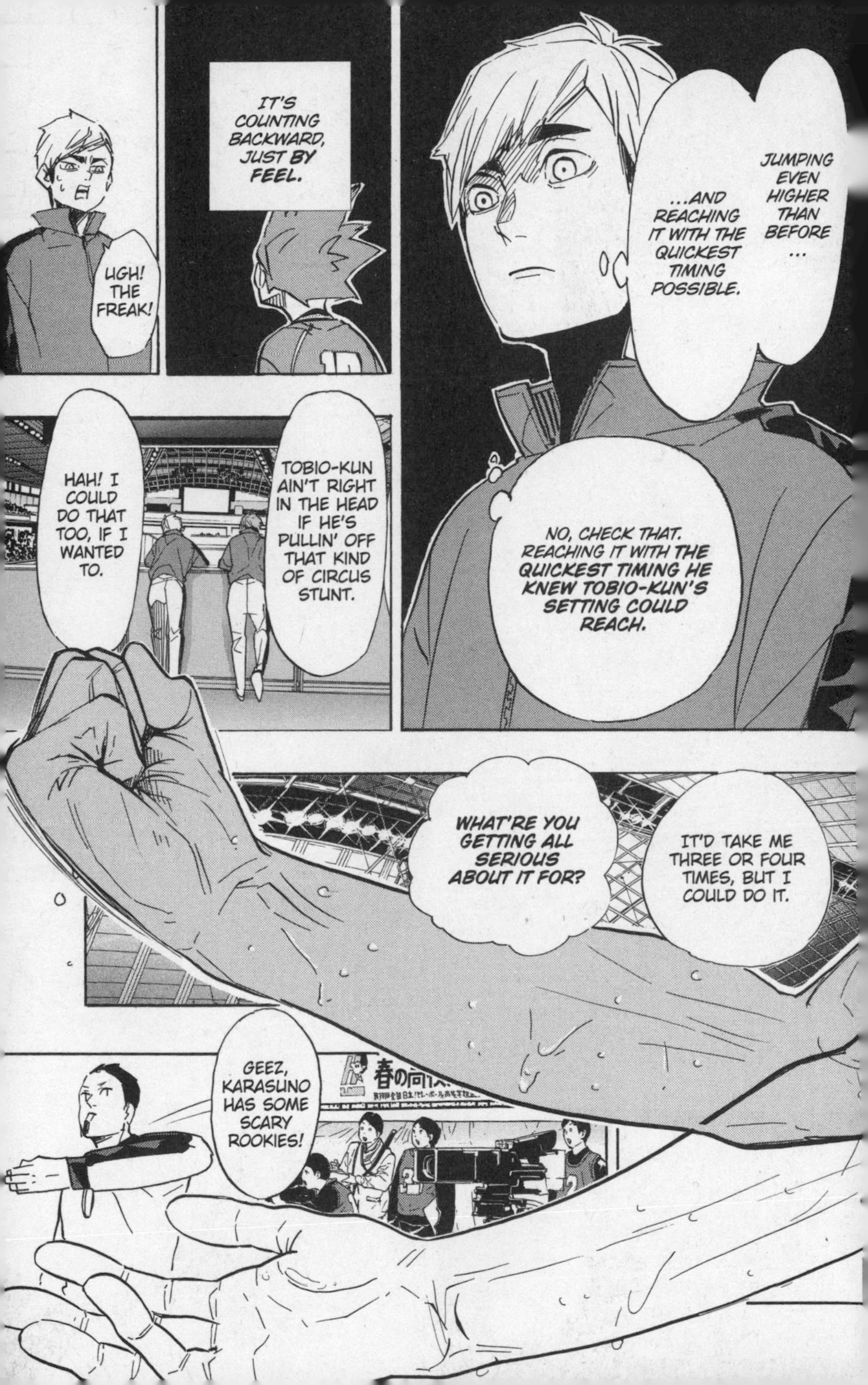
JUMPING EVEN HIGHER THAN BEFORE ...
...AND REACHING IT WITH THE QUICKEST TIMING POSSIBLE.
NO, CHECK THAT. REACHING IT WITH THE QUICKEST TIMING HE KNEW TOBIO-KUN'S SETTING COULD REACH.
IT'S COUNTING BACKWARD, JUST BY FEEL.
UGH! THE FREAK!
TOBIO-KUN AIN'T RIGHT IN THE HEAD IF HE'S PULLIN' OFF THAT KIND OF CIRCUS STUNT.
HAH! I COULD DO THAT TOO, IF I WANTED TO.
IT'D TAKE ME THREE OR FOUR TIMES, BUT I COULD DO IT.
WHAT'RE YOU GETTING ALL SERIOUS ABOUT IT FOR?
GEEZ, KARASUNO HAS SOME SCARY ROOKIES!

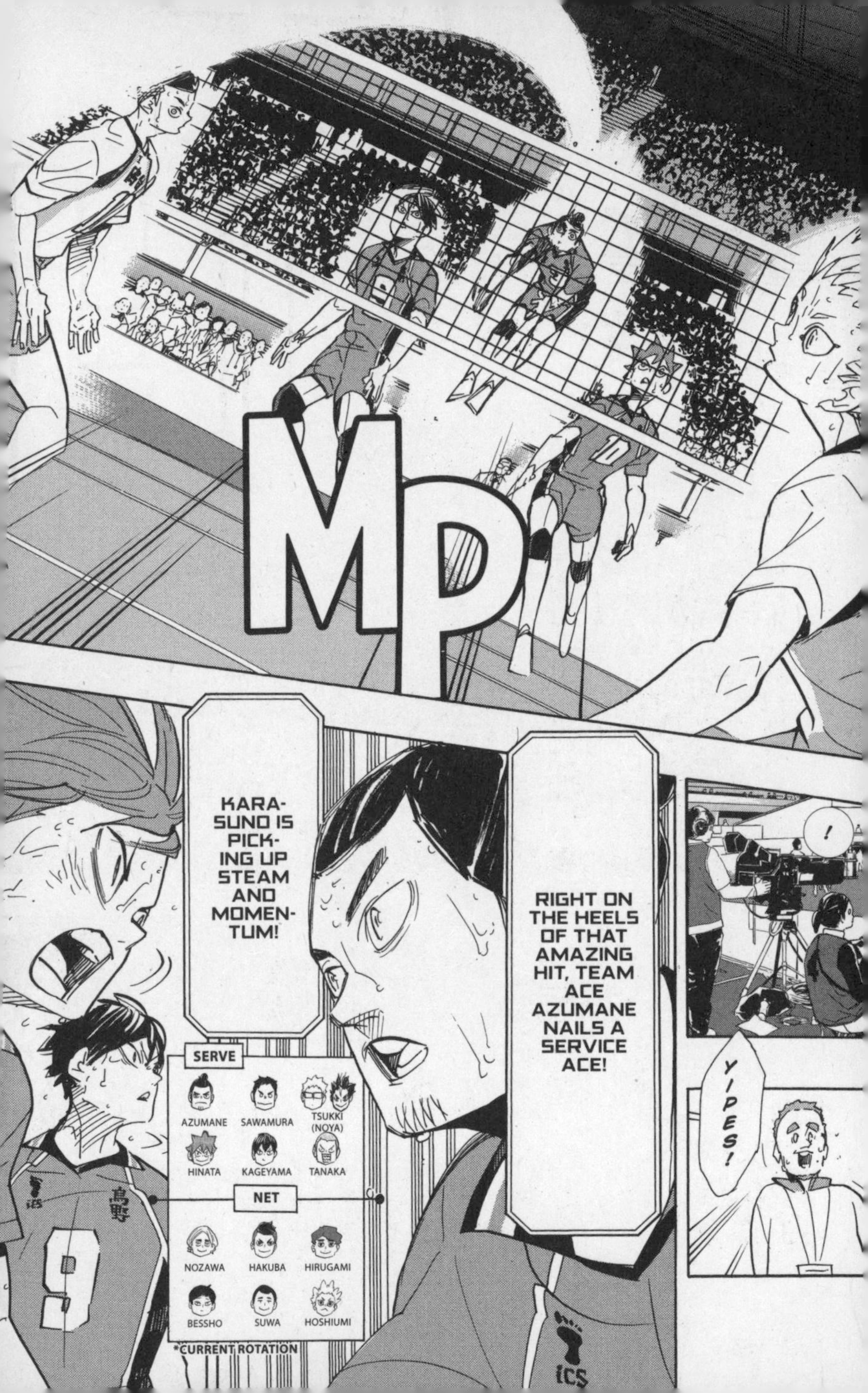
MP
!
YIPES!
RIGHT ON THE HEELS OF THAT AMAZING HIT, TEAM ACE AZUMANE NAILS A SERVICE ACE!
KARA-SUNO IS PICK-ING UP STEAM AND MOMEN-TUM!
SERVE
AZUMANE
SAWAMURA
TSUKKI (NOYA)
HINATA
KAGEYAMA
TANAKA
NET
NOZAWA
HAKUBA
HIRUGAMI
BESSHO
SUWA
HOSHIUMI
*CURRENT ROTATION

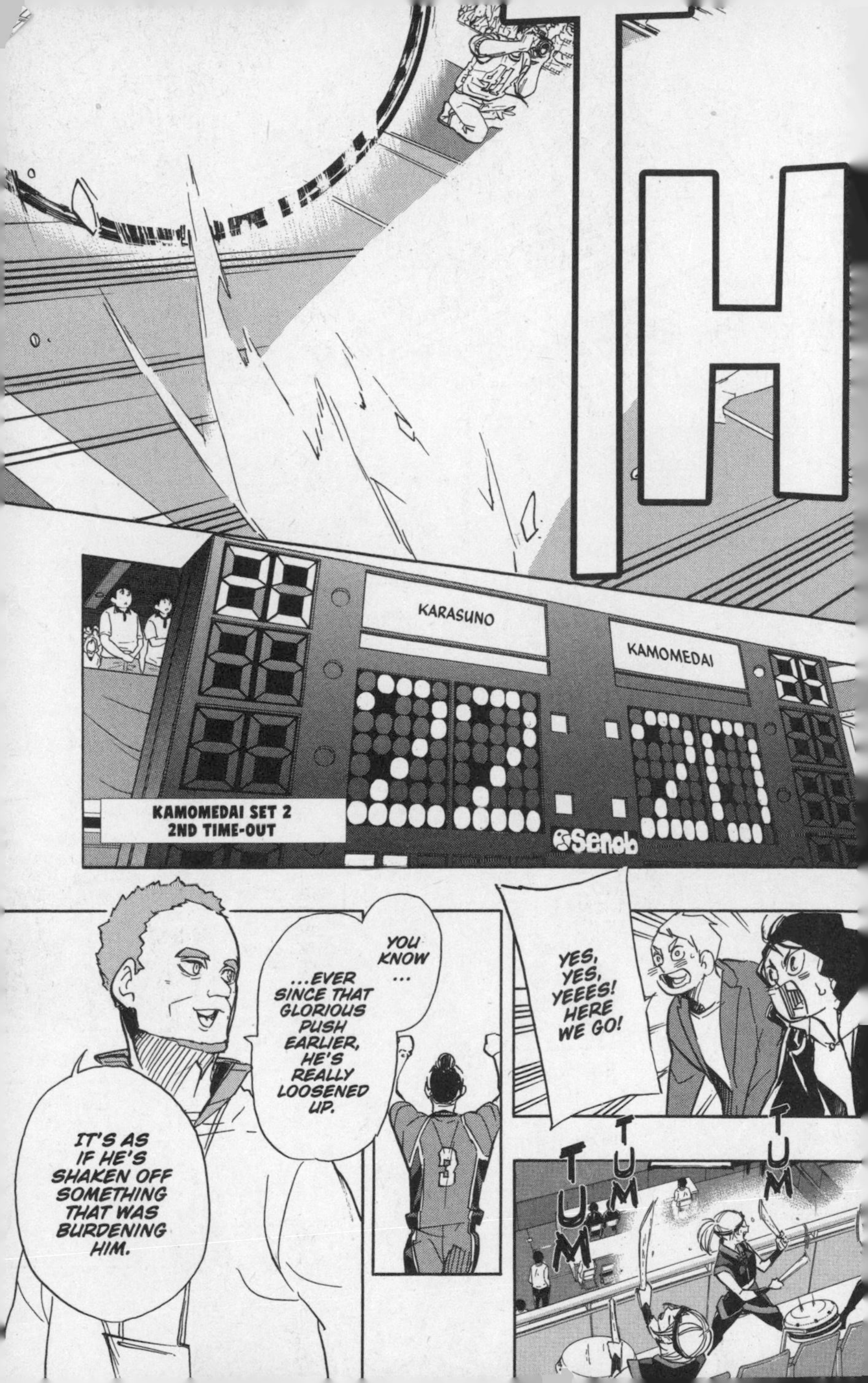
TH
KARASUNO
KAMOMEDAI
22 : 20
KAMOMEDAI SET 2
2ND TIME-OUT
YES, YES, YEEES! HERE WE GO!
TUM TUM TUM TUM
YOU KNOW ...
...EVER SINCE THAT GLORIOUS PUSH EARLIER, HE'S REALLY LOOSENED UP.
IT'S AS IF HE'S SHAKEN OFF SOMETHING THAT WAS BURDENING HIM.

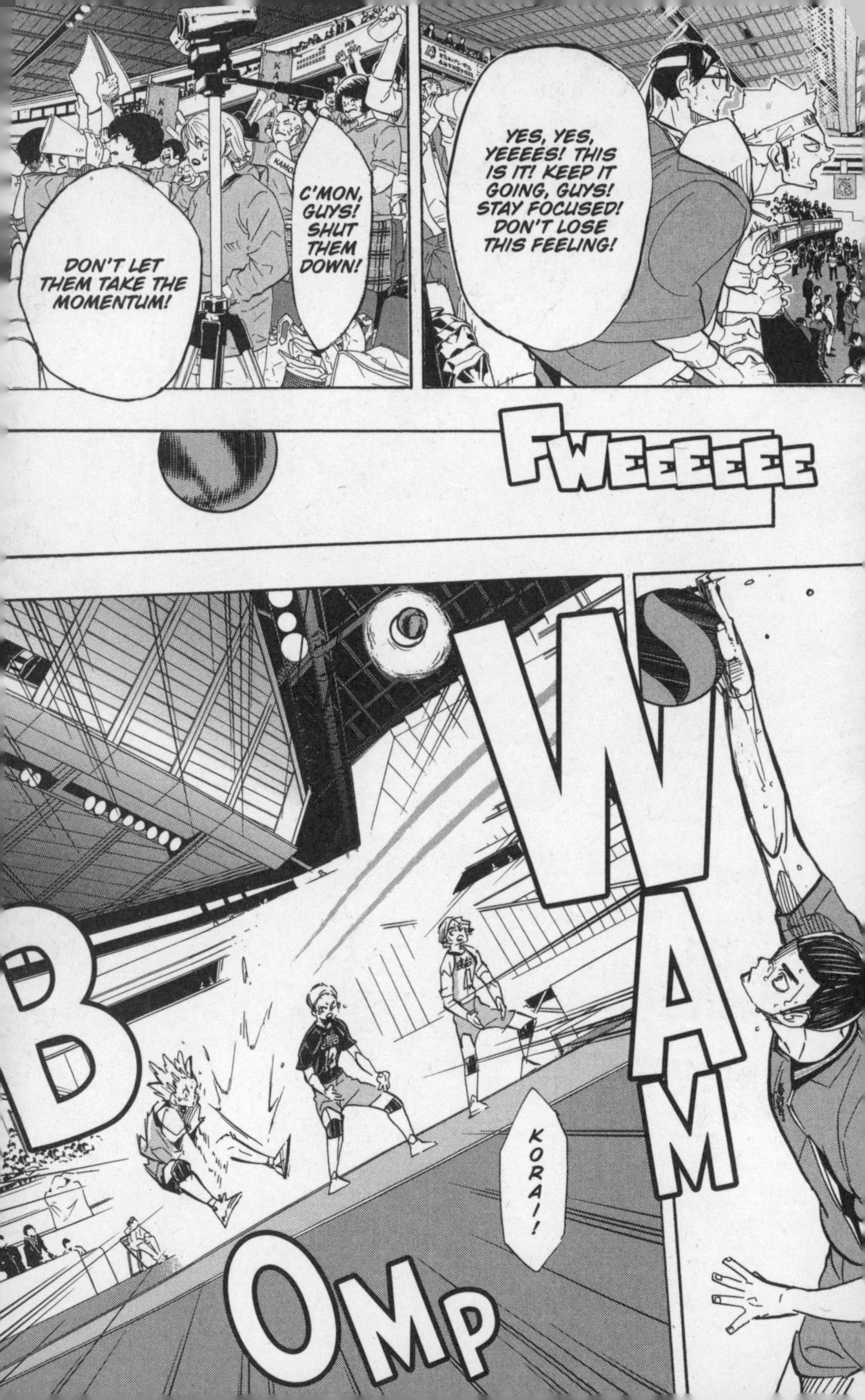
YES, YES, YEEEES! THIS IS IT! KEEP IT GOING, GUYS! STAY FOCUSED! DON'T LOSE THIS FEELING!
C'MON, GUYS! SHUT THEM DOWN!
DON'T LET THEM TAKE THE MOMENTUM!
FWEEEEEE
WAM
KORAI!
BOMP

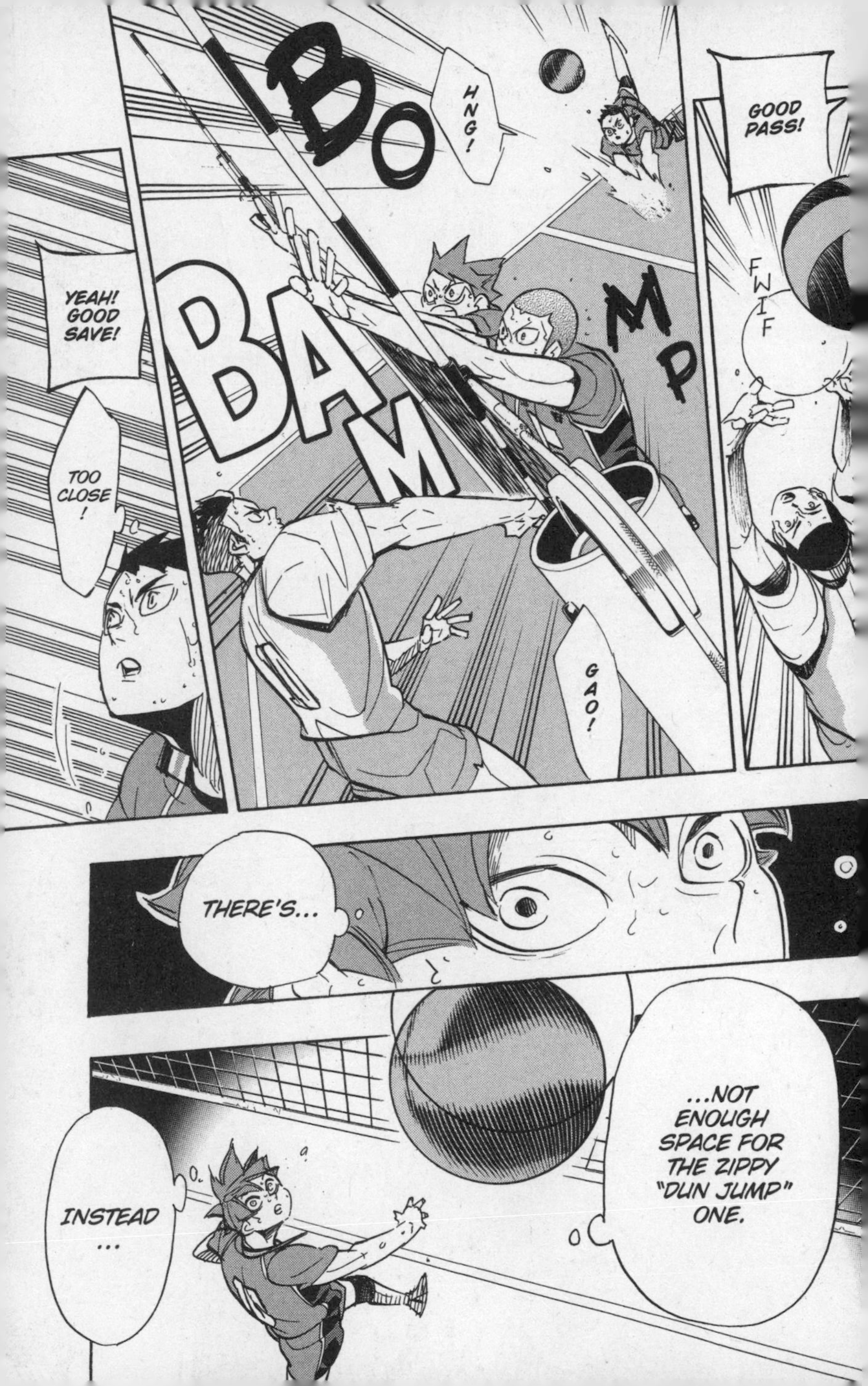
GOOD PASS!
FWIF
HNG!
BOMP
BAM
GAO!
YEAH! GOOD SAVE!
TOO CLOSE!
THERE'S...
...NOT ENOUGH SPACE FOR THE ZIPPY "DUN JUMP" ONE.
INSTEAD...

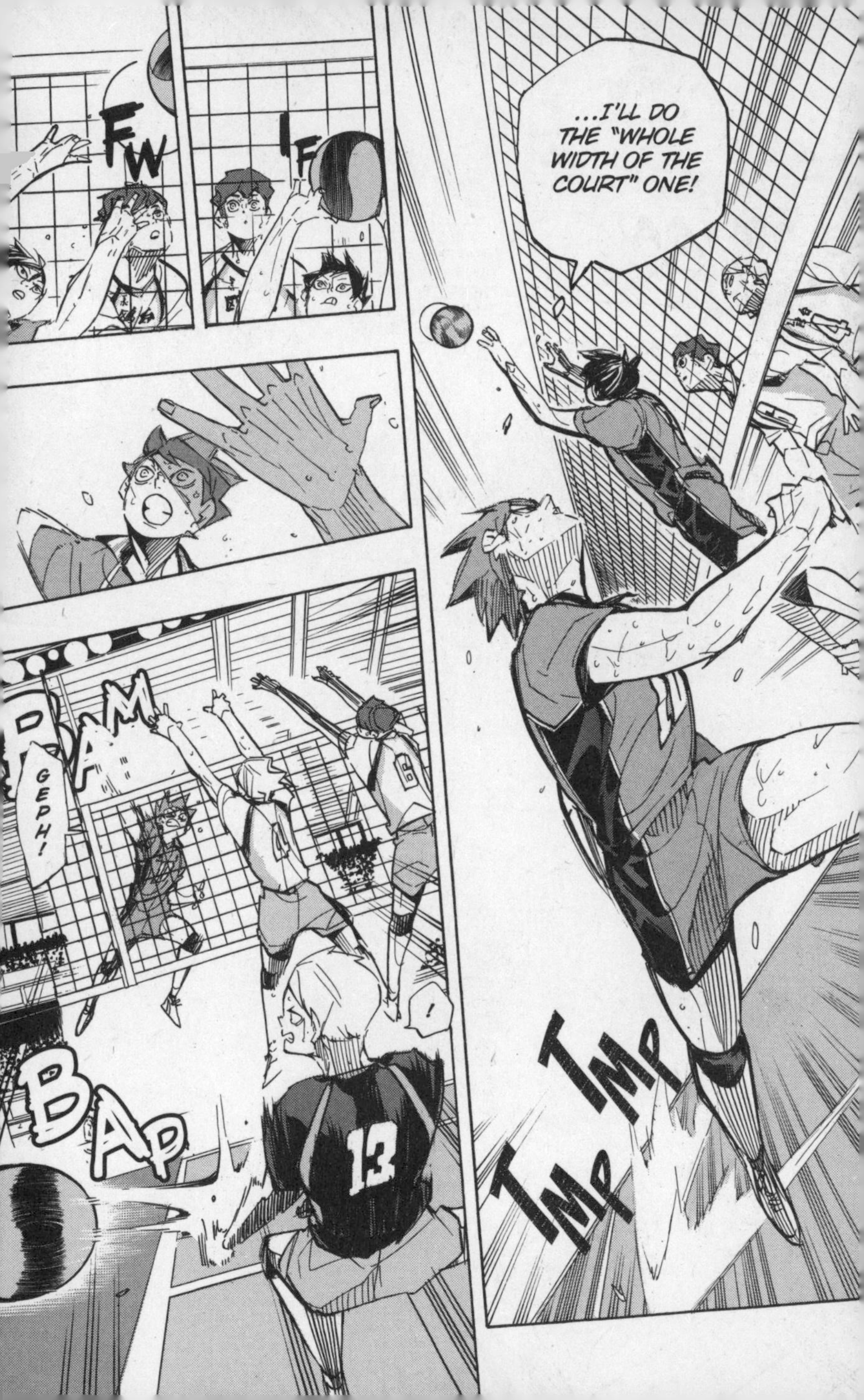
...I'LL DO THE "WHOLE WIDTH OF THE COURT" ONE!
TMP TMP
IF
FW
BAM
GEPH!
!
BAP

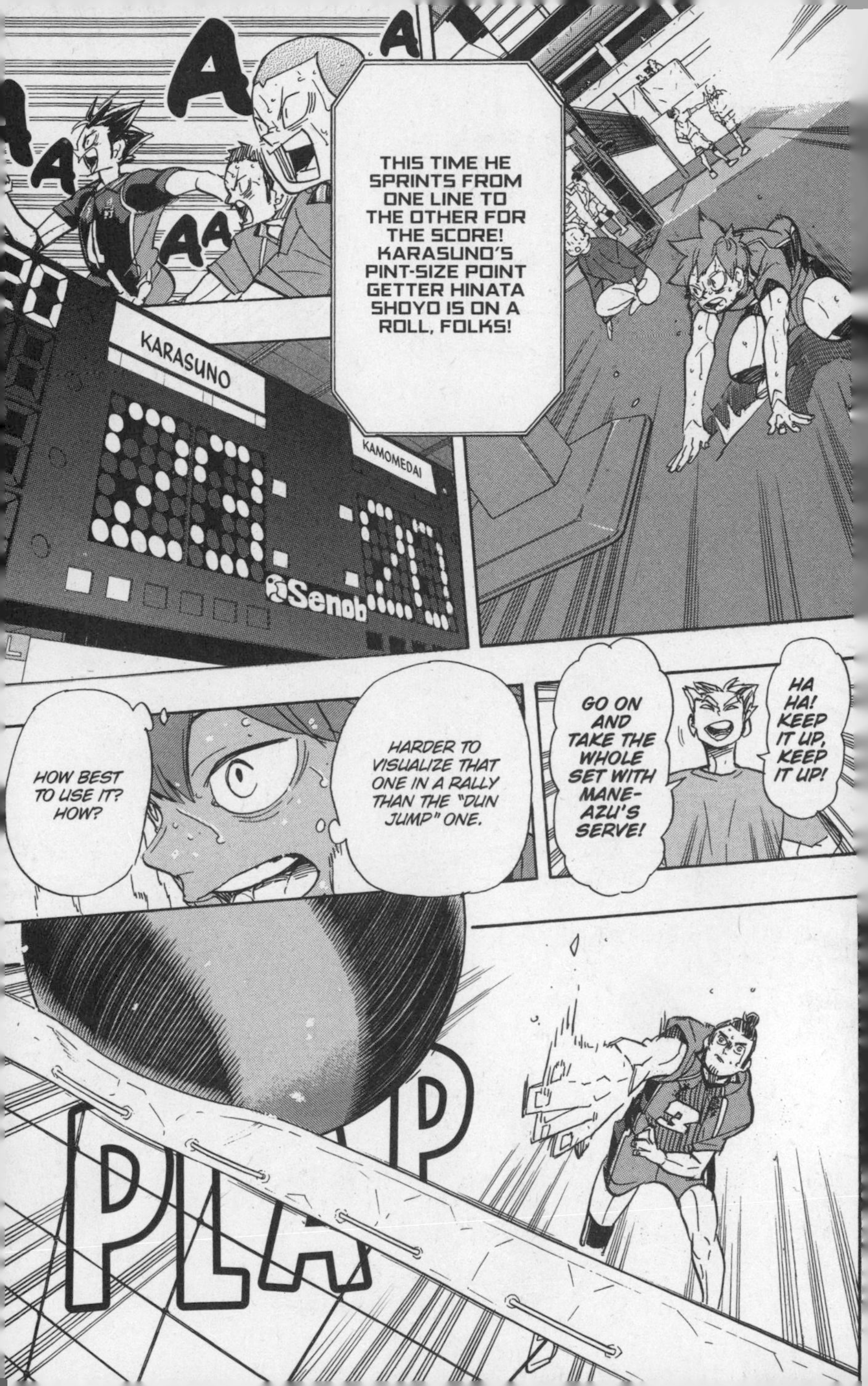
THIS TIME HE SPRINTS FROM ONE LINE TO THE OTHER FOR THE SCORE! KARASUNO'S PINT-SIZE POINT GETTER HINATA SHOYO IS ON A ROLL, FOLKS!
AAAAAA
KARASUNO
KAMOMEDAI
Senob
HA HA! KEEP IT UP, KEEP IT UP!
GO ON AND TAKE THE WHOLE SET WITH MANE-AZU'S SERVE!
HARDER TO VISUALIZE THAT ONE IN A RALLY THAN THE "DUN JUMP" ONE.
HOW BEST TO USE IT? HOW?
PLAP

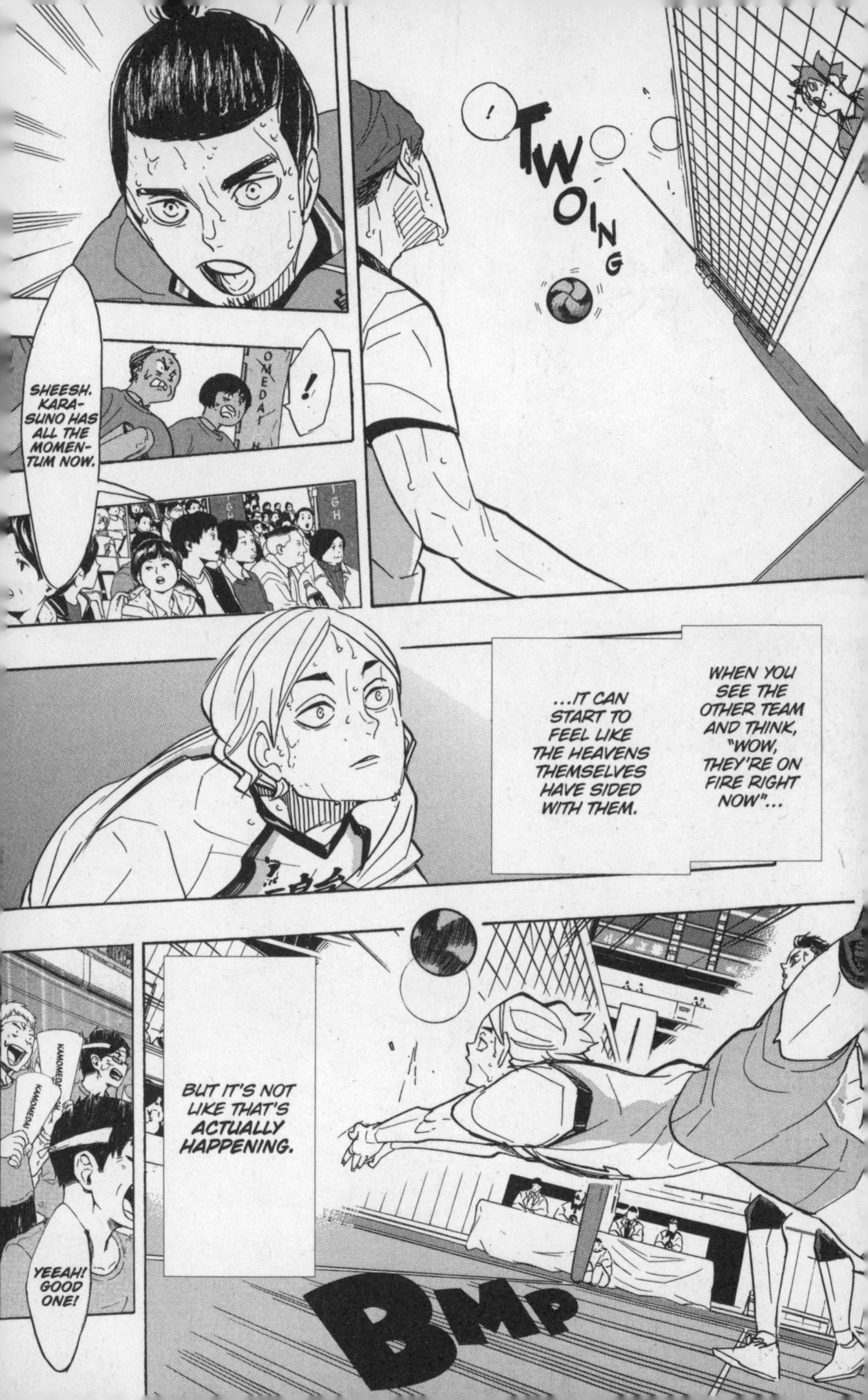
!
TWOING
!
SHEESH. KARA-SUNO HAS ALL THE MOMEN-TUM NOW.
WHEN YOU SEE THE OTHER TEAM AND THINK, "WOW, THEY'RE ON FIRE RIGHT NOW"...
...IT CAN START TO FEEL LIKE THE HEAVENS THEMSELVES HAVE SIDED WITH THEM.
BUT IT'S NOT LIKE THAT'S ACTUALLY HAPPENING.
BMP
KAMOMEDAI
KAMOMEDAI
YEEAH! GOOD ONE!

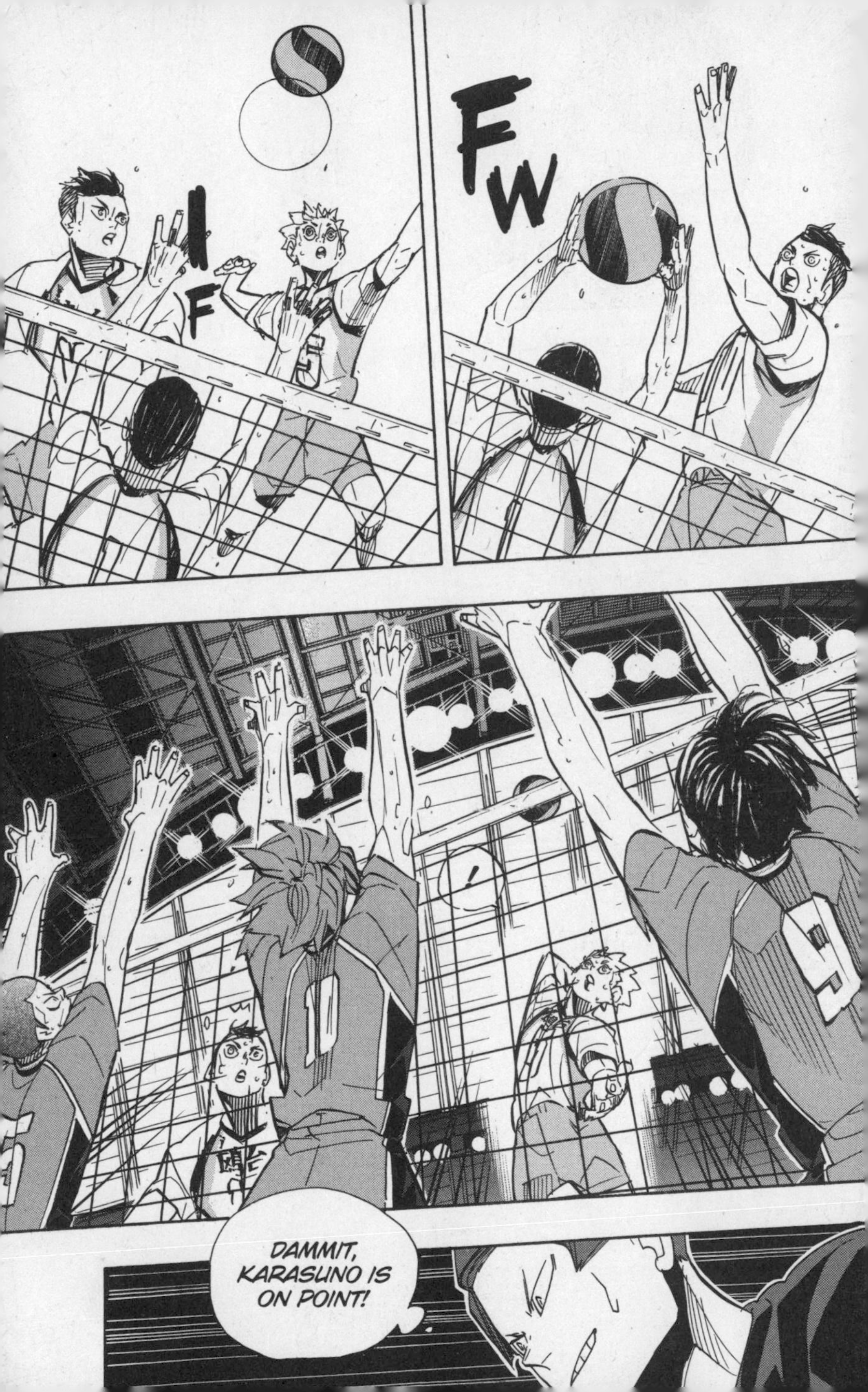
FW
IF
!
DAMMIT, KARASUNO IS ON POINT!

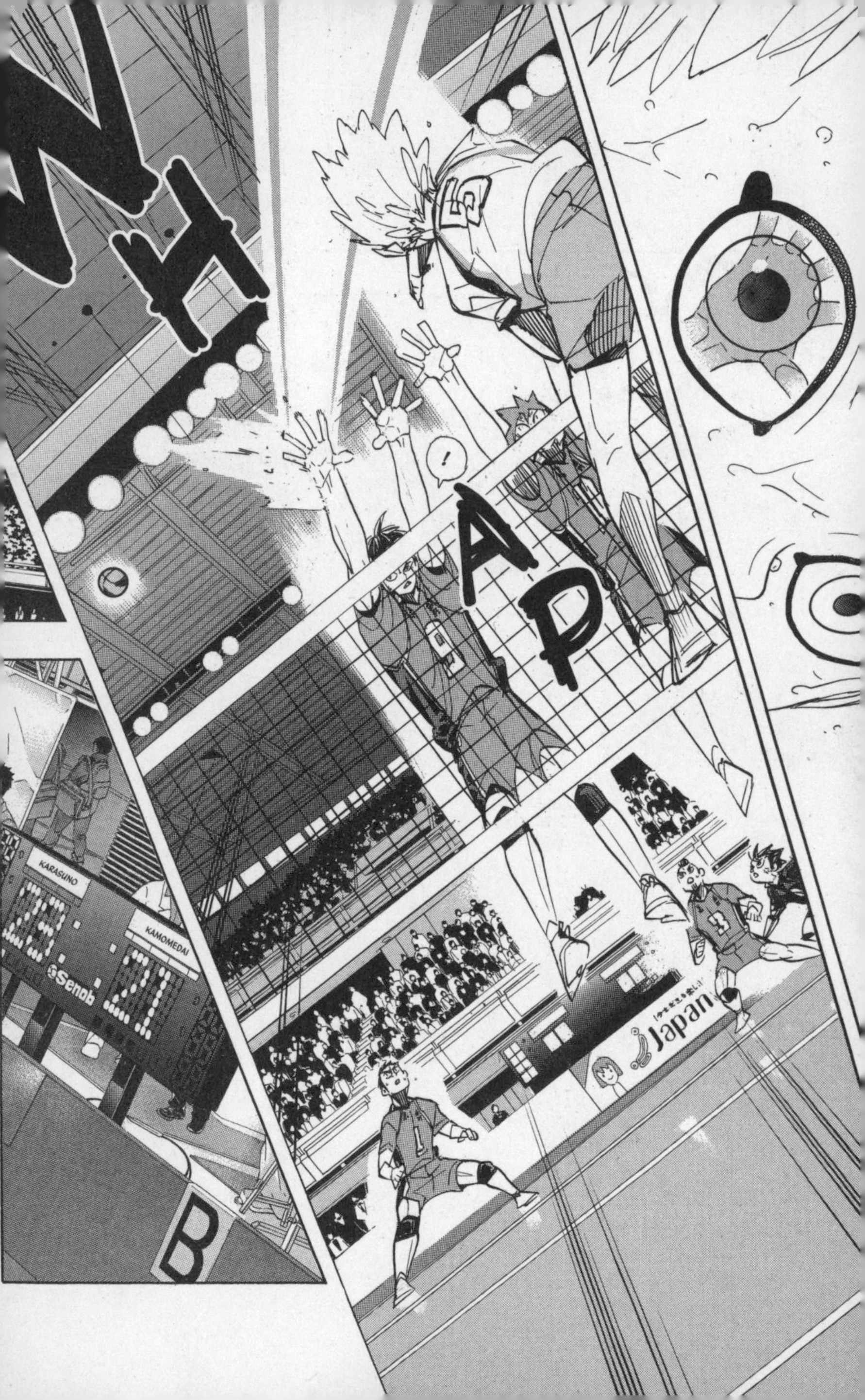
!
WH
AP
Japan
KARASUNO
KAMOMEDAI
Senob
27
B

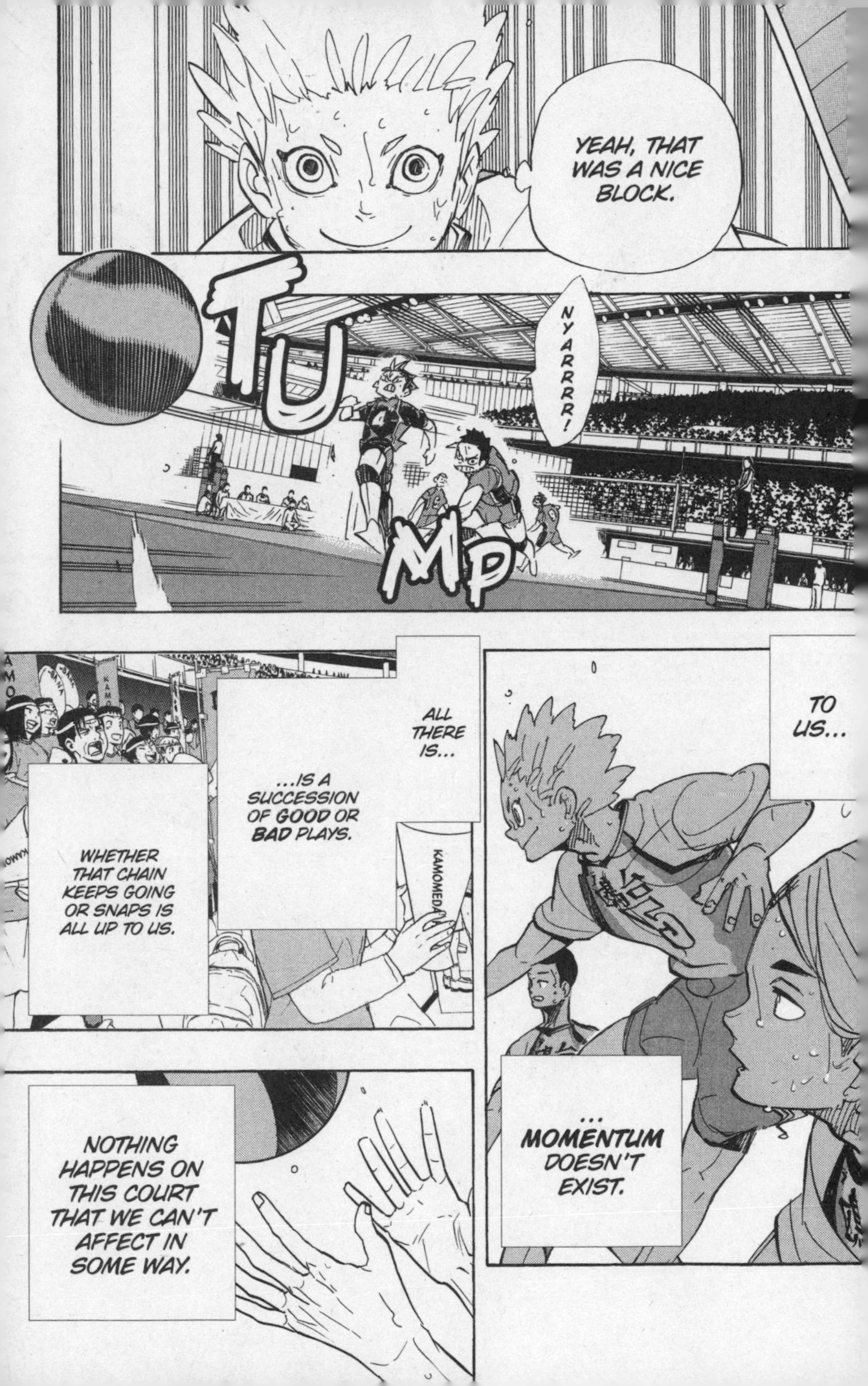
YEAH, THAT WAS A NICE BLOCK.
NYARRRR!
TUMP
TO US...
...MOMENTUM DOESN'T EXIST.
ALL THERE IS...
...IS A SUCCESSION OF GOOD OR BAD PLAYS.
KAMOMEDAI
WHETHER THAT CHAIN KEEPS GOING OR SNAPS IS ALL UP TO US.
NOTHING HAPPENS ON THIS COURT THAT WE CAN'T AFFECT IN SOME WAY.

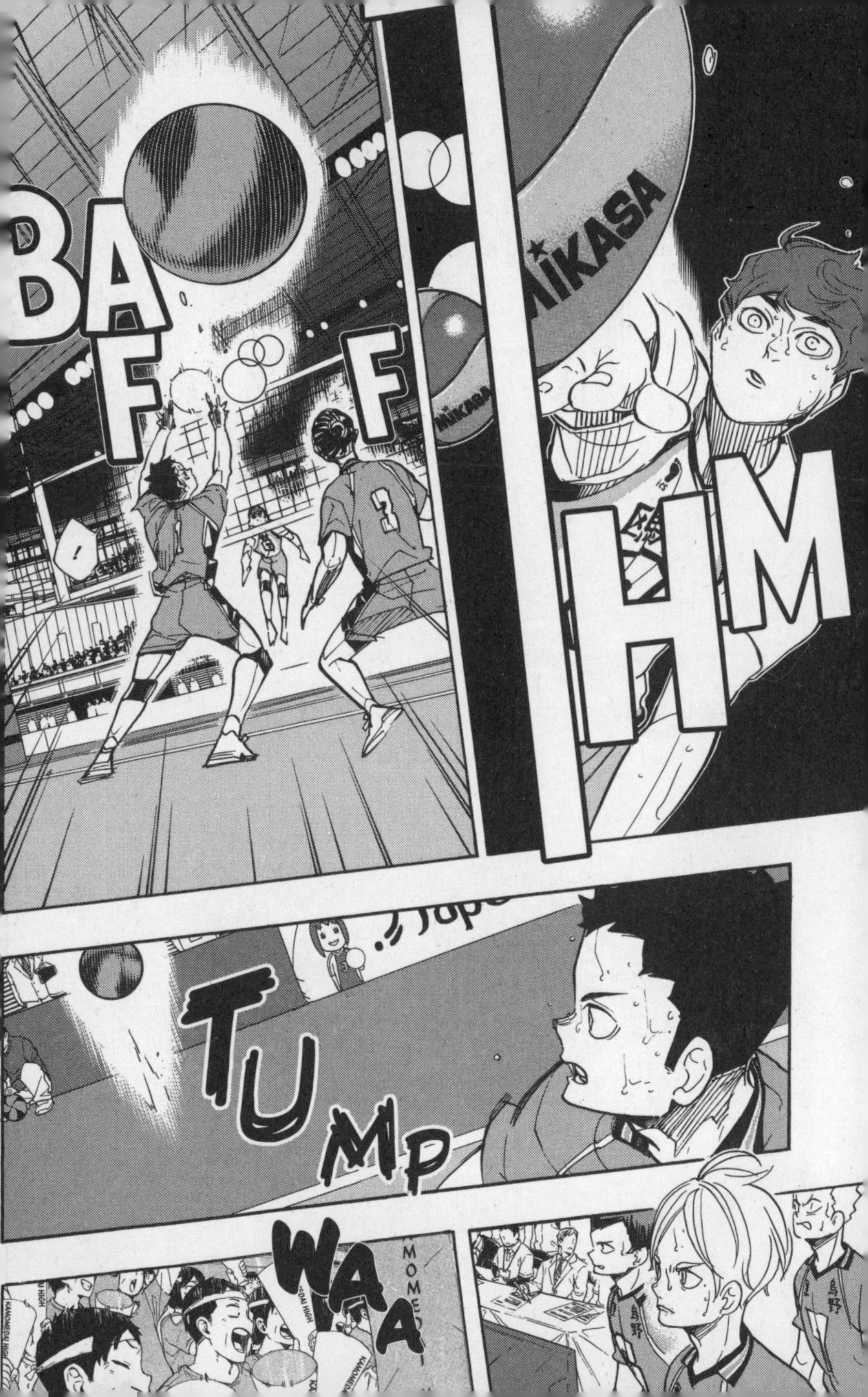
HM
MIKASA
BAFF
!
TUMP
WAAA

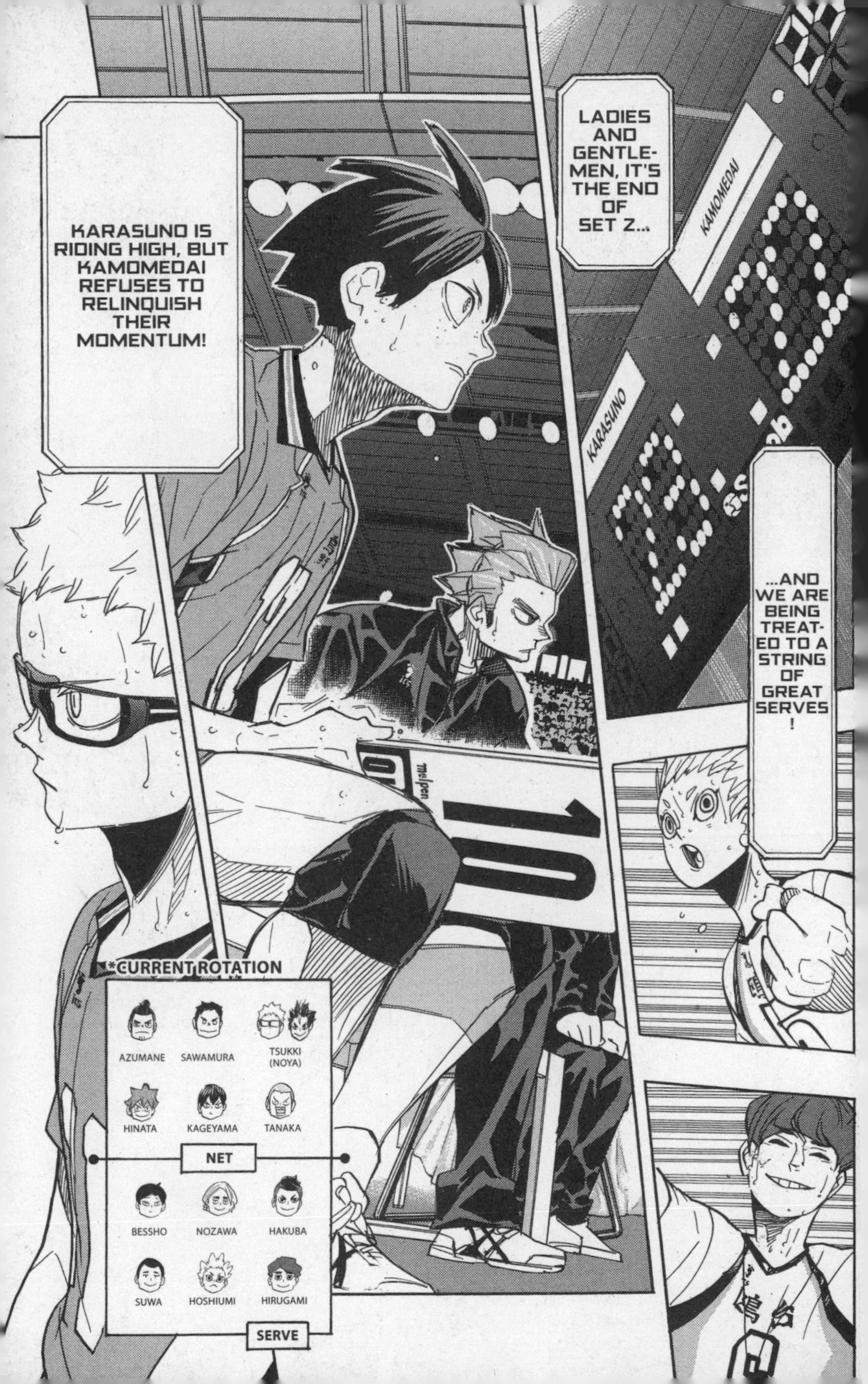
KAMOMEDAI
KARASUNO
LADIES AND GENTLEMEN, IT'S THE END OF SET 2...
...AND WE ARE BEING TREATED TO A STRING OF GREAT SERVES!
KARASUNO IS RIDING HIGH, BUT KAMOMEDAI REFUSES TO RELINQUISH THEIR MOMENTUM!
*CURRENT ROTATION
AZUMANE
SAWAMURA
TSUKKI (NOYA)
HINATA
KAGEYAMA
TANAKA
NET
BESSHO
NOZAWA
HAKUBA
SUWA
HOSHIUMI
HIRUGAMI
SERVE

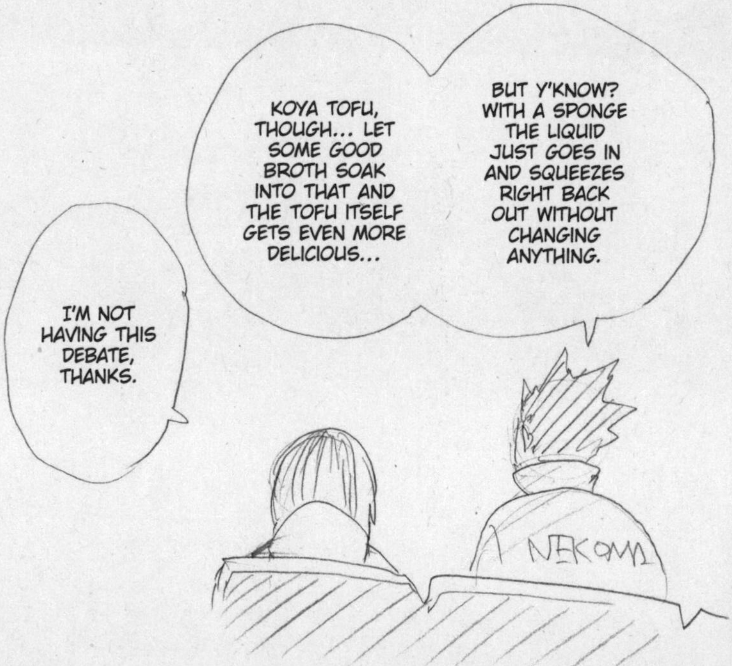
BUT Y'KNOW? WITH A SPONGE THE LIQUID JUST GOES IN AND SQUEEZES RIGHT BACK OUT WITHOUT CHANGING ANYTHING.
KOYA TOFU, THOUGH... LET SOME GOOD BROTH SOAK INTO THAT AND THE TOFU ITSELF GETS EVEN MORE DELICIOUS...
I'M NOT HAVING THIS DEBATE, THANKS.
NEKOMA

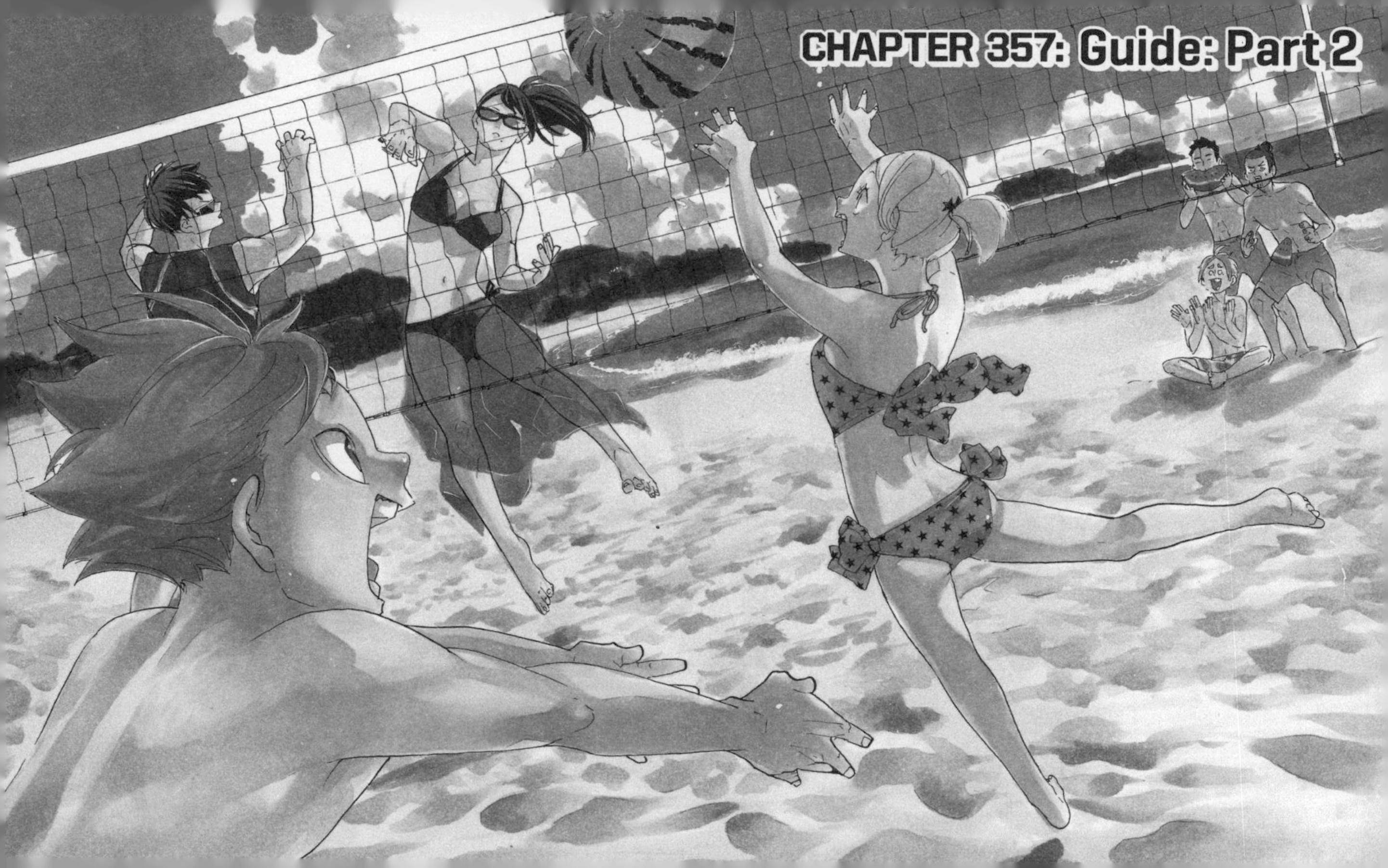
CHAPTER 357: Guide: Part 2

HAIKYU!!

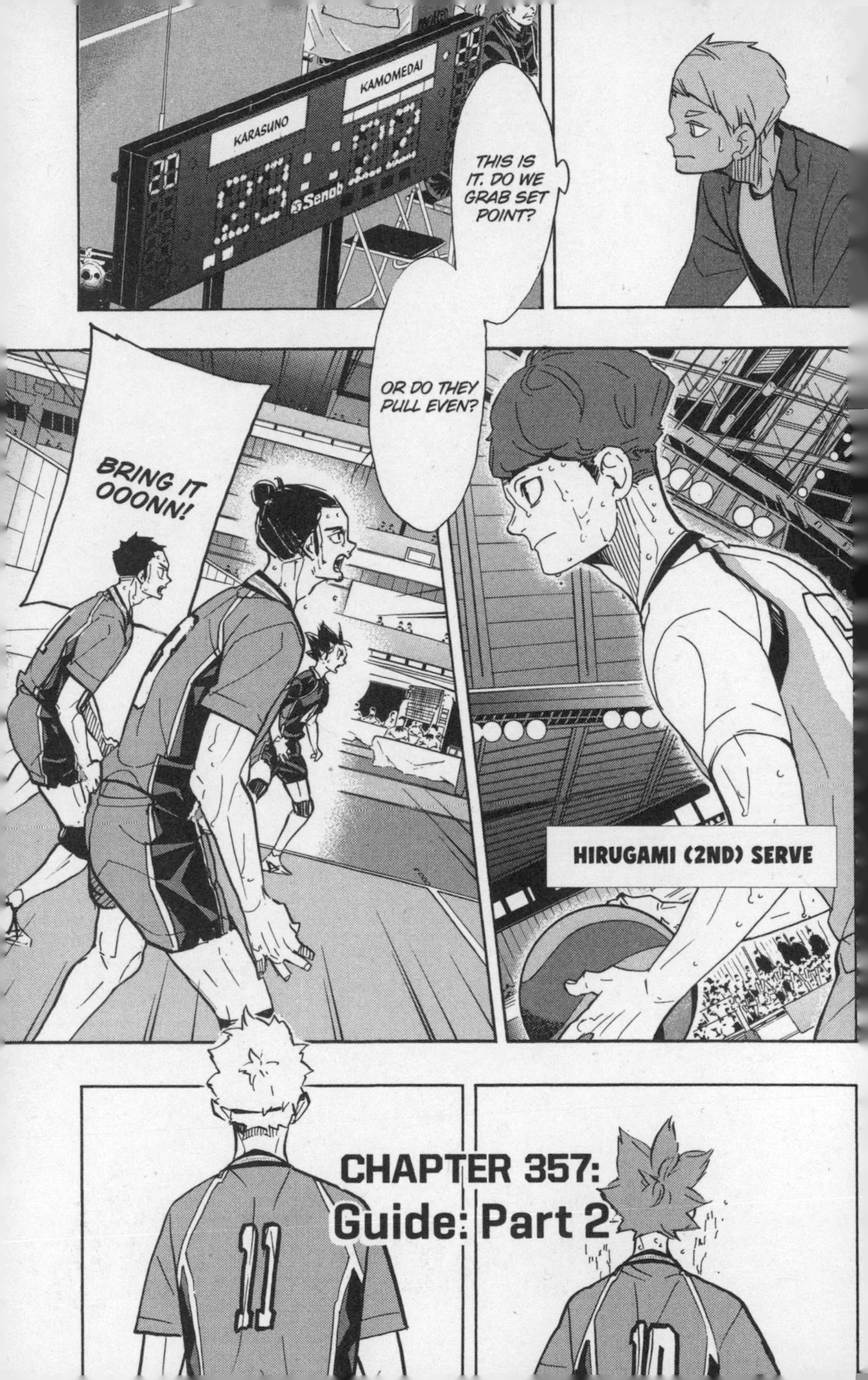
THIS IS IT. DO WE GRAB SET POINT?
KAMOMEDAI
KARASUNO
OR DO THEY PULL EVEN?
HIRUGAMI (2ND) SERVE
BRING IT OOONN!
CHAPTER 357:
Guide: Part 2

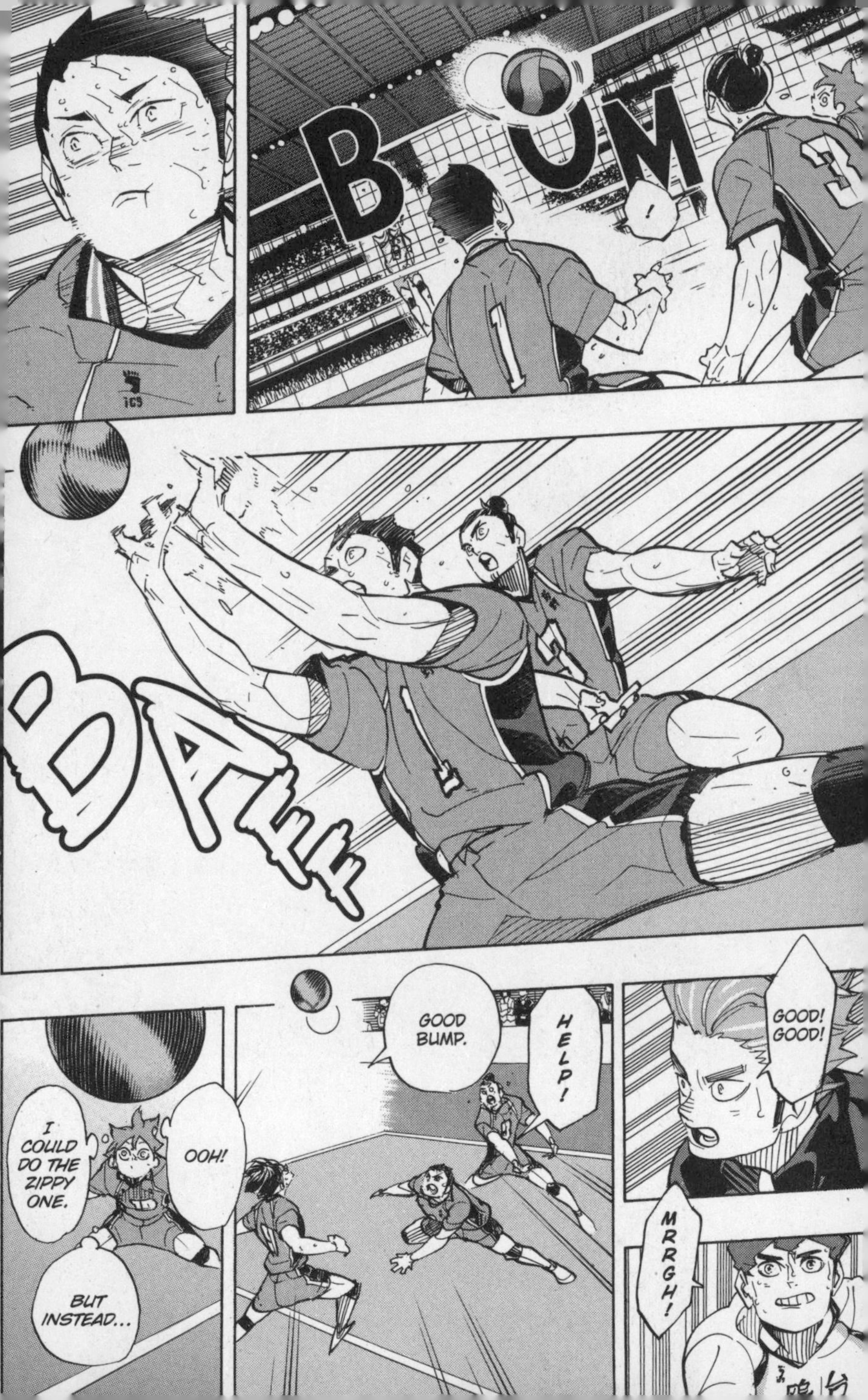
BUM
!
BA
GOOD! GOOD!
MRRGH!
HELP!
GOOD BUMP.
OOH!
I COULD DO THE ZIPPY ONE.
BUT INSTEAD...

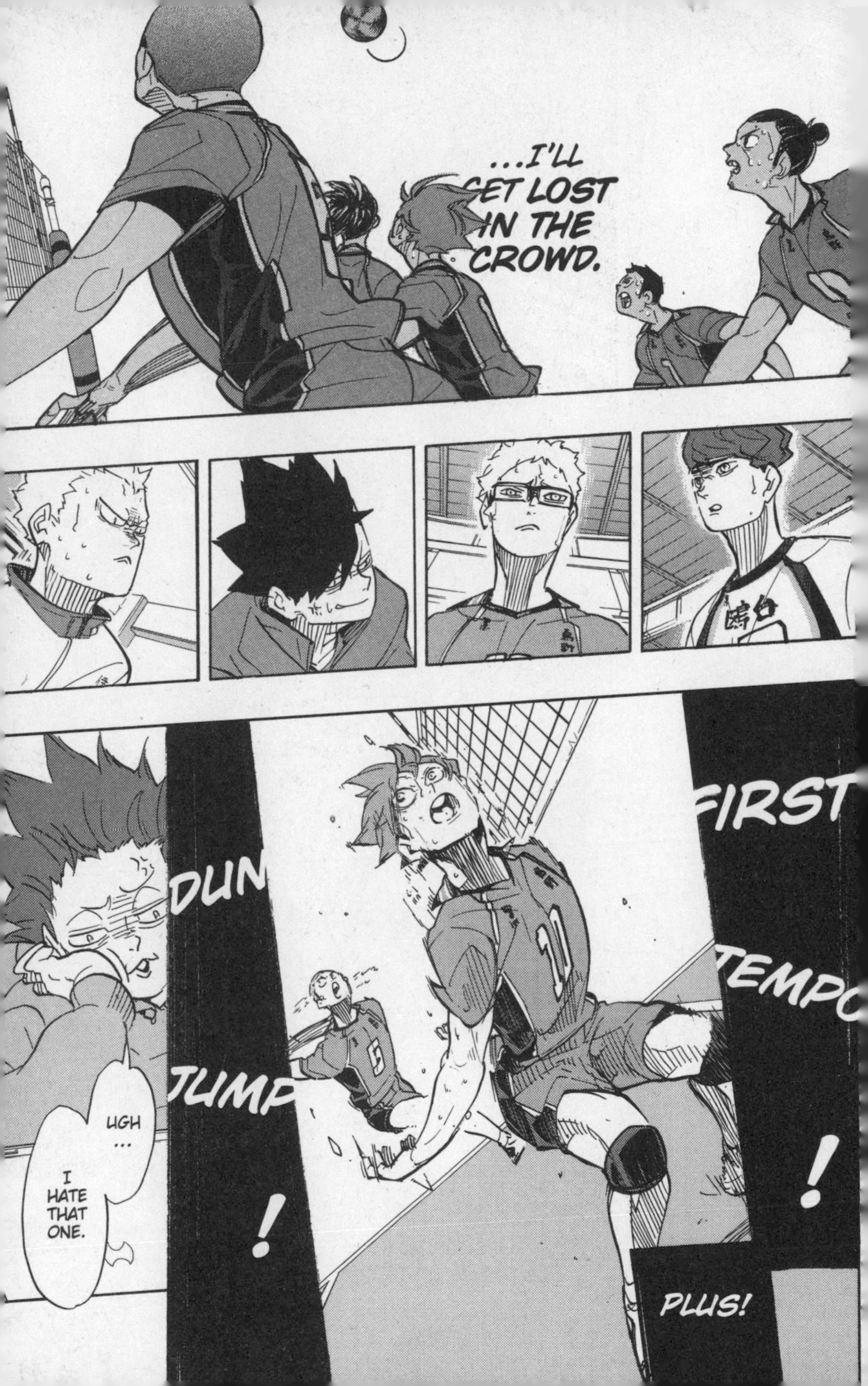
...I'LL GET LOST IN THE CROWD.
FIRST
TEMPO
!
PLUS!
DUN
JUMP
!
UGH ... I HATE THAT ONE.

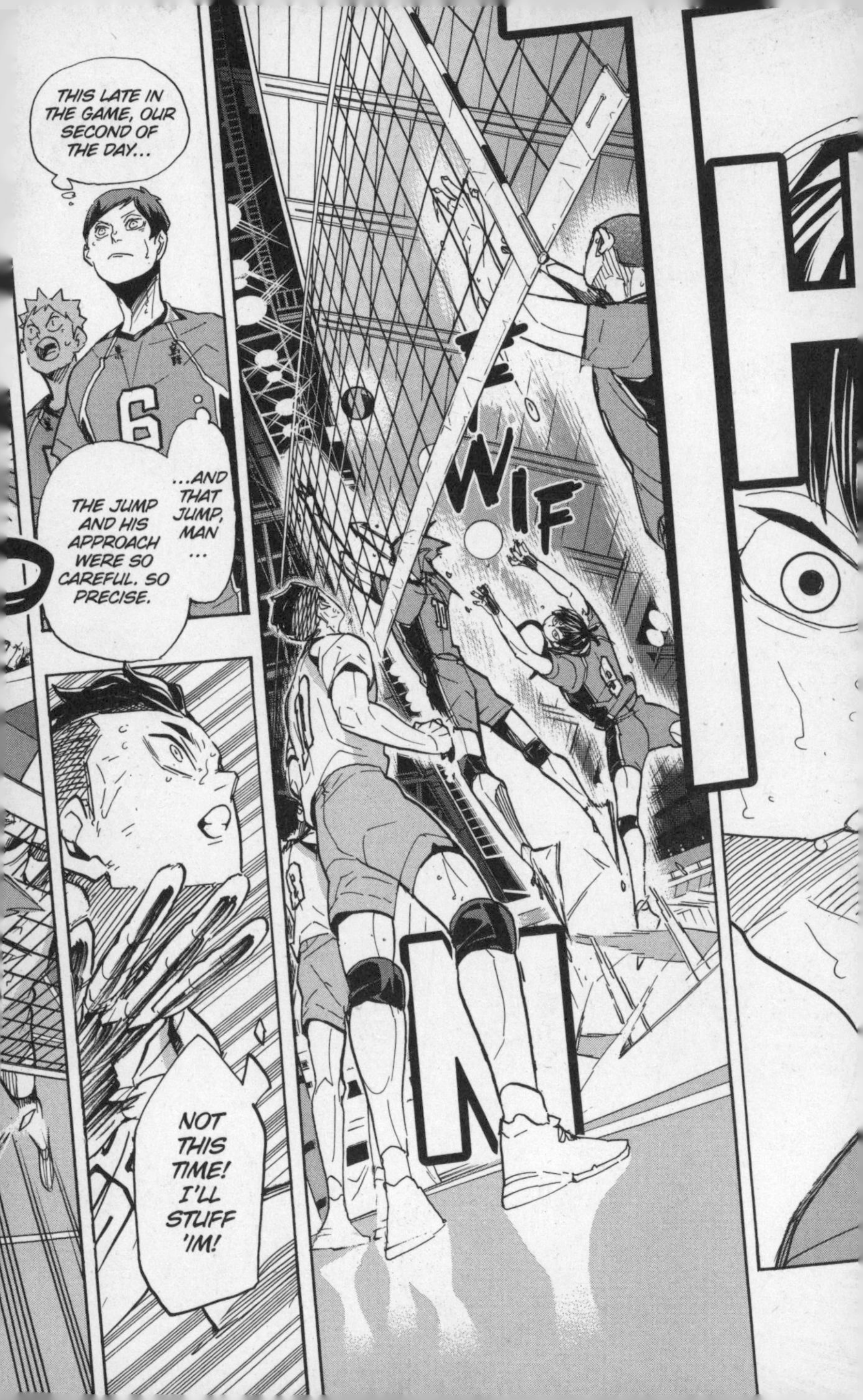
H
WIF
N
THIS LATE IN THE GAME, OUR SECOND OF THE DAY...
...AND THAT JUMP, MAN...
THE JUMP AND HIS APPROACH WERE SO CAREFUL. SO PRECISE.
NOT THIS TIME! I'LL STUFF 'IM!

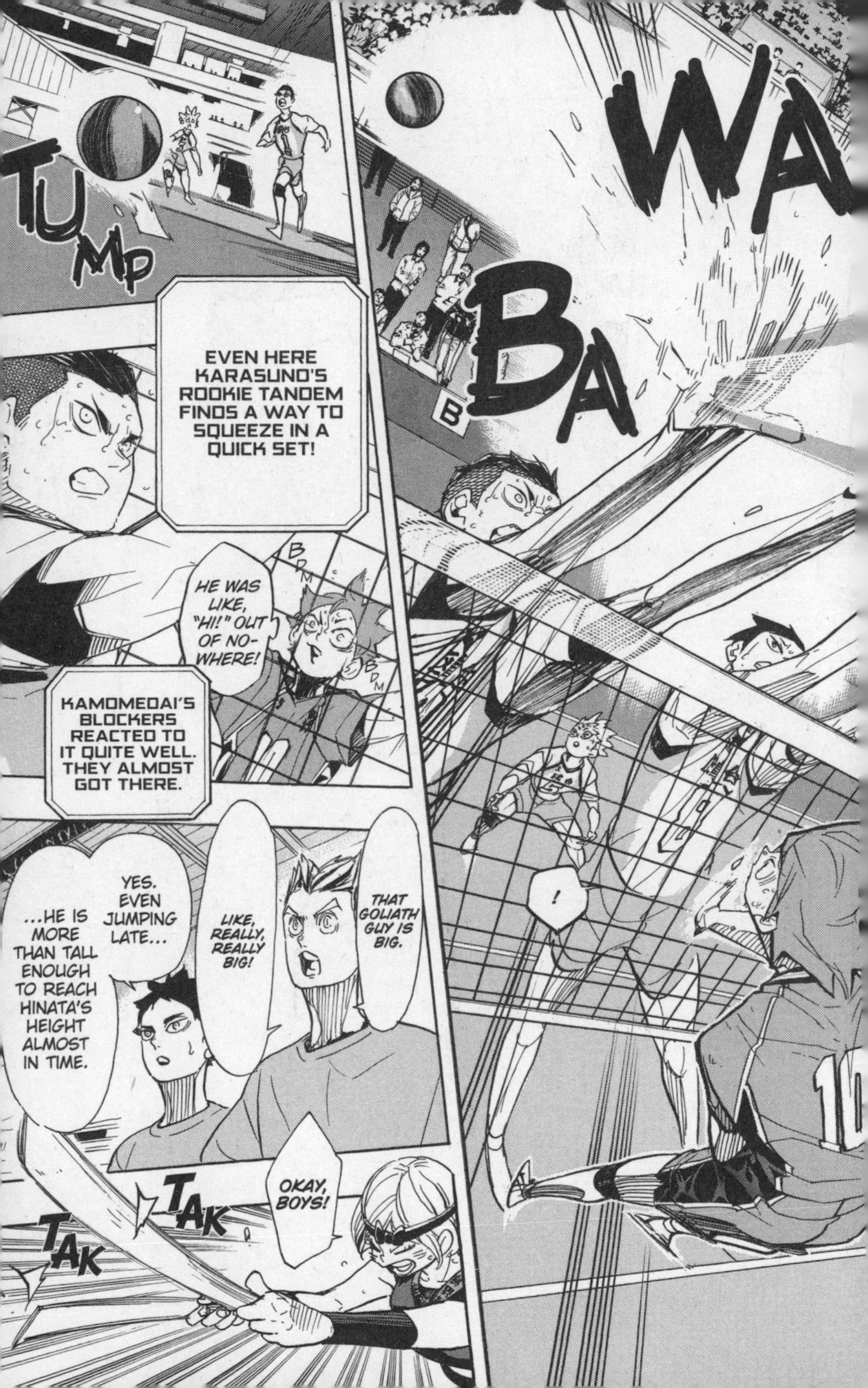
WA
BA
B
!
TUMP
EVEN HERE KARASUNO'S ROOKIE TANDEM FINDS A WAY TO SQUEEZE IN A QUICK SET!
HE WAS LIKE, "HI!" OUT OF NO-WHERE!
BDM
BDM
KAMOMEDAI'S BLOCKERS REACTED TO IT QUITE WELL. THEY ALMOST GOT THERE.
THAT GOLIATH GUY IS BIG.
LIKE, REALLY, REALLY BIG!
YES. EVEN JUMPING LATE...
...HE IS MORE THAN TALL ENOUGH TO REACH HINATA'S HEIGHT ALMOST IN TIME.
OKAY, BOYS!
TAK
TAK

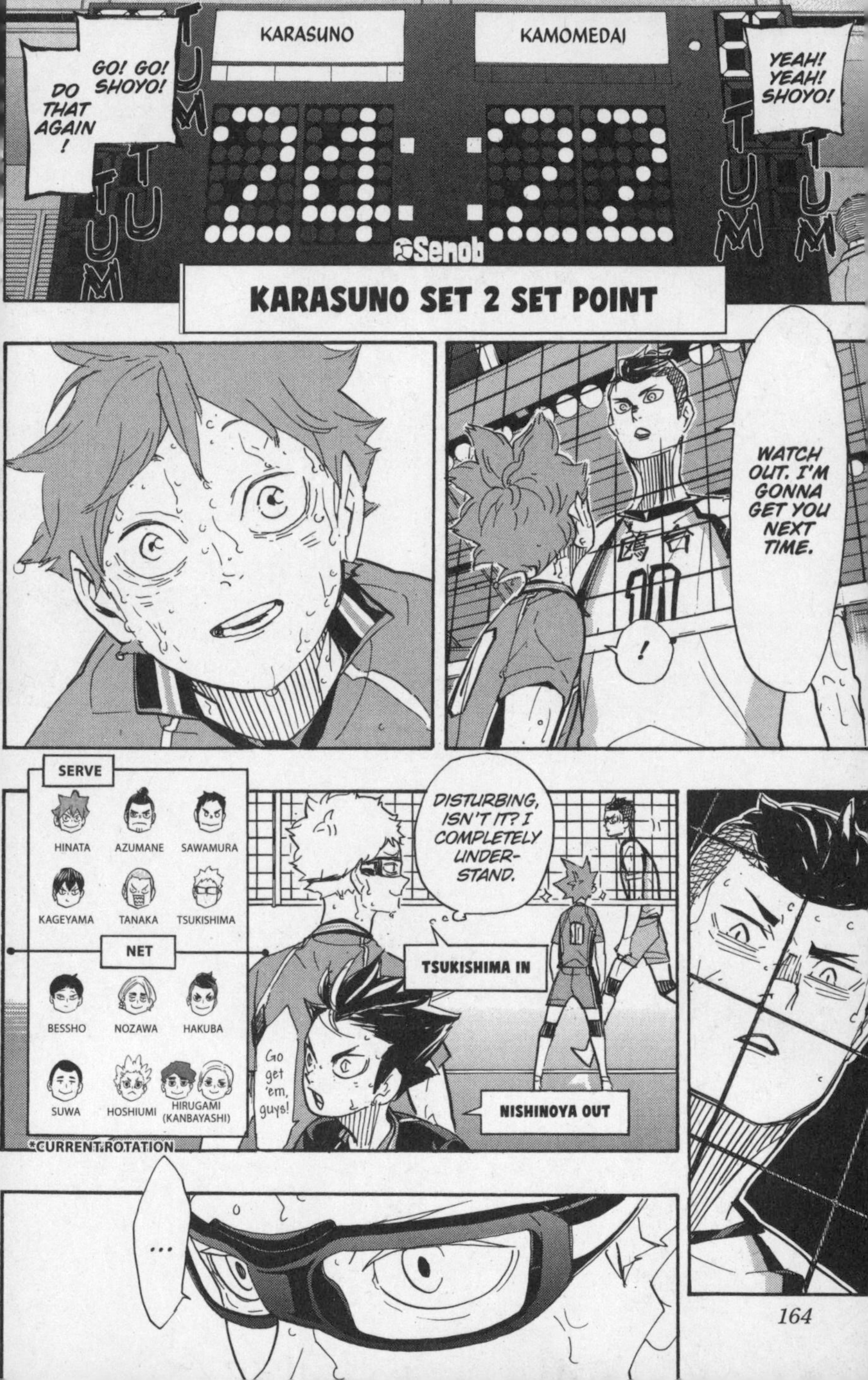
YEAH! YEAH! SHOYO!
TUM TUM TUM
KARASUNO
KAMOMEDAI
24 : 22
Senob
GO! GO! SHOYO! DO THAT AGAIN!
TUM TUM TUM
KARASUNO SET 2 SET POINT
WATCH OUT. I'M GONNA GET YOU NEXT TIME.
!
DISTURBING, ISN'T IT? I COMPLETELY UNDER-STAND.
TSUKISHIMA IN
NISHINOYA OUT
Go get 'em, guys!
SERVE
HINATA
AZUMANE
SAWAMURA
KAGEYAMA
TANAKA
TSUKISHIMA
NET
BESSHO
NOZAWA
HAKUBA
SUWA
HOSHIUMI
HIRUGAMI (KANBAYASHI)
*CURRENT ROTATION
...

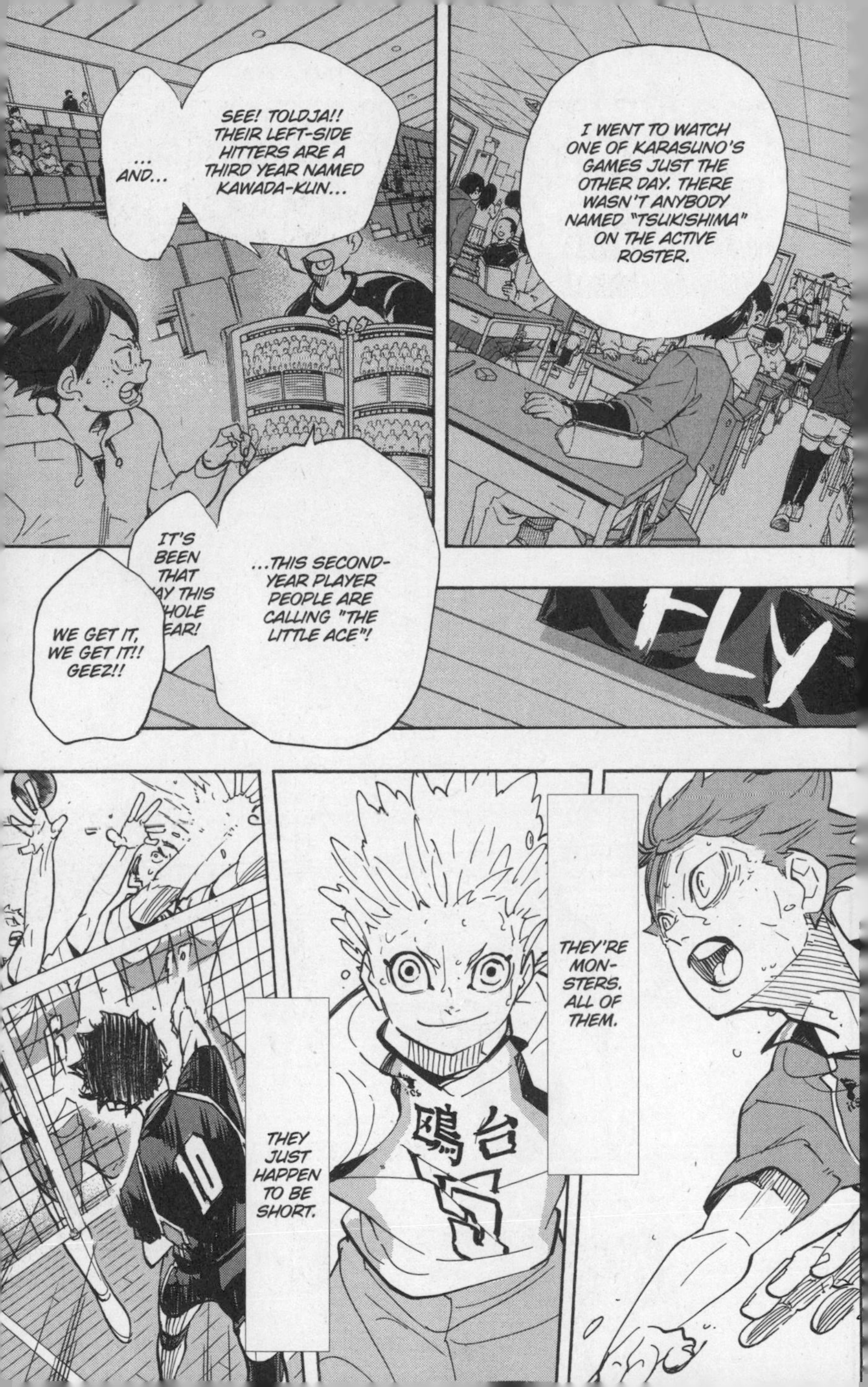
I WENT TO WATCH ONE OF KARASUNO'S GAMES JUST THE OTHER DAY. THERE WASN'T ANYBODY NAMED "TSUKISHIMA" ON THE ACTIVE ROSTER.
SEE! TOLDJA!! THEIR LEFT-SIDE HITTERS ARE A THIRD YEAR NAMED KAWADA-KUN...
...AND...
...THIS SECOND-YEAR PLAYER PEOPLE ARE CALLING "THE LITTLE ACE"!
IT'S BEEN THAT AY THIS HOLE EAR!
WE GET IT, WE GET IT!! GEEZ!!
FLY
THEY'RE MON-STERS. ALL OF THEM.
鴎台
THEY JUST HAPPEN TO BE SHORT.
10

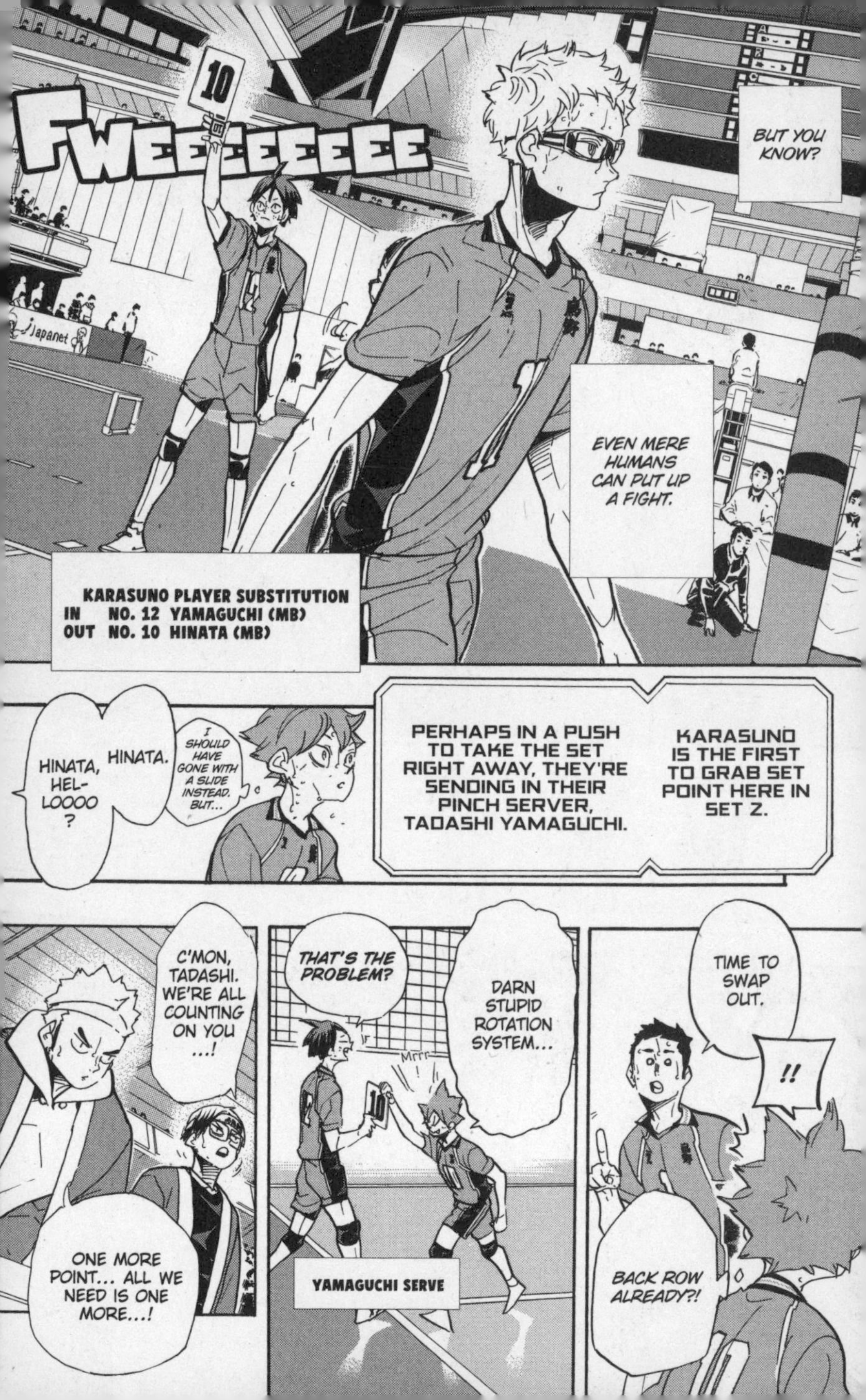
BUT YOU KNOW?
10
FWEEEEEEEE
EVEN MERE HUMANS CAN PUT UP A FIGHT.
KARASUNO PLAYER SUBSTITUTION
IN NO. 12 YAMAGUCHI (MB)
OUT NO. 10 HINATA (MB)
KARASUNO IS THE FIRST TO GRAB SET POINT HERE IN SET 2.
PERHAPS IN A PUSH TO TAKE THE SET RIGHT AWAY, THEY'RE SENDING IN THEIR PINCH SERVER, TADASHI YAMAGUCHI.
I SHOULD HAVE GONE WITH A SLIDE INSTEAD. BUT...
HINATA.
HINATA, HEL-LOOOO?
TIME TO SWAP OUT.
!!
BACK ROW ALREADY?!
DARN STUPID ROTATION SYSTEM...
THAT'S THE PROBLEM?
Mrrr
YAMAGUCHI SERVE
C'MON, TADASHI. WE'RE ALL COUNTING ON YOU ...!
ONE MORE POINT... ALL WE NEED IS ONE MORE...!

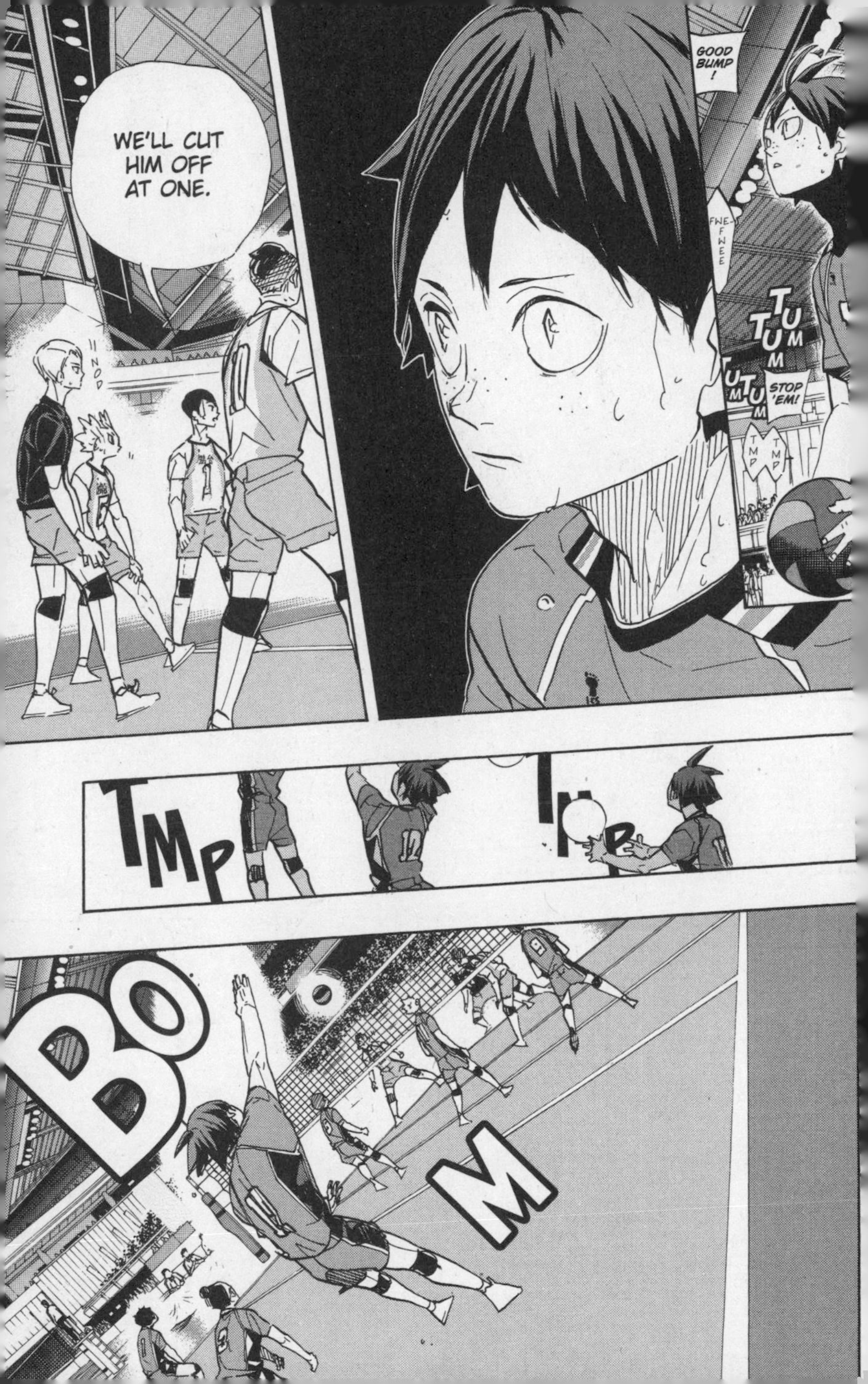
GOOD BUMP!
FWE-FWEE
TUM TUM TUM TUM
STOP 'EM!
TMP TMP
WE'LL CUT HIM OFF AT ONE.
NOD
TMP
TMP
BOOM

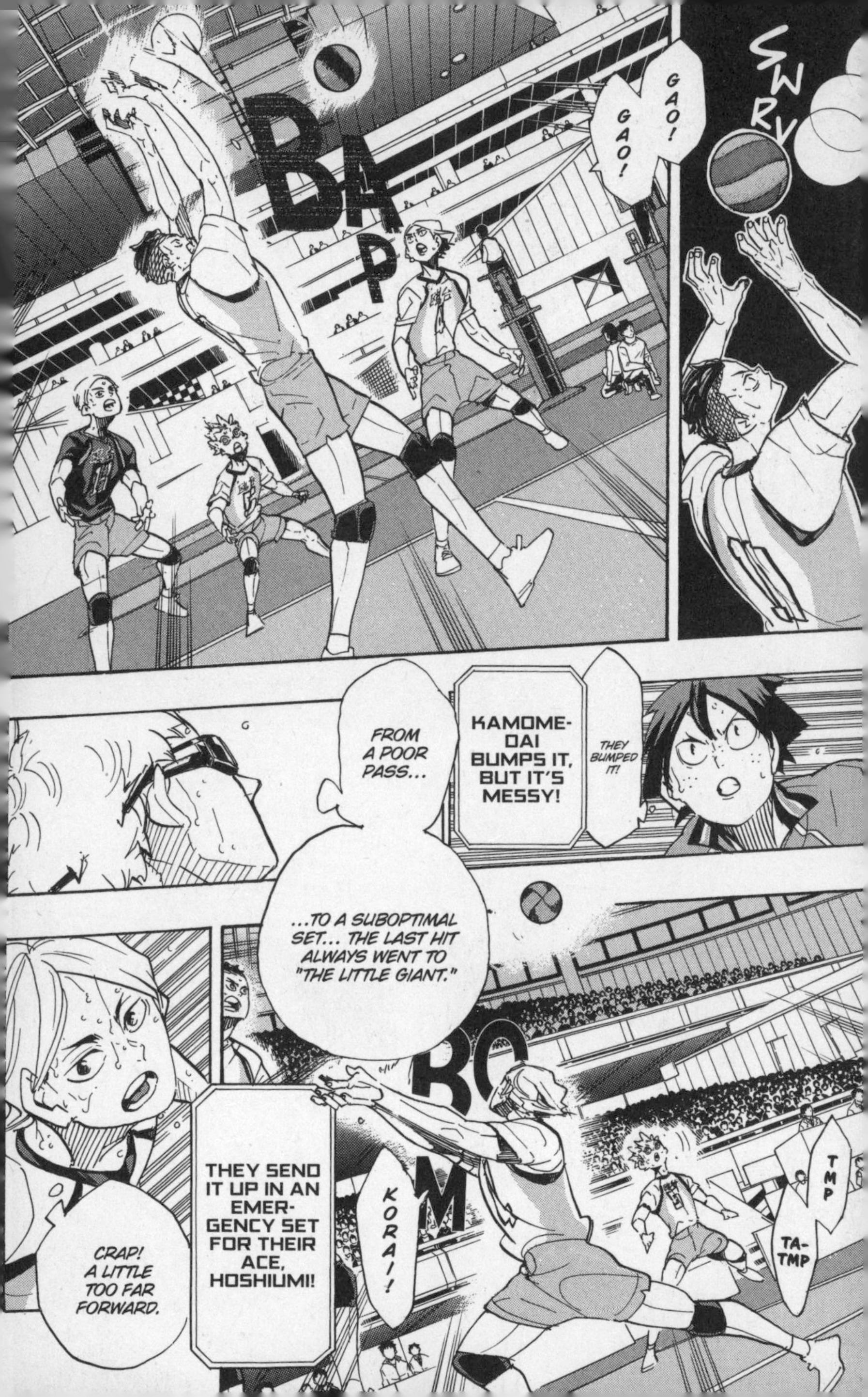
SWRV
BAP
GAO! GAO! GAO!
THEY BUMPED IT!
KAMOME-DAI BUMPS IT, BUT IT'S MESSY!
FROM A POOR PASS...
...TO A SUBOPTIMAL SET... THE LAST HIT ALWAYS WENT TO "THE LITTLE GIANT."
TMP
TA-TMP
BOOM
KORAI!
THEY SEND IT UP IN AN EMERGENCY SET FOR THEIR ACE, HOSHIUMI!
CRAP! A LITTLE TOO FAR FORWARD.

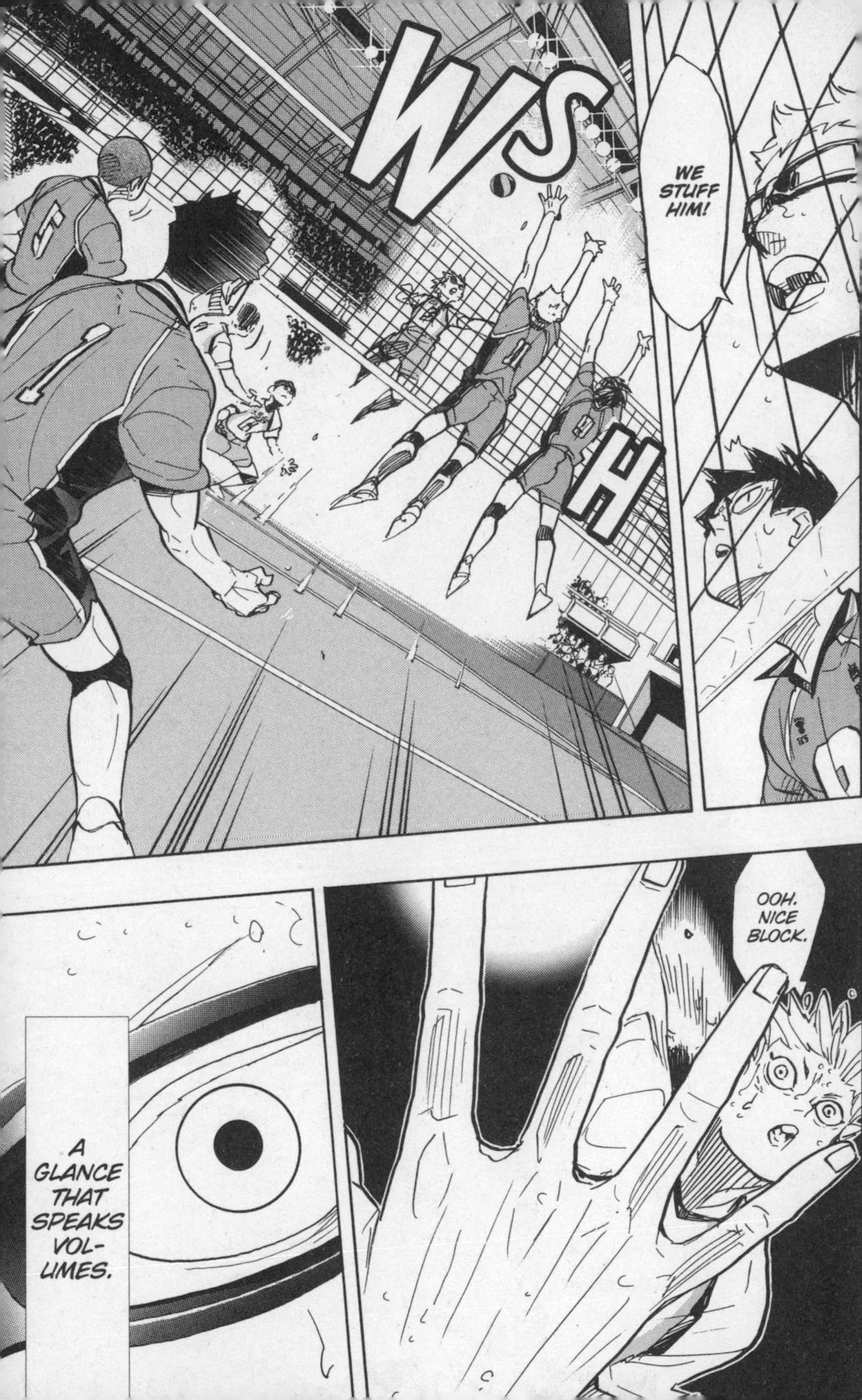
WE STUFF HIM!
WS
H
OOH. NICE BLOCK.
A GLANCE THAT SPEAKS VOL-UMES.

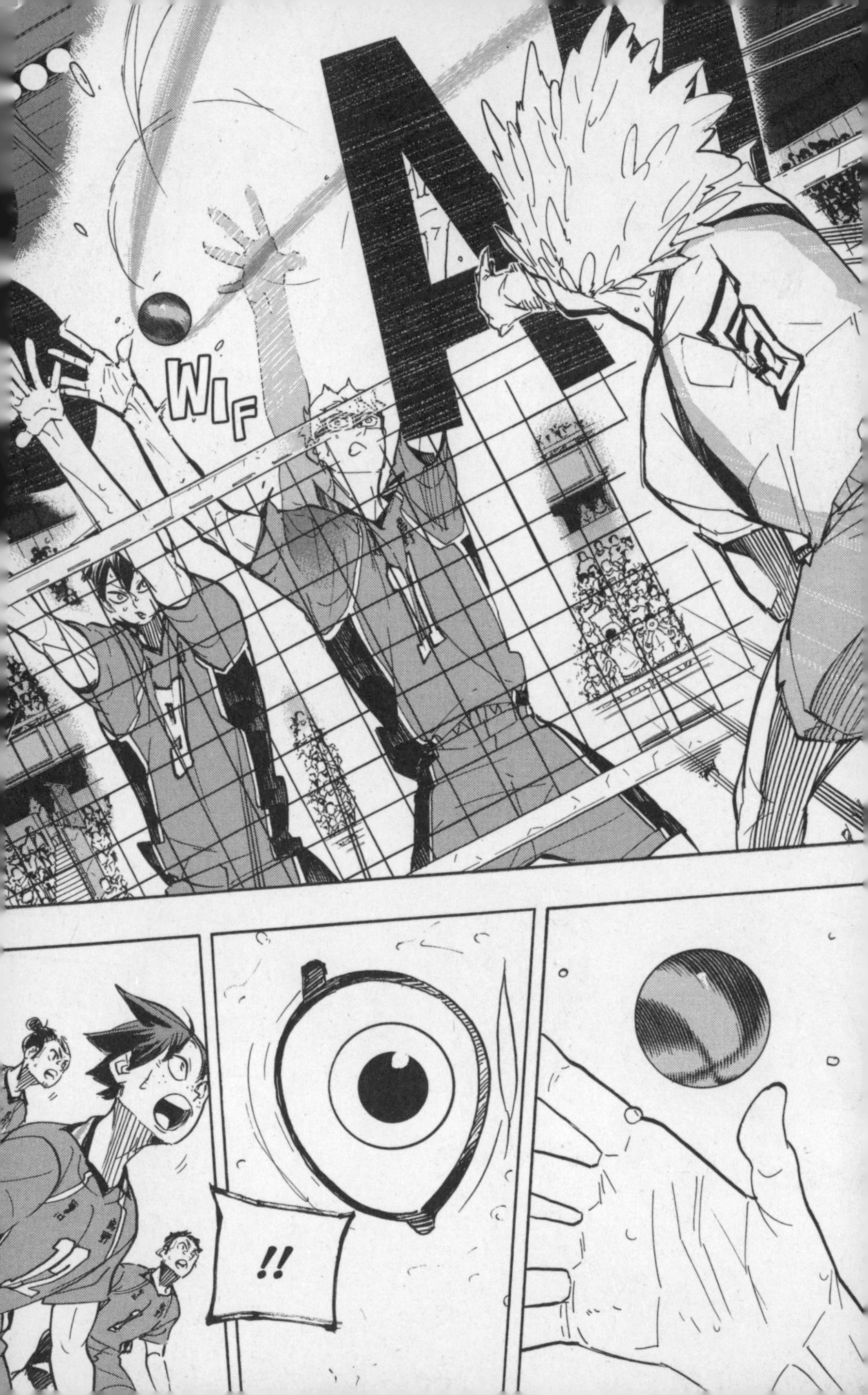
WIF
!!

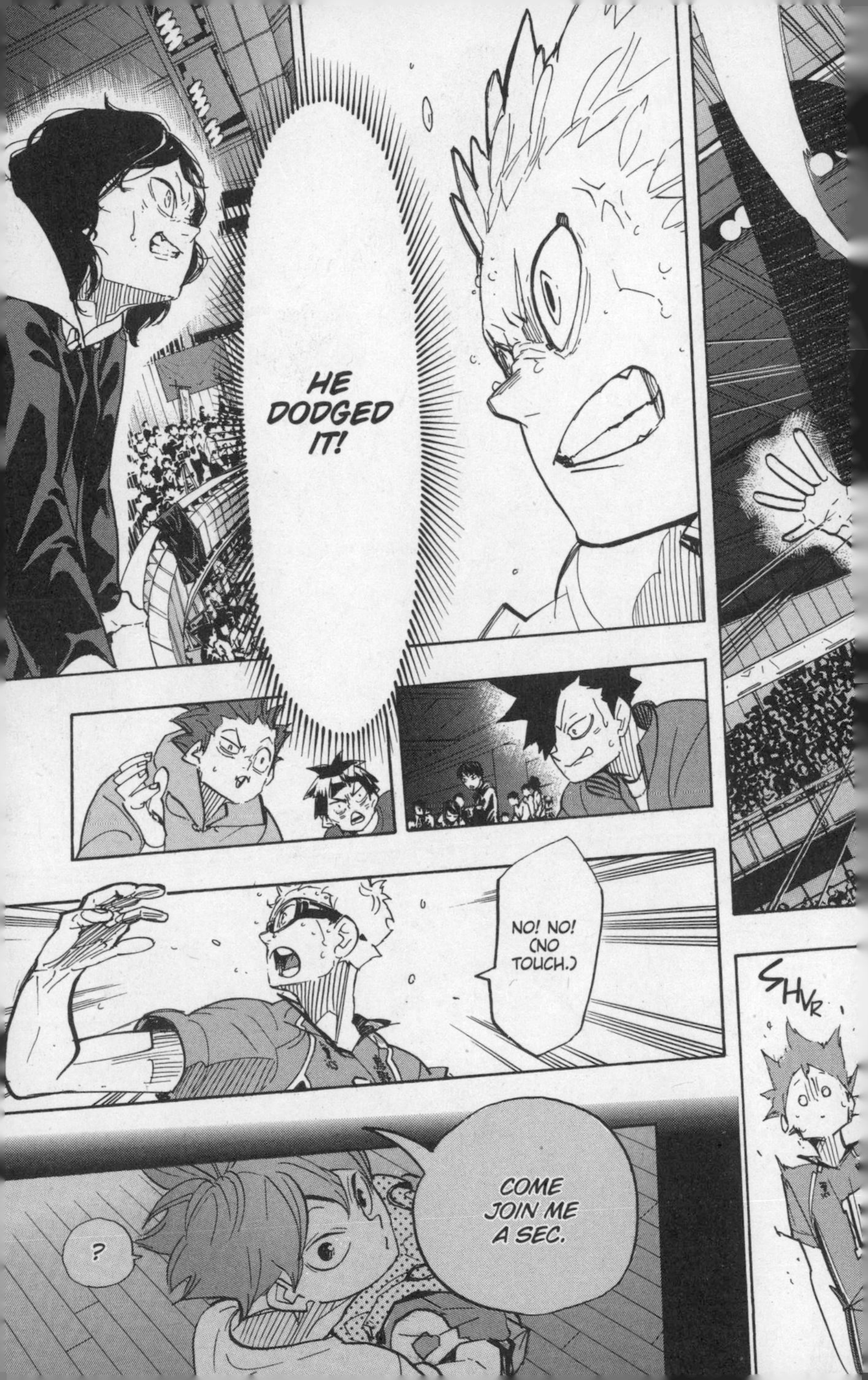
HE DODGED IT!
SHVR
NO! NO! (NO TOUCH.)
COME JOIN ME A SEC.
?

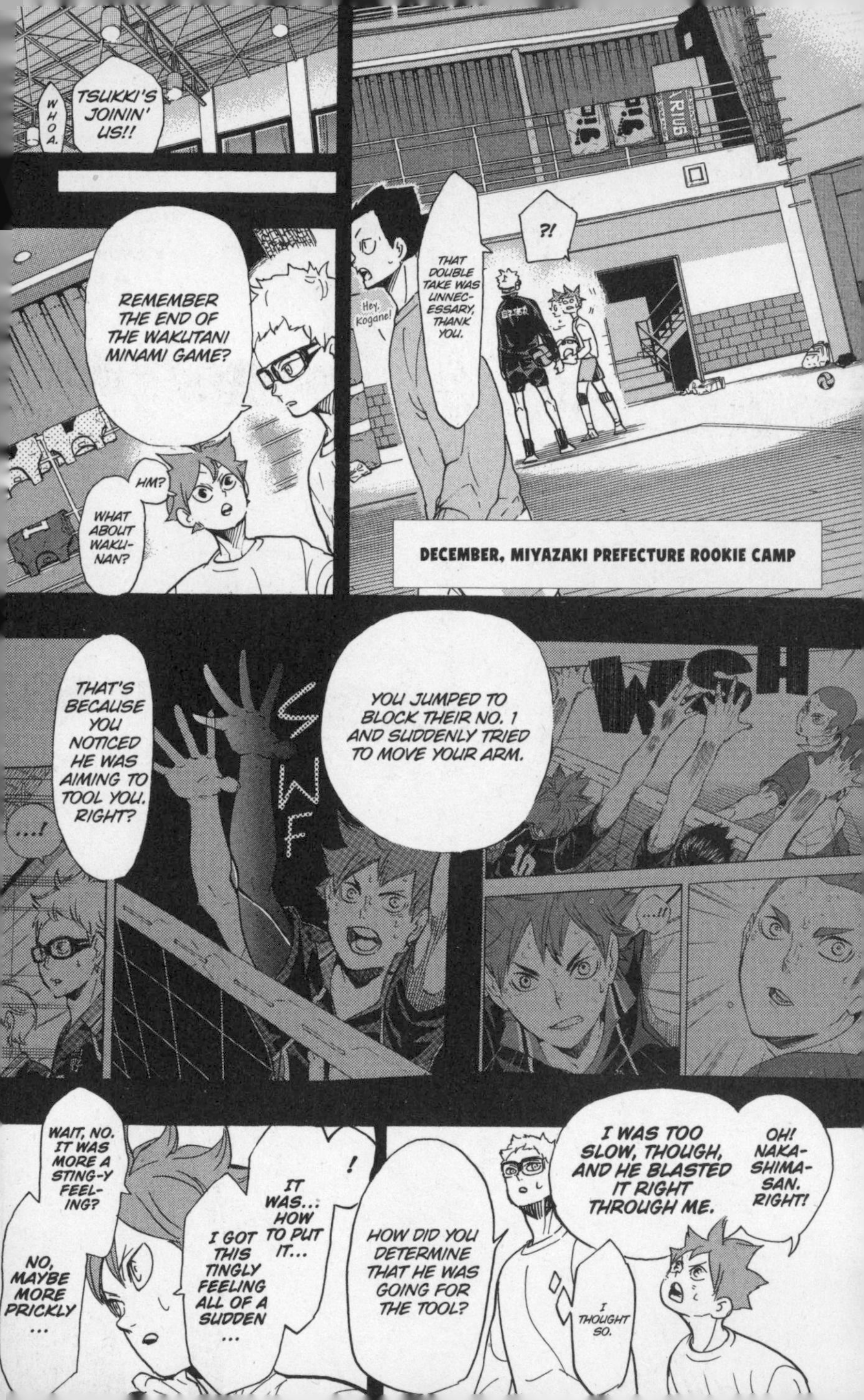
?!
THAT DOUBLE TAKE WAS UNNECESSARY, THANK YOU.
Hey, Kogane!
DECEMBER, MIYAZAKI PREFECTURE ROOKIE CAMP
TSUKKI'S JOININ' US!!
WHOA.
REMEMBER THE END OF THE WAKUTANI MINAMI GAME?
HM?
WHAT ABOUT WAKUNAN?
WSH
...!!
YOU JUMPED TO BLOCK THEIR NO. 1 AND SUDDENLY TRIED TO MOVE YOUR ARM.
SWF
THAT'S BECAUSE YOU NOTICED HE WAS AIMING TO TOOL YOU. RIGHT?
...!
OH! NAKASHIMA-SAN. RIGHT!
I WAS TOO SLOW, THOUGH, AND HE BLASTED IT RIGHT THROUGH ME.
I THOUGHT SO.
HOW DID YOU DETERMINE THAT HE WAS GOING FOR THE TOOL?
!
IT WAS... HOW TO PUT IT...
I GOT THIS TINGLY FEELING ALL OF A SUDDEN...
WAIT, NO. IT WAS MORE A STING-Y FEELING?
NO, MAYBE MORE PRICKLY...

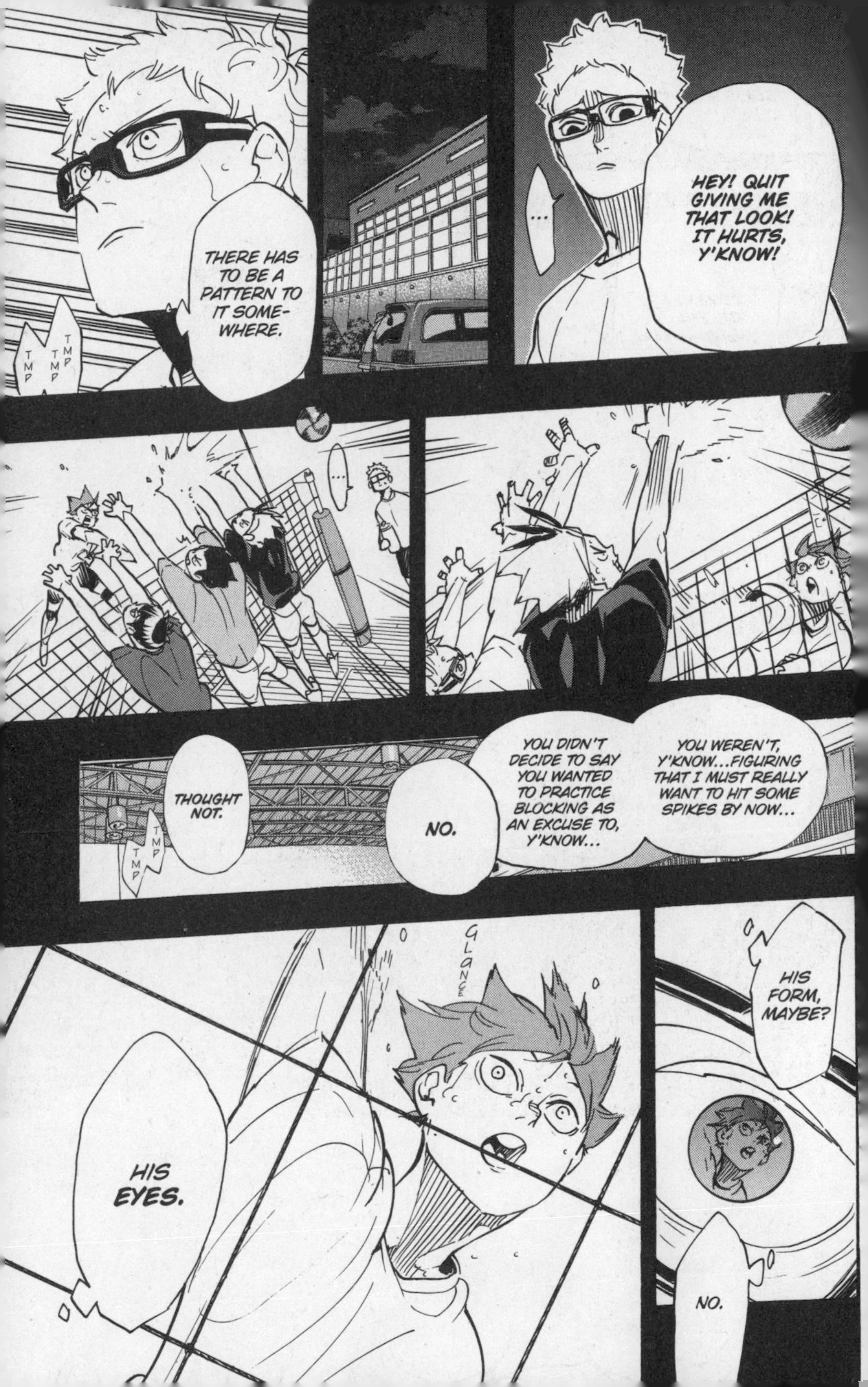
...
HEY! QUIT GIVING ME THAT LOOK! IT HURTS, Y'KNOW!
THERE HAS TO BE A PATTERN TO IT SOME-WHERE.
TMP TMP TMP
...
YOU WEREN'T, Y'KNOW...FIGURING THAT I MUST REALLY WANT TO HIT SOME SPIKES BY NOW...
YOU DIDN'T DECIDE TO SAY YOU WANTED TO PRACTICE BLOCKING AS AN EXCUSE TO, Y'KNOW...
NO.
THOUGHT NOT.
TMP TMP
HIS FORM, MAYBE?
NO.
GLANCE
HIS EYES.

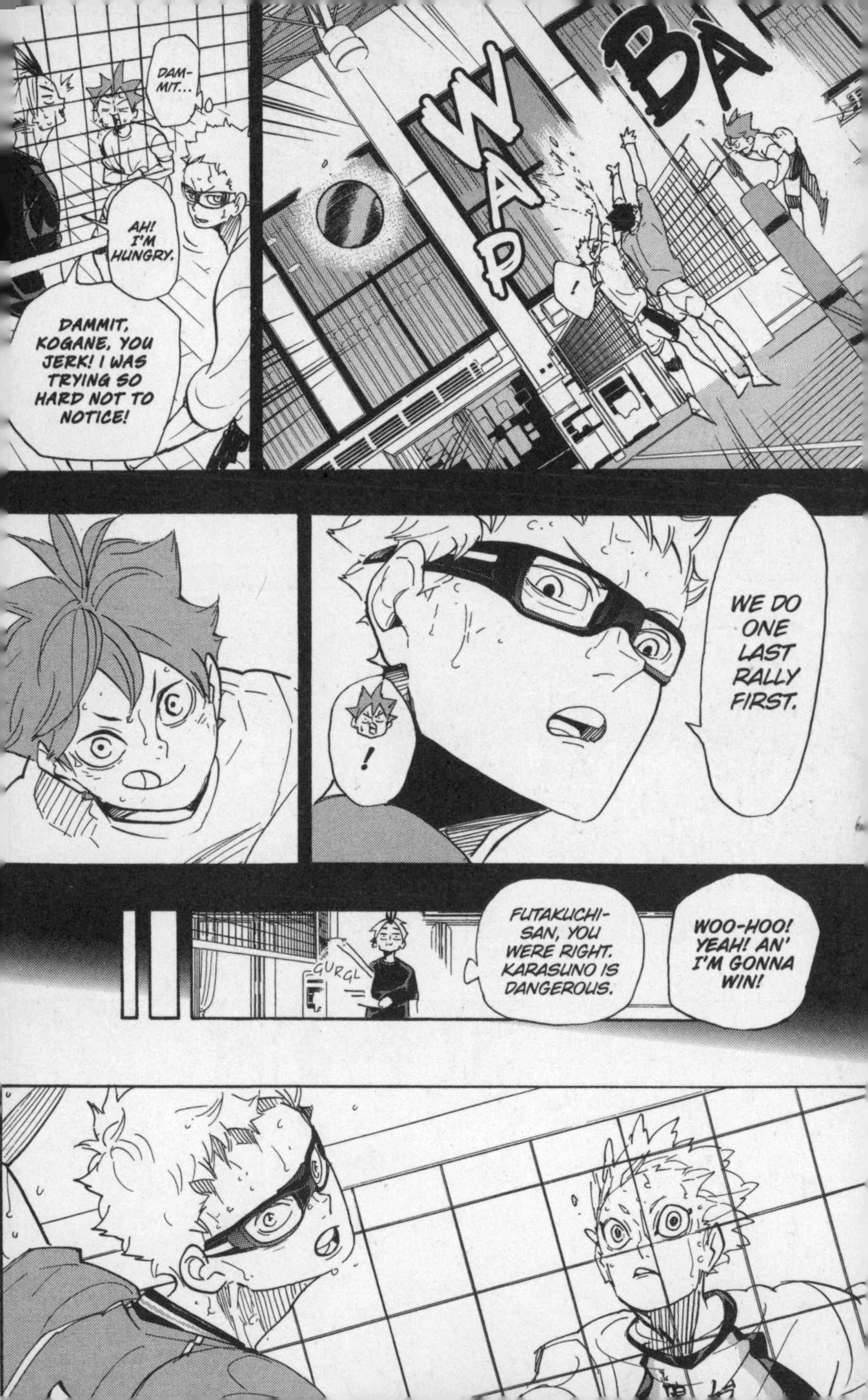
BA
WAP
!
DAM-MIT...
AH! I'M HUNGRY.
DAMMIT, KOGANE. YOU JERK! I WAS TRYING SO HARD NOT TO NOTICE!
WE DO ONE LAST RALLY FIRST.
!
WOO-HOO! YEAH! AN' I'M GONNA WIN!
FUTAKUCHI-SAN, YOU WERE RIGHT. KARASUNO IS DANGEROUS.
GURGL

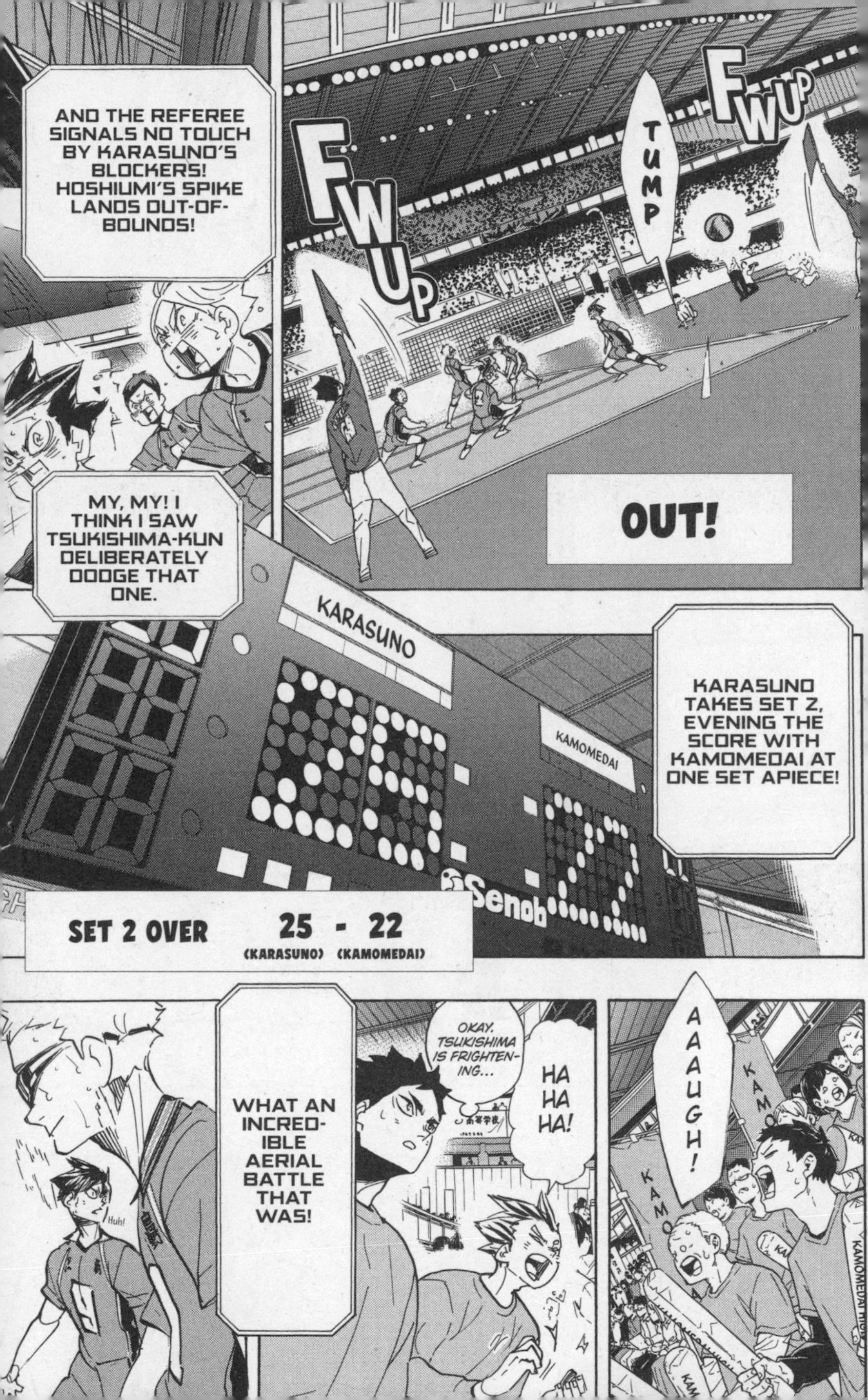
FWUP
TUMP
FWUP
OUT!
AND THE REFEREE SIGNALS NO TOUCH BY KARASUNO'S BLOCKERS! HOSHIUMI'S SPIKE LANDS OUT-OF-BOUNDS!
MY, MY! I THINK I SAW TSUKISHIMA-KUN DELIBERATELY DODGE THAT ONE.
KARASUNO TAKES SET 2, EVENING THE SCORE WITH KAMOMEDAI AT ONE SET APIECE!
KARASUNO
KAMOMEDAI
Senob
SET 2 OVER 25 - 22
(KARASUNO) (KAMOMEDAI)
AAAUGH!
KAM
KAM
KAMOMEDAI HIGH
HA HA HA!
OKAY. TSUKISHIMA IS FRIGHTENING...
WHAT AN INCREDIBLE AERIAL BATTLE THAT WAS!
Huh!

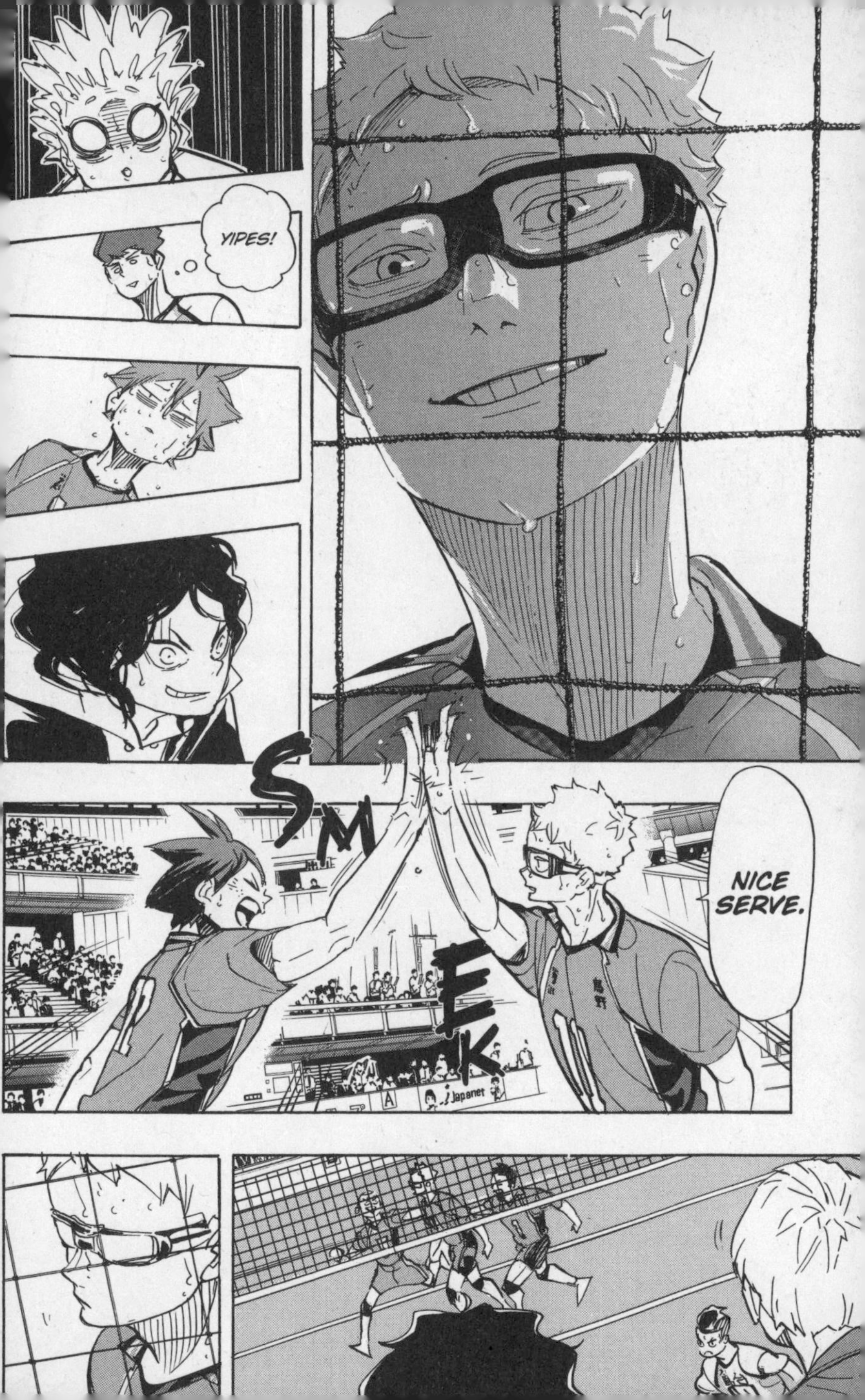
YIPES!
NICE SERVE.
SMEK

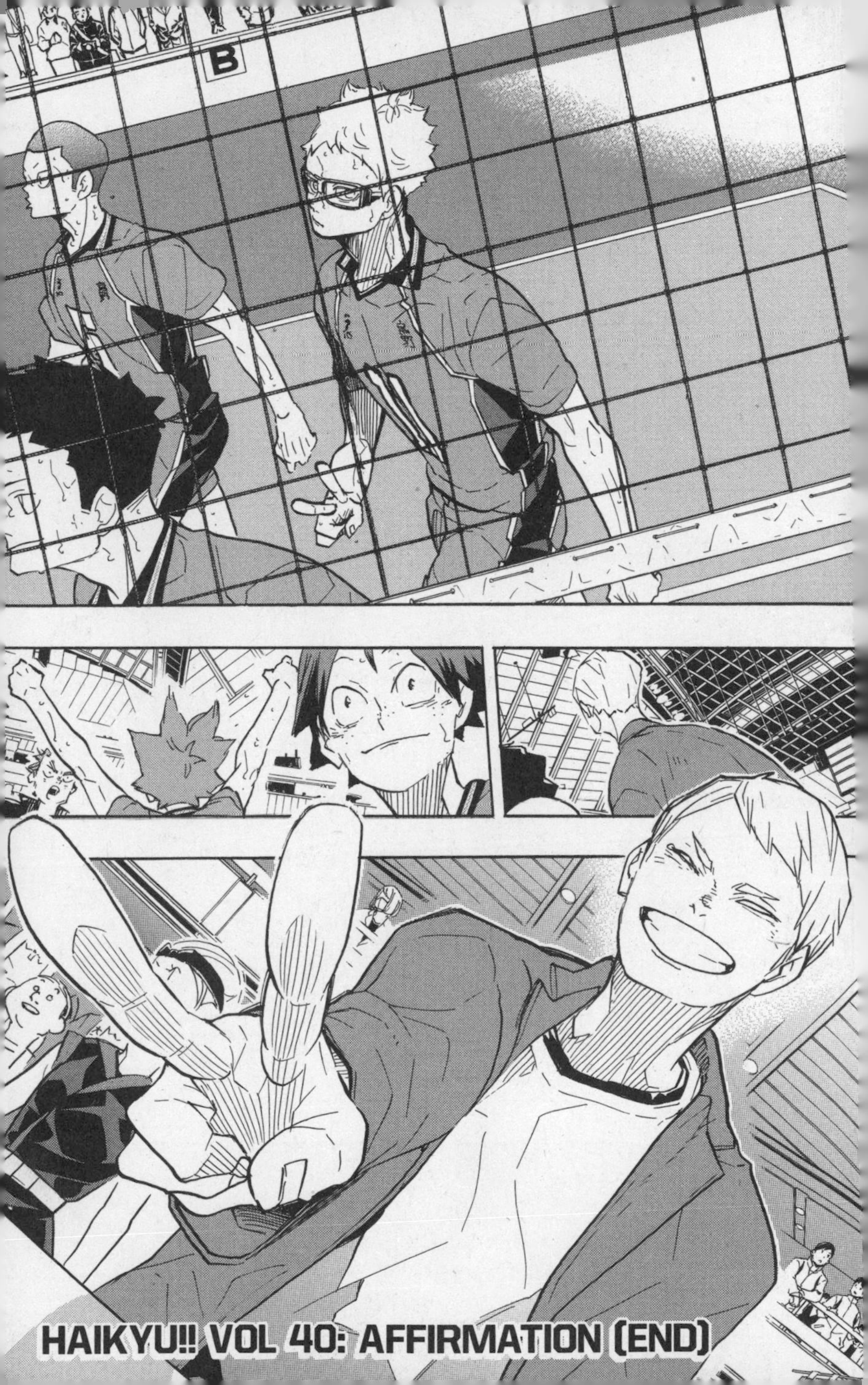
HAIKYU!! VOL 40: AFFIRMATION (END)

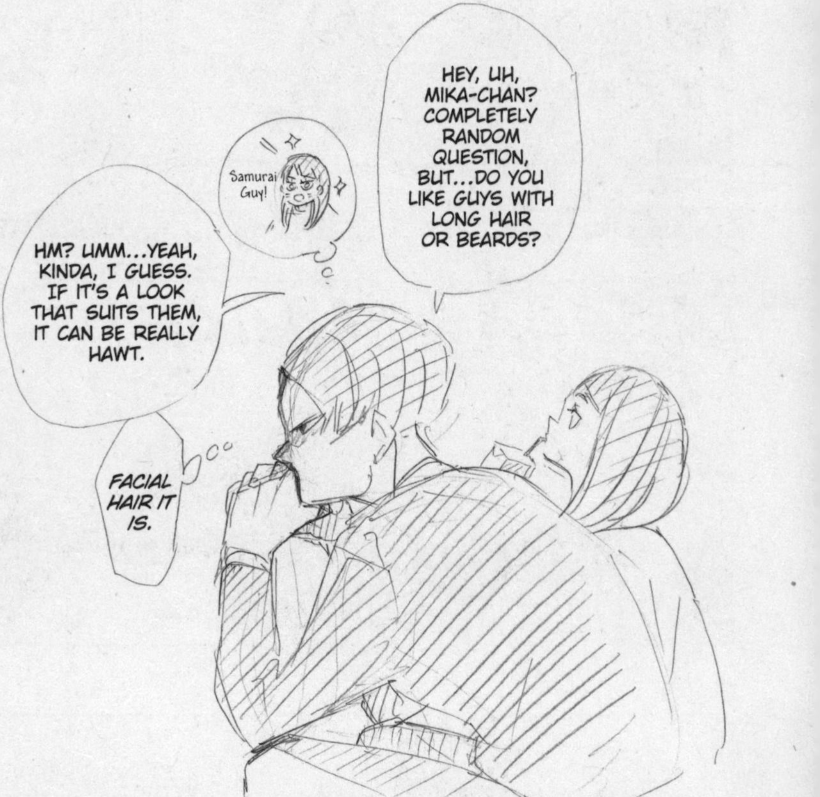
HEY, UH, MIKA-CHAN? COMPLETELY RANDOM QUESTION, BUT...DO YOU LIKE GUYS WITH LONG HAIR OR BEARDS?
Samurai Guy!
HM? UMM...YEAH, KINDA, I GUESS. IF IT'S A LOOK THAT SUITS THEM, IT CAN BE REALLY HAWT.
FACIAL HAIR IT IS.

← STARTING ON THE NEXT PAGE IS A SPECIAL BONUS MINI CHAPTER FROM THE SUMMER COMBINED ISSUE!

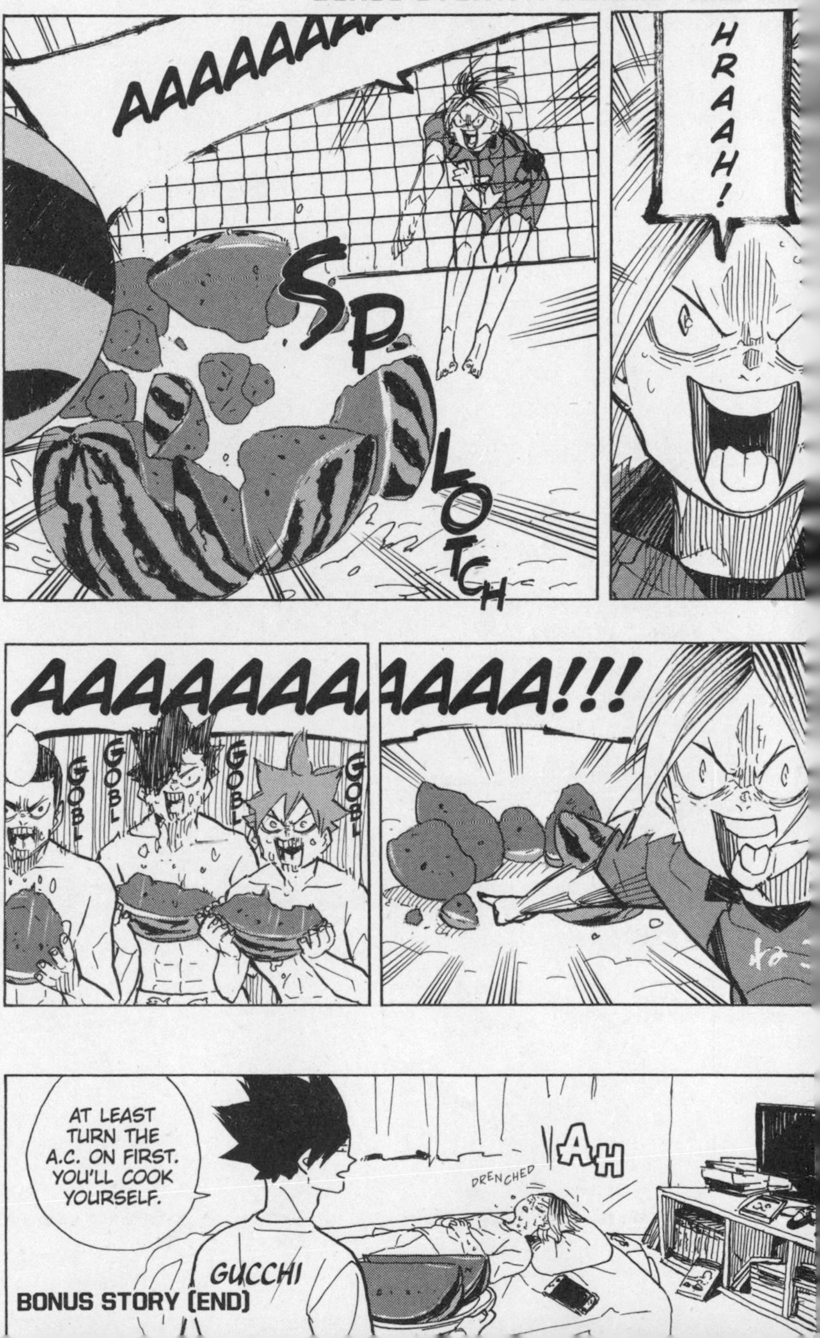
HRAAAH!
AAAAAAA
SPLOTCH
AAAAAAAAAAAA!!!
GOBL
GOBL
GOBL
GOBL
AT LEAST TURN THE A.C. ON FIRST. YOU'LL COOK YOURSELF.
AH
DRENCHED
GUCCHI
BONUS STORY (END)

# STAFF INTRODUCTIONS!!

## RYOTARO OGURA

**SPECIAL ABILITY:**
**CHEERING OTHERS ON**

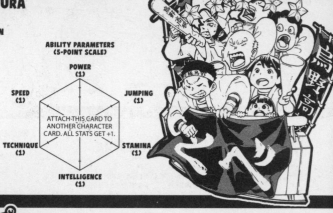

ABILITY PARAMETERS
(5-POINT SCALE)

POWER
(1)

SPEED
(1)

JUMPING
(1)

ATTACH THIS CARD TO
ANOTHER CHARACTER
CARD. ALL STATS GET +1.

TECHNIQUE
(1)

STAMINA
(1)

INTELLIGENCE
(1)

## SAKUJU KOIZUMI

**SPECIAL ABILITY:**
**FORGETFULNESS**

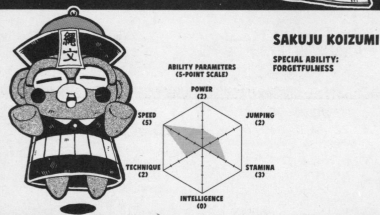

ABILITY PARAMETERS
(5-POINT SCALE)

POWER
(2)

SPEED
(5)

JUMPING
(2)

TECHNIQUE
(2)

STAMINA
(3)

INTELLIGENCE
(0)

## MIYAKO WATAHASHI

**SPECIAL ABILITY:**
**FORGETTING EVERYTHING**
**THEY BROUGHT WITH THEM**

ABILITY PARAMETERS
(5-POINT SCALE)

POWER
(1)

SPEED
(1)

JUMPING
(1)

TECHNIQUE
(2)

STAMINA
(1)

INTELLIGENCE
(3)

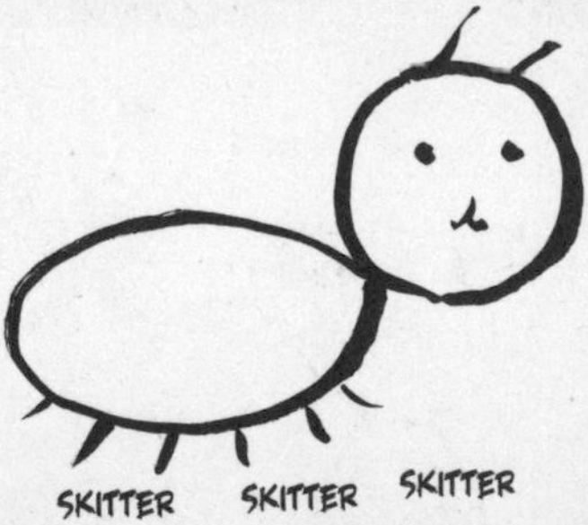

SKITTER    SKITTER    SKITTER

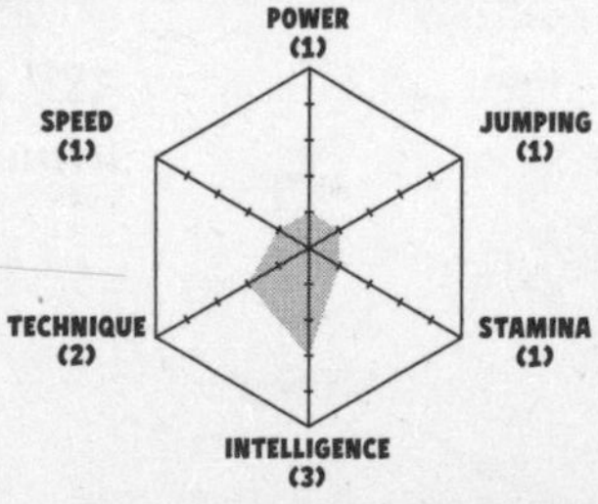

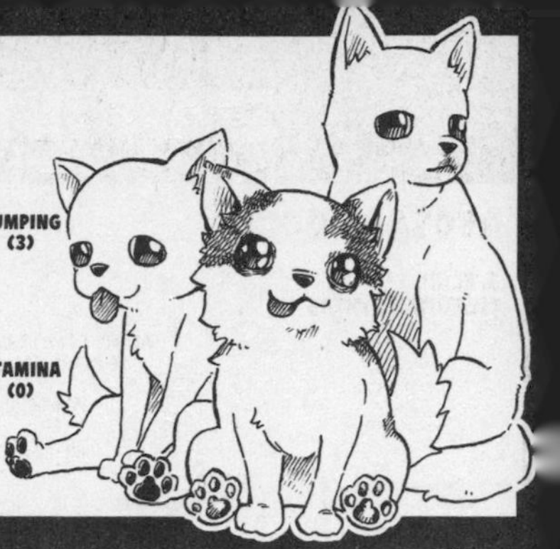

## YU AOKI

**SPECIAL ABILITY:**
**NOT LEAVING THE HOUSE**

ABILITY PARAMETERS
(5-POINT SCALE)

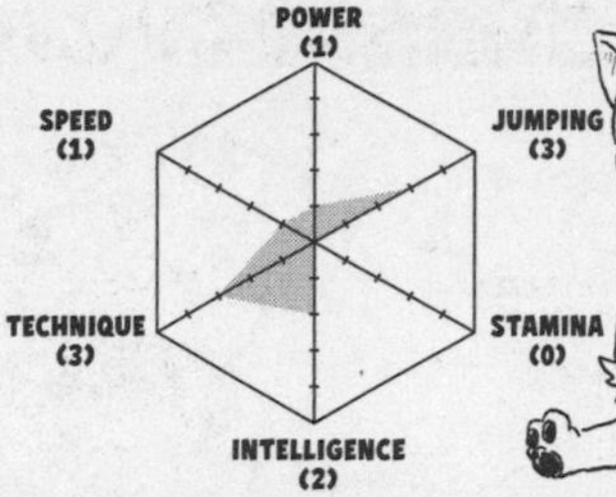
POWER
(1)
JUMPING
(3)
STAMINA
(0)
INTELLIGENCE
(2)
TECHNIQUE
(3)
SPEED
(1)

## DAI HOSHIKAWA

**SPECIAL ABILITY:**
**DRINKING IT DOWN AND SPITTING IT BACK UP AGAIN--IT KEEPS COMING BACK FOREVER AND EVER**

ABILITY PARAMETERS
(5-POINT SCALE)

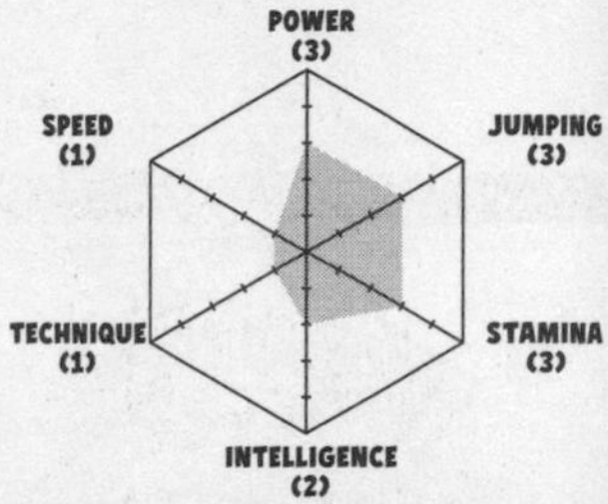
POWER
(3)
JUMPING
(3)
STAMINA
(3)
INTELLIGENCE
(2)
TECHNIQUE
(1)
SPEED
(1)

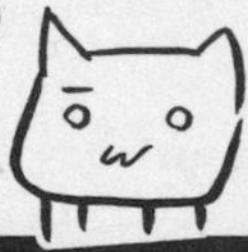

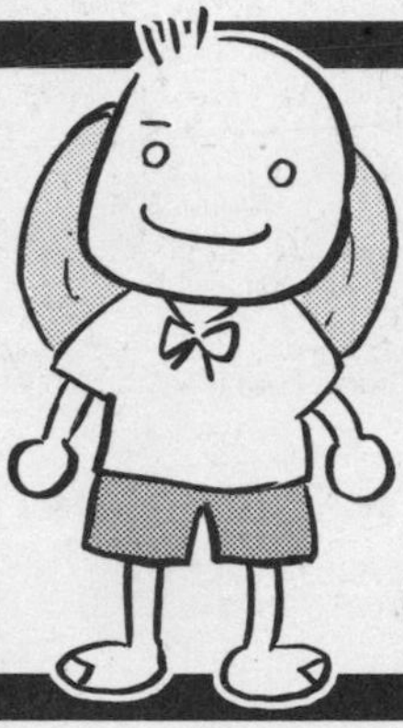

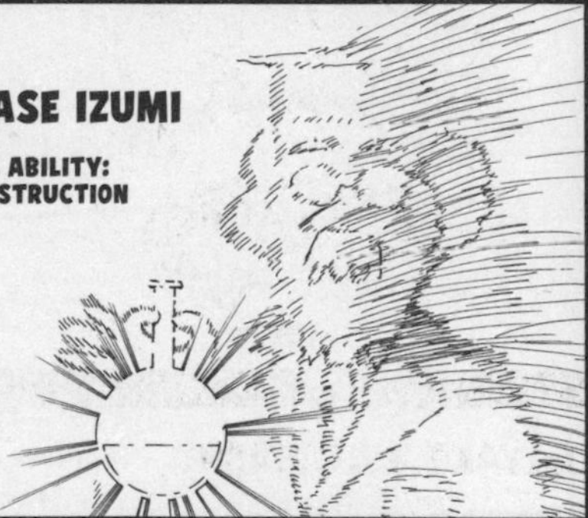

## HAKASE IZUMI

**SPECIAL ABILITY:**
**SELF-DESTRUCTION**

ABILITY PARAMETERS
(5-POINT SCALE)

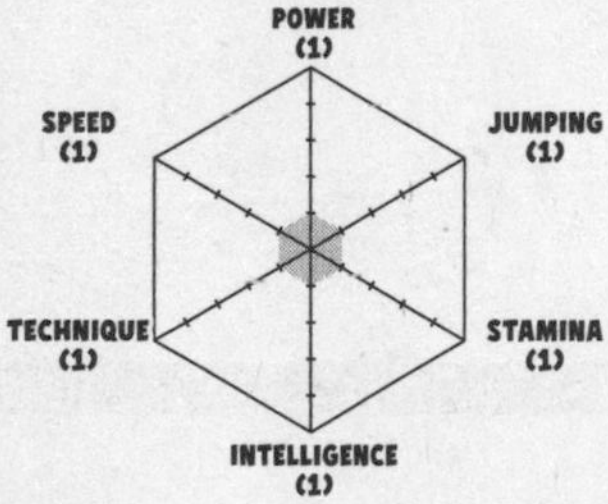
POWER
(1)
JUMPING
(1)
STAMINA
(1)
INTELLIGENCE
(1)
TECHNIQUE
(1)
SPEED
(1)

## KEN OGINO

**SPECIAL ABILITY:**
**SNACKING**

ABILITY PARAMETERS
(5-POINT SCALE)

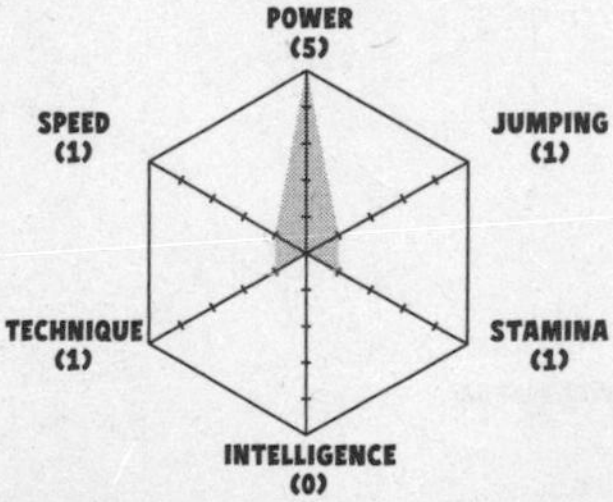
POWER
(5)
JUMPING
(1)
STAMINA
(1)
INTELLIGENCE
(0)
TECHNIQUE
(1)
SPEED
(1)

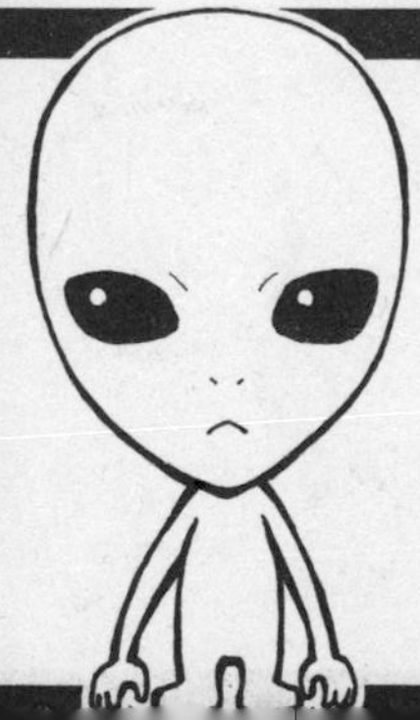

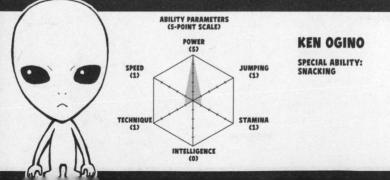

# EDITOR'S NOTES

The English edition of Haikyu!! maintains the honorifics used in the original Japanese version. For those of you who are new to these terms, here's a brief explanation to help with your reading experience!

When saying someone's name in Japanese, a suffix is often attached to indicate how familiar the speaker is with the person. Some are more polite and respectful, while others are endearing.

**1** *-kun* is often used for young men or boys, usually someone you are familiar with.

**2** *-chan* is used for young children and can be used as a term of endearment.

**3** *-san* is used for someone you respect or are not close to, or to be polite.

**4** *Senpai* is used for someone who is older than you or in a higher position or grade in school.

**5** *Kohai* is used for someone who is younger than you or in a lower position or grade in school.

**6** *Sensei* means teacher.

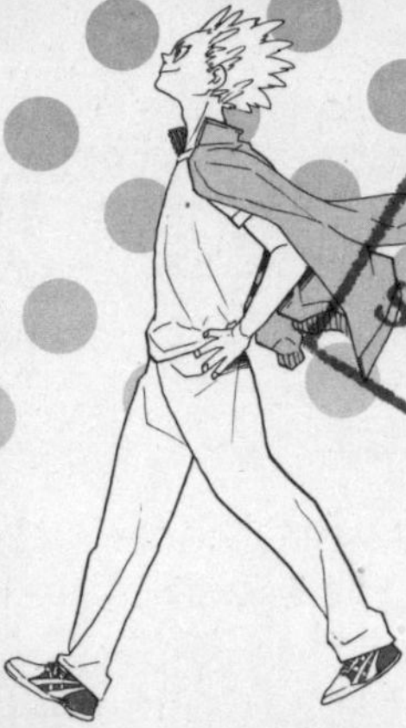

# You're Reading the WRONG WAY!

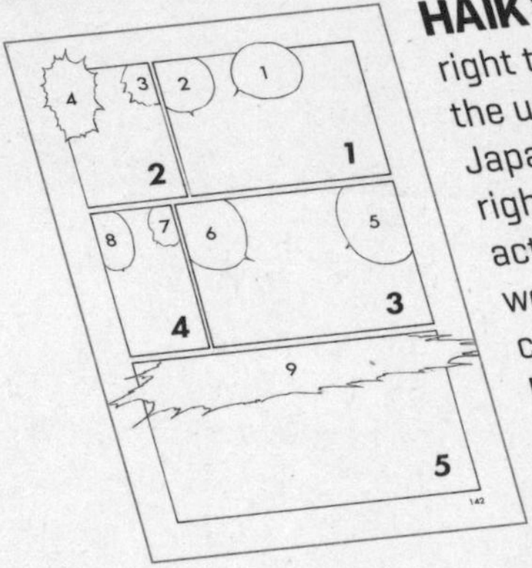

**HAIKYU!!** reads from right to left, starting in the upper-right corner. Japanese is read from right to left, meaning that action, sound effects and word-balloon order are completely reversed from English order.

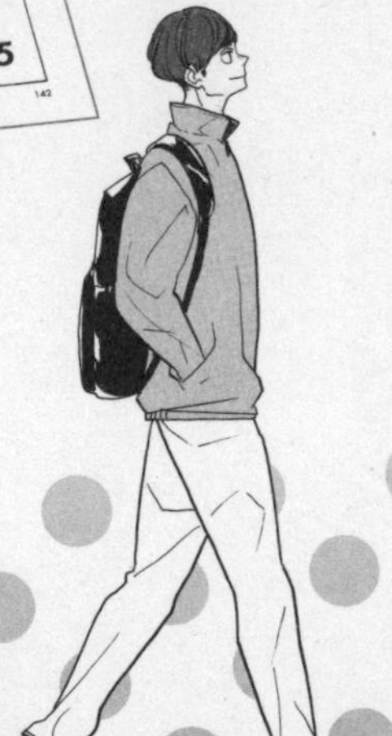